Mr. Cheap's® New York

Bargains, factory outlets, off-price stores, deep discount stores, cheap eats, cheap places to stay, and cheap fun things to do.

Mark Waldstein

Adams Media Corporation
HOLBROOK, MASSACHUSETTS

Published by Adams Media Corporation
260 Center Street, Holbrook, MA 02343

Mr. Cheap's® is a registered trademark of Adams Media Corporation

ISBN: 1-55850-256-4

Printed in Canada

J I H G F E D C

This publication is designed to provide accurate and authoritative information with regard to the subject matter covered. It is sold with the understanding that the publisher is not engaged in rendering legal, accounting, or other professional advice. If legal advice or other expert assistance is required, the services of a qualified professional person should be sought.

— From a *Declaration of Principles* jointly adopted by a Committee of the American Bar Association and a Committee of Publishers and Associations.

Cover design: Peter Gouck

This book is available at quantity discounts for bulk purchases. For information, call 1-800-872-5627 (In Massachusetts 617-767-8100).

Visit our home page at http://www.adamsmedia.com

CONTENTS

Acknowledgments

Mr. Cheap is never frugal when it comes to thanking the people who assisted him throughout this vast undertaking. First of all, thanks to editor Brandon Toropov, whose patience could fill five boroughs—and then some. Copyeditor Kate Layzer performed, as usual, with flawless accuracy under pressure. Production wizard Chris Ciaschini, forever asked to get things done yesterday, unfailingly did. For their help and their hospitality, thanks to John and Tina Bowen, John Havens, Nancy Wayne and Joshua Wesson. Thanks also to Paul Cortellesi, computer guru, and to Rebecca Fasanello, Jim Flaherty, Lynne Griffin, and Anne Hamilton. Finally, of course, gratitude goes out to the Waldstein and Wesson families in their entireties: Your time, energy and good leads made this huge project possible. More than that, you made it enjoyable. Thank you.

Some [Carefully Chosen] Words from Mr. Cheap

About this "cheap" business. I'll admit, there are more elegant ways to put the idea.

Just about everyone in and around the Big Apple wants to save money, especially with things being so tough lately. When you think about it, though, hasn't a keen appreciation for a good value always been an essential part of being a Real New Yorker? At any rate, when it comes to low *prices*, few know as many good places as I do.

Strictly speaking, that doesn't make these stores, entertainment options, eateries, and places to stay "cheap," nor does it make anyone who uses this book "cheap." *Thrifty* would be a better word, or perhaps *frugal*. A cheap person, to my way of thinking, is one who has plenty of money to burn and steadfastly refuses to spend it. Images of misanthropes and other spiritually suspect sorts automatically come to mind. A thrifty person, on the other hand, would probably spend the money if he or she had it, but is trying to get the best possible value right now—partially out of necessity, yes, but in part too as a kind of character-building exercise before actually hitting the lottery.

I think most of us fall into the latter category, don't you?

Most folks do love a bargain, and it's my happy mission to pass these hints along. It's only fair to point out, though, that assembling a book like this is much more an art than a science. That means that there were some interesting decisions to be made along the way. Consider, for example, the seemingly uncomplicated issue of how to categorize the listings.

I discovered, as I assembled the information, that a certain degree of overlap in the categories is inevitable. Many of the stores I have listed under, say, "Electronics" could also be considered to belong in the sections entitled "Cameras" or "Appliances." Where appropriate, I have included cross-references in the body of the text. Of course, this book features a detailed index section that will help you locate a particular establishment or product.

Categorizing things wasn't the only issue to confront. Just as significant an obstacle was the March Of Time, an enemy of all books which offer information about specific companies, people, prices, and places. Since it's taken me a while to put all this material together, some things will have changed by the time this book even reaches your hands. And price changes, alas, always seem to go in the wrong direction: Up. This isn't likely to be a particularly big deal if a poetry reading series I've recommended moves from "free" to a one-espresso minimum. On the other hand, if that stuffed moosehead you were after is suddenly unavailable at the price I've quoted, it may throw a monkey wrench in your redecorating plans.

We all whine about inflation, and no one more loudly than this writer, but the bottom line is this: Stores, restaurants, and hotels have to make money to stay in business. Much as it galls Mr. C's sensibilities, the establishments cited in these pages must, from time to time, be expected to raise their rates. Furthermore, they may not always have the exact items I describe. Some may nudge their prices up a bit (or more than a bit) for strategic reasons. Some may radically change their formats to target new groups of customers. A few shops will vanish entirely. Such variations come with the territory.

Even so, *Mr. Cheap's New York* provides an invaluable snapshot of the most compelling bargains in and around the Big Apple. Although no reference book from anyone, anywhere, about anything can claim to be completely accurate by the time it hits the bookstore shelves, I try to work with an accelerated (and then some) production schedule. That gives this volume an advantage in timeliness that the authors of most other guides and reference books would envy. Happily, future editions of the book are projected on a schedule that will keep all the information fresh and up-to-date. And by the way, there aren't really any moosehead retailers listed in this edition of the book. Maybe next time.

The book presents a one-of-a-kind look at a one-of-a-kind city—a road map for the thrifty, if you will. This, I hope, is a map that you will actually enjoy using to your benefit, one you will consult often as you navigate the often-tricky byways of that unpredictable journey known as Making Ends Meet In The Big Apple.

Mr. C strains modesty in pointing it out, perhaps, but the outlines of a New York that emerge in these pages create an image too many of us have given up on: An affordable city. Believe it or not, it's out there. This book shows you where.

✦ ✦ ✦

A few words of caution are in order: You get what you pay for.

That's been said many times, and it's usually true. With new merchandise especially, if the price is low, the quality may not be far behind. I have tried to point out, wherever I could, items that are cheap because they are less well made, or because they are irregulars or slightly damaged. Products that fall into these categories may still be of use to the reader who only needs something to last a short time (students furnishing a dorm room, for example). Sometimes, that's all you want. And that's fine.

In the other direction, there are a number of cases where particularly good values are attached to prices that rise above Mr. Cheap's standard limit. Take restaurants, for instance. As a general rule, I've included only eateries that feature menus that allow you to escape for about ten dollars, plus tip and taxes. Every once in a while, however, you will come across an exception—like L'Ecole in SoHo. This is an amazing place that offers an honest-to-goodness three-course gourmet French meal for fifteen dollars at lunchtime. As the name implies, it really is a school; a delightful restaurant setting for the benefit of students of the French Culinary Institute. The food is great, the atmosphere is not in the least low-budget, and the price—for food of this quality—is simply impossible to beat. Ten-dollar-limit or no ten-dollar-limit, this is one of the most unusual dining bargains to be found in the Big Apple . . . or anywhere else, for that matter. Accordingly, it has a place in this book.

The name of the game here is always the same: getting your money's worth no matter what. Often, that means tapping into the vast subculture of stores selling used and/or closeout items. These establishments are, admittedly, a rung below the standard levels of quality, dependability, and general atmosphere found at retail stores, but are still worth taking the time to investigate, as they can afford many pleasant surprises. But some precautionary measures are definitely in order, and this seems as good a place as any to review them.

Rule number one is: Look around first, buy later. My thinking in including these listings ran as follows: If you save money on something you want by spending some time searching out bargains in a less-than-aesthetically-stunning environment, you win—*and* get a certain predatory thrill at the same time. Mr. C actually found some of the quirks at these "second-tier" shops rather charming. Take for example Number One Closeout, a rather grungy job-lot store on Canal Street. This place is a real rarity of late-twentieth-century commerce—an electronics store without a telephone (they'll sell you one, though, for $7.99.)

When dealing with such outlets, a good dose of skepticism is definitely in order. Ask about warranties and exchange policies (actually, you should do this for just about any purchase, but it's particularly important in secondhand and closeout settings). You probably won't get the same warranty you would if you were buying the item new, but you should certainly be able to extract some commitment on the seller's part regarding the return of defective merchandise. Like the ability to return things that don't work for cash or credit within, say, thirty days of your purchase. At the risk of repeating advice you've probably heard elsewhere, I strongly recommend that you *always get and keep receipts when buying from durable goods retailers, especially secondhand or closeout establishments.*

One of the surprising things about secondhand outlets is that some of them actually represent opportunities for you to *make* money, rather than spend it (and if that's not a sure-fire way to get this author's attention, nothing is). Interested? Read on.

In reviewing the sections on used book and recording outlets, you'll notice that some of the places will indeed pay you cash on the barrelhead for your old books, tapes, or CDs (cashing in on old LPs is a much trickier business these days; maybe they'll qualify as antiques in a year or three). While this cash-for-things-you're-bored-with-now arrangement may be appealing in the short run, you should bear two important factors in mind.

First, the store is unlikely to buy something it can't reasonably expect to resell at a profit, which means that your boxed set of Guy Lombardo records may not represent the gold mine you expected. Second, if you read a lot of books or listen to a lot of music—in other words, if you are likely to turn around and purchase items from the same store, you should consider trading your old stuff in for credit, as this will usually mean a better value for you.

Buying everything used, of course, isn't Mr. Cheap's only buying strategy. In New York the spectrum of bargains is an extremely broad one, and I've done my level best to ensure that it's reflected in these pages. Sometimes that means not ignoring the big guys. *Mr. Cheap's New York* frankly admits when some large chain or other has a competitive price or selection advantage over smaller players in a particular category. Examples of this in the toys and games category, for instance, are both Kiddie City and Toys "R" Us. No accounting of the best toy values in the area could be called complete without acknowledging the deals to be found in the mega-stores run by these volume-driven, broad-inventory behemoths. Similarly, when it comes to good deals on mattresses, Sleepy's is clearly the city's dominant discount chain. Mr. C doesn't spend too much ink on such stores, though, since you probably know about them already.

But there are so many more remarkable deals to be found off the beaten track. You may not have known about Max Nass Jewelry on East 28th Street; it's a narrow little shop that somehow manages to cram what seems like a department store's worth of fine—and very affordable—jewelry items into cramped quarters. Similarly pleasant surprises await those who make their way to The Piano Store, a wonderfully offbeat place on the Lower East Side where you can purchase a quality refurbished piano for under a grand (no pun intended), and where the motto is a thought-provoking question: "What would you rather have, an old mink or a new rabbit?" Think about it. Or how about Marco's Art Gallery on Orchard Street, where the proprietor will let you choose a basic design from several hundred sketches, specify the size canvas you prefer, and a few days later, give you a unique oil painting for between $50.00

and $250.00? Try to find prices like *that* at those chi-chi galleries. Want a Picasso? Get a print. Want some unusual, affordable, real art to hang on your wall? Go see Marco.

The point is, bargains in New York come in all shapes, sizes, and denominations, and from a whole bunch of sources, large and small. In this book, I've tried to account for the most noteworthy deals to be had here in the greatest city in the world—but I'm always open to new suggestions about the best ways to make a dollar do a full day's work in the Big Apple.

I certainly expect to get mail from readers who insist I've left out their favorite diner, or some resale boutique they frequent. To which I say, Mr. C can't be *everywhere*, but please do pass along the information for our next edition. The address is:

Mr. Cheap
c/o Adams Media Corporation
260 Center St.
Holbrook, MA 02343

(Please use the correct stamp amounts. I can't abide those horrid "postage due" notices.)

✦ ✦ ✦

I wrote this book firm in the belief that there is nothing in the least embarrassing about saving a buck that you've worked hard to earn. My guess is that a lot of New Yorkers these days will agree with me.

Enough talk. On to the goodies!

Mark Waldstein
a.k.a.Mr. I.M. Cheap, Esquire

SHOPPING

APPLIANCES

There are hundreds of places to save money on home appliances in New York. Many of the discount places, unfortunately, are as far below repute as their prices are below retail. It happens that these stores are often foreign-owned and run; Mr. C says this not out of any kind of chauvinism, but because he wants you to be careful. This kind of merchandise, after all, is almost entirely imported from other countries, and so there is a greater possibility of a shady deal. This book should guide you to the more reliable retailers, but things can always change. One of the best ways to protect yourself while shopping around is to inquire about the store's guarantee policy: Make sure the item you want carries an American warranty. Since some stores deal directly with the manufacturers in the Far East, their merchandise may carry a foreign warranty instead, and that could make repairs a hassle. Remember, you are perfectly within your rights to ask about this in the store.

America Electronics—50 East 14th St., Manhattan; 212/353-0765. See listing under "Electronics."

Bernie's Discount Center—821 Sixth Ave. (28th St.), Manhattan; 212/564-8582. Bernie's is one of the best places in town for all kinds of household appliances, small and large. They have large-screen TVs from Sony and Mitsubishi, Brother fax machines and word processors, every kind of small kitchen appliance, and more. Nearly all of these are sold at prices around 10 percent above cost; they've been doing it since 1948.

They're one of the few dealers left in midtown selling big-ticket items like refrigerators and washers, yet the prices are still very competitive. Bernie himself related the story that employees of Krups were buying coffee machines here because his prices were better than their own employee discounts. The store has Bionaire humidifiers, and is one of the few in New York offering all the necessary support products as well. And it is a good place to get video camcorders and blank video tapes at discount prices.

The salespeople at Bernie's put no pressure on you—they know the prices will do the work, and it's always so busy that they don't have time to hassle you. Still, when you are ready to order, they'll give you all the time and attention you need.

Bloom & Krup—202-6 First Ave. (12th St.), Manhattan; 212/673-2760. What began as a basic hardware store back in 1928 has grown to become one of the city's most complete appliance and furniture centers, selling lots of big-name brands at discount. They have items large and small for every room in the house. Whether you're looking for a twelve-cubic foot Whirlpool refrigerator (retail price $649.00, here $519.00), or a twenty-six-inch RCA color TV ($200.00 below retail at $499.00), or even a La-Z-Boy recliner chair from just

$299.00, chances are you'll find it at B & K.

There are several large showrooms; the store seems to go on and on. Up front are the bathroom fixtures, from tubs to faucets (watch for their occasional floor model sales). Cut through the hardware store—yes, they still have all that stuff too—to the back rooms, filled with things like Whirlpool washers (one was $399.00, reduced from $529.00) and the above-mentioned kitchen appliances; plus smaller household items, such as a Welbilt 550-watt microwave oven for $119.00.

But wait—there's more. Head upstairs to the furniture area for beds, mattresses, sofas, and chairs, all at discount prices. You may find a Whitman and Clark loveseat that opens up into a bed, $100.00 off at $449.00. One recent closeout featured a Simmons Maxipedic twin mattress and boxspring for just $299.00, and you might have put a solid oak nighttable with opening doors next to it for $219.00, marked down from $300.00. Kitchen tables are here too, like a simple model topped in black or butcher-block formica for $140.00 It includes two ice-cream parlor chairs.

Bloom & Krup is open from 9:00 a.m. to 6:00 p.m. six days a week, and 11:00 a.m.-4:00p.m. on Sundays. Delivery is available for a nominal charge. Their service is impeccable—the sales staff will work with you to find just what you need to fit your home's dimensions—and they don't mind if you're "just looking." In fact, they *ask* you to come prepared with paper and pencil!

Bondy Export—40 Canal St., Manhattan; 212/925-7785. You know the old phrase, "I can get it for you wholesale"? Well, Bondy is that kind of place. For over thirty-five years this tiny shop on the eastern fringe of Chinatown has been getting tremendous prices on all kinds of small and large appliances for the home. The cramped, no-frills store stocks as many of the smaller items as it can; but anything you don't see, from almost any manufacturer, can be ordered at the same great prices—most of which are just above cost.

In addition to appliances, the same deals can be struck on luggage, watches, stereo, cameras, Ray-Ban sunglasses, and more. Luggage, for example, may be 50 percent or more below retail prices; Mr. C saw a Samsonite "Silhouette" briefcase, list price $330.00, selling here for $145.00. Bondy also specializes in appliances for overseas use, with the different voltage requirements for foreign countries. And with so many similar stores in the area, they are proud to be one of the only ones approved by the Better Business Bureau.

Eba's Appliance World—2361 Nostrand Ave. (Ave. J), Flatbush, Brooklyn; 718/252-3400. They do seem to have every appliance in the world at Eba's. Well okay, they don't carry small appliances. But otherwise, Wow. You can save over $100.00 on a Maytag extra-large washing machine, or on an Emerson air conditioner with a chillingly powerful 8,200 BTU. Find similar savings on refrigerators, stoves and other big-ticket items (but not as big as they could be!). All carry full manufacturer's warranties.

Eba's prices are good because they are part of a fifty-dealer buying group. Whatever it is, they can get a good deal on it and pass the savings along to you. But here's a special tip from Mr. C: Call them first. They are one of the very few retailers who will quote prices over the phone, and often they'll quote you a price that's closer to wholesale than the tag in the store itself. And you don't have to pretend to be a wholesaler to get that price. Try it.

They also carry a full line of electronic and video products,

Mr. Cheap's Picks

✔ **Bernie's Appliance Center**—Huge selection and great prices packed into a small space.

✔ **Bloom & Krup**—Since 1928, bargains for every room in the house—appliances large and small, hardware and fixtures, even furniture.

✔ **Eba's Appliance World**—Head to Flatbush for wholesale prices on major appliances and video stuff.

like a Sony 8mm camcorder—those new, hand-held babies—marked down from an $888.00 list price to $715.00. Or a Toshiba thirty-two-inch projection screen TV, reduced from $1,188.00 to a more watchable $930.00 With all their products, Eba's offers a thirty-day price guarantee; if you show them a lower price, they'll pay you the difference plus 10 percent. The huge warehouse-style store is open seven days a week.

47th St. Photo—67 West 47th St., Manhattan; 212/921-1287, and 115 West 45th St., Manhattan; 212/921-1287. See listing under "Cameras."

J & R Music World—23 Park Row, Manhattan; 212/732-8600. See listing under "Electronics."

Job Lot Pushcart—140 Church St., Manhattan; 212/962-4142, 80 Nassau St., Manhattan; 212/619-6868, and 1633 Broadway (50th St.), Manhattan; 212/245-0921. See listing under "Department Stores."

Kaufman Electric—365 Grand St., Manhattan; 212/475-8313. See listing under "Home Furnishings."

The Market Place—17 West 14th St., Manhattan; 212/620-0242. This large store sells a wide variety of electronics, from stereo to cameras to home appliances, all at pretty good discount prices. Find a Casio electric typewriter, with memory, for $90.00; a Samsung mini-microwave oven for $70.00; or an Olympus 8mm video camcorder for $550.00, about as low as they get. Larger appliances include a Eureka "Mighty Mite" vacuum cleaner for $70.00, and a Westinghouse 5000-B.T.U. air conditioner for $180.00. Some items may be factory-refurbished, so be sure to check out the warranty on any particular item.

National Wholesale Liquidators—632 Broadway, Manhattan; 212/979-2400, and 71-01 Kissena Blvd., Flushing, Queens; 718/591-3900. See listing under "Department Stores."

Odd-Job Trading—10 Cortlandt St., Manhattan; 212/571-0959, 149 West 32nd St., Manhattan; 212/564-7370, 7 East 40th St., Manhattan; 212/686-6825, and 66 West 48th St., Manhattan; 212/575-0477.

See listing under "Department Stores."

P.C. Richard and Son—576-80 86th St., Bay Ridge, Brooklyn; 718/745-7300, 450 Kings Hwy., Brooklyn; 718/382-5006, 2259 Ralph Ave. (Ave. M), Flatlands, Brooklyn; 718/968-9631, 2143 Flatbush Ave. (45th St.), Marine Park, Brooklyn; 718/377-5710, 36-01 Broadway (Steinway St.), Astoria, Queens; 718/204-0012, 113-14 Queens Blvd. (76th Ave.), Forest Hills, Queens; 718/896-6822, 103-54 94th St., Ozone Park, Queens; 718/848-6700, and 92-63 Queens Blvd.

(Woodhaven Blvd.), Rego Park, Queens; 718/268-8155.

Long established on Long Island, P.C. Richard has recently begun a wide-scale expansion into Brooklyn and Queens, including its newest "superstore" in Ozone Park. But each store has a huge selection of appliances for the home. Save big bucks on such big-ticket items as refrigerators, dishwashers, gas ranges, washers and dryers. They carry all major brands, sometimes featuring special sales on a particular manufacturer. One recent example found all General Electrics on sale, including a 20.7 cubic-foot refrigerator for $650.00 and a large, 800-watt microwave/convection oven for $380.00.

P.C. Richard guarantees to match the lowest advertised price you can find—even after your purchase, as long as you own it. And, for further bargains (if you can get out to the Island) check out their clearance outlet in Deer Park (516/254-0123).

Ralph's Discount City—95 Chambers St., Manhattan; 212/267-5567. See listing under "Department Stores."

Trader Horn—226 East 86th St., Manhattan; 212/535-3600, 1972 Ralph Ave., Flatbush, Brooklyn; 718/531-7000, and 89-59 Bay Pkwy., Bay Ridge, Brooklyn; 718/996-8800. Trader Horn is one of the metro area's big discount chains for large appliances, televisions, and stereo equipment. They sell first-quality major brands, at good prices; their huge showrooms have lots of stuff out on display. Find an eighteen-cubic-foot refrigerator/freezer by Frigidaire for $339.00, a Panasonic microwave oven for $120.00, or a Magnavox thirteen-inch color TV for $155.00. They also have VCRs as low as $129.00, telephones and answering machines, gas ranges, washers and dryers, and lots more. Open daily until 9:30 in the evening, except Sundays until 6:00 p.m.

Triest Export—560 Twelfth Ave. (44th St.), Manhattan; 212/246-1548. For over thirty years, Triest has been selling an eclectic assortment of appliances, luggage, stereo, clothing, and more, all at deep discounts. It's another store that epitomizes the phrase, "I can get it for you wholesale." For great prices on coffee makers, food processors, microwave ovens, telephones, and more, check 'em out. Be careful, though, that the machines are meant for American usage, as a lot of Triest's business is with overseas customers. Other countries use a different voltage system.

Meanwhile, Triest also has Olympus cameras, Sony Walkmans (use these anywhere), Ray-Ban sunglasses, luggage, binoculars (a pair of opera glasses for $38.00), watches, Parker pens, designer colognes (many in small, lower-priced travel sizes), linens, T-shirts, and even sporting goods. All of these are substantially below department store prices. It's a larger selection than their next-door neighbor, **Romino Boutique**, at 588 Twelfth Avenue (212/977-7751), though that place is well worth a look, too. Triest is closed on Fridays and Saturdays, but open on Sundays.

Weber's Closeouts—132 Church St., Manhattan; 212/571-3283, 475 Fifth Ave. (41st St.), Manhattan; 212/251-0613, 45 West 45th St., Manhattan; 212/819-9780, and 2064 Broadway (72nd St.), Manhattan; 212/787-1644. See listing under "Department Stores."

Willoughby's—110 West 32nd St., Manhattan; 212/790-1800. See listing under "Cameras."

BEDS AND MATTRESSES

Bella Furniture—107-08 Atlantic Ave., Ozone Park, Brooklyn; 718/441-6602. See listing under "Furniture: New."

Bloom & Krup—202-6 First Ave. (12th St.), Manhattan; 212/673-2760. See listing under "Appliances."

Dixie Foam Beds—611 Sixth Ave. (18th St.), Manhattan; 212/645-8999. Dixie offers an innovative approach to bedding—mattresses made of solid foam. These come in the same standard sizes as regular mattresses and in a range of thicknesses. According to the folks here, their best grade of foam offers better support and resilience than conventional innersprings and are frequently recommended by orthopedists. They can, meanwhile, give you that support for a lot less money. A full-size mattress in Dixie's top conventional grade is priced at $180.00; it's available in medium-firm and extra-firm and comes with a five-year warranty. The three top grades are guaranteed for fifteen years. There are seven different grades of density in all. What's more, you can also get bed foundations in foam as well. These are hard enough to be a solid yet lightweight platform—and a two-piece set can be as low as $225.00 in twin size. Not a bad idea for apartment dwellers on the move.

Furniture Gallery—581 Sixth Ave. (17th St.), Manhattan; 212/924-8802. See listing under "Furniture: New."

Furniture Land—1224 Liberty Ave., Ozone Park, Queens; 718/235-2759. See listing under "Furniture: New."

Gothic Cabinet Craft—360 Sixth Ave. (Waverly Pl.), Manhattan; 212/982-8539, 1601 Second Ave. (83rd St.), Manhattan; 212/472-7359, 1655 Second Ave. (86th St.), Manhattan; 212/288-2999, 2543 Broadway (95th St.). Manhattan; 212/749-2020, 27-50 First St., Astoria, Queens; 718/626-1480, 36-09 Main St., Flushing, Queens; 718/762-6246, 147-44 Jamaica Ave., Jamaica, Queens; 718/297-1109, 258-01 Union Turnpike, Glen Oaks, Queens; 718/347-5201, 31 Smith St. (Fulton St.), Brooklyn; 718/625-2333, 6929 Fifth Ave. (Ovington St.), Bay Ridge, Brooklyn; 718/745-0715, 2163 White Plains Rd., Bronx; 718/863-7440, and 2366 University Ave., Bronx; 718/365-9333. See listing under "New Furniture."

Kleinsleep Clearance Center—176 Sixth Ave. (Spring St.), Manhattan; 212/226-0900. This is the clearance outlet for the high-volume chain, which has ten stores in the New York area. Floor samples, final sales, and discontinued models offer you good quality at bargain prices—in mattresses, box springs, frames, daybeds, headboards, and the like. These go for about 25 percent to 35 percent below retail prices; sometimes even better. Mr. C saw a perfectly good daybed with a white lacquer frame, reduced from its $620.00 list price to just $399.00—essentially, at cost. Don't forget to look downstairs in the basement, which has recently been fixed up to be as bright and clean as the main level, for more bargains. And even at these prices you can have your bed delivered free within forty-eight hours. The store is open Tuesdays through Saturdays from 10:00 a.m. to 7:00 p.m.

Nationwide Warehouse & Storage—115 Allen St., Manhattan; 212/420-8590, 1991 Third Ave. (109th St.), Manhattan; 212/410-0707, 2102 Utica Ave., Flatlands, Brooklyn; 718/253-4200, and 152-65 Rockaway Blvd., Queens; 718/525-8700. See listing under "New Furniture."

Sleepy's—389 Sixth Ave. (8th St.), Manhattan; 212/243-9312, 25 West 34th St., 2nd Floor, Manhattan; 212/502-5307, 157 East 57th St., Manhattan; 212/308-8253, 2080 Broadway (72nd St.), 2nd Floor, Manhattan; 212/874-9812, and 337 East 86th St., Manhattan; 212/289-9714. Many other locations in the outer boroughs.

Sleepy's has become the city's largest chain for discount prices on name-brand bedding. This is the real stuff by Sealy, Serta, and many other major companies. The everyday prices here are always good, and frequent sales offer extra bargains. A recent offer featured Simmons Maxipedic Extra-Firm Deluxe mattresses for just $139.00 in twin size and $199.00 in full size. Furthermore, this particular sale added a matching box spring for 88¢ more. Check their big newspaper ads for current deals. Sleepy's also guarantees next-day delivery of stock items, or your purchase is free.

Sofa Works—48 West 8th St., Manhattan; 212/473-3023. See listing under "Furniture: New."

Town Bedding—205 Eighth Ave. (21st St.), Manhattan; 212/243-0426. A small, no-frills store, Town Bedding is able to offer great prices on all manner of mattresses, sofa beds, and futons. Find a Sealy Posturepedic or Serta Perfect Sleeper mattress and box spring for $750.00 in queen size, which ain't bad; and you can save even more with smaller, independent brands, which Town ensures are made to the same standards as the big names—or better. A similar queen set by Premier, for example, sells for just $500.00. Mattresses by these independent makers start as low as $49.00 for a twin-size and $78.00 full-size.

Town Bedding will deliver anywhere in the metro area, including Long Island and New Jersey. There is no charge for delivery of name-brand sets, and only a small fee for budget models.

Weissman-Heller Furniture—129 Fifth Ave. (19th St.), Manhattan; 212/673-2880. See listing under "Furniture: New."

Mr. Cheap's Picks

✔ **Dixie Foam Beds**—Consider these hard foam mattresses as a healthy and inexpensive alternative—also, a lot easier to move around.

✔ **Sleepy's**—The city's biggest discount chain can rest comfortably on its lead—with great selection and prices. Coming soon to a block near you.

BOOKS: NEW

Barnard Bookforum—2955 Broadway (116th St.), Manhattan; 212/749-5535. This Columbia-area bookshop is known to students for its outdoor tables offering all kinds of books for up to 40 percent off cover prices. Brush up your Shakespeare with a volume of his complete works—all for a mere $14.99. Not even Shylock could turn that down. John Updike's *Rabbit at Rest*, the most recent in his ongoing series, was seen for $4.99; similar markdowns can be found on politics, history, and computers. The store stays open nice and late; until 11:00 p.m. on weeknights, 8:00 p.m. on Saturdays, and 7:00 p.m. on Sundays.

Down the block, **Papyrus Books** at 2915 Broadway (212/222-3350) also offers remaindered books at discount. Check in with both.

Barnes and Noble Sale Annex—128 Fifth Ave. (18th St.), Manhattan; 212/633-3500. What can you say? It's just a monster of a book store. In fact, it's two stores right across from one another, forming the base of operations, if you will, for the vast B & N empire. Everything here is sold at some kind of discount, from 10 percent off new titles to remainders and damaged books at a fraction of their original cost. The sale annex is where you'll find the latter, in room after room of bargains. New overstocks are upstairs, diverse as any book store; from a biography section, where most books are $1.98 to $5.98, to coffee-table photo books on various arts. Stephen King's *Four Past Midnight* was seen here recently, reduced from $22.95 to a suspenseful $7.00; and the *New York Times Giant Crossword Puzzle Book* , originally $37.50, was just $10.00. With 250 puzzles, that works out to 4¢ apiece—can't beat that for cheap fun.

Back on the street level, the Annex also has its used and "hurt" books: Paperback fiction from 69¢ each, warehouse clearance items at half-price, and even used books from libraries—many for $3.39. Around the corner (and with its own entrance from the street), is the newest feature, "JR." No, "Dallas" has not risen again. This is a whole store within a store devoted to children's books—again, current titles and overstock bargains—all at discount.

Discount Bookshop—897 First Ave. (50th St.), Manhattan; 212/751-3839. The name says it all. In this pleasant, fairly large store a few blocks up from the United Nations buildings, all new hardcovers are discounted by 15 percent; new paperbacks by 5 percent. Ah, but if you pay in cold, hard cash, your discounts increase to 20 percent for hardcovers and 10 percent for paperbacks. Sign of the times; merchants want the money, pronto. Anyway, the store also sells a lot of used paperbacks, especially novels and mysteries, for half the original cover price; there are display tables outside, and more inside.

Drougas Books—34 Carmine St., Manhattan; 212/229-0078. If this

Mr. Cheap's Picks

✔ **Barnes and Noble Sale Annex**—One of the city's biggest and best stores for every kind of new book at discount.

✔ **Drougas Books**—A packed little shop, great for overstocks in the arts and politics.

small but surprising shop in Greenwich Village could cast itself as a book, it might be "The Little Politically Correct Engine That Could." With tongue in cheek, Drougas refers to its wares as "un-oppressive, non-imperialist discount books." Yes, these do include extensive selections in international relations, philosophy, poetry, and the like; but there are also books on movies and the arts, fiction, travel, and all the rest of the sections you'd find in any bookstore. All of these are overstocks at very low prices, with special tables of $2.99 books. Mr. C saw a Simpsons postcard book, originally $8.95, for just $3.00. Speaking of Hollywood, Penny Stallings' landmark *Flesh and Fantasy* was here for $8.00 in hardcover. And a.m. Sperber's well-received biography on Edward R. Murrow, all eight hundred pages of it, was reduced from $25.00 to a newsmaking $6.00.

SoHo Books—351 West Broadway (Spring St.) , Manhattan; 212/226-3395. You wouldn't expect to find a discount book store in the pricy environs of SoHo, but here it is. Opened just a year ago, SoHo Books sells publishers' overstocks and closeouts, as well as used books in near-new condition, with all the variety and choice of a full-price shop. Looks as pretty as one, too.

There are lots of artsy coffee-table books here, such as a large photo volume on John Lennon, half the original price at $15.00. A collection of three novels by Anne Tyler, including *The Accidental Tourist* , would total $47.00 in value; here it was an intentional $6.98. You'll also find all the knickknacks seen in most book stores—calendars, cards, and the like, at discount—as well as a selection of classical compact discs and cassette tapes selling for $5.98 and $3.98, respectively. The store is open into the evening hours, for a pleasant after-dinner browse.

BOOKS: USED

You can save money on books if you know the right places to shop—and used bookstores are the places to do it. New York is blessed with enough of these to give the hungriest bookworm indigestion. Save even more money at the used bookshops by bringing them books you no longer want. Most stores will give you cash or store credit; you'll usually get more by taking credit. It's a good, cheap way to check out new authors—and to keep your library lean.

Academy Book Store—10 West 18th St., Manhattan; 212/242-4848. The Flatiron District of lower Fifth Avenue is a great area for used bookstores, tucked away on the sidestreets and bounded by two literary lions—the Barnes and Noble Annex to the north and the Strand to the south, all within a square mile. Academy, and its neighbor across the street, Skyline Books (see listing below), can keep you browsing happily for hours.

Academy looks almost like a "regular" book store, big and bright, with good sections on the arts, history, poetry, philosophy, and more. Most are hardcovers, selling for half the original cover price or less; Mr. C found the hefty *Oxford Companion to the American Theatre*, like new, half-price at $25.00. Also the companion book to the television series *"The Civil War"*, reduced from $50.00 to just $15.00.

The store also has an extensive range of LPs and compact discs, focusing on classical music and jazz. Records are priced from $2.00-$5.00 and up, while CDs are mostly $5.99 to $8.99. These, in particular, represent a tremendous collection, with opera, orchestral, and early music recordings arranged according to composer, artist, and label. Most impressive.

Gryphon Bookshop—2246 Broadway (80th St.), Manhattan; 212/362-0706, and
Gryphon Book Annex—246 West 80th St.,Manhattan; 212/724-1541. A visit to the Gryphon is like a trip back to the nineteenth century—a narrow, handsome shop lined from floor to ceiling with dark wood shelves, rolling ladders, and, of course, books on every subject imaginable. Most of these are used, in both paperback and hardcover, and many are rare; especially those in the mezzanine gallery. Gryphon also has a large collection of used records and tapes, including rock, jazz and classical. Most are priced between $5.00 and $10.00. Mr. C even saw a five-album boxed set of Glenn Miller big band hits for $15.00.

The *real* place to prowl for book bargains is the Gryphon Book Annex, just around the corner. It's up on the fourth floor, down a winding hall from the elevator; but once you find it, you may think you've gone to book heaven. Here again, all popular and scholarly subjects are repre-

Mr. Cheap's Picks

✔ **Gryphon Book Annex**—Once you find your way up here, you'll be back again and again for incredible book deals.

✔ **Ruby's Book Sale**—Not only two storefronts of great bargains, but an encyclopedic collection of used magazines, too.

✔ **Strand Book Store**—What can be said that hasn't been said before? Absolutely New York's king of used book stores—like a library that's all for sale.

sented—but everything sells at 50 percent off the marked price. In hardcover, Mr. C found a copy of *Common Ground* by J. Anthony Lukas, in fine condition, and *Love Life*, the fine collection of short stories by Bobbie Ann Mason, each for $7.00; Sparky Lyle's autobiography about his days with the Yankees, *The Bronx Zoo*, for $5.00; and Laurence Olivier's own bio, *Confessions of an Actor,* both in hardcover ($7.50) and paperback ($2.50). For you mystery fiends, there are tons of used paperbacks to support your habit; and even general racks of $1.00 hardcovers and 50¢ paperbacks, including works by Anne Tyler, John Updike, and Frederick Forsyth.

Johnny's Books and Magazines—526A Columbus Ave. (85th St.), Manhattan; no phone. Barely a store, Johnny's is more like a bookmark wedged into the pages of Upper West Side storefronts. In fact, everything on display actually starts from the doorway and spills out onto the sidewalk. These are racks of used paperbacks, all at half their original cover prices; Mr. C found a like-new copy of Michael Crichton's *Jurassic Park* , reduced from $6.00 to $3.00. Johnny's also specializes in recent back issues of magazines, from the *New Yorker*, *Life* and *National Geographic* to *Gourmet*, *Newsweek* and *Playboy*. There are tons of 'em, all half-price.

Manhattan Books—154 Chambers St., Manhattan; 212/385-7395. Near Greenwich Street and the campus of Manhattan Community College, Manhattan Books sells used textbooks for as much as 75 percent to 90 percent off. A used copy of *The Norton Introduction to Literature by Women* , $30.00 if new, sells for $22.00 here. New editions, including general paperbacks, are discounted by about a dollar off the cover price; same deal on shelves of used Penguin editions of Shakespeare plays and other literature. You'll also find lots of used computer books at 50 percent off, along with bins of old magazines. This small but eclectic store is open weekdays only, from 10:00 a.m. to 6:00 p.m.

Louis J. Nathanson Books—219 East 85th St., Manhattan; 212/249-3235. Louis has clearly been here a long time. His narrow, cluttered shop looks more like one you'd expect to find in the Village—or in Dickens' London—than the Upper East Side. The walls are lined with bookshelves and display cases filled with antique spoons, engravings, and other curios. The occasional bit of wall space is sometimes filled by a framed, faded sign suggesting that you smile and be polite to your fellow man. The books are well worn, like those in a library, and they favor novels, political studies, and history. Hardcovers are mostly $7.00 to $10.00 each; tons of paperbacks, which go outside on tables when weather permits, are generally $1.50 to $3.00. Mr. Nathanson is also a political junkie, and when he creaks open the drawer to one of the antique hutches, it's filled like a treasure chest with campaign buttons from just about every election the city or country has held in the last century. Most of these are $1.00 to $3.00; the nostalgic conversations that inevitably follow are free.

Paperback Discounter—2517 Broadway (94th St.), Manhattan; 212/662-1718. Here's a great little neighborhood place for readers with ravenous appetites. The walls of this shop are lined with used paperbacks, mostly novels, all of which sell at 20 percent of their original cover prices. Note well, that's "20 percent *of* ", and not "20 percent *off* ". What a difference an "f" makes! But that's not all—most folks bring books in to swap for store credit. If you really work at it, you can probably keep a full reading list with almost no money changing hands. The store also sells bestselling hardcovers at 20 percent below cover price; and if there's one you want that's not on the bestseller list, they can order it for you at the same discount.

Ruby's Book Sale—119 Chambers St., Manhattan; 212/732-8676. Ruby's is a downtown mecca for new and used books and magazines, all at discount. The new books, sold from open tables, are mostly overstocks and slightly damaged books. You may find coffee-table picture books, like Eliot Porter's *Antarctica*, marked down from $35.00 to $12.00, or a John Jakes novel reduced from $20.00 to just $2.00. Plus greeting cards, maps, and novelties.

Next door, Ruby's goes on to sell used paperbacks at greatly reduced prices; this also looks more like a standard bookshop, with library shelves organized by subject and a wider selection. Better still is the used magazine section, where most copies sell for a dollar. These are arranged by title, and most well-known titles are represented, from *Life* to *Cosmopolitan* . There the system ends; once you've found the batch of, say, *New Yorkers*, you just have to plow through the pile and hope to see the particular back issue you're looking for. The chances are good that you will, if you're patient.

Science Fiction, Mysteries and More—140 Chambers St., Manhattan; 212/385-8798. It's no mystery what you'll find at this Financial District spot. Sci-fi fanatics should have a blast (phaser, that is) browsing through the shelves of new and used books of *Star Trek, Doctor Who, James Bond,* and other stories, as well as mysteries by everyone from good ol' Agatha Christie to bad ol' Stephen King. Used hardcovers are mostly $4.00, and used paperbacks are $2.00 (or half of the cover price, in some instances). SFM & M also has posters from all your favorite movies and TV shows, buys and sells vintage comic books, and even offers free monthly readings by science fiction and mystery authors. They're open weeknights until 7:00, and weekend afternoons until 6:30.

Skyline Books And Records—13 West 18th St., Manhattan; 212/759-5463. When similar stores gather themselves together, it's good for their business and great for shoppers. Skyline complements Academy Books (see above) just across the street, rather than competing with it. After all, you never know where that one lost title may turn up. Skyline is cramped and winding, like an eccentric old library, with a vast selection in all subjects—fun and serious. You'll find hardcovers and paperbacks mixed together, at good prices. The record room, way in the back, has lots of well-worn LPs in rock, jazz, and classical music. They start as low as 75¢, but most are in the $4.00-to-$9.00 range. In good weather you can browse the bins outside the shop—a cherished New York tradition.

The Strand Bookstore—828 Broadway (12th St.), Manhattan; 212/473-1452. Okay, here we go. The Strand is widely known as the mother of all discount book stores, and it well deserves the title. So many titles are here, in fact, that it looks as if your local library decided to sell everything off. The sign says, "Eight Miles of Books"; Mr. C says, "start jogging." There are so many books here, and almost as many ways to save money on them.

For starters, browse the racks outside the shop; they're filled with fiction and nonfiction, hardcover and soft, for $1.00 and $2.00 apiece. Many are a mere 48¢, or five for two bucks; why this odd price, who knows? Who cares?

Once inside, you'll find the recent overstocks and publishers' clearances. Mr. C noted David McCullough's best-selling bio of Harry Truman, originally $30.00, reduced to $23.00; and Anne Rice's *Cry to Heaven* in paper for just $4.00. Save $11.00 on a boxed set of Art Speigelman's clever and harrowing *Maus* books, here $25.95. And Martin Gottfried's *More Broadway Musicals*, filled with oversized, glossy color photos, sells here for $45.00, down from $60.00.

Move further in to the art section. Here, you can find a $70.00 edition on the works of Georges Seurat, with hundreds of color plates, for $52.95. And then you come to the shelves and shelves of general categories—the library part—with discounted books on every subject: History, drama, politics, science fiction, computer manuals, poetry, television, and everything in between.

But wait, there's more! Downstairs, they continue with all the subjects that couldn't fit on the huge main floor. Then there are shelves and shelves of reviewers' copies, tons of recent novels, and other releases in every subject at a straight 50 percent off cover price. Also, this area has the "hurt books" section, with slightly damaged bindings and such, for up to 80 percent off. You can even find various—vintage?—phone books for sale here.

The third floor houses rare and antiquarian books, not cheap, but considered to be reasonable amongst collectors' editions. Many are signed by famous authors. Strand has information desks on each floor, where helpful clerks can look up titles on their computers and in catalogs. The store is open daily until 9:30 in the evening; look for their outdoor bookstalls in parks around town, too.

CDS, RECORDS AND TAPES, VIDEO

Like used book shops, many of these stores will allow you to trade in the music you don't want anymore—though, alas, used LPs are getting harder to trade in these days. You can often get cash for the deal, but you'll get more in store credit. It's an easy way to try out artists you might not take a chance on at full price.

Academy Book Store—10 West 18th St., Manhattan; 212/242-4848. See listing under "Books: Used."

Downtown Music—211 East 5th St., Manhattan; 212/473-0043.

For such a small store, Downtown Music has lots of good old LPs, both new and used, along with its selection of cassettes and compact discs. Rock, jazz, reggae, and country are well-represented here, with most albums priced at $5.00 to $9.00 new, and $1.00 to $2.00 used. Lots of vintage jazz in the used bins, particularly; from Tony Bennett to George Benson to the Mahavishnu Orchestra. Used CDs are mostly $5.99 and $6.99, including such gems as Paul Simon's "Rhythm of the Saints"; and used cassettes are two for $5.00.

Entertainment Warehouse—835 Broadway (13th St.), Manhattan; 212/475-1844, and 1521 Third Ave. (86th St.), Manhattan; 212/717-4199. Here's a new development in second-hand music and video. Entertainment Warehouse buys and sells records, tapes and CDs; but they only take used items in like-new condition, which they shrink-wrap just as the original factories do. What you get is something that looks and sounds new, at used prices. Compact discs, mostly rock, pop and classical, are $5.99 to $7.99. Cassette tapes range from 99¢ to $3.99, with some unused clearance titles mixed in. The selection is quite good, almost what you'd find in any retail store; and unlike many such stores, you can bring anything back in for an exchange within seven days.

EW takes the same approach with VHS videotapes, most of which are priced at $9.99. The selection is as good as your corner video store, in both feature films and music videos. And for the kids, there are used computer games by Nintendo, from $7.95, and Sega, from $9.95. Finally, the store has good prices on blank audio and video tapes. These, of course, *are* brand new.

Don't forget, you can sell them your own used music and videos, if they are in good enough condition. A compact disc or video tape will usually net you $2.00 in cash or $2.50 in store credit; possibly more if it's a hot title. It's another great way to keep your library sounding good very cheaply.

Footlight Records—113 East 12th St., Manhattan; 212/533-1572. The name tells you that the specialty of the house here is Broadway...and then some. Footlight may be one of the city's most extensive selections of show tunes, movie soundtracks, spoken word, and similar recordings, both American and imported. And as the other half of the name implies, vinyl is still king here. It's a very impressive shop. Since many of the titles are rare or out of print, that's often the only way you can dig up some of these musicals. Rare albums are mostly priced around $15.00, but you'll find lots at lower prices. Footlight does buy and sell, and so you will find tapes and CDs—and you will find some rock and pop sections. One of Mr. C's money saving tricks is to "hit 'em where they ain't"; in other words, if you check rock & roll stores for classical discs, or this store for rock, you'll find them selling for less than those in which the store specializes. The choice may be slimmer, but you can get rock CDs here for $7.00 to $8.00. Worth a look.

The Golden Disc—239 Bleecker St., Manhattan; 212/255-7899. One of the bigger and better of Greenwich Village's many used music shops, Golden Disc specializes in imports and out-of-print discs—albums, 45s and CDs. Downstairs, in fact, is a whole room devoted mainly to new and used jazz LPs, and it's a fine collection. With an old-time dedication to service, the store will play any album for you to check the music and quality of the disc (they *expect* to do this for you!).

On the street level, they also have new jazz CDs at reduced prices; most of these range up to around $8.98, still below retail store prices. New cassettes are even better—Wynton Marsalis's "Think of One" for $5.98, and a Benny Carter Orchestra tape for $3.98. Lots of these to look at. The store also has a good selection in blues, rock oldies, and world beat.

Grand Prix Records—2327 Broadway (84th St.), Manhattan; 212/799-4590. Here's just what the Upper West Side ordered: A secondhand music store that's pleasant, is well stocked with a large range of styles, and doesn't blast hard rock. Grand Prix won't make you feel that you should be wearing a studded leather jacket, as so many of the downtown record shops do. The staff is so helpful that someone actually comes up to you and asks what you're looking for. And there's even a sense of decor, beyond the tattered Rolling Stones posters of downtown.

Don't get Mr. C wrong; those stores are great too, and they have lots of bargains; but sometimes you want a more relaxed place to browse, especially on a Sunday brunch stroll. Anyway, GP sells new and used music in jazz, classical, pop, new age, and much more. They

Mr. Cheap's Picks

✔ **J & R Music World**—Three stores on the same block offer fantastic bargains on records, tapes, CDs, and video, starting from just 99¢.

✔ **Tower Records Clearance Outlet**—Now roll all three into one, and you've got Tower's version of same. Located directly behind their Village store.

✔ **Triton**—Good prices on laser video discs, the next big thing in movies.

have lots of Broadway musicals and movie soundtracks, and international music from Europe, Brazil, Africa, etc.

New compact discs are $12.98, competitive with major music stores. Used CDs are mostly $7.98 to $8.98, while used cassettes are a mere $2.98, and in good condition. The store also sells video movies and concerts. On nice days they put bins out on the sidewalk for further browsing.

J & R Music World Outlets—23, 25 & 33 Park Row, Manhattan; 212/349-8400. Mixed into the many J & R storefronts that line the block across from City Hall Park are these goldmines for new records at discount. The Jazz Outlet, upstairs at 33 Park Row, features many of the latest compact disc releases for $10.99 each, with cassettes for $6.99. Whether your groove is big band, straight-ahead contemporary, or fusion, you'll find a lot to choose from here. Downstairs, you'll find similar savings on classical music. The store's top-ten best sellers are always at extra discount, and there are entire catalogues of budget-label CDs for $3.99 each.

A couple of doors down, at 23 Park Row, the bargains continue in the Budget Music Outlet. Along with more jazz and classical, this branch adds rock, pop, Broadway and international sounds. Most LPs, never-opened overstocks, are $3.99 to $5.99; however, some go as low as a dollar. Same price range for cassettes, while the CDs here range from $1.99 to $7.99. Yes, most of these are recordings that weren't hot sellers in retail stores; but you'll be surprised at how much there is to choose from—nearly as much variety and top artists as any full-price store.

Meanwhile, don't forget the J & R Video Outlet, at 23 Park Row; you'll find good prices on VHS movies and music videos here. A recent sale featured a wide selection on sale for $12.95 per title, including concert videos by Eric Clapton, Paul McCartney, James Brown, and Tina Turner.

Rebel Rebel—319 Bleecker St., Manhattan; 212/989-0770. The Bowie quote in this store's name tells you what you need to know: They specialize in rock. That includes alternative sounds and current dance styles such as hip-hop. Lots of new and used LPs, priced from $4.98, and CDs from about $8.98. It's a small store, but they do pack in a good selection.

Record Explosion—2 Broadway (Battery Pl.), Manhattan; 212/509-6444, 180 Broadway (John St.), Manhattan; 212/693-1510, 53 Nassau St., Manhattan; 212/233-3890, 384 Fifth Ave. (36th St.), Manhattan; 212/ 736-5624, and 469 Seventh Ave. (35th St.), Manhattan; 212/643-1030. This discount chain has standard prices on current-release rock and pop music. What is more interesting to Mr. C is their huge stock of closeout bargains. They have table after table of cassette tapes priced at three for $10.00; these are not your usual never-heard-of-'em bands but lots of big names, like The Beatles, Genesis, and plenty of Motown artists. The store also has wall racks filled with "previously viewed" videotapes from $5.99 to $9.99. Again, these are titles you'll definitely know and probably want. The tapes are all in very good condition, shrink-wrapped to look almost new.

Revolver Records—45 West 8th St., 2nd Floor, Manhattan; 212/982-6760. As you may guess from the name, the owner of this store is a Beatles freak. The bins are full of great records by the Fab Four and lots of other hot bands from the 1960s. While this is a house specialty, they do of course have rock & roll from all periods. Unless they are rare, most LPs go for $2.99 to $4.99, with cassettes around the same prices. They also have a large selection of used compact discs, most of which are $7.98 and up. Some new CDs are mixed in for $12.98, which is still a dollar or two better than most retail stores. Revolver also specializes in current and back issues of rock magazines, as well as tour posters for all your favorite bands from yesterday...and today.

Rock's In Your Head—157 Prince St., Manhattan; 212/475-6729. A used record shop in SoHo? What are things coming to? Well, you'll be coming to this store for a small but good variety of music—mostly rock & roll (naturally). Top-line used CDs go for $7.99 and $8.99; many others are priced at $5.00 each, or three for ten bucks. Even among these, Mr. C found controversial rapper Sister Souljah and once-controversial rocker Cyndi Lauper. There are some LPs and cassettes as well, but space is limited here, so there's not as much to choose from.

Second Coming Records—235 Sullivan St., Manhattan; 212/212-228-1313. Tucked away in a relatively quiet section of the Village, Second Coming has a large selection of used music. Most CDs range from $4.99 to $7.99; Suzanne Vega's "Days of Open Hand" was seen here for $5.99. New discs are blended in, usually priced at $11.99. Cassettes generally go for $2.99 to $4.99; in between was the Rolling Stones' "Under Cover" for $3.99. And records, of course, are plentiful. Joe Jackson's "Night and Day" was spotted, in good condition, for $2.99. Second Coming also has a good variety of music videos, most of which are in the vicinity of $19.99 or thereabouts.

Second Hand Rose's Record Shop—525 Sixth Ave. (14th Street), Manhattan; 212/675-3735. Vinyl is not dead! Of the city's many used music shops, few have as many good old LP record albums as Second Hand Rose's. The owner is clearly a jazz aficionado, lining the walls with bookcases stuffed with well-worn but well-loved records. Most of these are priced from $7.99 to $9.99—not as cheap as the records in other secondhand shops, but then, many of these titles have gone out of print. They should probably cost more. Along with jazz of all strains, Rose's is great for soul, R & B, oldies, and even—arrgh—disco. And they do have other formats, with most cassettes for $4.99 and $5.99, and compact discs as low as $3.99 and up. For higher-priced CDs, you can get a further discount if you buy three discs or more.

Smash Compact Discs—33 St. Mark's Place, Manhattan; 212/473-2200. That's not a suggestion, it's the name of this well-stocked shop. Smash has a whole wall of used CDs, mostly rock with some jazz and country mixed in; most of these are priced from $7.99 to $9.99. Mr. C found major albums by Van Morrison, R.E.M., Peter Gabriel, the Beatles, and many more. Even a double-length CD containing twenty hits by Sly and the Family Stone was only $11.99. One of the best record shops in the East Village.

Tower Records Clearance Outlet—20 East 4th St., Manhattan; 212/228-7317. Right around the corner from Tower's main megaplex, on the corner of Lafayette Street, is their Clearance Outlet. Here they sell cutouts and overstocks in all media—records, cassettes, CDs and videotapes—and all genres from rock to jazz to classical. These are unused, in their original packaging. Most CDs are just $5.99 to $7.99, with LPs and tapes a bit lower. Twelve-inch dance singles are as low as 49¢. In the classical section they have the entire Aurophon series of compact discs for $2.99 each, and opera cassettes for $3.99. The extensive section is arranged by composer, with as much to choose from as any full-price store. In the soundtrack area, Mr. C found a two-record set of the complete Les Miserables for $5.99.

Speaking of soundtracks, Tower has tons of pre-viewed VHS movies for $6.99 to $9.99; including such titles as *Rain Man, E.T.*, and *The Accidental Tourist*. Older movie "classics" (in glorious black and white) are just $4.99. Back in the music section, you can also find an "As Is" final sale display with records and tapes as low as $1.99; along with various music storage racks, like a fifteen-cassette carrying case for $2.49. Like its siblings, the Tower Clearance Outlet is open daily from 9:00 a.m. to midnight.

Triton—247 Bleecker St., Manhattan; 212/243-3610. Get with the modern world! Triton deals mainly in CDs, with some good prices on used and unused discs. All new jazz titles, except imports and sets, go for $9.99; new classical CDs sell for $8.99. There is also a good selection of used CDs in all categories, mostly $4.99 to $7.99, as well as some new and used cassettes.

But where the store *really* stands out is with laser video discs—no doubt the wave of the future. Unlike movies on VHS video tape, laser discs offer permanent, superior picture quality and digital sound. Triton is poised to become a major dealer in this format, using volume sales to keep prices low. Even before the laser video market began taking off, this tiny shop was selling discs at substantial discount. Most titles go for $15.00-$20.00, as much as half the price of other retail outlets. If you can't get into the store, call or send for a catalog; Triton does lots of business by mail order.

Venus Records—13 St. Mark's Place, Manhattan; 212/598-4459. Half a flight up from the hustle and bustle of St. Mark's Place, Venus has a big selection of what they themselves call "Cheap CDs." Mr. C was instantly attracted. Indeed, all of the discs in this section were priced at $4.00 and $5.00 each—with major artists like Bruce Springsteen, Julia Fordham, and Carly Simon. They also have plenty of cassette tapes, most $1.00 to $3.00, and LPs are generally $3.00 to $4.00. All of these, of course, are used, and the collection leans toward all varieties of rock & roll.

CAMERAS

As is the case with home appliances, there are hundreds of places to save money on cameras and electronics in New York. Many of the discount places are better avoided, however, because their merchandise may be almost entirely imported from other countries, opening up greater possibilities for shady deals. Protect yourself while shopping around by inquiring about the store's guarantee policy: Make sure the item you want carries an American warranty. Remember, you are perfectly within your rights to ask about this in the store.

Alkit Camera And Electronics—222 Park Ave. South (18th St.), Manhattan; 212/674-1515, and 866 Third Ave. (52nd St.), Manhattan; 212/832-2101. Alkit has been around for over fifty years, with competitive prices on all kinds of cameras and related equipment. These large stores are well stocked with all the big brands in 35mm cameras, instamatics, video camcorders, TVs and VCRs, and binoculars and accessories. They also have good discounts on film and blank audio and video tape. A Nikon N5005 semi automatic, with built-in flash, was recently on sale for $279.00; while the fully automatic Minolta "Freedom Zoom 70c" was selling for $189.00. Panasonic VCRs start under $200.00, with a four-head model for $229.00 Alkit also rents equipment and accepts trade-ins on purchases—another great way to save cash. The sales staff is very helpful; the atmosphere is pleasant and professional. Closed Sundays.

America Electronics—50 East 14th St., Manhattan; 212/353-0765. See listing under "Electronics."

Chambers Outlet—56 Reade St., Manhattan; 212/267-6910. Why isn't Chambers Outlet actually on Chambers Street? Who knows. Still, it's close enough, part of that vast area of discount shops small and large. This is a cozy old Mom 'n Pop photo store, selling lots of used cameras—from a Kodak Instamatic for $15.00 to a 35mm Olympus XA-1, with flash, for $100.00. They even have lots of Polaroid Land cameras, the original snap-and-pull, from about $65.00; or go modern with a Kodak Disc camera for $30.00. They also have lenses, flash units, Super-8 movie cameras and projectors, and more—all with a ninety-day store warranty. They do repairs on premises and will be happy to give you a free estimate.

47th St. Photo—67 West 47th St., Manhattan; 212/921-1287, and 115 West 45th St., Manhattan; 212/921-1287. 47th St. Photo is widely acknowledged as the king of New York's camera and electronics megastores. So big, in fact, that they have expanded to two midtown locations. At both addresses you'll find tremendous bargains in all departments. Like their nearby rival, Willoughby's, you'll do better here if you have already done your research and you're just shopping around for the lowest

Mr. Cheap's Picks

✔ **47th St. Photo/Willoughby's**—These two giants divide up the fiefdom of midtown Manhattan with great prices and terrible service.

✔ **Wall Street Camera**—Insider trading tip—it's worth a trip all the way downtown to get these unbelievable prices.

price. The sales staff always seems to be busy doing everything but serving you. Once you get someone's attention, however, throw a model number at the guy and he'll probably come back at you with a great price.

The camera department stocks every major brand: Canon, Minolta, Leica, Nikon, and all the rest. Fully automatic Nikons start at $144.00 for the "Zoom Touch 400." A Pentax auto-focus SLR, with power zoom and a retractable flash, was recently on sale for $419.00; it's a complete kit, with lens and case, with a list price of $935.00. The store also sells a full range of video camcorders by Panasonic, JVC, and Sony at very competitive prices.

Speaking of video, check out 47th St. if you're shopping around for a TV or VCR. They're also great for stereo; telephones, faxes and answering machines; computers (both PC and Macintosh styles) and software packages; and home appliances. Items recently on sale included a Compaq 386 notebook computer, with a 120mb hard drive, for $1,349.00 (sounds like a lot, but not for this latest of technologies), a Panasonic fax/answering machine combo for $388.00, and a portable CD player with headphones, also Panasonic, for $139.00. Good prices, too, on microwaves, juice machines, electric toothbrushes, and other vital necessities of modern life.

47th St. Photo is closed on Friday afternoons and all day Saturday, but re-opens on Sundays.

J & R Music World Camera Outlet—27 Park Row, Manhattan; 212/732-8600. Part of the J & R empire in the City Hall area, this shop stocks an extensive selection of cameras and optical equipment at rock-bottom prices. They can afford to, doing such a high-volume business. And yet the atmosphere, while busy, is more friendly and helpful—unlike its midtown competitors. Once you get someone to help you, he or she will take as much time as you need—depending, of course, on the amount of traffic in the store.

An Olympus 35mm zoom camera, fully automatic with a built-in flash, sells here for $199.95—$100 below the list price. It includes everything you need to start shooting but the film. A similar Nikon model, with a retail price of $550.00, sells here for $399.95. J & R also carries a full range of accessories, such as lenses, filters, tripods, and the rest. They also have good prices on telescopes and binoculars. Open seven days a week.

The Market Place—17 West 14th St., Manhattan; 212/620-0242. See listing under "Appliances."

Shifuran Photo—125 East 4th St., Manhattan; 212/533-9269. Shifuran is a full-service wholesale and retail camera shop in the East Village. In addition to good prices on new equipment, they buy and sell quality used cameras and other electronics. You may find a Vivitar auto-focus camera for as little as $39.95, or a Pentax 900 with a zoom lens for $160.00. There are always plenty to choose from: Minolta, Olympus, Polaroid and more. And, of course, you can get cash for your old camera too, if you want to sell or trade in.

Shifuran has great prices on film (developing, too) and lithium batteries. They also sell and connect Motorola beepers, take passport photos, send and receive faxes . . . kind of like a photographic general store. Open seven days a week.

Sixth Avenue Electronics City—1030 Sixth Ave. (39th St.), Manhattan; 212/391-2777. See listing under "Electronics."

Triest Export—560 Twelfth Ave. (44th St.), Manhattan; 212/246-1548. See listing under "Appliances."

Wall Street Camera—82 Wall St., Manhattan; 212/344-0011. If you're looking for fantastic prices from a solid, reputable dealer, here's an insider trading tip: Buy low at Wall Street Camera. They have Pentax, Olympus, Leica, Contax, and more, all at good prices. Snap the Olympus "Stylus" 35mm camera, with fully automatic focus and film handling, for just $109.00, or their "Infinity Zoom 200" power zoom model for $139.00. They also sell some demo cameras at further savings, such as the Leica "Mini" 35mm SLR—with a suggested retail price of $415.00—for a downright microscopic $249.00. Speaking of optics, Wall Street has binoculars by Leica, Pentax, and others too. New cameras carry American warranties, which are so important; and the store backs its merchandise up with technical support by phone, to answer any questions you may have. Any questions? Go!

Willoughby's —110 West 32nd St., Manhattan; 212/790-1800. Willoughby's claims to be the world's largest cameras and electronics store. Whether or not that is true, they certainly have a lot. Megavolume is the style here, which means it's best if you check out their prices after you already know exactly which model you want. Cameras come in every size, shape, and brand; you can find a fully automatic Fuji snapshot camera for as little as $37.00, or a 35mm Canon Max for $79.00. They also carry brands for professionals, such as Hasselblad, in stock. Mr. C found a 35mm Pentax with a zoom lens, built-in flash, and motorized winding on sale for $224.00. Willoughby's also takes trade-ins to help you save more money; which means that they have lots of used cameras for sale—like a Leica R-4 35mm camera for $140.00.

In the video department, you'll find competitive prices on camcorders, televisions, and VCRs. A JVC 8mm palmcorder was recently on sale for $549.00; and a Pioneer multi-CD laser disc player—that's audio and video—was $399.00. And we haven't even gotten to video games, telephones, stereo, fax machines, electronic organizers, and all the rest.

Willoughby's has a lot to choose from in computers, with 286 desktop systems as low as $348.00 (without monitor). Notebook computers begin around $1,200, including models with up-to-the-minute technical advances; and among the many computer printers, Mr. C found a Sharp laserjet model for $999.00. Needless to say, there's a lot to plow through here, so know what you want and you shouldn't get swamped. When you're at the pricing stage, this is one of the places to compare.

The Wiz—726 Broadway (4th St.), Manhattan; 212/475-1700, and many other locations in Brooklyn, Bronx, Manhattan, Queens and Staten Island. See listing under "Electronics."

CLOTHING—NEW

Know what you're buying! Clothes, like anything else, are sold at discount for many reasons. Let's go over some terms quickly. With new merchandise, *first quality* means perfect clothing that has no flaws of any kind. It may be reduced in price as a sales promotion, or because it's overstock or from a past season. *Discontinued* items are self-explanatory; again, most are new and perfectly good.

Seconds, or *irregulars*, are new clothes that have some slight mistakes in their manufacture or have been damaged in shipping. Often, these blemishes are hard to see. A reputable store will call your attention to the reason, either with a sign on the rack or a piece of masking tape on the problem area.

The "New Clothing" section below covers both these kinds of stores. It includes many shops around the ever-popular Orchard Street area of the Lower East Side. Remember that almost all stores in that neighborhood close at 2:00 p.m. on Friday and all day Saturday, in observance of the Sabbath. They reopen on Sundays.

A special tip from Mr. C: If you're a die-hard bargain shopper with a taste for designer clothes, consider subscribing to **The S & B Report**. It's a monthly publication that lists 50 to 250 designer showroom sales in every issue. This is real insider info, telling you where and when to get men's and women's clothing by Armani, Donna Karan, Escada, Betsy Johnson, Joseph Abboud, Kikit, and more—plus kids' stuff, shoes, jewelry, and things for the home—at savings of 50 percent to 80 percent. These are sales you'd probably never know about otherwise, taking place in office building showrooms and warehouses. Subscriptions cost $49.00 per year; call 1-800-283-6278, or write to: Lazar Media Group, Inc., 112 East 36th Street, New York, NY 10016.

MEN'S AND WOMEN'S WEAR—GENERAL

A & S Fashion Center—2496 Broadway (93rd St.), Manhattan; 212/873-6538. Not the famous old department store, just the same name. This cozy little Upper West Side boutique is ready to outfit the stylish woman from head to toe—all at discount. The walls are lined with racks and racks of collections by lesser-known designers like Mark Farrel, Pablo, Olga Chaus, and many others. In one example, a smart-looking Jessica Howard blazer and skirt set was reduced from $125.00 to just $70.00. A & S also has everything to accessorize these ensembles, from outerwear to jewelry, lingerie, and hosiery. They also specialize in petite and large sizes of clothing. Nice, helpful service, too.

Aaron's—627 Fifth Ave. (17th St.), Park Slope, Brooklyn; 718/768-5400. Okay, folks, here's one of the biggies. Aaron's is one of those places you have to go outside of Manhattan to find. One of those word-of-mouth legends. And because they don't have a high midtown rent, or advertising costs, Aaron's can save you 20 percent to 50 percent off women's designer fashions. These are big names, current styles, first quality, with a lot to choose from. In order to do this, of course, they cannot advertise the labels—but you'll know 'em, all right. Have a look for yourself. The store is open late on Thursdays (until 9:00 p.m.), otherwise until 6:00 p.m., and closed Sundays. Lots of free parking across the street.

A Real New York Bargain—253 Broadway (Murray St.), Manhattan; 212/587-9188, 1293 Broadway (Herald Center), Third Floor, Manhattan; 212/695-4776, and 380 Fifth Ave. (35th St.), Manhattan; 212/695-0430. This store's simple pricing philosophy has become the latest retail marketing rage: Every item in the store is $10.00. Judging by the crowds, and the expanding chain of stores, people seem to be convinced that the name is no lie. There are now branches as far away as Florida, where it is presumably something of a novelty; but here in the Big Apple, competition is stiff. ARNYB is probably the biggest and best of the lot. Their downtown outpost, right across from City Hall Park, offers two floors of clothing—women upstairs, and men downstairs. To be sure, you aren't going to find big-name designers for $10.00; but mixed into the good professional wear and casual sportswear, you may see names like Jordache, Forenza, and Atlantic Traders. Two-piece sets are $20.00; and downstairs, be sure to check out the clearance room, where everything is—yes—$5.00. Plenty of men's stuff too, from sports slacks and print shirts to exercise togs.

Many shops with the "Everything $10.00" approach have sprung up in the past year or so, including the similar-sounding **A Real Delancey Street Bargain** at 108 Delancey Street, Manhattan (212/228-4903) and 801 Manhattan Avenue, Brooklyn (718/383-4029). Mr. C found such items as Georgetown University and Hard Rock Cafe sweatshirts, a Jordache knit leotard with fishnet sleeves, and men's linen trousers by Basco, originally $40.00 All, of course, were $10.00.

"B" A Member—315 West 57th St., Manhattan; 212/581-5014, and 2011 Broadway (69th St.), Manhattan; 212/721-6013. What's the secret here? You have to be a member to shop in these two West Side boutiques. How do you become a member? You have to buy something. If this sounds like the biggest "Catch 22" this side of Actors Equity, well, it's not really so tough. Ring the bell at the front door and they'll let you in to look around. You'll find good prices on lesser-known designer names in professional and casual wear for women. Once you make a purchase, you become a member. That's not so hard, is it? The real story here is one of mailing lists and direct-marketing. Can't fault them for taking a novel approach to selling in these tricky economic times.

Bella Nassau Boutique—99 Nassau St., Manhattan; 212/227-3800. One of the many discount stores along this pedestrian shopping street below City Hall, Bella Nassau specializes in ladies' professional wear at good prices. Dealing in lesser-known brand names, the store buys in volume and sells first-quality merchandise at big discounts. A selection of Vivien Forest sweaters, sporty with gold-beaded applique, was recently found here for $40.00 The same sweaters sell at Macy's for over $100.00. Fiumicello skirt suits, made with a wool and silk blend, were reduced from $180.00 to just $50.00 And blouses by Lorelei and Yves St. Clair were on sale at two for $35.00. Have a look!

BFO Menswear—149 Fifth Ave. (21st St.), Manhattan; 212/254-0059. The main branch of this seven-store regional chain, BFO is another of lower Fifth Avenue's many discounters of designer suits. Right across the street from Moe Ginsburg, and a few blocks up from Eisenberg, Fenwick, Gilcrest, and others described in this section, this whole district allows you to compare bargains. BFO offers well-known name brands, which they cannot advertise (but they are many of the same names as the other stores), at $200.00 to $500.00 below retail prices. Of course, most retail prices are somewhat inflated, but don't worry—you're still getting a good deal on these suits. Wool/gabardine blends are in the $250.00 range, and a famous-name raincoat was recently seen here for just $129.00. Open seven days a week.

Bolton's—90 Broad St., Manhattan; 212/785-0513, 59 Liberty St., Manhattan; 212/349-7464, 17 East 8th St., Manhattan; 212/475-9547, 53 West 23rd St., Manhattan; 212/924-6860, 4 East 34th St., Manhattan; 212/684-3750, 685 Third Ave. (43rd St.), Manhattan; 212/682-5661, 110 West 51st St., Manhattan; 212/245-5227, 27 West 57th St., Manhattan; 212/935-4431, 225 East 57th St., Manhattan; 212/755-2527, 1191 Third Ave. (69th St.), Manhattan; 212/628-7553, 2251 Broadway (80th St.), Manhattan; 212/873-8545, and 1180 Madison Ave. (86th St.), Manhattan; 212/722-4419. Flash! Bolton's brandishes big discounts in no-holds-barred battle to be best

Mr. Cheap's Picks

✔ MEN'S SUITS—A three-way tie (no pun intended): **Gorsart**, **LS Men's Clothing**, and **Rothman's** are classy standouts for classic suits, hundreds of dollars below retail.

✔ WOMEN'S DESIGNER MEGA-STORES—**Aaron's and Loehmann's** in the outer boroughs, and **S & W** near Chelsea, offer incredible savings on designer fashions from top to toe—and vast stocks to choose from.

✔ DESIGNER DEPARTMENT STORES—Down in the Financial District, men and women can maintain their personal wealth in high style at both **Century 21** and the **Burlington Coat Factory**. In midtown, fashion plates will go crazy for **Daffy's**.

✔ **Cheap & Chic**—This East Village discovery will keep you in hip Euro-fashion without spending *molto lire*.

✔ **Fishkin Knitwear**—One of the best shops on the Lower East Side for current women's designer fashions at "last-season" prices.

✔ **Nice Price**—Very popular bargain boutiques, with markdowns on cool casual wear and party clothes.

✔ **Simply Samples**—One of the most consistent outlets for designer sample selloffs, right in the Garment District.

bargain chain! Yes, Bolton's continues to expand its empire, as does Labels for Less (see below), and the winner is—you. Both have plenty of branches scattered about town, and both offer good bargains on designer clothing for ladies. Because of its relationships with the manufacturers, the store prefers not to advertise the names you'll find here; but trust Mr. C, they're top-notch and first-quality.

Most of the looks here are for the professional set. A European-style blazer and skirt set, by a well-known name indeed, was recently seen for just $149.00; a 100-percent-silk-washed running suit, in two-tone purple and pink, was $59.99. And the clearance racks offer further discounts, like half-price on a designer name silk dress. Then there is the separate room filled with the real high-end names, with plenty of fancy evening wear. Bolton's is also great for accessories, like hats, gloves, scarves, and belts.

Bruce Elliott Clothiers—43 Park Place, 5th floor, Manhattan; 212/962-1117. Here's a Financial District bargain that's blue-chip all the way. At Bruce Elliott (actually the two first names of its co-owners), there's nothing cheap about the men's suits except the prices. An out-of-the-way location and no advertising keep the costs low and the emphasis on service. The company makes its own line of top-quality clothing, mixing a few other names in on the racks.

All-wool suits, most of which would retail for $700.00 to $800.00, sell here around $300.00. Wool blends sell in the $150.00 to $200.00 range, with values of up to $300.00. These are traditional styles and are fully-constructed suits made from two-ply woolens. Seasonal suits, like summertime cotton poplins, are further reduced at the end of that season; that's when you can get one for as little as $75.00 from the half-price rack. Mr. C also saw a 100-percent-silk blazer there for the same price. There are also lots of accessories—dress shirts, silk ties, and the like. Often these run as special promotions, like three silk ties for $20.00.

Again, service is a key element at Bruce Elliott. The store offers free alterations, one of the very few in this class who do. They can also recut their suits to fit a more athletic build, if necessary, though there is a fee for that. The folks here really work to build a permanent, but easy-going relationship with each customer; and it works, leading to many repeat customers.

Burlington Coat Factory—45 Park Place, Manhattan; 212/571-2630. Bargains, bargains, bargains! This place has five floors of 'em. There's plenty to see here, in designer and casual fashions for men, women, and children. Ladies may find a belted dress by John Roberts, in bright fuchsia with white lapels, reduced from $90.00 to $25.00; Evan Picone blazers as low as $20.00; and the same price for a variety of suede skirts. On the men's floors, wool-blend suits by Egon von Furstenburg were seen for $89.00; Botany 500 raincoats reduced from $170.00 to $100.00; and John Weitz cashmere-blend overcoats, originally $200.00, here just $90.00. For sporty guys, 100-percent-silk shirts in bold colors by Bogari were marked down from $50.00 to $20.00. And for the kids, there is an entire room filled with racks of jeans, tops, and outerwear. A pair of Little Levis overalls with a list price of $32.00, sells here for $22.00.

Canal Jean Company—504 Broadway (Broome St.), Manhattan; 212/226-1130. This store is so big it must be described in both the "new" and "used" clothing sections of this book. Five floors and fifty-thousand square feet of clothing bargains make Canal Jean (yes, which used to be on Canal Street) a must for the latest in hip at low prices. In new clothes, hip always seems to include Levi's jeans; Canal claims to be the largest Levi's outlet in the city. Prices here start as low as $17.99 for the ever-popular 501 button-fly, and $26.99 for the basic zipper. From there it's on to dyed, silver tab, baggy, denim jackets, and the rest.

First-quality leather fashions from baseball jackets to full-length coats are sold at up to 50 percent off including such makers as Schott, U-2, M. Julian and more. Some begin at just $40.00. Other outerwear bargains include men's and women's trenchcoats for $30.00 and up.

Ladies will love the mezzanine lingerie section, with dancewear, cotton tights at half-price, and some naughtily seductive stylings; not to mention dresses from $5.00 to $10.00 and up. Shoes are here too, including black patent-leather varieties as low as $30.00 to $40.00. The store just goes on and on, and is open seven days a week into the evenings. Why, it could almost be listed under Mr. Cheap's "Entertainment" section too; it's an experience just to walk around and observe the scene.

The Catwalk—440 East 9th St., Manhattan; 212/330-8304. For shoppers, one of the joys of walking the sidestreets of New York is the discovery of a little storefront where some up-and-coming designer is making his or her latest creations and selling them on the spot. The Catwalk is just that for designer Shin Yee Man, who opened for business in the spring of '92. Ms. Man makes classy fashions for women and sells them for below retail prices. She calls her styles "timeless", and they are simple: Dresses and skirts in wool, lace, cotton-lycra, and stretch velvet. The dresses go for $60.00 and up, while skirts start around $25.00. She also has handmade jewelry from places like Indonesia and Thailand, from $10.00 and up. Discover it for yourself.

Century 21—22 Cortlandt St., Manhattan; 212/227-9092. See listing under "Department Stores."

Cheap & Chic—81 Third Ave., Manhattan; 212/995-2395. This East Village place is really cool. They have incredible prices on trendy European sportswear for men and women. Guys will love Italian suits and blazers, such as a 100-percent-wool suit from Profilo, originally $225.00, here just $125.00. Trousers from Basco are $35.00; they can go for upwards of $100.00 at Barney's. For women there are lots of designer skirts at $15.00 and $25.00; Mr. C noticed an Armani vest for $45.00. as well as sweaters by Kikit for the same price. Other names you'll find here include Matinique, C.P. Company, and Willi Wear. They also have leather jackets; one from M. Julian was half-price at $400.00, but some go for as little as $75.00.

The store is open daily from 11:00 a.m. to 8:00 p.m., and Sundays from noon to 7 p.m. The stock moves quickly at these prices, so people stop in here regularly. Cheap & Chic is both.

City-Lite Men's Clothing—142 West 14th St., Manhattan; 212/366-1842, and 575 Eighth Ave. (38th St.), Manhattan; 212/695-5399. These stores sell a mix of name brands and cheap imports, but they can be worth a look if you like to prowl around the crowded racks. You can find Jordache jeans for $20.00, or Buffalino shoes—part leather, in sporty multicolored designs—for $29.00. You may even find some of these on sale for $19.99. Plus lots of casual separates, from bright T-shirts with roll-up sleeves ($5.99) to cotton trousers ($9.99, or three for $25.99).

Daffy's—111 Fifth Ave. (18th St.), Manhattan; 212/529-4477, and 333 Madison Ave. (44th St.), Manhattan; 212/557-4422.

There's nothing daffy about shopping here—unless you think it's crazy to save lots of money on designer clothing. Daffy's has two floors of clothing bargains, both fancy and casual, for men, women and children. For the smart-looking exec type, there are lots of imported European suits and jackets. Mr. C found a Louis Raphael blazer, originally $430.00, selling here for $70.00. On the women's side, a blazer by Semplice (worthy of Jackie O) was reduced from $350.00 to just $50.00. Women will also like wool skirts by various designers starting at just $40.00 (some have retail prices as high as $170.00), and blouses for $6.00 and up.

Returning to the guys, there are imported Italian wool sweaters marked down from $120.00 to $36.00; designer jeans reduced from $48.00 to $15.00; silk ties from Saks Fifth Avenue, originally $52.00, now just $14.00; and silk boxer shorts slimmed down from $20.00 to $12.00. Downstairs, along with more women's fashions, you'll find sections for boys and girls at similar discounts. A young girl's velour party dress was reduced from $120.00 to $50.00, and a boy's fleece pullover from Italy, originally $140.00, was just $30.00. These are the kinds of prices Mr. C thinks people should really pay for clothing—and it's all great stuff.

Dollar Bills—99 East 42nd St., Manhattan; 212/867-0212. Near Grand Central Station, Dollar Bills caters to the well-dressed gentleman or lady who likes designer fashions but wants to keep a few dollar bills in his or her pocket. The selection does favor the men, with racks of designer suits from $399.00 and fancy Italian wool sweaters for $59.00. Mr. C can't tell you the names, but they're big. Move further into the store and check out the clearance sections, where you may find a men's sport jacket half-price at $135.00, or a pair of women's slacks marked down from $100.00 all the way to $10.00. The store has all the furnishings to complete the outfit, with the exception of shoes. For the latest in European fashions at terrific savings, don't miss it.

Eisenberg & Eisenberg—85 Fifth Ave. (16th St.), 6th Floor, Manhattan; 212/627-1290. Up in this great old New York building, the Eisenberg family continues a tradition begun in 1898 of great men's clothing at great prices. Most of the suits are Eisenberg's own label, so you're buying directly from the manufacturer. These lean toward the European, double-breasted styles, all wool, priced from $150.00 to $400.00. They compare favorably with suits at twice the price in the uptown department stores. You'll also find designers like Perry Ellis, Ralph Lauren, Tallia, Dior, Lagerfeld and others, at up to half the retail prices; as well as shirts and ties, slacks, raincoats, and accessories.

Formal wear is a big seller here, with some of the latest contemporary fashions. A double-breasted "shawl" style, *trés chic*, is less than half of its uptown price at $500.00. And there are plenty of other styles, starting around $180.00 Eisenberg's offers lots of low-key personal attention; you'll want to become a regular and call the place "your" tailor. Alterations are inexpensive and fast. These guys will even beat the prices in other stores' ads, plus 10 percent of the difference, for up to thirty days *after* you buy a suit!

The Explorer's Company—27 Seventh Ave. (12th St.), Manhattan; 212/255-2322, and 228 Seventh Ave. (23rd St.), Manhattan; 212/255-4686. With one foot in Greenwich Village and the other in Chelsea, this store is worth exploring if you love the great outdoors. Mr. C found racks of ski parkas reduced from their original prices of up to $160.00 all selling at $69.00 each. Full-length stadium coats, with the logo of your favorite NFL team, were seen here for $59.00. London Fog raincoats with zip-out linings were marked down from $165.00 to $79.00, along with lots of London Fog sweaters for just $14.00. They also have tons of casual print cotton shirts to chose from for $9.00 to $12.00. While most of the clothing here is for men, they do have some ladies' fashions at similar savings.

Fenwick Clothes—22 West 19th St., 5th Floor, Manhattan; 212/243-1100. You can *see* the factory in this factory-direct men's clothing store, in a warehouse setting five floors up. They have racks and racks of suits, sport coats, raincoats, tuxedos, and accessories. Fenwick's buyers even select the ties that will be sold here specifically to match the colors of the suits. Another specialty here is Fenwick's own label of European-style suits, many made in the same factories as Armani and other designers. But instead of paying $425.00 to $795.00 for these, they go for about $260.00 to $450.00 at Fenwick. Alterations are made on the premises for a small charge; service is a high priority to the folks here, where they say, "We cater to our customer."

Aldo Ferrari Inc.—321 Fifth Ave. (32nd St.) 2nd Floor, Manhattan; 212/685-5131. Here is another one of the Garment District's wholesale showrooms that occasionally open up to the public (keep an eye out for someone handing out flyers on the corner). With offices in New York and Paris, Aldo Ferrari may not sell Italian sportscars but he definitely has the clothing you should wear when driving one. European suits with retail prices of $600.00 to $750.00 may sell here for $200.00 to $270.00. Dressy Italian shirts to go with these may be half-price at $25.00, and there are similar savings on designer raincoats, lambskin jackets, cashmere sweaters, and silk ties. Call them to find out the date of their next public sale.

Fishkin Knitwear—314 Grand St., Manhattan; 212/226-6538. Fishkin is one of the great finds of the Lower East Side. More like a department store than the area's many no-frills shops, Fishkin offers big discounts on women's designer fashions—all first-quality, current-season styles. On their many racks you may find a Liz Claiborne blazer marked down from $178.00 to $143.00; or a ribbed black and white wool dress by Adrienne Vittadini reduced from $216.00 to $173.00. Silk blouses by Starington sell for 20 percent to 50 percent less than at Saks. Fishkin also specializes in cashmere sweaters, for men and women, at the same discounts. Past-season clearances offer more savings, like a pair of Harve Bernard jeans reduced from $66.00 to just $30.00. Don't forget to check the basement for more clearance items.

Women's shoes, fancy and casual, are another specialty here. Again, these are current collections that start at 20 percent below department store prices. A pair of pumps by Nickels, list price $88.00, sell here for $60.00. End-of-season sales (late in summer and winter) bring further reductions, like a pair of Justin cowboy boots marked down from $165.00 to $130.00. While Fishkin does not stock men's shoes, they will be happy to order them for you at the same rates. Big on personal service, they will also ship your purchases anywhere in the country at no charge.

Fishkin also has a separate outlet store a couple of doors down at 318 Grand Street, where they sell off slow-moving items at up to 75 percent discounts. Check out the $10.00 racks, which may hold corduroy slacks (originally $44.00) or John Meyer sweaters (originally $50.00).

Fowad—2554 Broadway (96th St.), Manhattan; 212/222-8000. What does this mean? Is it "forward" in a bad New York dialect? Doesn't matter. Fowad is a huge, sprawling clothing store selling good brands and designer labels—often irregulars—at big discounts. They have lots of every kind of item for men and women. Find men's blazers by Stanley Blacker for $40.00, and Perry Ellis silk ties to go with them for $9.99. London Fog raincoats for $145.00. Plus lesser-known brands of slacks and shirts, sweaters and more; and of course, a similar selection for women. Mr. C also heard a tip that this is where all the musicians go for inexpensive formal wear. Well, maybe not *all*, but you get the idea.

Gabay's—225 First Ave. (14th St.), Manhattan; 212/254-3180. This is what New York bargain shopping is all about. A small, cramped, dingy storefront that happens to get seconds and irregulars shipped in daily from fancy department stores. You may not find anything today, but come back tomorrow—or next week—because people know about this place, and the stock really moves. Most of it sits out on open tables and bins; better-quality pieces go on the racks along the walls. Mr. C saw a men's wool overcoat by Christian Dior for $50.00 (yes!), and a properly-fatigued leather bomber jacket for $90.00. Barrels of hosiery from Bloomingdale's and Givenchy are $2.00. There are linens here too, like complete sheet sets by Esprit for $20.00 to $50.00 Get there as close to the 9:30 a.m. opening as you can for the best selection; and Saturday mornings are apparently the best time for men's stuff.

Gilcrest Clothes—900 Broadway (20th St.), 3rd Floor, Manhattan; 212/254-8933. Gilcrest is another of this area's many upstairs-warehouse-type men's clothiers. They have a huge selling floor; you can lose yourself in a sea of suits by such designers as Perry Ellis, Ungaro, Valentino, and Ralph Lauren, along with Gilcrest's own private label. An Ungaro suit, retailing for $850.00, was seen here for just $399.00. This includes a fitting; Gilcrest offers free alterations, done on the premises—one of the few to do this at no charge.

Gilcrest's private label offers further savings; these suits are generally priced $100.00 or so lower than the designer brands. Of course, they have all the accoutrements—separates, neckties, raincoats, and a large selection of formal wear in many styles. The atmosphere is quiet and relaxed, with careful attention to each customer, but no pressure. The store is open seven days a week (except weekends in summer); and their hours are from 7:30 in the morning, in case you need something in a hurry for that big meeting, to 5:30 p.m.

Moe Ginsburg—162 Fifth Ave. (21st St.), Manhattan; 212/242-3482. Most guys know of this longtime institution for discounted dressy clothing. Five—count 'em, five—floors of showrooms cover the gamut from suits to outerwear to shoes to accessories. The styles include both classic and Eurocontemporary. A snazzy olive-colored suit in a silk/wool blend by Perry Ellis was recently seen for $230.00, marked down from $495.00; similar savings could be had on an Yves St. Laurent. A Stanley Blacker raincoat was reduced from $295.00 to $180.00 A Calvin Klein print sweatshirt, originally $85.00, went for $48.00.

The clothing here is first quality; the discounts come from volume sales. There are special sections for "Big and Tall" and athletic-fit suits. On the third floor, you'll find good deals in tuxedos and formal wear; and the fourth floor has shoes from casual to the shiny and sharp, most at $15.00 to $25.00 off list prices.

Be sure not to miss the "Red Dot" areas, where the last few stragglers of many items sell for 50 percent off. Among the items on the table during Mr. C's visit were a pair of Bugle Boy men's pants, originally $38.50, now $19.00. The courteous salesmen know their stuff and don't pressure you. Moe Ginsburg is open seven days a week, into the early evening.

Gorsart—9 Murray St., 2nd Floor, Manhattan; 212/962-0024, and 10 East 44th St., Manhattan; 212/557-0200. This has got to be one of the city's classiest secrets. For over seventy years Gorsart has been quietly selling the *crème de la crème* of men's suits and furnishings, all at discount, from a second-floor shop in the Financial District. There is no awning at the street level, just the word "Gorsart" on a door that you can easily miss if you're not looking. Similarly, the store never advertises, doing business simply by word-of-mouth. And those words come from some of New York's most influential men.

Current owner Moe Davidson is proud of the prices and service his store offers. Thanks to its low-rent location, Gorsart can sell designer suits as much as 35 percent below retail. Take note, these suits still cost anywhere from $300.00 to $700.00 each, with names such as Hickey-Freeman, Freedberg's of Boston, and the like. But if top names in conservative styles are what you wear, you can save hundreds of dollars by shopping here.

The atmosphere is refined and casual, with natural wood floors and comfortable surroundings—not the common "upstairs warehouse" look. Salesmen help you without pressure. And there are thirty tailors on the premises; this is, in fact, one of the few discount stores offering free alterations.

Gorsart also carries everything else you'll need to make that stylish impression, from Robert Talbot neckties to Alden shoes—*the* tassled loafers of choice—at $30.00 to $40.00 below certain well-known midtown clothiers. Mr. C wished he had the budget—and the wardrobe—to show off a set of Trafalgar suspenders woven with images of 19th-century baseball players; this limited (numbered!) edition retails for $135.00, but was selling for $99.50 here. Gorsart also sells several designs of formal wear from Lord West and Diamond, as well as Timberland outdoor coats.

Recently Mr. Davidson decided to tackle one of his famous competitors head on, opening a second store just off Fifth Avenue in midtown. You'll find the same great prices and service there, though you stand less chance of bumping into the head of the New York Stock Exchange.

Kami—302 East 23rd St., Manhattan; 212/598-9059, and 30 West 39th St., Manhattan; 212/391-2287. Kami is a small men's shop with big savings on classic styles of professional wear. Suits that retail up to $400.00 can be found here for $195.00; blazers are also about half their retail prices at $125.00, and raincoats go for around $99.00. You'll also find sweaters, silk ties, belts, socks, and just about any other accessory you may need. Alterations are available at an extra charge.

Klein's Of Monticello—105 Orchard St., Manhattan; 212/966-1453. This Klein seems very much out of place on the Lower East Side. Mixed in with no-frills wholesalers, the shop seems more like something you'd find on the Upper East Side. It's a true boutique, with natural wood floors, glass display cases, fitting rooms and a quietly chic atmosphere. And yet for over thirty years Klein's has been selling men's and women's tailored clothing for 20 percent to 40 percent below major stores. Mind you, these clothes begin at much higher prices, so they can still be expensive, even with a discount. But if your style runs to small specialty European brands, this is the place for you. Display cases are even filled out with imported gourmet foods and antique watches.

LS Men's Clothing—19 West 44th St., Suite 403, Manhattan; 212/575-0933. Here is another one of the best treasures New York City has to offer for the well-dressed gentleman, with suits at up to 60 percent off retail. It's one of the few shops offering downtown prices without leaving midtown. You'll have to look hard for it, though: Past the lobby, up the elevator and down the hall. While the prices may be cheap, the quality definitely is not. As the owner put it, "If you can only spend $150.00 on a suit, you should go somewhere else. If you want an $800.00 suit for $300.00, this is the place." Indeed, you'll find many classic American designs, all hand-tailored, ranging from $225.00 to $440.00. The retail prices for these same suits can be over $1,000 elsewhere.

LS can also fit you out in a custom-made suit for $465.00 complete. They will proudly show you the hand-sewn linings, reinforced arm holes, and shoulders that will last and last without stretching out of shape. This is career clothing that can really last your entire career. All tailoring is done on the premises; alterations do cost extra, but don't forget how much you're saving in the first place. Hours are Monday through Thursday from 9:00 a.m. to 7:00 p.m.; Friday 9:00 a.m. to 4:00 p.m.; and Sunday 10:00 a.m. to 5:00 p.m. They are closed on Saturdays.

Labels for Less—204 Park Ave. South (18th St.), Manhattan; 212/529-7440, 329 First Ave. (19th St.), Manhattan; 212/529-5075, 415 Seventh Ave. (33rd St.), Manhattan; 212/594-4571, 130 East 34th St., Manhattan; 212/689-3455, 639 Third Ave. (41st St.), Manhattan; 212/682-3330, 1124 Sixth Ave. (43rd St.), Manhattan; 212/302-7808, 130 West 48th St., Manhattan; 212/997-1032, 800 Third Ave. (50th St.), Manhattan; 212/752-2443, 551 Madison Ave. (53rd St.), Manhattan; 212/888-8390, 619 West 54th St., Manhattan; 212/957-9150, 1345 Sixth Ave. (54th St.), Manhattan; 212/956-2450, 1302 First Ave. (68th St.), Manhattan; 212/249-4800, 186 Amsterdam Ave. (69th St.), Manhattan; 212/787-0850, and 1430 Second Ave. (74th St.), Manhattan; 212/249-4080. Along with Bolton's (see above), Labels for Less has been carving out a big slice of the women's discounting pie all around town. Again, the forte is high-quality designer clothing for the professional woman; again, the names are biggies; again, you'll have to go in and see for yourself just which names they are. But, as there's probably a branch opening this week in the lobby of your apartment building, that should be no problem.

The bargains are good ones, and some are terrific. A houndstooth blazer by a famous European designer was recently marked down from $196.00 to $99.75; a "name" silk blouse was reduced from $46.00 to $30.00, as an everyday price. Save $20.00 on an angora sweater with a bright multicolored pattern, and find good prices on accessories like belts and handbags. One recent deal offered wool shaker-style sweaters, normally $30.00, for just $10.00 with any other purchase. And for the politically correct among us, one of Mr. C's experts notes that L For L is a good place to find synthetic fur coats at great prices. Spray-paint cans optional.

Lea's—119 Orchard St., Manhattan; 212/677-7637. Half a flight up from the Lower East Side's famous Fine and Klein, Lea's sells high-fashion women's sportswear at prices about 30 percent lower than in department stores. These include all kinds of blazers, suits, skirts, and slacks by well-known European designers. Mr. C was asked not to mention the names, but you'll know them when you see them. Whenever the end of a season approaches, slower moving items are further reduced to 50 percent off.

Leather 99—976 Sixth Ave. (36th St.), Manhattan; 212/563-1828. This small Garment District shop sells a variety of leather jackets at up to half-off the list price. These may not be designer quality—many of them being made in Korea and Pakistan—but you may find that the price is right. Motorcycle jackets can be as low as $79.00; and full-length leather coats, meant to sell for $400.00 were seen here for $200.00.

Leather Outlet—327 Sixth Ave. (4th St.), Manhattan; 212/229-1500. Many stores abuse the word "outlet." They are not really discount outlets for a particular manufacturer; they just want to get your attention, lending some confusion to the term. This Greenwich Village store is a bit of both, selling leather jackets, skirts and pants by several manufacturers, including their own London Leatherwear label. Men's full-length soft black leather coats, for example, which may sell for as much as $400.00 elsewhere, are $300.00 here. Better still, there are usually several racks of final sale items, such as a green suede short jacket with sixties-style fringe for only $90.00. Black motorcycle jackets were seen here for $69.00, about as low as they get in the city.

Lion One—135 West 36th St., 14th Floor, Manhattan; 212/584-6510. Most of the year, you can't shop at this Garment District showroom. Lion One is New York's largest wholesaler of shearling coats. But each fall, for just a month or so, they open up to the public and sell hundreds of coats for hundreds of dollars off. Short jackets, for men and women, start at just $75.00. Three-quarter-length coats are $175.00, and full-length ones go for $300.00. There are racks and racks of styles and colors to chose from, whether you like a basic, natural look or something dyed and trendy. If this is what you're after when it comes to keeping warm, give Lion One a call around September to find out when the sale begins.

Loehmann's—19 Duryea Place, Flatbush, Brooklyn; 718/469-9800, 5746 Broadway, Bronx; 718/543-6420, and 60-06 99th St., Rego Park, Queens; 718/271-4000. For over seventy years, women have known of Loehmann's as *the* place to shop for designer fashions at discount. Today, the store still lives up to its reputation, and the constant crowds prove it. Wander through the sea of clothing racks and you may come up with a bright red skirt suit by Oleg Cassini, once $310.00, reduced to $139.00 and finally to $99.00. Shiny raincoats by Adrienne Vittadini, dozens of them in a variety of irridescent colors, were on sale for just $30.00 each. Speaking of coats, there are always lots of leather coats and furs to look at; one full-length model by Spring West combined black leather with fox trim, also dyed black, marked down from $500.00 to $300.00. And there's plenty of casual and sports wear, like leotards by Gilda Marx, half-price at $12.99, and Italian jogging suits for $59.00. For something extra-special, check into "The Back Room," where they keep the real fancy evening stuff. It's all first quality, all at discount. Loehmann's also sells designer perfumes at up to 50 percent off retail prices, as well as cosmetics and jewelry. If you live in Manhattan, it may be a schlep to get out to one of these stores, but if you're a bargain hound, there are few places like Loehmann's.

Mano à Mano—580 Broadway (Prince St.), Manhattan; 212/219-9602. What an experience *this* place is. Never mind the great discounts on contemporary men's fashions; the store is a maze of narrow, winding aisles, each laid out differently, all done in natural woods. Live monkeys or dogs may appear around any corner. It's kind of like a GQ jungle—with plenty of native guides to assist you, don't worry.

Meanwhile, the savings are just as impressive as the decor. Fashions include everything from traditional American to trendy European. Find all-wool blazers from London and Paris for as low as $89.00 to $139.00, and tweed sportcoats for just $59.00. Mr. C also saw some classic American "country" looks, including cotton trousers from $14.00 and tweed jackets from $55.00. Plus sport shirts at two for $25.00, dress shirts, heavy cotton sweaters for $15.00, soft Italian leather jackets for $99.00, leather belts for $6.00, raincoats, winter gear, and lots more, all at discount. On-premises tailoring is available. The store is open all week, with evening hours.

Marco's Tee Shirt Factory—37 Orchard St., Manhattan; 212/219-2738. Marco is a character who could only spring up from the streets of New York City. He describes himself as an "unschooled, self-taught artist who paints in an expressionistic style influenced by Picasso, Matisse, Van Gogh, and Modigliani." All of which does little to describe the crazy look of his work. For two years he sold his made-to-order art from a SoHo street corner; last year he moved into an industrial space down on the Lower East Side. Rock music blares from his gallery, which is lined with hundreds of sketches—any one of which can be made into a T-shirt (or a canvas for your wall). The designs are raw, gritty, visual puns that may not appeal to every taste, but they show an edgy sense of humor with a touch of political correctness. His "Pancake Batter" cartoon, for example, depicts a very round fellow wearing a cap and swinging a bat.

These unique shirts sell for $10.00 apiece, whether in stock or custom-chosen. However, Marco encourages his customers to bring in their own shirts, onto which he will print many of the designs for just 75¢ per color. And since he is located amidst the wholesale/retail garment dealers of Orchard Street, you can pop out to any of several T-shirt vendors who sell a dozen plain shirts for the price of one uptown "creation."

Marco's fertile, clever imagination adds new designs all the time. He will also create designs for you at wholesale prices for quantities of six dozen or more. The store is open daily from 8:00 a.m. to 8:00 p.m. Check it out.

Marun Fashions—10 West 28th St., Manhattan; 212/683-9055. Deep in the heart of the sometimes impenetrable Garment District, where there seem to be an endless array of boutiques in which the public cannot shop, is this interesting little place. Marun sells an eclectic variety of imported casual fashions and basic accessories at bargain prices. You may find a pair of Bugle Boy jeans for $12.99, or women's full-length down coats for $40.00. Other jeans often discounted here include Lee and Calvin Klein—along with colorful sweatshirts, down vests, and more. Men may want to stock up on Fruit of the Loom underwear, just $5.00 for a three-pack of briefs. You can even find European-style dress shirts for $7.00, and tuxedo shirts for $10.00. The atmosphere is strictly no-frills, with bins and hanging racks. In good weather, extra bargains are displayed in front of the store for browsers.

Miriam—146 Atlantic Ave., Brooklyn Heights, Brooklyn; 718/834-

9062. Not far from the Promenade in Brooklyn Heights, this cozy little shop quietly sells women's designer clothing at discount. The styles tend to be splashy and colorful, something you'll wear out on the town. Print blazers by Adrienne Vittadini were recently on sale for $50.00 apiece, and angora sweaters by Rafaella were $45.00. There was also a rack of cocktail party dresses in bold, shiny colors by A. J. Bari at reasonable prices. Miriam also sells costume jewelry to complete the outfit, as well as belts, handbags, and perfumes.

NBO Men's Wear—1965 Broadway, (67th St.), Manhattan; 212/595-1550, 8973 Bay Pkwy., Brooklyn; 718/266-8180, 1100-02 Kings Hwy., Brooklyn; 718/645-8098, 2283 Ralph Ave., Brooklyn; 718/763-3115, and 6407 18th Ave., Brooklyn; 718/331-0411. National Brands Outlet offers savings on men's suits, casual wear and furnishings. Wool suits by Christian Dior, Ungaro and Ralph Lauren's "Chaps" start at $299.00. Wool blends by such makers as Jeffrey Allen can be found for $119.00, and Brett Lawrence navy blazers for $79.00. Finish off these outfits with a pair of Eastwick dress shirts for $25.00, silk ties for $10.00 and up, and cotton socks by Givenchy or Pierre Cardin at three pairs for $9.00.

On the casual side, Mr. C loved a suede bomber jacket by U2 Wear Me Out, a hot brand for $165.00. NBO also has closeout tables stacked with items at 50 percent off. Terrific sweaters by Ralph Lauren are among some of the treasures you can find in these bins.

Nakazawa Art Wear—147 Spring St., 2nd Floor, Manhattan; 212/226-5336. Here's another great New York discovery. In this workshop/showroom, designer Shizuka Nakazawa creates dresses, blouses, and all kinds of casual wear for women that is unique—and very fashionable. An oversized blazer, meant to be worn open-style, is almost like an Oriental kimono; at $65.00 it may not be cheap, but remember—this is one-of-a-kind art. Blouses in bright, bold colors start around $35.00, in turtleneck and scoopneck cuts. And Nakazawa's hand-painted giant T-shirts, with elaborate Asian illustrations, can be worn as minidresses or nightshirts. These are done in full color for $30.00, or black-and-white sketches for just $15.00. Also, there is usually a rack of special sale items, reduced for clearance. You're sure to come away with something chic that your friends won't have also.

New York Army Navy—328 Bleecker St., Manhattan; 212/242-6665, 110 Eighth Ave. (15th St.), Manhattan; 212/645-7420, 221 East 59th St., Manhattan; 212/755-1855, and 1598 Second Ave. (83rd St.), Manhattan; 212/737-4661. These places have a more upscale atmosphere than army/navy stores used to, and the clothing they sell has more to do with fighting your way through New York crowds than through foxholes. But one of Mr. C's shopping mavens likes these stores for good prices on the basic uniforms of jeans and sweats—especially because the displays are so neatly arranged by type and color. Recent finds here included Levi's 501 jeans for $19.99 a pair, and bright Jerzees sweatshirts for $12.99.

New York Fur Manufacturer's Clearance Center—150 West 30th St., 11th Floor, Manhattan; 212/244-0773. This is kind of a Garment District version of the more famous Ritz Thrift Shop (see listing under "Used Clothing"). Unlike Ritz, though, NY Fur sells new fur coats by top designer names at substantial markdowns. Those names can't be printed, but when you see a full-length mink with a list price of $12,000.00, you know it's the real thing. And when you see it reduced for clearance to a price of $2,495.00, you know it's a bargain. The store is open Mondays through Fridays from 10:00 a.m. to 6:00 p.m., and Saturdays from 10:00 a.m. to 4:00 p.m. They accept credit cards (and Swiss bank accounts).

Nice Price—513 Broadway (Spring St.), Manhattan; 212/966-6000, and 493 Columbus Ave. (84th St.), Manhattan; 212/362-1020. Here is a find. Nice Price is one of those shops that snaps up major brands of contemporary fashions, both first quality and irregulars, and sells them way below retail. Mr. C was asked not to print the names, but you won't be disappointed. Most of the clothing is women's, though there is some men's stuff too—denim shirts marked down from $42.00 to $20.00, sweaters reduced from $80.00 to $25.00, and a designer blazer of handwoven silk, originally $245.00, here just $60.00.

Women will love such items as a multicolored leather baseball jacket, first quality, half-price at $250.00; a black lace minidress, slightly imperfect, marked down from $120.00 to $40.00; and the same price for one designer's wool blazer, or another's grey pinstripe trousers. Nice Price is open seven days a week, and they allow returns for exchange or store credit. There's a lot packed into these shops; on the weekends, that includes wild-eyed shoppers. Try to go on a weekday!

O.M.G. Jeans—555 Broadway (Prince St.), Manhattan; 212/925-9513, 55 Third Ave., Manhattan; 212/533-8549, and 217 Seventh Ave., Manhattan; 212/807-8650. "The Jeans Store," they call themselves, and they have quite a lot. Lee Riders are $25.00 here, and Wranglers start at $20.00; same price for Levi's "Dockers" dress slacks for men. O.M.G. also has lots of other activewear for men, women and kids; find Danskin aerobic fashions, Speedo swimwear, and much more, all at good, competitive prices.

One Price Concepts—35 West 39th St., Manhattan; 212/921-0135. This is one of the flashier of the ten-dollar clothing stores that have taken New York City by storm. It has the spare look of a SoHo boutique, with sporty women's fashions—all, you guessed it, for ten dollars. These include tops, stretch leggings, and other separates in lycra and velour prints. Also, slightly more traditional (but still very smart) herringbone blazers and slacks. Most of the merchandise here is overstock and closeouts in first quality.

Orva—155 East 86th St., Manhattan; 212/369-3448. This Upper East Side women's retailer has recently opened a "Sample Sale Room", making a formality of what designers have done for years. Clothing samples from the latest collections, after being taken around to various stores, cannot be sold at full price; manufacturers then get rid of these for something close to actual cost. Orva has a big selection of skirts for $25.00 to $30.00, about half of their original prices; "men's style" tweed blazers for $20.00; suede jackets for $99.00; and the store has always sold a wide variety of lingerie, hosiery, shoes, and other basic necessities at nearly half the price of other stores. There's certainly nothing like it in this pricey neighborhood.

PRG Sportswear—160 West 26th St., Manhattan; 212/620-0409, and 307 Seventh Ave. (28th St.), Manhattan; 212/627-1132.

Not far from the Garment District are these two women's fashion shops, offering the latest in designer lines at discounts of 20 percent to 50 percent. For over twelve years PRG has been satisfying women from New York and around the country; many folks make an annual pilgrimmage to stoke up their closets. They book appointments and have the goods shipped back home, though neither of these is necessary.

Though the store features the latest collections, its buyers look for classic styles—clothing that will last longer than next season. And the prices: One designer blazer, which would be $475.00 retail, sells here for $340.00—except at the end of the season, when it was further reduced by another 40 percent. These designer collections are mostly found in the 26th Street store; the Seventh Avenue branch focuses more on career and casual wear for the professional woman.

Pan Am Menswear—50 Orchard St., Manhattan; 212/925-7032. Pan Am is a full-service men's store selling everything you need from top to toe at savings of 30 percent or more. They have suits by Perry Ellis, Ralph Lauren, Hugo Boss and others in current season styles. The looks here are classic and fairly conservative. A dark navy suit by Perry Ellis, with a retail price of $530.00, will sell here for $369.00. The price includes free alterations—a rarity in men's clothing stores nowadays. After the season, further reductions may bring the price as far down as $199.00. Pan Am also has raincoats from such names as Christian Dior and Austin Reed. Open daily 9:00 a.m. to 6:00 p.m. and Thursday until 8:00 p.m.

Prato Men's Wear—41 John St., Manhattan; 212/619-9017, 122 Nassau St., Manhattan; 212/349-4150, 28 West 34th St., Manhattan; 212/629-4730, 492 Seventh Ave. (36th St.), Manhattan; 212/564-9683. These small shops—two in the Nassau Street mall downtown and two in the Garment District—carry designer sportswear at very good prices. Get a pair of Calvin Klein jeans for $28.00 and Jordache for $15.00; sweaters by Pierre Cardin for $28.00; and silk shirts for $15.00. They also have lots of Italian wool-blend suits priced around $150.00; and leather jackets that would retail for over $300.00 sell here for $100.00 to $150.00. There is not a large selection, but it is definitely worth a look.

Prolix Inc.—860 Sixth Ave. (30th St.), Manhattan; 212/545-9775. Mr. C entered this Garment District store in the midst of a good-natured argument between a customer and a salesperson. The customer was trying on a leather jacket that he obviously liked, but the price was so low he couldn't believe it was *really* leather. A close examination by nearly everyone in the store finally convinced him. Leather clothing is what this store is all about, with its own line of fashions as well as other brands. You can get a black motorcycle-style jacket for as little as $70.00, one of the lowest prices Mr. C has found. A rack of baseball-style leather jackets with colored sleeves was on sale, reduced from $240.00 to $160.00 Along with these savings, Prolix had black Durango boots for only $100.00 and Buffalino shoes priced between $39.00 and $49.00.

Robbins—48 West 14th St., Manhattan; 212/691-2573, 162 West 23rd St., Manhattan; 212/627-9085, 609 Eighth Ave. (40th St.), Manhattan; 212/564-1194, 1717 Broadway (55th St.), Manhattan; 212/581-7033, and other locations throughout the boroughs. The main merchandise at this discount chain is men's and boys' clothing; but they also have some women's accessories, as well as health and beauty aids, luggage, and backpacks. Among the clothing bargains, Mr. C found Jordache jeans for $19.95, with generic import brands for $9.95. Fruit of the Loom sweatpants were $7.99, sport shirts by McGregor were $16.95, and Sasson dress shirts were $10.95. They have lots of racks jammed with all kinds of clothing, which are a mix of first-quality and closeouts. It's also a good place to stock up on basics like underwear and socks. Open seven days a week.

Daniel Rochas—244 West 35th St., Manhattan; 212/239-0106. If you dream of penetrating the walls of the Garment District, with its many "Wholesale Only" boutiques, this is the place to do it. Daniel Rochas manufactures and imports sporty clothing for women, and this is one of the few factory showrooms open to the public on a regular basis. The clothing is all first-quality, current-season styles, and the huge store goes on and on with racks of dresses, blazers, pantsuits, and more. The service here is very personal, and the prices excellent. Mr. C was shown a Compagnie International Express dress with a white blouse top and black pinstripe bottom, selling here for just $19.99. A full-length pantsuit by Spasso, retailing for $50.00, sells for $18.00; and a black gauze dress by The Limited was marked down from $84.00 to $25.00. There are lots of items priced from $5.00 to $30.00, including racks of basic white cotton/poly blouses for $5.00 each. The store has a good stock of large and full sizes as well, ranging from size 14 up to size 30. The store is open daily, including Sundays from noon to 5:00 p.m.

Rothman's—200 Park Ave. South (17th St.), Manhattan; 212/777-7400. Along with Gorsart, mentioned above, Rothman's is one of the classiest and best of the men's suit discounters. The store even feels classy, being in a former bank building; the top-line suits are kept in the (open) vault room downstairs.

Rothman's has all the big names, such as Hickey-Freeman, Joseph Abboud, and Aquascutum; and not only suits but raincoats, shirts, ties, socks, and all the other accessories. Owner Ken Giddon has taken over the business begun on the Lower East Side by his grandfather, and he does the old man proud. The average price of a suit here is around $350.00, easily half the going rate at many other upscale men's stores. You'll find Hickey-Freeman suits at discount *in season* , a true rarity; one model, retailing for $975.00, sells here for $585.00. Wool-blends suits are even more reasonable, in the $200.00 range, and there are racks and racks of all of these.

Back upstairs, check out the various furnishings. Kenneth Gordon basic dress shirts, which retail for $65.00, are $39.00 here. Neckties by the Italian label Aquascutum, as much as $95.00 in department stores, sell here for $40.00. For all the fanciness of the clothing, the atmosphere at Rothman's is quite casual, and the service is polite and friendly.

S & W—165 West 26th St., Manhattan; 212/924-6656, and 4217 Thirteenth Ave., Borough Park, Brooklyn; 718/438-9679. For over thirty years, S & W has been a legend in women's designer clothing. They sell current-season styles, all first quality, at 25 percent to 50 percent below list prices. This rambling store's main branch is wrapped around the corner of Seventh Avenue, with room after room on two levels—each of which offers a different kind of clothing. You want a coat? S & W has five thousand in stock. Shearlings, leathers, and wool coats in all styles and lengths are discounted; check the upstairs clearance room for further markdowns of 50 percent off the lowest price. That can get you a shearling coat, originally $1,625.00, for $650.00. Usually such reductions are made at the end of the season.

The boutique department features the collections of Escada, Dior, Lagerfeld, Della Spiga, and many, many others. They have everything you need to create a full wardrobe, including accessories. Again, there is a clearance section with discounts up to 80 percent. Alterations are available on the premises, though there is an extra charge for this service.

And don't forget the separate but related shoe store. Here you may find a pair of patent-leather pumps by Bandolino for $63.00. Other brands here include Bally, Stuart Weitzman, Ungaro, Via Spiga, and many others, at up to 25 percent off retail. Leather handbags, too. A recent sale offered a second pair of shoes for an additional $10.00.

S & W is closed on Saturdays; they are open Sundays through Wednesdays until 6:00 p.m., Thursdays until 8:00 p.m. and Fridays until 5:00 p.m.

Sample Sale Center—1410 Broadway (40th St.), Basement level, Manhattan; no phone. This is not a store but rather a central location for designers and manufacturers to sell samples and overstocks directly to the public. You never know who may be selling this week; perhaps it's Brett Harrison sportswear, leather fashions by Vakko, or the latest Lagerfeld collection. The day that Mr. C dropped in, women's 100 percent wool tweed overcoats by Paul Levy were selling for $85.00. There were also Jantzen crewneck sweaters in heavy cable knits for $25.00. Each sale may last a week or two, usually with daytime hours Monday through Friday only. If you pass through this area on a regular basis, look for people handing out flyers.

Simply Samples—150 West 36th St., 3rd Floor, Manhattan; 212/268-0448. This shop is really something to see—however, Mr. C was unable to see very much of it. This store is for women only, and because of open dressing rooms, men cannot come in. Simply Samples offers women's designer sportswear at wholesale prices, and sometimes even below wholesale. Smart-looking suits with retail prices of up to $500.00 may sell here for as little as $60.00 to $100.00. The merchandise has never been worn; it comes directly from the manufacturers after they have used it to market their newest designs. But someone's got to wear this stuff—why not you? The stock changes all the time, and all sizes are available, so stop in, ladies, and have a look. They are open from 11:00 a.m. to 7:00 p.m. Monday through Friday.

Spitzer's—15 Ann St., Manhattan; 212/393-9709, 156 Orchard St., Manhattan; 212/473-1515, and 101 Rivington St., Manhattan; 212/477-4088. Among the many clothing bargains to be found on the Lower East Side, Spitzer's is a gem for women's dresses, suits, sportswear, and outerwear. You'll find serious discounts on designer labels—which they would prefer Mr. C not to mention, but you won't be disappointed. In fact, there is so much to choose from that you can barely squeeze through the aisles of these small shops. There are attendants to help you with sizes and such; they can be brusque, since they appear to have been doing this for, well, a long time. But they do know their stuff.

Street Life Outlet—422 Columbus Ave. (81st St.), Manhattan; 212/769-8858. Street Life is a very popular women's boutique, selling the work of two very contemporary designers. They have shops in SoHo and on lower Fifth Avenue, and their clothes are also sold in other stores around the city. In September of 1992 they decided to turn their Upper West Side branch into a clearance outlet, selling the same merchandise at 25 percent to 75 percent off. These are not irregulars! The clothing here is first quality, whether current overstock or leftovers from a previous season. Mr. C noticed an all-silk dress, in silver or fuchsia, marked down from $120.00 to a slinky $30.00. A pair of walking shorts, originally $52.00, was on sale for $13.00. The fashions here are casual but definitely eye-catching.

The outlet was begun on a trial basis, so it's possible things may have changed by the time you read this; judging by the eager traffic in this small shop, however, that seems unlikely.

Tates Boutique—130 Church St., Manhattan; 212/766-8000, 310 Broadway (Reade St.), Manhattan; 212/619-4821, 1039 Sixth Ave. (39th St.), Manhattan; 212/354-7091, and 2490 Broadway (93rd St.), Manhattan; 212/787-5396. Most of the clothing here consists of irregulars and second-quality stuff, but you may find perfectly acceptable deals on men's and boys' semi-casual clothing. The walls are lined with tightly filled racks above and below you. Mr. C found lots of nice suits in the $80.00 to $130.00 range; a selection of Polo wool-blend suits was $90.00 each. Snappy, urban-chic blazers by Cotler were $10.99 and $12.99, while Cotler jeans were available for $12.99 and chino pants were $13.00 to $16.00. Plenty of styles for boys and teens as well. Good place to stock up.

Tobaldi—83 Rivington St., Manhattan; 212/260-4330. For an unexpectedly upscale experience on the Lower East Side, Tobaldi has incredibly elegant men's suits and accessories at big discounts. Of course, with this echelon of clothing, most of which is imported from Europe, you may still pay over $1,000.00 for a single suit. So, why is Tobaldi in this book? Well, they can save you hundreds of dollars on these well-known designer names, which cannot be mentioned here, so the prices are cheap*er*, if not exactly cheap. An Italian suit of 100 percent wool, for example, was seen here for $898.00—and would have been $1,100.00 in a fancy uptown boutique. An outer jacket of black brushed suede from Spain, retailing for $1,080.00, sells instead for $798.00. They do have simpler items, like sweaters, shirts, and silk ties. Tobaldi will save you money, if this is your style. And who knows? It may bring one special suit just within range for you.

Townie Merchandise—212 West 14th St., Manhattan; 212/929-8060. For basic casual supplies, Townie has good prices on T-shirts and underwear, sweat shirts and pants, socks, thermal underwear and the rest. The brands you'll find here are well known: Fruit of the Loom, Hanes, Osh Kosh, and more. They have a complete stock of colors to choose from, and you can buy in quantity.

Trend Clothiers—274 Madison Ave. (39th St.), 2nd Floor, Manhattan; 212/889-4686. After twenty years in the same location, this gentleman's shop recently moved around the corner to a new address and larger quarters. They've quadrupled their space, but their prices are as low as ever on all kinds of men's suits and accessories. Trend specializes in importing suits by French and Italian designers in nifty double-breasted looks; the shop also sells its own line of traditional American styles. In both cases, all-wool suits start as low as $175.00, ranging up to around $250.00. Tailoring is done on the premises, and on many suits they offer two pairs of pants for the same price—or one pair, in any waist size you need. This is old-fashioned service to match their old-fashioned prices. Trend also has overcoats, shirts, ties, and shoes; they deal in tuxedo sales and rentals as well. Open Monday through Friday, 11:00 a.m. to 7:00 p.m.

Trocadero—1466 Broadway (52nd St.), Manhattan; 212/302-0137, and 159 Columbus Ave. (67th St.), Manhattan; 212/724-0900. You may not have expected to find this European high-fashion women's boutique in Mr. C's book, but don't count them out. Trocadero's back rooms have a large quantity of clearance sale items at greatly reduced prices.

Among the items found there on a recent visit were a pair of black stirrup pants by Guess, originally $89.00, marked down to $62.00. And a frilly, floral-print top, short enough to expose a bit of the midriff was reduced from $48.00 to $19.00. There are always lots of sporty separates to check out.

V.I.M. Jeans, 16 West 14th St., Manhattan; 212/255-2662, 15 West 34th St., Manhattan; 212/736-4989, 388 Fulton St., Brooklyn; 718/855-0112, and other locations around the city.

For jeans, sneakers, and all of the fashions that go with them, V.I.M. has very good prices. Current-style Levis start around $25.00 and up; there are lots of cheap import jeans for less, including women's stretch jeans from $19.99. Along with these are men's casual print shirts for $9.99, and women's Gitano tops for $5.99 and acrylic sweaters for as little as $3.99. The place is great for a lot of outfitting in a hurry. The stores have special clearance sections as well.

The other real bargains here are in sneakers for men, women and kids. The vast stock includes current styles at good prices and last year's closeouts at even better prices. Among these are such varieties as Etonic high-tops and running shoes for $19.99; Reeboks for $30.00 and up; and L.A. Gear from $25.00. Children's sneakers may start as low as $15.00, in many of the same brand names. Because these are leftovers, they may not have all sizes for each style; but the big and open displays, with all the shoes in labeled boxes, make it easy for you to rummage through.

Charles Weiss Fashions—331 Grand St., Manhattan; 212/966-1143. Ladies, here's a find for all kinds of clothing needs. Charles Weiss prides himself on a large selection of activewear and lingerie, all at least 25 percent below retail. He specializes in Danskin, along with many other big-name brands. And when these items go on his clearance racks, you can get them as much as 70 percent off. For example, a snazzy Danskin sweatshirt with a snap-up collar, originally $40.00, was seen on sale here for $13.00. Satin-look jogging suits by Lavon, in colorful prints with a "crinkly" finish, were reduced from $66.00 to $50.00 per set.

Of all the Lower East Side clothing stores, Weiss is one of the few selling bathing suits at discount all year round, by such names as Roxanne and Gottex. More significantly, this store is one of the very few with fitting rooms for you to try things on—and everything they sell is always out on display with clearly-marked prices.

Weiss Tees—91 Orchard St., Manhattan; 212/966-2293. No relation to the Weiss above, Weiss Tees specializes in—guess what? T-shirts. Get 'em here at close to wholesale prices. Brands like Lee and Fruit of the Loom are available individually or in quantity. And, you can take them down the street to Marco's (see above) for cheap-chic prints. There are sweatshirts and sweatpants too, such as Lee Heavyweights for $25.00 apiece—they'd be $35.00 in full-price stores. Hours here can be very irregular—unlike the shirts—so it's best to call ahead.

What's New—176 Madison Ave. (34th St.),Manhattan; 212/532-9226, and 122 East 42nd St. (subway level), Manhattan; 212/867-0574. What's new? The fashions at these women's stores, that's what. For the latest looks in professional and casual wear by lesser-known designers, check 'em out. You'll find first-quality blazers from $17.00 and stretch leggings from $10.00; in irregulars, you may see blazer and skirt sets from just $25.00. There are also lots of clearance racks to peruse. Sure, it ain't Ralph Lauren; but if you want something you can do everyday work in without worrying about wear and tear, this may be for you.

Wings—666 Broadway (Bond St.), Manhattan; 212/254-9002, 388 Sixth Ave. (Waverly Place), Manhattan; 212/505-7140, 155 East 23rd St., Manhattan; 212/460-8963, 270 West 38th St., Manhattan; 212/768-4220, 18 East 42nd St., Manhattan; 212/983-0533, 210 East 86th St., Manhattan; 212/879-2575, 2491 Broadway (95th St.),Manhattan; 212/595-6662, 2824 Broadway (110th St.), Manhattan; 212/666-8330, and many other locations around New York. Yes, you've seen these folks all over town. This chain is indeed a good place to check out for good prices on name-brand jeans and other casual wear. Jordache, Levis and Wrangler often go on sale here for as little as $20.00 a pair. Dyed jeans by Jon Taylor NY may only be ten dollars more, in a variety of bright colors. And for the kiddies, lots of Osh Kosh jeans too. Athletic clothing is great here; a recent sale featured Champion walking shorts reduced from $25.00 to $10.00. And they have plenty of clearance deals in sneakers too, with models originally priced from $27.00 to $40.00 selling for just $10.00 to $15.00.

CHILDREN'S WEAR

Nathan Borlam—266 South 2nd St., Williamsburg, Brooklyn; 718/387-2983. Manhattan's Lower East Side spills across the Williamsburg Bridge to this similarly ethnic, commercial neighborhood; while it's not the shopping destination that Orchard Street is, Williamsburg is definitely one of Brooklyn's up-and-coming areas. This store is one of the best in the city for children's clothing, and has been for over fifty years. You'll find discounts of 20 percent, 30 percent and perhaps more on all kinds of classic and trendy fashions for kids, from tots up to teens. There's a lot to see, much of which could just as easily show up at Bloomie's for a lot more money. The store is open from Sunday through Thursday from 10:00 a.m. to 5 p.m.; closed on Friday afternoons and all day Saturdays.

Bunnie's Children's World—116 West 14th St., Manhattan; 212/989-9011. There's nothing small about this Bunnie. Big as any department store, Bunnie's has two floors of clothing bargains for infants, toddlers, and children up to teenagers.

Nearby, another store with a large selection for children is called **Best for Kids**, at 152 West 14th Street (212/633-6951). They have lots of clothes priced at $5.00 and $10.00, including matched complete sets.

Burlington Coat Factory—45 Park Place, Manhattan; 212/571-2630. See listing under "Men's and Womens's General Wear," above.

Jay's Bargain Store—40 West 14th St., Manhattan; 212/691-1563. Along the 14th Street stretch of inexpensive stores, Jay's specializes in clothing for infants and kids. There's a huge selection of decent stuff, from girls' denim skirts ($7.00) and wide-wale corduroy jumpers ($8.00) to boys' nylon warmup suits ($19.99). Plus lots of clothing and outerwear for infants, for as little as $2.99.

Kids Are Magic—2287 Broadway (83rd St.), Manhattan; 212/875-9240. Well, you'll think so when you see what discounts they can get you on clothing in this new store—not even up to its first birthday party yet. The large, fun place, with two levels of dazzling displays sells most major brands of children's clothing at 40 percent to 60 percent below retail prices. Sizes range from infants' clothing, up to boys' size 20 and girls' size 14. It's like a whole de-

Mr. Cheap's Picks

✔ **Nathan Borlam/Rachel's Boutique**—Two great Brooklyn spots for huge savings on little clothes.

✔ **Kids Are Magic**—Are they, now? Well anyway, this bright and gigantic store works its magic with a vast selection that won't make your wallet disappear.

partment store. KAM has a twelve-day return policy, with receipt, for cash, credit, or exchange; the salespeople are quite friendly and helpful. Open seven days a week.

Rachel's Boutique—4218-22 13th Ave. (43rd St.), Borough Park, Brooklyn; 718/435-6875. First of all, Rachel's has kids clothing. Then they have more kids clothing. And still more kids clothing. Old Mother Hubbard couldn't begin to make a dent in this stock—it's truly a vast amount of stuff to choose from. You can outfit your child completely from head to toe, from underwear to raincoats and everything in between, for very few shekels. The prices here are like those of the Orchard Street shops—appropriate enough, since this area of Brooklyn has much in common with the Lower East Side. And, like that area, the shops in this old-world neighborhood close up early on Friday and reopen on Sunday.

Tates Boutique—130 Church St., Manhattan; 212/766-8000, 310 Broadway (Reade St.), Manhattan; 212/619-4821, 1039 Sixth Ave. (39th St.), Manhattan; 212/354-7091, and 2490 Broadway (93rd St.), Manhattan; 212/787-5396. See listing under "Men's and Women's Wear—General," above.

Tobaldini—140 Orchard St., Manhattan; 212/477-0507. Not far from Tobaldi, the discounter of expensive men's suits, is this version offering discounts on designer clothing for the young set. Here you'll find names such as New Man, Guess, Moschino, Mona Lisa and Baby Minnie at discounts of 20 percent to 25 percent. Most of these are sold in complete outfits; a young girl's ensemble by Guess, with a list price of $85.00, sells here for $69.00. The shop is small but has a lot to offer, which is probably the way you feel about your tots! If so, you'll want to dress them up here. Don't forget this is the Lower East Side, so the store is closed on Saturday and open on Sunday.

ACCESSORIES

Ananias Leather—197 Bleecker St., Manhattan; 212/254-9540, 367 West Broadway, Manhattan; 212/274-9229, and A & S Plaza, Sixth Ave. (33rd St.), Fifth floor, Manhattan; 212/947-4814.

See listing under "Shoes."

The Dress—103 Stanton St., Manhattan; 212/473-0237. Perhaps named to complement the Mexican restaurant across the street—"El Sombrero"—The Dress is a real find on the Lower East Side. Designers Amy Downs and Mary Adams create dresses and accessories that are practically works of art, and alas, priced to match. But don't despair! If you're looking to add an ultra-hip touch to something you already have, you should have a look at their hat collection. With most of these in the $25.00-to-$60.00 range, you'll get something unique and dazzling, probably for less than at some Upper East chic chapeau shop. The styles and colors are bold throwbacks to the days of "mod." They also make specially designed makeup bags to go with these for just $10.00 apiece. And after you've bought your hat, you can go across the street and eat enchiladas in one.

Fine and Klein—119 Orchard St., Manhattan; 212/674-6720. One of the landmarks of the Lower East Side bargain area, F & K has been retailing all kinds of handbags at wholesale prices for nearly fifty years. These include leather bags, wallets, and evening bags, in casual and handwoven styles from such makers as Finesse, Susan Gail, Sharif, Stefon, and many others. All are current styles, first quality at about 30 percent off retail prices. Upstairs in the same location is a terrific women's clothing discounter, Lea's (see listing above). Both stores are open all day, Sunday through Friday, and closed on Saturday.

Barbara Gee Danskin Center—2282 Broadway (82nd St.), Manhattan; 212/769-2923, and 2487 Broadway (92nd St.), Manhattan; 212/769-1564. These Upper West Side twins have good prices on underwear, lingerie and activewear for women. Save 10 percent to 20 percent on Danskin tights and leotards for dance class or the gym; save 20 percent also on a variety of sports bras. Lacy lingerie by Christian Dior and Lily of France may be discounted by as much as 20 percent to 40 percent below list prices; ditto for hosiery by Calvin Klein, Berkshire, and many others. It's all comparable to Lower East Side prices—without the long ride from this neighborhood.

A.W. Kaufman—73 Orchard St., Manhattan; 212/226-1629. Kaufman's is one of the traditional Lower East Side cubbyholes offering great prices with no frills. They leave the frills to the daywear and lingerie they sell by such makers as Christian Dior, Hanro, and Calida. Most of these are imported from makers in Switzerland, Belgium, and France. Their customers, too, come from all over the world to stock up on bargains; prices here average 20 to 25 percent off retail. You name it, chances are they've got it.

Bernard Krieger and Son—316 Grand St., Manhattan; 212/226-1929. For that dashing accessory to spruce up your wardrobe, you'll want to keep dashing into Bernard Krieger and Son. Whether it's a set of men's gloves or handkerchiefs or ladies' scarves and hats, you can find that extra something in this narrow but well-stocked shop. And everything here is about 40 percent below prices in the big department stores. Princess Diana may have lost a bit of her image, but her favorite hats will never go out of style. Krieger has lots to choose from, as well as tam o'shanters, berets and more, many priced around $20.00.

Lismore Hosiery—334 Grand St., Manhattan; 212/674-3440. This stretch of Grand Street, from Allen to Essex Streets, is lined with warehouse-style hosiery shops. If you're the sort of person who likes to stock up on stockings, you've got to come down here and browse these stores. Each has its specialty, but Lismore is one of the best. For over fifty years this service-oriented shop has worked to fill every need and preference. They have a huge selection, at 20 to 30 percent off name brands. They also manufacture their own line, patterned after antique styles; and they have lots of hard-to-find items, including support hose for men and women, cotton-lined health socks, and more. They also allow exchanges within thirty days, with receipt.

Among the other hosiery

shops worth looking into around here is **Friedman Hosiery** (326 Grand St.; 212/674-3292), with 25 percent and more off on a variety of stockings, underwear, pajamas, athletic socks, and so on by Jockey, Perry Ellis, Totes and others. At **Grand Lingerie** (330 Grand St.; 212/473-0969) you can save 25 to 50 percent on brand-name underwear and sleepwear; **Sultan Shop** (also at 330 Grand St.; 212/998-0979), specializes in men's socks by Pierre Cardin, Hanes, and Dior. Many of these are irregulars; you can get some varieties at $10.00 a dozen. And across the street, **Ideal Hosiery** (339 Grand St.; 212/226-4792) specializes in pantyhose, though they prefer to sell in quantity.

Steuer Hosiery—31 West 32nd St., Manhattan; 212/563-0052. This is the central branch of the Value Hosiery Center chain, which has locations all around town (see listings under that name). Their large but humble shop just east of Herald Square sells first-quality and irregular hosiery as much as two-thirds below department store prices. You may find, for example, 'Round the Clock pantyhose (irregulars) selling here at three pair for the price of one regular pair at a major store. They also have first-quality activewear and leotards at very low prices, all on display for you to look at. The service is very attentive here, one of New York's few wholesale stores where ordinary people are welcome to come in and shop also. Most of the other Value Hosiery outposts are smaller, but just as well stocked (no pun intended there).

Ties Plus—41 Orchard St., Manhattan; 212/925-6285. This is one of the many discount men's accessory stores on the Lower East Side. Designer silk ties, Italian imports, and other high-priced furnishings are easily half the price of fancy uptown boutiques. A silk tie that might retail for $50.00 at Bloomie's probably sells for $20.00 here. They also have good prices on socks by Calvin Klein, dress shirts by After Six, leather belts, and more.

Tompkins Park Shop—147 Avenue A (10th St.), Manhattan; 212/677-5001. This terrific little East Village storefront is packed

Mr. Cheap's Picks

✔ **Fine and Klein**—The Lower East Side's longtime landmark continues to offer great savings on handbags and leather goods.

✔ **Tompkins Park Shop**—A great discovery in the East Village; suede and woven handbags in casual designer styles, at very casual prices.

✔ **Kaufman Lingerie**—Perhaps the best of Orchard Street's many no-frills shops for frilly lingerie at great prices.

✔ **Lismore Hosiery**—For those who like to stock up at low prices, Lismore has the biggest selection and the most helpful service.

✔ **Ties Plus**—Another great thing to buy on the Lower East Side—silk ties at half-price. This is one of the best.

with bargains on handbags, belts, scarves, and other accessories. These are mainly buyouts on brand-new merchandise in perfect condition. You may find a silk belt with a floral print, meant to sell for $38.00 at Express, selling here for a mere $5.00. Incredible! A suede bag by Tano was seen here for $18.00, and a black leather one by Barganza—originally $120.00—was just $25.00. The store also has finds in handcrafted items from around the world, like Indonesian carry bags made of woven straw and decorated with seashells, reduced from $22.00 to $7.00; and also jewelry, such as Rosecraft earrings, originally $9.00 to $11.00, marked down to $5.00. There's a lot to see, and with new closeouts to be snapped up all the time, their selection changes over quite rapidly.

Value Hosiery Center—255 West 23rd Street, Manhattan; 212/243-7243, 221 East 86th Street, Manhattan; 212/289-1515, 2345 Broadway (85th St.), Manhattan; 212/769-0594, 4615 13th Avenue, Brooklyn; 718/853-4296, and 107-10 71st Avenue, Forest Hills, Queens; 718/544-3699. See listing under "Steuer Hosiery" elsewhere in this section.

Vesture—141 Atlantic Ave., Brooklyn Heights, Brooklyn; 718/ 237-4126. Straddling the border of Brooklyn Heights and Cobble Hill are several inexpensive clothing shops. Vesture is a combination workshop and showroom for designer Akio Jow and company. They make a wild variety of women's hats at prices from just $20.00 and up. The styles range from the Victorian era right up through today and just about everything in between. There were even some fun, floppy, unconstructed hats in richly colored velvets. Everybody has fun just trying these on.

TRULY CHEAP STUFF

Mr. Cheap wants to save you money on all kinds of good-quality merchandise; but this book wouldn't be complete—especially in New York—without covering every part of the discount spectrum. Most of the clothing at these stores is not from recognizeable name brands, yet you may find it suitable for everyday wear. Besides, they're just fun to browse. You never know when you may stumble across some buried treasure!

Clothes-Out Store—25 Murray St., Manhattan; 212/587-0571. Amidst the basement-style discounters of this neighborhood (see "Damages!" below), the Clothes-Out Store is a rung up on the close-out ladder. It looks more like a bona fide boutique and carries a decent selection of disposable clothing, including some recognizable brands. These are first-quality clothes, only some of which are irregulars (clearly marked). Most of the fashions are for women; professional dresses that would cost around $40.00 in other stores can be found here for $12.99 and $19.99. Most of these, of course, are polyesters. Mr. C found a Kathryn Deene suit, in rayon/linen blend, still bearing a $79.00 price tag from Lane Bryant; here, it sold for $19.99. There are funky fashions as well, like a mesh top for nightclubbing, just $4.99.

There are some men's and children's clothes; you may find men's cotton work shirts reduced from $25.00 to $7.99, or a bin offering T-shirts and tank tops at four for $10. Clothing can be returned, if damaged, for exchange only.

Damages!—27 Murray St., Manhattan; 212/608-0024. This area of the Financial District, especially the blocks of Murray and Warren Streets between Broadway and

Mr. Cheap's Picks

✔ **Clothes-Out Store**—Definitely the nicest of the many bargain-basement stores just north of the World Trade Center area.

✔ **International L'Atmosphere**—One of the city's nicer chains of disposable fashions for women.

West Broadway, is literally lined with ultra-discount clothing stores. At most of these places, "cheap" refers to price *and* quality; Damages! makes no apologies for its merchandise. This is the lowest end of the new clothing chain, but such stores deserve mention—there are so many of them, and folks do shop there. They look more like rummage sales, with clothing piled into open bins. As the names imply, the goods are usually damaged or irregular in some way. Still, you can find some useful items, such as stockings for fifty cents (yes, in unopened packages) and sweaters for $1.99. At these prices, it can be fun to browse around.

Other such stores in the area include **Wild Deals** at 23 Park Place, **This 'n That** at 23 Warren Street, and **Great Expectations** at 30 Warren Street. Another entry in the damage derby, a store so humble it bears no name outside, is located at 12 Warren Street. Yet it has one of the better selections of the bunch, with men's suits for $30.00 (new, but don't forget, damaged; examine them well), sweaters for $12.00, and Timberland-style workboots for $15.00. Amazingly enough, such an area can also boast an elegant discounter like Gorsart (see above); ya gotta love New York.

International L'Atmosphere Clothing Company—152 Fulton St., Manhattan; 212/732-7063, 550 Broadway (Prince St.), Manhattan; 212/966-6051, 329 Sixth Ave. (4th St.), Manhattan; 212/229-2957, and 420 Columbus Ave. (80th St.), Manhattan; 212/595-7922. They may not have the best grammar, but International L'Atmosphere has prices that are easy to say: Everything in the store is $10.00. They carry lots of casual clothing for women, not famous brands but well made for the price. Brightly colored floral print dresses, sporty separates like applique sweaters and stirrup pants, and accessories are the main commodity here. For everyday stuff, it's worth a look. The stores are open seven days a week, and they accept credit cards along with good ol' greenbacks.

J & S Fashion Express—34 West 14th St., Manhattan; 212/255-5959. Among the vast cheap wonderland of 14th Street, you'll find one shop after another spilling out onto the sidewalk with racks of jeans, sportswear, handbags, and much more. J & S is a good example of such places, where you can get knockoff brands of blue jeans for $12.99 or women's stirrup leggings for as little as $4.99. You may find Sergio Valente hi-top sneakers for $19.99, or "New York" cotton sweatshirts for $6.99.

These stores also have things like cheap housewares, luggage, and the ubiquitous $2.99 umbrella. Most of these are closeouts, so you never quite know what they'll have. Sure, this merchandise won't last forever; at these stores, you definitely get what you pay for. But hey, if you're getting wet, does it matter how good the umbrella is? You're only going to leave it on a bus next week anyway.

Krazy Bargain—104 West 14th St., Manhattan; 212/924-4336. A cute name for a fairly run-of-the-mill clothing store, but one of the better ones along the junk mile of 14th Street. There are dressy, contemporary fashions for men and women here, all new and first quality. Men can find lots of Italian-style suits, for example, which are in fact imported from Seoul rather than Rome. Made with synthetic fabrics and priced at only $115.00, they may work for you as an inexpensive outfit that you won't have to worry about at the dance clubs. Same for women's dresses and separates, such as a black pullover sweater with gold applique for $35.00.

7th Avenue Saver's Paradise—450 Seventh Ave. (35th St.), Manhattan; 212/279-7022. The streets surrounding Macy's are lined with bargain clothing shops, small and large. Such is the attraction of the city's most famous department store, located smack in the middle of the Garment District. Wander the area and you never know what you may find; many of these shops, especially the smaller ones, come and go. Mr. C found this narrow storefront selling casual stuff with all items priced, as the current fad has it, at $10.00 apiece. These included blouses, leggings, men's and women's sweaters, and slacks. For the most part, you're dealing with synthetic fabrics at this price, of course, but the designs were up-to-the-minute prints and colors.

Shayo Stores—138 West 14th St., Manhattan; 212/242-0325. For inexpensive women's fashions, Shayo is a step above the riff-raff of 14th Street. The brands are not big names, but most are first quality and not irregulars. There's lots to choose from in casual wear and shoes, like cotton-lycra bodysuits or the popular quilted satin-look jackets, all from just $9.99. Black patent-leather boots, military-style, go for $14.99; and there are plenty of accessories too.

Sunny Shop—204 West 14th St., Manhattan; 212/243-4647. Well to the west of the main shopping area on 14th Street, Sunny Shop is a jam-packed little place for women's casual fashions, most of which are unknown imports. But they are first quality, and you may find stuff here that's fun anyway. Gold-lame (polyester) tops are just $9.99, perfect for club-hopping; matching pants are $11.99. Linen-look blazers, again synthetic, are $18.99; and floral-print full-length skirts are $9.99.

Or just stock up on dependable basics, like tank-tops for $4.99 and cotton leggings for $3.99 ($7.99 with stirrups). Solid cotton long-sleeve pullover shirt-and-skirt sets, in basic black, go for $14.99. The mood here is friendly, and items may be exchanged for store credit.

CLOTHING—USED

Used clothing is another great way to save lots of money—and don't turn up your nose at this idea. Recycling doesn't just mean bottles and cans, y'know. There is a wide range of options here, from trashy stuff to designer labels.

Consignment shops sell clothing they call "gently used"—by the original owner, who chose to wear the article once, maybe a few times, and then resell it. These are the places where you can get top-name fashions at incredibly low prices—and no one will ever know you didn't buy them new, though you'll probably want to brag about your "find" anyway. You can also, of course, sell things from your own closet at these shops, and split the profits, for another way to save money.

Vintage clothing is usually well worn but may still cost a bit more than you'd expect for used clothing, because it's from a trendy "retro" era. But there are great bargains out there for the persistent vintage hound.

Thrift shops sell used clothing that may have seen better days, and has been donated to benefit the charity that runs the particular store. In New York there are all kinds of organizations you can support by thrift shopping, from schools to health causes to the opera. And there is just as wide a range of quality; some of these shops are hard to tell from commercial boutiques.

CONSIGNMENT SHOPS

Allan & Suzi—416 Amsterdam Ave. (80th St.), Manhattan; 212/724-7445, and 1713 Sheepshead Bay Rd., Sheepshead Bay, Brooklyn; 718/332-7003. This is quite a place. Allan & Suzi resell dressy women's fashions by the *really* big designers like Bob Mackie (you know, the one who barely dresses Cher), John Paul Gaultier, Isabelle Allard, and many others. One dress, which sold originally for $3,600.00 was reduced here to $1,000.00. If that's still out of your range, there are even less expensive designs, like a black-sequined gown with feather trim for $80.00. Just about everything in these stores is dramatic; movie stars and the people who costume them shop here frequently. The stores sell a good stock of new clothes from past seasons, too, for as much as 70 percent off the original prices.

Allan & Suzi will also work with you to complete the outfit, perhaps with a pair of $900.00 earrings for just $275.00 And they sell Chanel cosmetics at discount. If you want to make a bold statement, or just have a lot of fun, drop into their Upper West Side boutique, or the original Brooklyn location.

A Women's Consignment Shoppe—177 Court St., Cobble Hill, Brooklyn; 718/596-1639. Two blocks below Atlantic Avenue, Susan Carole runs this very stylish resale shop, with great prices on gently used designer clothing. There is a lot to see packed into a relatively small store front. The Kleins, Calvin and Anne, are both here, as well as Liz Claiborne, Ralph Lauren, and other major names. On Mr. C's visit, a wool overcoat by Larry Levine was selling for $41.00; and a pair of Escada leather pants, which Susan said would have been $950.00 at Barney's, was just $250.00 here. There were also Kikit tops, with retail prices at $35.00 to $40.00, selling for a mere $5.25. The store also specializes in vintage fashions from the 1920s through the 1940s. It's open Wednesdays through Saturdays from noon to 6:30 p.m..

Debut II—136 West 83rd St., Manhattan; 212/875-8809. This Upper West Side consignment store just off of Amsterdam Avenue made its debut late last year. It specializes in women's designer clothing that is either unused or gently worn. You'll find names like Calvin Klein, Christian Dior, Laura Ashley, Donna Karan, Fendi, Armani, and many others. These are all priced substantially lower than their original costs. Along with clothing, Debut has lots of shoes from $35.00 to $45.00, and a sale rack of shirts and sweaters for $7.00 each. Furthermore, this store has an automatic markdown policy, which reduces the already-low prices by 20 percent after thirty days and by 50 percent after sixty days. The store is open Monday through Friday from 11:00 a.m. to 6:30 p.m., and an hour later on Thursdays; on Saturdays they close at 6:00 p.m.

Encore—1132 Madison Ave. (84th St.), 2nd Floor, Manhattan; 212/879-2850. This packed resale shop sells designer clothing in very good condition, barely used, at a fraction of their original prices. An ivory-colored wool sweater by Ungaro, in fact, was recently on sale with a Saks price tag still on it. So, it had *never* been worn; yet it was reduced from Saks' $700.00 to Encore's $200.00. Unused clothes are the exception, of course. Other items seen included an Anne Klein wool minidress for $50.00, and splashy evening dresses in bright colors by various designers, most from $200.00 to $300.00.

Encore is unusual in that it has some men's clothes too, though most of the merchandise is for women. Most resale shops have no men's clothes at all, simply because guys hang on to their clothing for years. Anyway, Mr. C found a navy-blue cashmere overcoat for $90.00, and a Rodier sweater for $45.00. Get on Encore's mailing list, and they'll notify you of special clearance sales for even better bargains.

Good-byes—230 East 78th St., Manhattan; 212/794-2301. Good-Byes is a child's version of the consignment shops listed in this section; it sells high-quality clothing and accessories for infants

Mr. Cheap's Picks

- ✔ **Allan & Suzi**—Be grand! The biggest designer names (from both Italy *and* Hollywood, dahling) at the lowest prices.
- ✔ **Michael's Resale Dress Shop**—Great prices and great service on women's designer names.
- ✔ **One Night Stand**—A novel approach—rent the fancy gown you could never hope to own.

through size 14. Recent items included a Health-Tex snowsuit in a leopard-skin print for $10.00, as well as a young girl's wool overcoat in a smart-looking magenta with black trim for $50.00. Lots of sweaters, too, for boys and girls, most $10.00 to $15.00. Everything has been cleaned, and it's all in great condition. They even have toys. Considering how soon youngsters outgrow their clothing, consignment stores are a great way to keep your investments down as your kids grow up.

Michael's Resale Dress Shop—1041 Madison Ave. (79th St.), 2nd Floor, Manhattan; 212/737-7273. The emphasis at Michael's is on personal service as much as great clothes. A smaller shop than the nearby Encore, it nevertheless has a well-stocked selection of such merchandise as a full-length black dress by Giorgio Armani, seen recently for $250.00 (well, no doubt it's gone by now!), Kenzo wool blouses for $39.00, and shoes by Ferragamo, Charles Jourdan, and Kenneth Cole, all under $50.00 a pair. Mr. C's shopping expert also loved a stylish wool coat in bright red by the Italian designer Galanos, for $350.00.

Mr. C had to rely very much upon his companion here, because this is a women's shop only. Men are requested to sit in a large, comfy chair and yap with the store's playful dog. Ladies pop in and out of the dressing rooms, you see, to get a good look in the light as they model various items. As they usually find a lot to try on, guys may prefer a walk around the block instead. The store is open Mondays through Saturdays from 9:30 a.m. to 6:00 p.m.

One Night Stand—905 Madison Ave. (72nd St.), Manhattan; 212/772-7720. Ladies, here's a very interesting alternative to buying expensive designer clothing that you'll never want to be seen in twice anyway. Creative guru Joanna Doniger buys the latest fashions from the biggest names and rents them to you for just $150.00 to $350.00. That's for a four-day period, so you can make sure you won't clash with your best friend's dress. It also means you can relax the day after the ball, instead of rushing in to return your glass slippers by the stroke of midnight.

With over eight hundred dresses to choose from, there's sure to be something here you'll like. Rent a de la Renta, or a Guy LaRoche, or one of many British designers (through the English Ms. Doniger's exclusive contacts). How about a $3,000.00 black sequined creation by Bob Mackie for $300.00? Sure! Some of these dresses—from short cocktail to full-length evening gown—cost as much as $5,000.00. All sizes from 2 to 14/16 are available.

Service is up-close and personal, as they say, and by appointment only; that's to give you as much time and attention as you need. The four-day rental will give you more time to accessorize the outfit, though Ms. Doniger can take care of that for you in the store; she has wraps, jackets, and lots of good-quality costume jewelry.

So, what happens to the dresses after they've been to a few galas, you ask? Yes, she does eventually sell some off, "when I'm fed up with them." There are usually a few on the sale rack, for a mere $50.00 to $250.00. Definitely worth a look. Meanwhile, the unique rental concept will save you a fortune—and you'll definitely look like a million. Furthermore, Ms. Doniger is quick to point out, renting for business purposes is a tax deduction!

The Ritz Thrift Shop—107 West 57th St., Manhattan; 212/265-4559. Notice the category in which this appears—no ordinary thrift shop *this*. For over 50 years Ritz has been reselling top-quality fur coats at a fraction of their original price. Actually, they prefer the phrase, "gently used." Customers come from all over the world to bargain shop here, regularly trading in one style for another. This ensures a large and ever-changing variety of mink, sable, beaver, fox, and more. Ritz also gets trade-ins from other furriers. Each item is one of a kind; recently on the racks were a Pierre Cardin raccoon jacket for $295.00, and a Dior mink coat, originally $8,000.00, reduced to $2,900.00. A jet-black rabbit fur jacket by Fendi was selling for $1,000.00. "Fendi is one of the big names in the business," noted one of the salesmen. "They can get any price they want for a jacket like this."

Ritz also has hats, stoles, and other smaller items. Service is very personal without being high-pressured. Mr. C, who does not even come *close* to looking like a fur coat type, was greeted just as readily as anyone else coming through the door.

VINTAGE CLOTHING

Alice Underground—481 Broadway (Broome St.), Manhattan; 212/431-9067, and 380 Columbus Ave. (78th St.), Manhattan; 212/724-6682. Definitely among the city's best vintage clothing stores, Alice Underground has lots and lots of clothing from Victorian to contemporary, much of it at terrific prices. The SoHo branch takes its cue from the nearby Canal Jeans and its many competitors on downtown Broadway, with boutique-style displays of mainly 1950s and 1960s clothing. Lots of jeans, wild shirts, and cool dresses. The uptown shop is more of a traditional vintage store—more like a romp through Grandma's attic. It's quieter, with several packed rooms to wander through.

In the first rooms, you'll find lots of formal wear; many styles of tuxedos and tails, with a whole outfit for as little as $50.00. A men's Botany 500 raincoat was seen for $22.50, and Harris Tweed blazers for $40.00. Then again, a sixties sleeveless minidress in great condition was also seen for just $12.00. But it's in the back rooms that you'll see some real deals; this is where the sale racks are. Get an Italian raincoat, in black, of course, for $10.00. Traditional and flashy sweaters, normally $15.00 to $20.00, are two-for-one. A woman's silk blouse, boldly purple, was seen for $5.00. Well-worn leather jackets go for $10.00. There are also $5.00 bins filled with accessories, fun to rummage through. And to the side, yet another room of linens—tablecloths, draperies, bedspreads and remnants.

The salespeople know their stuff and will help you with finding items and fitting them in front of the tri-folding mirror. They also sell cosmetics at discount; "Paint" matte lipsticks, normally $20.00 elsewhere, are just $6.50 here, and rice-based facial powder is $10.00 for a huge container. Plus brushes, liners and pencils, all at discount.

Andy's Chee-Pees—691 Broadway (4th St.), Manhattan; 212/420-5980, and 16 West 8th St. (Fifth Ave.), Manhattan; 212/460-8488. With a name like this, says Mr. C, how can you go wrong? Andy's is crammed with racks and racks of men's and women's antique clothing. In fact, the prices are not as good as some other vintage stores in this book, but the quality is high and there is so much to chose from. A selection of handsome buckskin fringe jackets in clean, brushed suede was seen for $110.00 each; black-velvet cocktail dresses for $55.00; and a sleeveless dress done up in a rainbow of sequins for $65.00. Men will find tweed blazers starting at $35.00 and three-quarter-length winter coats, when the season demands, for $55.00. Both stores stay open late, seven days a week.

The Antique Boutique—712 Broadway (Waverly Place), Manhattan; 212/460-8830, and 227 East 59th St., Manhattan; 212/752-1680. Antique Boutique is tremendously popular with the art crowd/student set, especially at its base camp near Washington Square Park. The store sells a mix of vintage clothing and new items manufactured in retro styles, for men and women. There are two large floors crammed with clothes; the newer fashions are on the street level, and the more vintage stuff is underneath. Upstairs, you may find unisex flight jackets for $60.00 (on a recent sale, marked down to $48.00), or floral-print rayon minidresses for $30.00. This area is also good for women's accessories, like lingerie and jewelry.

Downstairs, in AB's "Bargain Basement," they have an entire room filled with leather coats in a variety of lengths and styles. Studded motorcycle jackets by Schott, new factory irregulars, were marked down from $350.00 to $225.00; vintage leather is sold on racks designated $19.99, $29.99, $39.99 and $49.99. Lots of military coats in this room, too. You'll also find Harris tweed jackets for $29.00, along with the ever-popular selection of jeans, baseball shirts, overcoats and much more.

Canal Jean Company—504 Broadway (Broome St.), Manhattan; 212/226-1130. As noted in the "New Clothing" section, Canal Jeans is a downtown institution for cheap chic—but discounts on the latest fashions tell only half the story. Downstairs in the basement, Canal has upped the ante in what it's best known for: "Recycled clothing" is what they call it. Hey, these days, that's the perfect way to think of these fashions. After all, every style comes back sooner or later, right?

What they've done, y'see, is to renovate the basement into fifteen thousand square feet of new and used clothing bargains—none of which is priced over $10.00. That's right. Wool overcoats, blazers, sweaters, dresses, skirts, military styles....you name it, they've probably got it, and the highest price you'll see is $10.00 per item. It's really huge, and lots of stuff is still in very good condition. Some of the clothing is new, too; closeouts and irregulars. And this doesn't even include the 99¢ bargain bins, filled with accessories, hosiery, T-shirts, sleepwear, and more. The stuff keeps pouring in all the time, so check out the bargains whenever you can! Canal Jean Company is open seven days a week.

Cheap Jack's Vintage Clothing—841 Broadway (13th St.), Manhattan; 212/777-9564. Cheap Jack could learn a thing or two from Mr. Cheap. For all its publicity, this store is one of the more expensive vintage shops in town. They do have a huge selection, on two floors; and while there are bargains to be found here, the prices overall are not that great. You can find suede jackets from $20.00 and up, heavy wool military jackets for $19.00, lots and lots of wool overcoats for $50.00 to $75.00, dresses for $25.00 and up, and ties, ties, ties. They also have unusual clothes with an international flair, such as daishiki shirts and Japanese kimonos. These are priced under $20.00. Periodic sales afford better savings—as much as 30 to 50 percent off regular prices. Jack's is also more service-oriented than other vintage shops, offering layaway plans and alterations while you wait.

Dorothy's Reruns—117 Perry St., Manhattan; 212/229-2606. This cozy West Village shop, on a sidestreet just off of Hudson, has a bit of everything—vintage wear

Mr. Cheap's Picks

✔ **Alice Underground**—Step through the looking glass and find the lowest prices on a wide range of vintage threads.

✔ **Canal Jeans**—As if this SoHo giant wasn't big enough, they've added a bargain basement for super-cheap downscale fashion.

✔ **Love Saves the Day**—Probably the most fun vintage shop—as devoted to Elvis, the Bradys, and lava lamps as it is to clothing.

✔ **Rose's Vintage**—Definitely the best prices in town for vintage jeans.

✔ **Tuxedo and Clothing Liquidators**—Used formal wear—a great idea for musicians and people who go to lots of weddings.

from every decade, second-hand designer clothing, and even one-of-a-kind artsy pieces, such as painted jeans and tie-dyed shirts. Regular jeans, including Levis and Guess, go for $10.00; black-velvet cocktail dresses around $40; shoes from $10.00 to $20.00 and up (a pair of black pumps by Chanel for $50.00), lots of period hats from $15.00 to $25.00, costume jewelry, and much more. Dorothy herself hand-picks what she will sell, with a careful eye for style and quality. There's also a $5.00 and $10.00 rack at the rear of the narrow store, with more "grab-bag" bargains out in front, when weather permits. The shop is open seven days a week.

The Family Jewels—832 Sixth Ave. (29th St.), 2nd Floor, Manhattan; 212/679-5023. Now, this makes perfect sense—a vintage clothing store in the Garment District. This place is great. It's jammed with racks and racks of men's and women's coats, jeans, formal wear, shoes, and accessories. Bag a leopard-skin coat for $59.00, or a Pierre Cardin tweed sport jacket for $21.00. A sleeveless dress of black lace was seen for $39.00; add a pair of strap sandals by Halston for $35.00 more. An array of hats ranges from $15.00 to $45.00, and there's lots of jewelry (natch!), gloves, handbags, and other add-ons. The shop is lots of fun to browse; it's even been the backdrop for photo sessions for fashion magazines such as Bazaar. Open daily from 11:00 a.m. to 7:00 p.m.

Jana Starr/Jean Hoffman Antique Clothing—236 East 80th St., Manhattan; 212/861-8256 or 212/535-6930. This narrow Upper East Side shop houses two experts in antique clothing and linens, along with piles of the same stacked up, shelved, and hanging from the rafters. Starr and Hoffman collect everything from bridal gowns to shoes, hats, and costume jewelry. Many of these items date from the Victorian era onward, and just about all are one-of-a-kind. So, for that very special outfit, you can find something unique or have it assembled from separate pieces, and then accessorize it from head to toe. A wedding gown of this sort can cost as little as $200.00, or as much as $3,000.00.

These folks have an encyclopedic knowledge of the history of clothing, plus scrapbooks filled with patterns; designers like Ralph Lauren come here to copy antique styles for their own work. But you don't have to be a big name to get ultra-personal service. "We give our customers a lot of support," says Starr. Like its dresses, the shop itself is one-of-a-kind.

Live Shop Die—151 Avenue A (10th St.), Manhattan; 212/674-7265. Kind of says it all, huh? Live Shop Die has something a little different from the rest of the East Village's many vintage shops—original, *unused* period clothing. Not exclusively, of course, but you will find lots of clothing, shoes, and memorabilia from the 1950s, 1960s, and 1970s that was never sold and has been well preserved. Mr. C found a pair of platform shoes, for example, that look so good they seem to be modern-day reproductions—but they're the genuine article. At $40.00 the pair, they're not exactly cheap—but hey, this is an investment in *culture*, man. Get a real pair of bell-bottom jeans to go with the shoes for $25.00. Or go further back for a 1950s red cocktail dress, also $25.00. There's also plenty of vintage and costume jewelry—rings, earrings, even belt buckles—posters, decorative items, and some small pieces of furniture. "I try to keep the New York-sized apartment in mind," says Trixie, the charming owner who finds all this great stuff. Adding to the fun of the store is a black-and-white photo booth, in which you can still get four poses for $1.50—good, cheap entertainment! Oh, and of course it's genuine, rescued from an Asbury Park arcade.

Love Saves The Day—119 Second Ave. (7th St.), Manhattan; 212/228-3802. Besides being remembered as the pivotal store in the film *Desperately Seeking Susan*, Love Saves the Day is one of the East Village's longtime greats for funky clothing and memorabilia. Find an antique bridal gown from the 1930s for just $45.00, or an equally timeless black spaghetti-strap party dress for $15.00. Blue satin poodle skirts (definitely fifties) are $45.00. Plus jeans for as low as $12.00, felt fedora hats for $10.00, and vests for just $2.50.

The shop also has a tremendous collection of period collectibles, from lava lamps ($55.00) to packs of Elvis playing cards ($5.50). Not to mention tons of toys and paraphernalia from all of those keen TV shows from yesteryear, like *"Star Trek"* and *"Batman"*; as well as current favorites like, er, *"Star Trek"* and *"Batman."* Some things truly are timeless.

Panache—525 Hudson St., Manhattan; 212/242-5115. A beautifully appointed women's vintage clothing store, Panache's prices are a bit out of Mr. C's range, even for used clothing. The quality and taste found here is exceptional, you see, keeping prices higher than many other vintage shops. Still, they do have an "Ultra Sale" rack at the rear, where you may find dresses, blouses, and sweaters for $5.00 and up—or a genuine 1940s black "poodle coat" reduced from $350.00 to $250.00.

Pow-Wow Vintage Clothing—149 Avenue A (10th St.), Manhattan; no phone. One of the more recent additions to the East Village scene, Pow-Wow has a nice selection of hip clothing, mostly for women, and very reasonable prices. Fashions lean towards the 1950s and 1960s, with fake-fur overcoats (you may even find the popular leopard-skin look) for $25.00 and up; and cocktail dresses from $25.00 to $45.00. Add a gold-lame handbag for $15.00 and a pair of go-go boots, and you're ready for a night on the town. Pow-Wow has leather jackets from $30.00 to $50.00, well broken-in. And Mr. C did find some men's sweaters priced around $25.00.

Reminiscence Garage—175 MacDougal St.; 212/979-9440. The popular Reminiscence stores, which sell wonderful styles from the 1950s through the 1970s, run this Greenwich Village branch as sort of a clearance center, with reduced prices on many of the items. It's still a large selection. You can find good-quality vintage jeans for as little as $9.00, which some places sell for up to $30.00. Men's blazers go for $18.00, with silk ties for $3.00. There are lots of accessories, from earrings for $3.00 to velvet caps for $6.00—made new from recycled vintage fabrics. Reminiscence sells its own entire line of new clothing made in 1940s styles, such as pleated trousers for $18.00. And they have lots of kitschy toys and novelty items, including all of your television sitcom needs.

A Repeat Performance—156 First Ave. (9th St.), Manhattan; 212/529-0832. See listing under "Home Furnishings."

Rose's Vintage—96 East 7th St., Manhattan; 212/533-8550, and 350 East 9th St., Manhattan; 212/979-7660. These two East Village shops are crammed from floor to ceiling with great vintage clothing buys. A recent sale featured stacks and stacks of denim jeans for an incredibly low $12.00 a pair; Mr. C has found few such places with this quantity of jeans in good shape for that price. Rose also has things like vintage coats, including men's cashmere overcoats from $50.00. Mr. C even saw a woman's 1950s-style leopard-skin coat for $75.00—and it was real. Now, *that's* unusual. Plus, lots of sequined dresses, formal wear, and other fancy stuff. The 7th Street shop is larger and has more to see, but both are gems.

The Second Coming—72 Greene St., Manhattan; 212/431-4424. Given the neighborhood, it shouldn't be surprising that this is one of the fanciest vintage stores you'll ever see. It is impressive, if not always inexpensive; but then, vintage can be tricky that way. Still, you will find some good deals here. The front of this vast store, as well as its mezzanine level, are crammed full of clothing that is a mix of true vintage stuff and modern items done in retro styles. Suits, tuxedos, dresses, and blouses abound here, but they are not necessarily cheap. Accessories are better bargains: you may find a pair of Italian women's shoes, with stiletto heels and pointed toes, for $25.00, or a wide-brimmed hat of straw and velvet, with netting over the front for $35.00. A new pair of men's suede western boots was seen for $95.00. There are lots of handbags, costume jewelry, sunglasses, and scarves, all reasonably priced.

Second Coming also has furniture and home decorations, much of which are set up in displays that make the store look like a museum for living rooms through the decades. That's the true fun of the place. The couches, chairs, and tables are not particularly cheap, though you never know what will turn up. Smaller accessories, again, save the day. Get a deco-style chrome candy dish and lid for $15.00, or an eight-piece cocktail mixer and glassware set that came straight out of some fifties suburban basement rec-room for $45.00. Meanwhile, as much as any SoHo gallery, just browsing through Second Coming is good, cheap entertainment.

Star Struck—270 Bleecker St., Manhattan; 212/366-9826, and 47 Greenwich Ave., Manhattan; 212/691-5357. This pair of Greenwich Village boutiques sells very good-quality vintage wear, in styles from traditional to outrageous. You can find great black cocktail dresses from $30.00 to $55.00, and men's tweed blazers in the same price range. There are lots of blue jeans from $25.00 and up. The prices are not as low as other vintage stores around town, but again, this stock is mostly in good condition and there is a lot to choose from.

Tuxedo and Clothing Liquidators—2 East 14th St., Manhattan; 212/691-0502. Now, *here's* a great idea. This packed little store resells tuxedos of every style, along with the accessories, from the past few decades. These are clothes that have come from rental stores and may not look brand-new anymore, but still have a lot of life in them. Some are factory samples that have never been worn. All are high-quality wool tuxes from such designers as Christian Dior, Pierre Cardin, After Six, and others. Some of these cost as little as $70.00 for a jacket and pants set. A set of tails can be just $25.00. Ruffled shirts start at $2.99, black or red bowties are $5.00, sashes $9.00, those shiny black plastic shoes are $3.00...you get the idea.

There are even fancier savings, like a Raffinatti tux—which originally sold for $450.00—here, just $150.00. And they have far-out styles from the seventies, including prints and velours. Why rent, when you can own at these prices?

The Usual Suspects—337 East 9th St., Manhattan; 212/677-2644. Here's a cozy, narrow little shop specializing in new and used clothing of a dressy nature—from uniforms to splashy evening wear. Round up a velour blazer for $20.00, or a 1950s satin dress for just $10.00; they recently had a selection of glittery, colorful "Peacock" jackets for women, $30.00 each. Men can find tweed sportcoats for $20.00 and up, as well as things like military jackets and marching band uniforms, and unused tuxedo separates from $30.00. The store also has $1.00 and $5.00 bins filled with shirts, jackets, and sweaters.

Vintage Antique Clothing—111 Seventh Ave. (Carroll St.), Park Slope, Brooklyn; 718/638-7451. It's small, "but what's there is cherse." Vintage sells a nice mix of new and used clothing at good, if not sensational, prices. Most everything is in fine condition, even styles that date all the way back to the 1940s. Just about all of it is for women, from coats and dresses to interesting hats. They also have a wide assortment of real and costume jewelry, also at good prices. Open daily from 11:00 a.m. to 8:00 p.m.

Vintage Circus—9 East 4th St., Manhattan; no phone. Mr. C loves this funky shop right across the street from Tower Records. They have a huge collection of fashions from the 1950s, 1960s, and onward. Lots of used Levis jeans are priced between $15.00 and $30.00, and there were also some denim shirts, just in time for their re-emergence in the fashion world, for $15.00. Men's and women's shirts and blouses start as low as $5.00, including plenty of Hawaiian, baseball, and military styles. A ladies' glittery top in black see-through mesh was $12.00, and a rabbit-fur short coat was $45.00. Vintage Circus also gets closeouts on new clothing; during Mr. C's visit, the latest arrival was a shipment of military overcoats from the East German army for $60.00 apiece. Evidently, they won't be needing them anymore. Like so many shops in this young and happening area, the store is open evenings.

THRIFT SHOPS

When you buy at thrift shops, you can not only find some fantastic bargains on nice clothing and housewares, but almost all of the stores described below benefit good causes, from schools and medical facilities to even the New York City Opera! Don't be put off by the idea of these places; yes, some are grungy, but many are quite fancy, especially those on the Upper East Side. You may not believe the things to be found there until you see for yourself.

Calvary/St. George's Thrift Shop—208 East 16th St., Manhattan; 212/475-5510. Calvary/St. George's easily wins the prize for most dramatic thrift store. Tucked into the basement of a marvelous old brownstone church, the exposed stone walls and stone steps give the shop an almost medieval atmosphere. The prices are almost as old-fashioned; the clothing styles, however, are quite current. Mr. C found an olive Italian-style blazer from Brooks Brothers for $10.00, and a young girl's down jacket for $15.00. Wool overcoats for men and women are $10.00 to $25.00; there are racks of dresses for just $5.00 each; and sweaters for all at $2.00 and $3.50.

A couple of blocks away, through picturesque Stuyvesant Square, is the **Calvary/St. George Furniture Thrift Shop**. This has amazing bargains that also benefit the church; see the listing under "Used Furniture."

Chelsea Thrift Store—201 Eighth Ave. (19th St.), Manhattan; 212/675-1520. A run-of-the-mill store much like a Salvation Army post. You'll find jeans for $7.00 to $10.00, sweaters from $5.00, dresses for $15.00, and men's suits from $15.00 to $25.00. The selection is somewhat limited. There is a 25 percent discount for senior citizens on Mondays.

Everybody's Thrift Shop—261 Park Ave. South (21st St.), Manhattan; 212/355-9263. Everybody must donate to this store, because it has such an interesting assortment of clothing and housewares. The clothing selection leans toward the women; one item spotted was a lavender-colored cashmere blouse and skirt. It had never been worn, and still bore its original price tag of $145.00; the price here was $75.00. You could also get a pair of Ferragamo heels to go with the outfit for $15.00. The main level also has china and silverware, some small appliances, and furniture. Upstairs, you'll find several attics' worth of books and records, most selling for a dollar or two. There is also some good artwork to be found; Mr. C saw a large framed poster from a Metropolitan Museum of Art exhibition for $40.00. Proceeds benefit the Columbia College Fund and several related charities.

Girls Club Thrift Shop—202 East 77th St., Manhattan; 212/535-8570. Of the many Upper East Side thrift stores filled with ritzy clothing, this is one of the biggest. They have a huge selection of designer fashions for men and women. Most of these are in great shape and at even greater prices. Among the bargains Mr. C found were a men's Adolfo suit for $90.00; and for women, a pair of Pappagallo shoes for $25.00. And that was just a quick pass-through. The store also has good-quality handbags, as well as lots of books and furniture. Proceeds, of course, benefit The Girls Club of New York.

Godmothers' League Thrift Shop—1457 Third Ave. (82nd St.), Manhattan; 212/988-2858. This narrow and cluttered thrift shop is a bit more of what you'd expect from a thrift shop. Clothing is hung on racks and piled on top of them; it's not all in the best of shape, but if you rummage through you may find a diamond in the rough. Mr. C came up with a Ralph Lauren tweed suit; at $250.00 it's still a bargain even if it is much more expensive than anything else in the store. Other discoveries included a brightly colored ski jacket for $35.00 and a Pringle Scottish wool sweater for $10.00. If you're brave and can find the back steps, there is a basement area stacked with dusty old furniture. But again, there may be something buried down here that you can use. This charity benefits The West End Day School, an elementary school for children with special needs.

Goodwill Thrift Shop—217 West 79th St., Manhattan; 212/874-5050. One of the more nicely kept thrift stores of this type, Goodwill is just off of Broadway on this popular stretch of the Upper West Side. You'll probably find some nice things among the racks of men's dress shirts for $4.00, jeans for $8.00, suits for $20.00, skirts for $8.00, and shoes for $6.00. Each day, tickets of a particular color will be half-price. There is also some small furniture here ($25.00 to $50.00), along with lots of books and records. It's worth a look.

Help Line Thrift Shop—382 Third Ave. (27th St.), Manhattan; 212/532-5136. This basic thrift shop is just a step or so above the Salvation Army variety, but you can find some nice things here, like a black Dior women's blazer, in good shape, $12.00; men's tweed jackets from $10.00 to $20.00, and winter overcoats from $15.00 and up. Sales benefit this twenty-four-hour counseling hotline, founded in 1969 by Norman Vincent Peale.

Irvington Institute Thrift Shop—1534 Second Ave. (80th St.), Manhattan; 212/879-4555. You'll hardly think you're in a thrift shop when you walk into this place. It's large and comfortable, with neatly displayed clothing that includes a lot of designer names. Well, this *is* the Upper East Side, dahling. You may find a grey pinstripe blazer and skirt by Anne Taylor for a mere $50.00, or a men's Perry Ellis raincoat for $20.00. In fact, men's overcoats are grouped by price: $25.00

Mr. Cheap's Picks

✔ UPPER EAST SIDE THRIFT TOUR—Second and Third Avenues in this area are lined with charitable thrift stores, to which charitable people donate furs and designer clothing. Among the best are the **Irvington Institite Thrift Shop** and the **Spence-Chapin Thrift Shop**. Both feel more like fancy boutiques.

✔ **Out of the Closet Thrift Shop**—Another Upper East Sider, this store benefits AIDS groups. It's more hodge-podgey, stuffed with clothes, books, home furnishings, and collectibles.

✔ **Repeat Performance**—Part of the other great neighborhood for thrift shops, the east twenties. This one benefits the New York City Opera, and sells clothing you could wear to opening night.

coats, $50.00 and $100.00. Who ever thought a thrift store could charge $100.00 for *anything*? And yet, they're still bargains.

Racks and racks of shirts and blouses, too, for $2.00, $5.00 and $10.00 Plus jewelry, neckties, and other accessories. And the store runs such special sales as, "All Bric-A-Brac, $2.00 Today."

Memorial Sloan-Kettering Thrift Store—1440 Third Ave. (81st St.), Manhattan; 212/535-1250. Part of the Upper East Side thrift shop district, this store has lots of high-quality fashions for men and women. Mr. C found a Brooks Brothers classic blue pin-stripe suit for $25.00. Same price for a woman's houndstooth blazer and skirt set by Jones New York. Another find in the women's section was a black rain poncho from Bergdorf Goodman for $75.00. And women will like the shoe section, where they may find a pair of Maud Frizon alligator heels for $25.00. The store also has lots of books, like a two-volume edition of *Who's Who in America* for $10.00, as well as housewares and some furniture. Proceeds benefit the Memorial Sloan-Kettering Cancer Center.

One block up the street is another thrift shop dedicated to the same cause, **The Cancer Care Thrift Shop**, 1480 Third Avenue, (212/879-9868). Here Mr. C found a men's Nino Cerruti blazer for $30.00, and a black lace dress by Fiandaga for $40.00.

Out of The Closet Thrift Shop—220 East 81st St., Manhattan; 212/472-3573. Yes, the name is a pun. Out Of The Closet benefits community organizations and institutions fighting AIDS. This packed store goes on and on with great fashions, small appliances, antiques and collectibles. The front of the store features women's clothes, like a black and red print top by Donald Brooks for Lord & Taylor, just $20.00 A red knit dress from Victoria's Secret was seen for $10.00, and there is a big selection of women's shoes. For men's clothing you actually go out the back of the store to a separate building, which is even larger. Here, you'll see suits for $45.00, and racks of shirts and trousers for $10.00. This area is also lined with bookshelves featuring hundreds of fiction and nonfiction titles; you"ll also find linens, rugs, and appliances back here.

Repeat Performance—220 East 23rd St., Manhattan; 212/684-5344. This thrift store benefits the New York City Opera; one visit will have you singing its praises. Find lots of good-quality clothing, like a Jacqueline de Ribes evening dress in black silk with rhinestone buttons for $75.00, or a brushed suede lavender skirt for $40.00. Men will find lots of classic looks, like a Nino Cerruti corduroy blazer for $20.00. Lots of shoes, too; a pair of high heels in gold lame by Andrew Geller, like new, were seen for $30.00.

Upstairs there is furniture, artwork, books, and all kinds of things for the home. Among the recent booty were a Smith-Corona manual typewriter for $30.00, a great-looking sofa bed upholstered in grey and white striped cloth for $350.00, and a framed poster from "A Chorus Line" for $30.00. Speaking of music, you will, of course, find records here, many for a dollar each; same price for a library full of used books. Items marked with a red dot are on sale for half-price.

Right next door, sharing the same address, is **Second Time Around** (212/685-2170), a thrift shop benefiting Planned Parenthood of New York City. They have a big selection of clothing at uniform prices (excuse the pun). Men's suits are all $30.00, blazers $15.00, shirts $7.00; women's outfits are $20.00, sweaters $8.00, shoes $4.00. The condition is quite good. Often certain sections are further discounted; a recent sale offered 30 percent off anything with a designer label.

The Salvation Army Thrift Stores—536 West 46th St., Manhattan; 212/664-8563, 112 Fourth Ave., Manhattan; 212/673-2741, 26 East 125th St., Manhattan; 212/289-9617, 208 Eighth Ave., Manhattan; 212/929-5214, 40 Ave. B, Manhattan; 212/473-9492, 268 West 96th St., Manhattan; 212/663-2258, 220 East 23rd St., Manhattan; 212/532-8115, 268 Knickerbocker Ave., Brooklyn; 718/821-7477, 572 Fifth Ave., Brooklyn; 718/499-6557, 963 Coney Island Ave., Brooklyn; 718/856-5280, 282 Broadway, Brooklyn; 718/387-9286, 39-11 61st St., Woodside, Queens; 718/426-9222. You hardly need Mr. C to describe the scene at the Salvation Army. Suffice it to say, they're everywhere, and tend to have a decent selection of clothing at rock-bottom prices. Men's sport coats for $15.00, women's for $10.00, jeans for $5.00, T-shirts for $2.00. And you never know what labels may turn up; at one location Mr. C even spotted a Ralph Lauren dress shirt for $3.99. Oh sure, most of this clothing has seen better days, but then, who hasn't? For bulk buying in the downscale nineties you can't beat these prices—or the work your few dollars will help support.

Spence-Chapin Thrift Shop—1430 Third Ave. (80th St.), Manhattan; 212/737-8448. Spence-Chapin is a most impressive thrift store, more typical of its posh East Side environs than the rock-bottom prices found inside. Their two floors of clothing and accessories feel like a fancy boutique. Right up in the front window, in fact, is a rack of fur coats selling for a fraction of their original prices. Next to them is a separate designer room, with women's dressy fashions like a Nina Ricci blue and black knit dress for $125.00. An Adolfo blazer and skirt, like new, in a black and red print was seen for $250.00.

Elsewhere in the store, women will find lots of shoes by such designers as Ferragamo, Charles Jourdan, and Kenneth Cole. A pair of Bandolino heels was just $20.00. Plus lots of handbags, jewelry, and other accessories. Men may find a London Fog raincoat or a Jaguar herringbone blazer, each for $45.00. And we haven't even gotten downstairs to the basement, where everything is either $5.00 or $10.00. These clearance racks include shirts, pants, sweaters, dresses, coats, and more. This area also has furniture and housewares. The proceeds benefit Spence-Chapin's Adoption Resource Center.

COSMETICS AND PERFUMES

Alice Underground—481 Broadway (Broome St.), Manhattan; 212/431-9067, and 380 Columbus Ave. (78th St.), Manhattan; 212/724-6682. See listing under "Clothing—Used; Vintage Clothing."

Century 21—22 Cortlandt St., Manhattan; 212/227-9092. See listing under "Department Stores."

Cosmetic Boutique—52 West 8th St., Manhattan; 212/254-0151. If you're in Greenwich Village and you like perfumes and makeup, you'll want to check this one out for sure. Jackie Harvey, the woman who began the store just over a year ago, had you in mind. Here you can get name brand cosmetics for as much as 30 to 50 percent lower than department store prices: Chanel lipsticks for $12.00 ($18.50 elsewhere); Chanel eye pencils for $8.00 instead of up to $23.00. Clinique lipsticks half-price at $5.00. A Shiseido makeup compact, reduced from $30.00 to $18.00. Colognes are about 30 percent off, and there are plenty of skin care products too. She can also place custom orders for your favorite items, if you wish—and returns for exchange are allowed. Go.

Cosmetics Plus—605 Third Ave. (40th St.), Manhattan; 212/986-1407, 275 Seventh Ave. (26th St.), Manhattan; 212/727-0705, 501 Seventh Ave. (40th St.), Manhattan; 212/768-4696, 175 West 57th St., Manhattan; 212/399-9783, 1920 Broadway (65th St.), Manhattan; 212/875-8604, 518 Fifth Ave. (53rd St.), Manhattan; 212/221-6560, 515 Madison Ave. (53rd St.), Manhattan; 212/644-1911, 666 Fifth Ave. (52nd St.), Manhattan; 212/757-2895, and 1201 Third Ave. (70th St.), Manhattan; 212/628-5600. As you can see, what we've got here is a discount cosmetics chain. Cosmetics Plus is like a cross between a drugstore and the perfumes section of Bloomingdales: The shelves are filled with shampoos, toiletries, and beauty products, while there are also glass display counters featuring all kinds of colognes, eye makeup, nail care items, and people to demonstrate them. Just about all of this stuff is sold at 10 to 15 percent off the retail list prices. That includes Paul Mitchell's "Nexus" hair care, Revlon facial products, and designer name brand perfumes. There is also a special counter featuring thirty perfumes and colognes that are sold at 20 to 70 percent off for the week. During Mr. C's visit, these included Calvin Klein's "Obsession," as well as scents by Lagerfeld and Givenchy. Most items may be exchanged for store credit within seven days of purchase; that makes CP a good place to do gift shopping as well as personal shopping.

Jay's Perfume Bar—14 East 17th St., Manhattan; 212/243-7743. This block of 17th Street, between Fifth Avenue and Broadway, is another one of those New York shopping miracles: The Enclave. Here, more than half a dozen perfume discounters work both sides of the street, allowing you the consumer to find the

Mr. Cheap's Picks

✔ **Cosmetic Boutique**—This average-looking Greenwich Village shop has tremendous discounts on fragrances and makeup.

✔ **Parisian Perfumes**—An upstairs treasure chest of perfume bargains.

✔ **Jay's Perfume Bar**—One of the many bustling no-frills perfume shops along this block of 17th Street; big selection, low prices, McDonald's service.

✔ **Perfumania**—This national discounter truly has great savings on designer fragrances.

best deals easily. Jay's is one of the better shops of the group; the difficulty in getting to the counter, and then getting someone to help you, proves its popularity. Go ahead, be a pushy New Yorker, like everyone else in the store. Meanwhile, you'll find great discounts on all your favorites: Halston Z-14 men's cologne, list price $36.00, here $25.00. Pavlova light cologne splash for women, an eight-ounce bottle for $2.00. A 3.4-ounce bottle of Paloma Picasso perfume, listing for $80.00, sells for $52.00. Plus other cosmetics, like Chaps deodorant stick for $2.50 or a pound of Nivea skin lotion for $5.00. Funny name for a store, though. Makes it sound like you should drink the stuff.

Directly across the street, check out **Bizzarro Turci**, 9 East 17th St. (212/741-1632) for a similar selection, as well as good prices on lots of gift sets. And, down the block from Turci is another winner, **The Perfume Encounter**, 25 East 17th St. (212/645-8868), which has more great deals on men's and women's scents, yet in a quieter and more refined atmosphere. Ask them if they have your choice in a blank, "no frills" box; it'll save you a couple dollars more.

Loehmann's—19 Duryea Place, Flatbush, Brooklyn; 718/469-9800, 5746 Broadway, Bronx; 718/543-6420, and 60-06 99th St., Rego Park, Queens; 718/271-4000. See listing under "Clothing–New."

National Wholesale Liquidators—632 Broadway (Bleecker St.), Manhattan; 212/979-2400, and 71-01 Kissena Blvd., Flushing, Queens; 718/591-3900. See listing under "Department Stores."

Parisian Perfumes and Cosmetics—123 Fifth Ave. (19th St.), Manhattan; 212/254-5300. Walk up to the second floor and you'll find terrific bargains on a truly vast selection of perfumes and colognes, cosmetic products, and gifts. There are over six hundred items in this packed store, most of which are sold at up to 60 and 70 percent off list prices. Find a Replique gift set marked down from $45.00 to $20.00; or a Helena Rubinstein set reduced from $22.50 to just $5.00. There are even gifts like leather bags from just $5. Also, full lines of makeup products, all on display. The place may be cluttered, but owner Arnold Weiner knows where everything is and can find what you want in a jiffy. The store is relaxed and quiet, above the bustle of lower Fifth Avenue's bargain haven.

Perfumania—One Times Square, Manhattan; 212/944-2311, 782 Lexington Ave. (61st St.), Manhattan; 212/750-2810, and 342 Madison Ave. (43rd St.), Manhattan; 212/330-0146. Perfumania is a nationwide chain whose buying power allows them to offer deep discounts on designer perfumes and colognes for men and women. Generally they divide into three pricing categories: 20, 40, and 60 percent off list prices. These may include Cher's "Uninhibited," which lists at $45.00 for a three-ounce spray bottle; Perfumania's price is a cher-ifically revealing $17.95. A 1.6-ounce bottle of eau de toilette by Balenciaga is reduced from $27.50 to just $5.95. And you'll find similar savings all the time on Oleg Cassini, Shalimar, Anne Klein, Alfred Sung, Halston, Gucci, and many others.

Perfumania also discounts gift sets, such as a Giorgio sampler for men nearly half-price at $34.95. There are lots of items to chose from for under $10.00, for that inexpensive (and always last-minute) gift idea.

Ralph's Discount City—95 Chambers St., Manhattan; 212/267-5567. See listing under "Department Stores."

Triest Export—560 Twelfth Ave. (44th St.), Manhattan; 212/246-1548. See listing under "Appliances—Home."

DISCOUNT DEPARTMENT STORES

These are some of Mr. Cheap's favorite playgrounds. Keep an open mind about the vast subculture of stores that have sprung up to sell what did not sell before; for basic necessities and splurges you'd never make at full price, these places can be lots of fun. And you may be amazed at what hidden, name-brand treasure may await you down the next aisle!

DISCOUNT DEPARTMENT STORES

American Liquidators—367 Canal St., Manhattan; 212/219-8521. No, not that late-night TV sports show. This is one of the best of the Canal Street junk shops, where you may find just about *anything* being sold on a given day—from Panama hats to fax machines to dentists' tools (but would you want your dentist to shop at a closeout store?). The electronics—stereos, computers, phones—are a combination of unused overstocks and older, refurbished models. The used machines have been checked by technicians, Mr. C was assured, and a three-month money-back return policy (no questions asked) stands behind their word. You can get a computer system for as little as $200.00, along with software; or a Tappan microwave oven for $75.00. In stereo, you can even buy used components that haven't been repaired yet, like a Mitsubishi CD player for $25.00; techies take note!

What else can you find? Blank videotapes for $1.50 (or movies like *Teenage Mutant Ninja Turtles* for $7.99), embroidered patches from famous soda and beer brands for 49¢, compact disks at three for $5.00, rolls of fax paper for $2.00, and all sorts of hardware, tools, extension cords and the like. The folks in here are nice and friendly and will help you look for something you need. They're open from 10:00 a.m. to 7:00 p.m. every day.

The Bargain Depot—510 Fulton St., Brooklyn; 718/243-0700. Part of the Bargain Bazaar, a mini-mall that's not so mini, Bargain Depot sells all those little odds and ends that you may actually need, like film, recording tape, paper supplies, cosmetics and so on. They have weekly sales that offer very good prices, such as a two-pack of Duracell "AA" batteries for 89¢, TDK blank video cassettes for $2.39, or even a box of Ginseng tea for $4.00.

The rest of the mall is filled with cut-price vendors of clothing, jewelry, records, food, and the like. It's not all name-brand stuff, so Mr. C makes no guarantees on quality, but in fact the entire Fulton Street shopping district is like Discount Heaven. The streets are lined with cheap stores. Some are good, some ain't; if you're born to shop, chances are you'll find something good in the area, which by the way is right on the subway line.

Bargain Hunters—519 Eighth Ave. (36th St.), Manhattan; 212/564-8451, 10 Flatbush Ave., Brooklyn; 718/875-1939, 387 Bridge St., Brooklyn; 718/875-2613, 1530 Pitkin Ave., Brooklyn; 718/346-3774, and 92-30 Guy R. Brewer Blvd., Jamaica, Queens; 718/526-5307. From within the deepest jungles of closeouts and irregulars, Bargain Hunters bring back untold treasures in clothing and household goods—and now Mr. C is here to tell you of them. Yes, these stores snap up all kinds of stuff, some good, some of it junk, and sell it off cheap from rows and rows of open bins. For stocking up on basics, like Fruit of the Loom underwear or your favorite brand of shaving cream, BH can save you bucks. Clothing items can yield some good values; men's casual print cotton shirts, reduced from $28.00 in department stores to $5.99 here. There are lots of household products, cleaners, and so forth, at good prices; unlike the zillions of "everything $1.00" stores, these are real brands, not the knock-offs. You can also find a pretty good selection of cosmetics, toys, candy, and things for the kitchen. Mr. C found a Mirro seven-piece set of pots and saucepans for $19.99.

The Bargain Store—27-29 West 14th St., Manhattan; 212/924-3531. Part of 14th Street's junk row, the Bargain Store is perhaps the bottom of the barrel for things like housewares and domestics. Clothing—unused, but knocked around a bit—sells at prices like shirts for a $1.00 and pants for $5.00. Downstairs, racks and racks of video movies sell for $7.99 each. Some are new, mixed in with the rest, with lots of popular titles. Rummage around.

Century 21—22 Cortlandt St., Manhattan; 212/227-9092, and 472 86th St., Bay Ridge, Brooklyn; 718/748-3266. Century 21 may be unique in New York; a complete department store in which everything is discounted. They have not only well-known brands, but also lots of designer clothing at bargain prices. Among these, men can find soft-leather Italian loafers by Caporicci reduced from $145.00 to $60.00. Sport shirts by Bill Blass sell for $29.00, well below the retail price of $55.00; and for the stylish, a Versace raincoat

Mr. Cheap's Picks

✔ LEFTOVERS APLENTY—The city has several great chains of job lot stores, selling overstock and second-quality merchandise with all the selection of a department store. **Job Lot Pushcart**, **National Wholesale Liquidators**, **NYC Liquidators**, **Odd Job Trading**, and **Weber's** are all fun to browse.

✔ **Century 21**—Face creams, toys, and designer clothing all in one discount store? This is it—one of New York's unique places.

✔ **G and Sons**—Submitted for your approval—a department store that defies the march of time. This Brooklyn store looks like it hasn't changed in fifty years—nor have the prices.

marked down from $780.00 to $250.00. Women may go for cashmere sweaters, half-price at $99.00; and they'll love the designer samples section, where exotic fashions are sold below half-price. Of course, these can still run you over $1,000.00, even on clearance. Bargains are relative, no?

C21 sells an extensive section of cosmetics, all at discount. It's a good place to stock up on the basics. Nearby, you'll find counters lined with jewelry and watches for men and women, along with gloves, handbags, and other accessories. And then there are sections of toys, seasonal gifts, and miscelleaneous clearance items. Century 21 is a huge store for the Mr. (or Ms.) Cheap in everyone.

Conway—111 Fulton St., Manhattan; 212/374-1072, 37 Broad St., Manhattan; 212/943-8900,450 Seventh Ave., Manhattan; 212/967-1371,1333 Broadway (Herald Sq.), Manhattan; 212/967-3460, 11 West 34th St., Manhattan; 212/967-1370, 49 West 34th St., Manhattan; 212/967-6454, 225 West 34th St., Manhattan; 212/967-7390, 201 East 42nd St., Manhattan; 212/922-5030, 505 Fulton St., Brooklyn; 718/522-9200. Conway is a full clothing and housewares department store that is in the midst of a major expansion, capturing a big share of the discount market. For many it has become the place to stock up on health and beauty aids, linens, toys, and clothing basics. The stores are big and well stocked with first-quality merchandise. Regular weekly specials make for further savings on such items as White Rain shampoo, Arm & Hammer laundry detergent, Revlon cosmetics, Fruit of the Loom underwear, and Kodak film, as well as small appliances by Hamilton Beach and Proctor Silex, Barbie and Sesame Street toys, and Fieldcrest towels. They also have inexpensive sportswear fashions, like men's sweaters for $15.99 and women's dress blazers for $39.00 to $49.00.

One extra note: With so many stores concentrated in the midtown area, not all branches carry every department. Women's larger-size clothing, for example, is a specialty at certain locations.

Dee & Dee—97 Chambers St., Manhattan; 212/233-3830, and 39 West 14th St., Manhattan; 212/243-5620. Another of the closeout specialists, there's a lot of junk here—though you can find name brands among the various bins. The store mainly sells clothing, with lots of cheap jeans and underwear; it can be a good place to stock up on the basics. You may find Lee Riders jeans (irregulars) for $12.00, or Fruit of the Loom sweat pants for $7.99. Also, cheap things for the home, such as draperies, bathroom accessories, and linens. They have many other branches around the boroughs.

Everyone's Superstores—853 Broadway (14th St.), Manhattan; 212/228-6149, 47 West 34th St., Manhattan; 212/279-2900, 112 West 72nd St., Manhattan; 212/721-8651, 1950 Third Ave. (107th St.), Manhattan; 212/348-6486, 2567 Broadway (97th St.), Manhattan; 212/866-4303, 256 West 125th St., Manhattan; 212/866-3536, 471 Fulton St., Brooklyn; 718/852-1321, 136-14 Roosevelt Ave., Queens; 718/539-4024, and 162 Jamaica Ave., Queens; 718/739-5428. Everyone's is for anyone who wants to save money on health and beauty aids, household products, small appliances, and various other sundries (Mr. C has never been quite sure what "sundries" really are, but this place must have them at discount). Stock up on things like Alberto VO5 shampoo at 99¢ for a large bottle, a sixty-four-ounce jug of All liquid detergent for $2.59, Mentadent toothpaste—y'know, that new one with the two sides that you mix together—for $1.99, and more. You may also find a Proctor-Silex coffee maker for $14.99, Isotoner ladies' slippers for $3.99 a pair, sweat pants for $9.99, or a set of three nonstick cooking pans for $4.88. There's a grocery section as well, with such things as Pfeiffer salad dressing for 79¢ or a can of Planters peanuts for $1.99. Different items go on sale each week; stop in or grab a circular.

G and Sons Department Store—4806 New Utrecht Ave. (48th St.), Borough Park, Brooklyn; 718/438-2604. Want to take a trip back to the turn of the century—but your time machine is on the fritz? Go to this Brooklyn neighborhood instead and pay a visit to G and Sons. Talk about a blast from the past. Nice, creaky wooden floors, helpful service, and old-time prices on nearly everything in the world you could want. They've got clothing. They've got toys. They've got luggage. They've got kitchen gadgets and appliances. The place is huge; it goes on and on, and the prices are all seriously discounted. Remember, like the Lower East Side, this area closes up tightly by Friday afternoons; and the store is open on Sundays.

Global Imports—160 Fifth Ave. (21st St.), Manhattan; 212/741-0700. Mr. C thought this was one of the best of the smaller closeout bargain shops he found. Global has the usual array of overstock household items, packaged foods and sodas, linens, and cheap clothing items at bargain basement prices. Where this store really excels, though, is in its audio/video department. They sell new and used VHS videos, priced from $4.00 to about $15.00, with almost as much of a selection as your local video store. You'll find plenty of popular titles in comedy, drama and music. Global also has great prices on blank audio and video cassettes, with a full range of quality and lengths, as well as batteries. There is a big record section, too, with lots of movie soundtrack LPs for 50¢ each. Another good buy here is in photo albums and lucite picture frames, most of which are priced from $2.50 to $5.00.

Holly's Dollar Store—103 West 14th St., Manhattan; 212/924-8960. One of the better deals along 14th Street, Holly's is actually two stores in one. The main part sells good-quality clothing at discount. Bugle Boy shirts were recently on sale for $19.99; Wrangler denim shirts, originally $30.00, were $20.00 here. For women there were rayon blazers with tie-dyed prints, just $15.00. Some of these are irregulars, such as men's Wrangler jeans for $12.99.

Off to one side is the "dollar store," where most items cost—yep—a dollar. These consist mainly of household products, cleaners, and such, in copycat brands of well-known stuff. There are some packaged foods, kitchen gadgets, toys, and also used videos for $10.00 each. Holly's is open seven days a week.

Job Lot Pushcart—140 Church St., Manhattan; 212/962-4142, 80 Nassau St., Manhattan; 212/619-6868, and 1633 Broadway (50th St.), Manhattan; 212/245-0921. "Since 1943, Bargains Are Our Business," state the ads for Job Lot. It seems to be true. Of course, a lot of the bargains are on things you may not want, such as lesser-quality brands of things like clock radios, videotapes, and housewares. However, you may see a table lamp for $7.99, a five-piece bathroom rug set for $10.00, and good prices on things like toys, packaged foods, and batteries. And there are real names mixed in with the knock-offs: A Black and Decker coffee maker for $15.00, half of the retail price; or a Welbilt mini-microwave oven reduced from $170.00 to just $80.00. In fact, Job Lot has a separate section for electronics, and here they do have many good deals on name brands. These carry the full manufacturer's warranties, along with a two-week return policy.

The Marketplace—1481 Third Ave. (84th St.), Manhattan; 212/472-1900. How'd this place get into the Upper East Side? It looks more like a Canal Street junk emporium, filled with overstock merchandise of all kinds. Mr. C found men's high-top basketball sneakers by Voit and Sergio Valente for $18.99 a pair, reversible cotton outerwear vests for $12.99, and lots of children's clothes, toys, housewares, and kitchen products—all at basement prices.

National Wholesale Liquidators—632 Broadway (Bleecker St.), Manhattan; 212/979-2400, and 71-01 Kissena Blvd., Flushing, Queens; 718/591-3900. This is perhaps Mr. C's favorite among New York's many closeout specialists. The selection is vast, and more importantly, it includes lots of well-known names; not just junk and copycat brands. Find a "Dirt Devil" vacuum cleaner marked down from $70.00 to $50.00; a twenty-piece Corelle dinnerware set, $15.00 off at $34.00; women's sweaters from The Limited, half-price at $26.00; and more.

The cosmetics section alone features everything from Paul Mitchell conditioner, reduced from $11.00 to $7.00; colognes and perfumes by Ralph Lauren, Elizabeth Taylor, and Calvin Klein, at bargain-basement prices; and every vitamin from A to Z. Plus housewares, hardware, toys, candy, videos, you name it. For a store that relies on getting its stuff from manufacturers' overstocks and seconds, they maintain almost as good a variety as a "real" department store—for a lot less money.

NYC Liquidators—158 West 27th St., Manhattan; 212/675-7400. If you enjoy browsing through aisles and aisles of, well, *stuff*—the flotsam and jetsam left over from what seems to be every store in the city—you'll love NYC Liquidators. They've got so much more, with much less space, than many of the other job lot stores. What do you need? An oil-filled electric space heater, half-price at $35.00; silk ties by Ralph Lauren (can it be true?), originally $60.00, here $10.00; a quartz wall clock by Westclox for $8.00; a box of one dozen magic markers for $1.50....

For kids, there are plenty of toys and games, most at half their original prices. Mr. C noticed a Teenage Mutant Ninja Turtle "Killer Bee" doll for $12.50, and an HO scale "Silver Shadow" four-car train set for $30.00. Other brands include Fisher-Price, Playskool, and Milton Bradley.

Music is big here. NYC has lots of unopened classical and jazz compact discs for $3.98, by the likes of Andre Previn or Fats Waller; or rock & roll, like the Pretenders, for $6.98. Cassettes are priced from 50¢ to $4.50; most fall somewhere in between. And the record section, at the other end of the store, is a vast treasure trove of cutouts and overstocks in all categories, from rap singles to Broadway shows. Most of these, unused, are just $1.00 each—making this a popular stop for disc jockeys who want to fill out their collections cheaply or replace worn-out albums.

There are tons of videos, from half-hour cartoons ($1.50) to pre-viewed movies like *Sophie's Choice, Royal Wedding*, and *Drugstore Cowboy* ($3.98). And then there's a whole separate room filled with X-rated movies. Say what you will, the store does lots of business in all of these.

And then there's the rest of the odds and ends—paper supplies, cosmetics, handbags, Christmas decorations as the season approaches, and lots more. The store is a mix of new, used, and slightly imperfect merchandise; but if you're dissatisfied with any purchase, you can bring it back for an exchange. The folks in here are friendly and helpful. And it sure is cheap!

Odd-Job Trading—10 Cortlandt St., Manhattan; 212/571-0959, 149 West 32nd St., Manhattan; 212/564-7370, 7 East 40th St., Manhattan; 212/686-6825, and 66 West 48th St., Manhattan; 212/575-0477. One of the big boys in the closeout business, Odd-Job's stores boast two floors of savings on just about anything imaginable. You'll find chino pants marked down from $45.00 to $15.00; Franklin baseball mitts reduced from $80.00 to $30.00; acrylic sweaters for just $3.99; a Profile fan-resist exercise bicycle for $100.00, a third of its original price; $60.00 Regal deep-pile bathroom rugs for $18.00; a one-ounce bottle of Chaps Musk aftershave, reduced from $10.00 to $2.99; plus toys and games, hardware, gardening tools and shovels, kitchen gadgets and major cookware. You can even find a box of thirty Christmas cards marked down from $12.00 to $2.99—and that's *before* Christmas!

Pearl River Mart—277 Canal St., Manhattan; 212/431-4770, and 200 Grand St., Manhattan; 212/966-1010. These Chinatown department stores feature some ten thousand unusual bargains on all sorts of Oriental merchandise, from food to clothing to housewares. If you like silk, you'll love their imported silk dresses—just $42.00—as well as the traditional embroidered robes and kimonos. Imported canvas flat shoes are $6.50 a pair. Get a set of Chinese checkers for $4.50, or a tube of ginseng toothpaste for $1.50. They also have linens, silk lampshades, china (naturally), woks and bamboo steamers (the real thing, not those TV types), herbs and imported foods, and even traditional Eastern musical instruments. It's a fascinating place to roam around. Both branches of Pearl River Mart are open from 10:00 a.m. to 8:00 p.m., seven days a week.

Ralph's Discount City—95 Chambers St., Manhattan; 212/267-5567. Ralph's is the king of discount department stores. You can find everything here from a fifteen-ounce bottle of Jheri Rhedding Biotin shampoo for just $2.99 to a Conair "Pro-Style" mini hair blower to dry you off for $11.99. Two floors of discount prices on current products and closeouts include cosmetics, health and beauty items, candy, household cleaning products, small appliances, and all the other essential and not-so-essential stuff found in your average pharmacy or convenience store. What's not so convenient, of course, is the fact that Ralph's is so far downtown; but then, it's in the heart of a whole cut-price bazaar of stores (for clothing, electronics, books and more). You may find it worth making a regular trip to the area every week or two.

Two doors down the street, check out **Ralph's Thrift Store** for similar bargains on packaged foods (see listing under "Food Stores—General"). Meanwhile, over on the Nassau Street pedestrian mall—another budget shopping area—there is a second **Ralph's Discount City** (80 Nassau St.; 212/964-9386), which claims to be unrelated to the Chambers Street store. Yet Mr. C found almost all of the same kinds of merchandise here, again at bargain-basement prices. In fact, the store itself is downstairs one level from the street. This Ralph's has an even larger selection of cosmetics, plus more in the way of small appliances. There was a Hamilton Beach juice machine for $29.99, and a Black & Decker "Cup at a Time" coffee maker was seen for a mere $9.99. Brew your own for a week and it's paid for itself !

Weber's Closeouts—132 Church St., Manhattan; 212/571-3283, 475 Fifth Ave. (41st St.), Manhattan; 212/251-0613, 45 West 45th St., Manhattan; 212/819-9780, and 2064 Broadway (72nd St.), Manhattan; 212/787-1644. Weber's is one of the biggest of the job-lot sellers, specializing in designer names wherever possible. Here, among the two or three floors of manufacturers' closeouts, you may find a pair of ladies' casual shoes by Perry Ellis, originally priced at $45.00, selling for $14.99—or a pair of Converse hi-top sneakers for $9.99. During Mr. C's visit, he also saw: Men's dress shirts by Botany 500, reduced from $30.00 to $9.99; down vests for $19.99; leather portfolios for $30.00, Pierre Cardin tweed-sided luggage marked down from $105.00 to $30.00, a selection of compact discs for $4.99; gold-plated monogram flatware for 99¢ per piece, plus colognes, cosmetics, teas and jams, woven baskets, kitchen gadgets, tools, books, and toys. Many clothing items are irregulars; check carefully to see if these meet with your approval. All sales are final.

DISCOUNT DRUGSTORES

For discounts on cosmetics and household products, don't overlook your local drugstore. Many of these are chain stores, offering excellent deals on certain selected items each week. Thus, you may find a sixteen-ounce bottle of Vitamin E lotion for a dollar, name-brands of roll-on deodorant for $1.39, a three-pack of blank videotapes for $10.00, or three light bulbs for 99¢. Some of these drugstores sell designer perfumes at discounts of 20 percent or more, and many have good prices on small appliances too. Look for weekly sales!

Here are just a few of the places to try:

Bottom Line Health and Beauty Center, various locations.

Discount Beauty Supply, 599 Sixth Ave. (17th St.), Manhattan; 212/741-3132.

Duane Reade, various locations.

Love's Health and Beauty Aids, various locations.

McKay's Drugs, various East and West Village locations.

Mr. M Discount Center, 192 Seventh Ave. South (11th St.), Manhattan; 212/741-2225.

Price-Wise Discount, various Upper West and East Side locations.

Rite-Aid Discount Pharmacy, 148 East 86th St., Manhattan, with other branches in the outer boroughs.

Plus many, many more, all around the city.

ELECTRONICS

STEREO AND VIDEO EQUIPMENT, AND COMPUTERS

There are hundreds of places to save money on electronics in New York. Many of the discount places, unfortunately, are as far below repute as their prices are below retail. It happens that these stores are often foreign-owned and run; Mr. C says this not out of any kind of chauvinism, but because he wants you to be careful. This kind of merchandise, after all, is almost entirely imported from other countries, and so there is a greater possibility of a shady deal. This book should guide you to the more reliable retailers, but things can always change. One of the best ways to protect yourself while shopping around is to inquire about the store's guarantee policy: Make sure the item you want carries an American warranty. Since some stores deal directly with the manufacturers in the Far East, their merchandise may carry a foreign warranty instead, and that could make repairs a hassle. Remember, you are perfectly within your rights to ask about this in the store.

America Electronics—50 East 14th St., Manhattan; 212/353-0765. At the southern tip of Union Square Park, America has two floors of good prices on stereo and electronics, cameras and home appliances. The street-level floor looks like any of New York's five zillion electronics shops, but it does have a much larger selection and better service than any Times Square hole-in-the-wall. Upstairs they have a large selling floor with large appliances on display. Major brands of refrigerators, microwave ovens, vacuum cleaners, and such all sell at good prices. Salespeople are on hand to assist you just as you'd find in a department store. There is also a small section of computers, making this a very well-rounded store indeed. Mr. C even found a couple of used and refurbished items here, such as a Panasonic computer printer reduced from $280.00 to an even $200.00.

American Liquidators—367 Canal St., Manhattan; 212/219-8521. See listing under "Discount Department Stores."

Bernie's Discount Center—821 Sixth Ave. (28th St.), Manhattan; 212/564-8582. See listing under "Appliances."

Bondy Export—40 Canal St., Manhattan; 212/925-7785. See listing under "Appliances."

Canal Hi-Fi—319 Canal St., Manhattan; 212/925-6575. Of Canal Street's many stereo shops, Canal Hi-Fi has one of the best selections of quality audio components at competitive prices. They actually specialize in professional sound equipment, the stuff used by disc jock-

Mr. Cheap's Picks

✔ **J & R Music World**—Perhaps New York's biggest electronics stores, more like a marketplace along Park Row. You may find a lower price now and then, but J & R has the most consistent discounts on the widest selection of stereo, video, cameras, and computers.

✔ **Mashugana Ike**—The best deals here are refurbished stereo and video, with a more substantial warranty/return policy than most others.

✔ **Stereo Exchange**—Great bargains on used high-fidelity components, an inexpensive route to the best names in audio.

eys and recording studios; toward the back, a separate room has lots of speakers, tape decks, and compact disc players for home use. Usually there are a couple of models of each on sale, stacked in the center of the room. These can include a Pioneer dual-cassette dubbing deck marked down from $160.00 to $140.00, or a Sony CD player for $150.00. The staff is fairly helpful.

Eba's Appliance World—2361 Nostrand Ave. (Ave. J), Flatbush, Brooklyn; 718/252-3400. See listing under "Appliances."

Electro Brands—43 Warren St., Manhattan; 212/619-5605. Primarily a place to stock up on accessories, Electro Brands sells miles of recording tape, braces of batteries, stacks of computer disks, and more. A recent sale included Fuji VHS videotapes for $1.99, a pair of Duracell "AA" batteries for 88¢, and a box of ten floppy disks by 3M for $7.99 (3.5 inch, double-sided, double-density). Electro does have some components, many of which are factory refurbished, such as a Samsung videocassette recorder for $119.00. These come with a three-month in-store warranty. They also sell beepers, cordless telephones, and other communications stuff.

Many of their sale items are cash and carry, with no limit on quantity. Electro Brands is open six days a week, closed Sundays.

47th St. Photo—67 West 47th St., Manhattan; 212/921-1287, 115 West 45th St., Manhattan; 212/921-1287. See listing under "Cameras."

J & R Music World—23 Park Row, Manhattan; 212/732-8600. It seems as if you can find everything in the world at J & R Music World. From half-a-dozen storefronts along one block, they sell full lines of audio, video, and home office equipment (plus cameras, computers, and music) from all major brands at discount. Recent examples include things like a Sony "Mega Watchman" portable TV for $99.00; an Aiwa mini-component stereo rack with a radio, CD player, double cassette deck, and speakers for $399.00; a Panasonic Super-VHS videotape recorder for $229.00; a Sony cordless phone for $69.00; and a JVC boom box with AM/FM radio and an auto-reverse cassette player for $69.00.

Whatever you're looking for, J & R stocks a full range of products, from budget lines to professional-quality components. In home stereo speakers, you can get a pair by Technics for $99.95, or the Bose 901 "Classic" directional speakers for $1,399.95. Both pairs are at good, competitive prices for their levels of performance.

And then you have disco equipment, car stereos, blank recording tape, portable electronic music keyboards, fax machines, copiers, electronic games, clock radios, electric razors, vacuum cleaners, juice extractors, air conditioners, microwave ovens, and every single accessory you could possibly need to run all these babies. Get the idea? The salespeople are helpful in the midst of all this mega-marketing, and the store is open seven days a week.

The Market Place—17 West 14th St., Manhattan; 212/620-0242. See listing under "Appliances."

Mashugana Ike—111 Chambers St., Manhattan; 212/267-1140. Downtown's answer to Crazy Eddie, Mashugana Ike has outlasted the original crazy man, selling a wide selection of audio and video equipment and accessories at bargain prices. This includes televisions, stereo, car phones, small appliances, and beepers. New equipment, by most major brands, sells for about 20 percent below many other electronics stores in town; Ike also sells factory-refurbished equipment at even bigger discounts. Not only do these components carry a full one-year warranty from the manufacturer, they can also be exchanged for credit in the store for up to thirty days—a relatively rare combination in used electronics.

Number 1 Closeout—383 Canal St., Manhattan; no phone. Yes, it's strange—an electronics store without a telephone. They'll sell you one, though, for $7.99, guaranteed to work. This job-lot store is tucked into an open-fronted garage, and browsing here feels like going to a garage sale. A lot of what they have is just plain junk looking for a home—but no doubt there are lots of techies who are keen to give them one. For those of us who do not own soldering irons, there are some interesting bargains: Color TVs for $99.00, perhaps a set of speakers for $30.00, or even a portable Karaoke machine—just plug it in and sing—for $75.00. Unless it's sold "as is," defective equipment may be returned within thirty days for an exchange.

A few doors down, **Argo Electronics** at 391 Canal Street is a similar operation, whose stock may include used computer monitors and printers along with the audio and video stuff. They even have a phone number: 212/226-4945.

Rabson's Audio Video—119 West 57th St., Manhattan; 212/247-0070. On pricey 57th Street, home of the Russian Tea Room and Carnegie Hall, sits this long-established stereo shop with prices that are, well, not especially cheap, except for particular sales. But don't pass them up completely! Because inside there are some shelves with brand-new components that are closeouts or discontinued stock, being sold off at bargain prices. Anything wrong with them? Well, maybe this year's line has come out in silver instead of black, that sort of thing. You may see something like a Yamaha dual cassette deck, originally priced at $299.00, now going for $179.00, or a high-end Mitsubishi audio/video receiver, originally $1,000.00, now $499.00. Although they are closeouts, they do carry the full manufacturer's warranty. At any given time, Rabson's may only have a few closeouts on a particular kind of item, but it's always worth stopping in during your research phase. Unlike many of the discount shops profiled elsewhere in this book, you'll benefit from serious, legit salespeople who may have a real deal for you.

Romino Boutique—588 Twelfth Ave. (44th St.), Manhattan; 212/977-7751. See listing under "Luggage."

Seven Stars Audio—46 West 14th St., Manhattan; 212/727-9105. In addition to selling new stereo equipment at good prices, with brands like JVC, Pioneer, and Blaupunkt, Seven Stars also sells a lot of factory-refurbished pieces. These are items which have most likely been bought at department stores, returned for some reason, and sent back to the manufacturer—which fixes the problem but cannot resell it at full price. You may therefore find a bargain like a Magnavox portable stereo (that's a boombox, son) with dual cassette and CD players, reduced from an original $330.00 to just $199.00. Many other home stereo items, fairly current models, are as much as 50 percent below their retail prices.

You may return such an item yourself, within seven days, for an exchange or credit; you also get a ninety-day manufacturer's warranty. Seven Stars also has lots of car stereos, watches, cameras, and other small electronics.

A few doors down, **USA Shopping Center** at 56 West 14th Street (212/727-2197) is another shop selling refurbished stereo and camera equipment. Recent finds here included a Pioneer cassette deck, originally $250.00, selling for $139.00, and an Epson LQ-510 letter-quality computer printer for just $200.00. They also have small appliances, like microwave ovens from $80.00 and fax machines from $299.00. USA offers a manufacturer's warranty on rehabbed items.

Sixth Avenue Electronics City—1030 Sixth Ave. (39th St.), Manhattan; 212/391-2777. This place looks quite identical to the millions of stereo/camera stores you see up and down the streets of the city; but, while most of those are wheeler-dealers trying to fleece innocent tourists, don't pass this one by so quickly. Sixth Ave. is more legitimate than its many local competitors, and is growing into a more substantial chain, adding branches in the 'burbs. More importantly, they back up their products with their own, American warranty—one of the best signs of a reputable dealer.

So, what have they got? Everything, it seems. For stereo equipment, Mr. C found bargains on Bose speakers, about $150 below retail; an Aiwa complete mini-system for $416.00, a savings of about $80.00; and a fancy NAD three-head tape deck at $100 below list price. Plus plenty of portable and car stereo stuff at good savings.

In video, there are regular and projector-screen TVs, laser disk players (a Pioneer model for $346.00), VCRs and all the rest. They recently had a Canon 8mm camcorder on sale for $546.00, as low as you're likely to find this still-hot technology. Good prices on blank videotapes too, in all sizes and formats.

Sixth Ave. also has 35mm cameras, like a Nikon "Zoom Touch" for $156.00, over a hundred dollars off retail. And then there are fax machines, cordless and cellular phones (a Motorola cordless for $46.00) and more. The company guarantees that it will beat any advertised price you show them; they also offer a ten-day return policy, giving you a full refund (if you paid in cash) or credit (if you didn't). Open seven days a week.

Stereo City—123 Chambers St., Manhattan; 212/385-2111.

This may be the bottom of the line for bargain electronics, but hey—it's all part of Mr. Cheap's New York. After all, you may be a technical whiz who enjoys a good project—or someone who wants a car stereo that no one would even consider stealing. Stereo City has a large collection of these, for example, all for $50.00 each. They include brand names like Pioneer, which could sell for as much as $200.00 new. Here everything is used, and looks it; but they have been repaired, and they carry a ninety-day store warranty for exchange or repair at no cost.

Mr. C also saw home stereo components, such as a

Sony cassette deck for $50.00; a variety of stereo speakers for $25.00 apiece; plus boom boxes, walkmans, and more. Some have not yet been repaired and are sold "as is"; that's when you techies can get a tremendous deal. Oh, there may be a knob or two missing, but for some people, who cares as long as it works?

Stereo Exchange—627 Broadway (Houston St.), Manhattan; 212/505-1111. If your tastes in high-fidelity sound equipment run to the exotic, but your bank account does not, this may be the place for you. Stereo Exchange, as the name implies, repairs and sells used components from the very best high-end brands at a fraction of their original costs. Thus, you may find things like a Teac compact disc player, once $1,100.00, selling here for $500.00. A pair of Bose 901 speakers, the classic directional design, was seen for $899.00, well below the original $1,400.00. And an Onkyo cassette deck was reduced from $300.00 to $160.00. These all carry a thirty-day store warranty covering parts and labor, if you should find that a unit has not been properly rehabbed. But you'll realize once you go in that this is a store for the serious audiophile, not just some resale joint; and the people in here know what they're doing.

Trader Horn—226 East 86th St., Manhattan; 212/535-3600, 1972 Ralph Ave., Flatbush, Brooklyn; 718/531-7000, and 89-59 Bay Pkwy., Bay Ridge, Brooklyn; 718/996-8800. See listing under "Appliances."

Triest Export—560 Twelfth Ave. (44th St.), Manhattan; 212/246-1548. See listing under "Appliances."

Uncle Uncle—343 Canal St., Manhattan; 212/226-4010. Probably the biggest and best-stocked of the Canal Street stereo shops, Uncle Uncle is evidently a distant relative of Uncle Steve's, a longtime stereo store at the same location. Very little seems to have changed. The store carries two floors of VCRs, camcorders, receivers, speakers, tape decks, answering machines, car alarm systems, and all the necessary accessories—cables, stands, blank tapes, etc.—at discount prices. The salespeople are quite aggressive in here, so beware of the hard sell. Yet even in this higher-profile store than its many neighbors, you can turn on the hard sell yourself; try a little haggling and see how you do.

Van Win—331 Canal St., Manhattan; 212/334-0378. See listing under "Unusual Gifts."

Vicmarr Stereo and TV—88 Delancey St., Manhattan; 212/505-0380. Way down on the Lower East Side, Vicmarr sells sound and video systems for the home and car at very competitive prices. Among these, Mr. C found a Kenwood dual-cassette recorder, with auto-reverse and other nice features, on sale for $189.00; full retail price would be $299.00. Some items are floor samples on sale, such as a Sony thirteen-inch color TV for $279.00. In addition to new items in most major brands, the store also sells factory-refurbished units at further discounts—like a JVC four-head VCR, reduced from $299.00 to $179.00. They have a big selection, filling several rooms in this large store. Vicmarr is open six days a week, closed on Saturdays.

Nearby, you may also want to check out **Hi Fi Electronics** at 152 Delancey Street (212/260-7222) for further options in new and refurbished equipment. They are a licensed dealer of Sony, Pioneer, and other brands; a new Sony cassette deck was recently seen there for $129.00. Their refurbs are guaranteed for a period of ninety days, during which you can bring a defective unit in for repair or exchange. Among these bargains may be a Pioneer stereo receiver, originally $190.00, now selling for $155.00. The store is open until 7:30 most evenings.

Willoughby's—110 West 32nd St., Manhattan; 212/790-1800. See listing under "Cameras."

The Wiz—726 Broadway (4th St.), Manhattan; 212/475-1700, and many other locations in Brooklyn, Bronx, Manhattan, Queens and Staten Island. "Nobody Beats the Wiz," claims the advertising for this fast-growing chain of audio/video stores. Indeed, if you've managed to miss their blitz of TV and radio ads, it must be because you're the sort of person who ignores such outlets completely—and therefore won't be shopping here anyway.

Meanwhile, though Mr. C prefers to guide you to the lesser-known bargain spots, no picture of the discount electronics scene would be complete without the Wiz. If, for example, you'd like to see that picture on a forty-eight-inch stereo projection TV by Toshiba, you might find such an animal here for about $2,500.00—almost one thousand dollars below retail. A more manageable RCA twenty-inch model, list price $379.00, was recently on sale for $250.00.

In stereo, you may find a $200.00 Technics CD player, with remote control, as low as $130.00; or a bevy of boomboxes well under $100.00 each. This is also a good place to check for prices on computers, fax machines and other appliances for the home office; as well as a limited selection of compact automatic cameras, like the Nikon "Lite Touch," recently on sale for $149.98.

Further, you'll find Walkmans, Nintendo games, cordless phones, and whatever else may be the latest rage. The Wiz makes its best-price claim by offering a guarantee in which they'll beat any advertised price plus 10 percent of the difference. They are also reputable, factory-authorized dealers for every brand they carry. And chances are, if you hold still long enough, they'll be building another branch on the very spot where you stand.

COMPUTERS

Crocodile Computers—240 West 73rd St., Manhattan; 212/769-3400. Just west of Broadway, Crocodile offers an interesting option for saving money on computers: Buy one used. Not unlike the used-car market, used computers—starting off as such a big-ticket purchase—have become a whole new field. You never know what they'll have, but Crocodile always maintains a good stock of various models, both IBM-types and Mac-types. The lowest-priced systems may be a bit out of date, without the latest bells and whistles, but they're all refurbished to work just fine. You may find an IBM-compatible 286 system, complete with keyboard and monitor, for as little as $300.00; and it probably cost over $1,000.00 when it was new.

You can often find more recent used models here too; though these are in a higher price range, they're still well below retail prices. In any case, the memory will be completely erased and checked for problems. All computers carry a warranty, with repairs done in the store. If you're looking to get into the computer game and don't have a lot of cash to spend, this is definitely the way to go. It's an especially good idea for parents who want an inexpensive starter setup for their kids, or for grad students looking for something basic for writing a thesis.

47th St. Photo—67 West 47th St., Manhattan; 212/921-1287, and 115 West 45th St., Manhattan; 212/921-1287. See listing under "Cameras."

J & R Computer World—15 Park Row, Manhattan; 212/732-8600.

One of the many J & R stores, this place has two levels with great prices on everything in hardware, software, and whatever's in between. They are authorized dealers for AST, Epson, Okidata, NEC, Toshiba, and many other brands, all sold at discount. Mr. C found an Epson 24-pin printer, one of the few to use regular typing paper, for about $20.00 less than any other competitor. J & R carries the full line of Apple and Macintosh computers, including PowerBooks from $999.00. On the PC side, Leading Edge 386 systems start from $799.00 (without monitor), and they have the Hewlett-Packard DeskJet 500 priced at $399.95.

Plus discount prices on monitors, modems, scanners, external drives, internal parts, diskettes, paper, ribbon cartridges—and every kind of business or entertainment software. They even have instructional videos. It's all here. The salespeople know their stuff, and give you all the info you need. You can order by fax, twenty-four-hour toll-free phone, or (it's old-fashioned, yes) by just stopping in, seven days a week.

Manhattan Electronics Corporation—17 West 45th St., Manhattan; 212/354-6462. Along with new computers, parts, and accessories, this small midtown shop sells used computers at very low prices. These may be old and outdated, but they have been refurbished in the shop to perfect working order. This means that you can get an IBM PC, with 640K of memory, dual floppy-disk drives, and a monochrome monitor all for $150.00 You may also find an NEC letter-quality printer for $80.00, and monitors from $50.00. All of these items carry a short-term warrenty, in case any problems should arise immediately; but the chances are that any such bugs have already been worked out. The store's open seven days a week.

Micro U.S.A. Computer Depot—55 Sixth Ave. (Canal St.), Manhattan; 212/941-0270. At the western end of the Canal Street shopping area, Micro U.S.A. is a clean, bright store with a good variety of computer merchandise for a small place. Its salespeople are low-key friendly and quite knowledgeable. You can buy systems, components, and accessories; a complete PC system, with a 386 processor, can be gotten for under $1,000.00. Simpler systems, with monchrome monitors, are in the $600.00 range. And accessories are very cheap, whether it's a surge-suppressor six-outlet strip for $7.00, or a glare filter for your screen for $10.00 They also sell blank disks, software, and shareware at good prices.

Willoughby's—110 West 32nd St., Manhattan; 212/790-1800. See listing under "Cameras."

Mr. Cheap's Picks

✔ **Crocodile Computers**—The newest thing in computers is (drum roll, please)—*Used* computers. Get a complete system in fine shape for $300.00. Perfect for the downscale, recycling-conscious nineties.

✔ **J & R Computer World**—Two floors of good prices on absolutely everything, inside and out. Hardware, software, peripherals, paper, cables; you name it, they've got it.

FLEA MARKETS AND EMPORIA

Flea markets are fun to explore and can turn up some super bargains. There are two main varieties, though they all call themselves "flea markets;" the easiest way to describe the difference is to say "new" and "used." Several locations in SoHo and the Village sell new merchandise, mostly clothing and jewelry, usually from booths. The other kind of market has a more spread-out look and tends to consist mainly of antiques, used wares, and memorabilia.

Like the nomadic wanderers who sell at them, flea markets may come and go with the wind. Listed below are some of Mr. C's well-established favorites. Almost all of them operate on one or both days of the weekend, in large parking lots that they've bought out for the day, and charge no admission. They could almost go into the "Entertainment" section of this book as good, cheap fun.

Annex Antiques Market—Sixth Ave., between 24th and 27th Sts., Manhattan. Probably the largest of the outdoor weekend markets, Annex Antiques stretches through several parking lots on both sides of Sixth Avenue every Saturday and Sunday, from roughly 9:00 a.m. to 5:00 p.m. As the name suggests, most of the dealers here are selling furniture and decorative items for the home. So if you'd like to find a full-size brass bed frame, a dining table and chair set, lamps, or more unusual items (Say, honey, isn't a four-foot-tall African conga drum *just* the thing for our living room?), you'll have lots to look at here. See if you can work out a bargain with the dealer!

Broadway Flea Market—Corner of Broadway and Grand St., Manhattan. Every Saturday and Sunday throughout the year, this parking lot becomes one of the city's best outdoor flea markets. Dozens of vendors set up tables of clothing, art, records, cameras, furniture, and more. Just about everything is used, vintage or antique. Mr. C rambled around and saw a fur coat for $180.00, compact discs for $6.00, and even a framed painting by Peter Max. At $6,000.00, this was easily the most expensive item in the whole lot, but the dealer insisted that it should sell for $28,000; so technically it *was* a bargain. Hours here are usually about 10:00 a.m. to 6:00 p.m.; they bend a bit for bad weather or early winter dusks.

Chinatown Phoenix Mall—277 Canal St. and 428 Broadway, Manhattan. Chinatown holds many surprises. You can walk through one of the millions of identical stores along Canal Street and suddenly discover a world of other stores hidden inside it. One of the biggest of these indoor malls is the Phoenix Mall, which straddles a corner and can be entered from a jewelry store on Canal or a clothing store on Broadway. Inside, the tiny store opens up into a huge bazaar of booths, selling jeans, T-shirts, sneakers, coats, silk ties,

Mr. Cheap's Picks

✔ **Broadway Flea Market**—Big and wacky; where else can you get bargains on cheap jewelry and a Peter Max painting?

✔ **Chinatown Phoenix Mall**—Of Chinatown's many indoor bazaars, this is the biggest—like stepping into another world.

✔ **I.S. 44 Flea Market**—Week in and week out, one of the most diverse and interesting flea markets in the city.

jewelry, electronics, and more. Each of these is a permanent, individually owned and operated business. Some are large, with racks and racks of clothes (including some good bargains on American and Oriental styles), and some are as small as a jewelry counter selling gold chains of all varieties.

There are similar, though smaller malls up and down Canal Street; some of the ones Mr. C found are located at 264 Canal and 374 Canal. You can explore these or find your own.

Designer's Co-op—512 Broadway (Spring St.), Manhattan; 212/226-8535. Actually between Spring and Broome Streets, this emporium along the cheap-chic stretch of SoHo's Broadway consists of some twenty booths and shops featuring the wares of small local designers, along with the usual melange of other trinkets. Find leather motorcycle jackets for $99.00, vintage clothing for $5.00 to $15.00 and up, jewelry, posters, and more. There is also the Oasis Cafe in the back of this mini-mall, a simple and cheap eatery where you can cool your heels over a quick snack. Designer's Co-Op is open seven days a week.

Doc's Rock & Roll Flea Market—Corner of Atlantic and Flatbush Aves., Brooklyn; 718/858-6903. Every Saturday and Sunday, from February (or whenever the air warms up) into the fall, Doc—a nearby antiques dealer—runs this big outdoor market. Anywhere from twenty to a hundred vendors are likely to be here, selling all kinds of used furniture in all ranges of condition and price. It's worth checking out, taking a chance that you may come up empty-handed. Ya never know.

The market is open each weekend day from 8:00 a.m. to 5:00 p.m., but the real twist is the live rock & roll music that kicks up around noon and goes through the rest of the day. Local bands of all sorts appreciate the exposure and lend a festival atmosphere to the proceedings. Admission is free.

Around the corner is **Doc's Antiques** itself (490 Atlantic Ave.; phone number above). Doc sells primarily antiques, a subject Mr. C does not cover; but again, on weekends throughout the year, Doc puts lesser-quality used furniture out on the sidewalk in front of the store. These pieces may be scuffed up, but he says it sells just like *that*; people snap up chairs for $5.00 and $10.00, dressers for $75.00, and so on. A young, friendly guy himself, Doc has clearly cornered the youth market for cheap furniture.

Flea and Farmer's Market—East 67th St., between York and First Aves., Manhattan. Every Saturday the blacktop lot at P.S. 183 turns into a carnival of delights. It's one of the few flea markets to combine food with browsing—why don't more do this? Buy all kinds of wonderful fresh produce, in season, direct from the farmers who grow it. Some turn their produce into further goodies, like fresh apple and cherry pies for just $4.50. Others sell exotic flowers and plants; find a large and colorful orchid plant for $25.00. Plus children's clothing, cosmetics, used CDs and more. Hours here are 6 a.m. to 6 p.m.; those farmers wake up mighty early, y'know.

I.S. 44 Flea Market—Columbus Ave. at 76th St., Manhattan; 212/947-6302. Here's another schoolyard flea market, one of the city's best. It's a sprawling setup inside and out, with a tremendous variety of goods from necessities to splurges. There are lots of vintage clothing dealers, selling things like buckskin jackets for $45.00; new clothing, like unique art T-shirts for $10.00; antique, new, and African jewelry; Revlon cosmetics; comic books, engravings, and other collectibles; even optical frames at wholesale prices. These sell here for $39.00 and up, with values that are claimed to be up to $200.00; since Mr. C doesn't wear glasses, he cannot vouch for their authenticity.

There are also more farmers selling fresh produce, along with the hot snacks and drinks available inside. The market runs from 10:00 a.m. to 5:30 p.m. (sharp!), every Sunday except Easter.

Jan Hus Church Flea Market—351 East 74th St., Manhattan; 212/535-5235. One of the few such fleas that are held indoors, this church basement packs a pretty good selection of used and new clothing, jewelry, linens, nostalgia collectibles, and the ever-popular "bric-a-brac." There are also snacks and beverages for sale. The market runs from 9:00 a.m. to 4:00 p.m. every Saturday, except in summer. It's a small but friendly operation; check it out on your way to the much bigger Flea and Farmer's Market (see above).

Soho Flea Market—503 Broadway (Spring St.), Manhattan; no phone. Right across from the venerable Canal Jean Company (see listing under "New Clothing"), and a block up from the fantastic Broadway Flea Market (see above), is a wide alley that houses one of SoHo's newest outdoor emporia. The SoHo Flea Market, like many others around the area, is a coming-together of a dozen or so vendors, mostly selling new merchandise of all sorts, often at good prices. Since they are independent sellers, if the price is not good enough, you can probably haggle a bit. Among the things you may see are Gap jeans for $20.00, all-wool handcrafted sweaters from South America for $25.00, and the ubiquitous brightly printed T-shirts for $12.00. Books, jewelry, cosmetics, and snacks are some of the other booths you'll find here.

Soho Market—376 West Broadway, Manhattan; no phone. This emporium seems to specialize in African arts and crafts, such as malachite rings from Zaire for $5.00 and bronze bracelets for $10.00; at the various booths in this mini-mall you'll also find more jewelry, as well as tie-dyed jeans, cotton skirts, and leggings from $10.00 and up.

Directly across the street is another similar emporium, with such businesses as Spring Breezes, which specializes in Chinese arts and crafts, masks, and antiques at reasonable prices. They have lots of inexpensive jewelry too. Other vendors sell silk-screened T-shirts, clothing, and collectibles.

Tower Flea Market—Broadway at East 4th Street, Manhattan; no phone.

Named for its illustrious neighbor, Tower Records, this is a SoHo-like bazaar of hip new clothing, jewelry, and trinkets. Find a Calvin and Hobbes T-shirt for $11.00, a full-length velour dress by Body Basics for $35.00, or two pairs of earrings for $5.00. Being in the Village, this market keeps somewhat later hours than most other outdoor venues; it runs on Saturdays and Sundays.

FOOD STORES

BAKERIES

Addeo's Bakery—2352 Arthur Ave., Belmont, Bronx; 718/367-8316. This, tiny, spare bakery in the old-world Italian section of the Bronx doesn't offer much in the way of variety, but oh, is their stuff good. For a dollar, grab a hot loaf of the *pane di casa*—literally, the house bread—and tear into it as soon as you reasonably can without making a scene. It's a crusty bread on the outside, but so soft and tasty in the inside. How do they *do* that?

Bagel Buffet—406 Sixth Ave. (8th St.), Manhattan; 212/477-0448. See listing under "Restaurants: Greenwich Village."

Cupcake Cafe—522 Ninth Ave. (39th St.), Manhattan; 212/465-1530. See listing under "Restaurants: Midtown West."

D & G Bakery—45 Spring St., Manhattan; 212/226-6688. A longtime favorite in Little Italy, D & G bakes up loaves of fresh, hot oven-baked bread—scali, Italian bread, whole wheat, and more. The prices are as good as the aroma. Get there early, though; the place is open seven days a week, but it closes up by 2:00 p.m. each afternoon.

Jumbo Bagels And Bialys—1070 Second Ave. (56th St.), Manhattan; 212/355-6185. Want a real "insider's New York" tip? Check out Jumbo Bagels, a bakery that is well loved in its neighborhood but hardly known outside. They offer more than a dozen varieties of bagels that, true to the name, are big indeed. These are baked up fresh throughout the day (Jumbo's is open twenty-four hours). They also have plenty of cream cheese and lox spreads to slather onto one of these bready delights—plus muffins, croissants, and Jewish pastries.

Kossar's Bialys—367 Grand St., Manhattan; 212/473-4810. Kossar's is a longstanding tradition on the Lower East Side. Alas, the neighborhood is not what it once was, making a trip to this tiny bakery a somewhat unpleasant proposition—but people do go, and once you bite into one of their hot-from-the-oven breads, you'll know why you came. The place is literally just a bakery, without even so much as a counter; the selection is small but "cherse." Bagels and bialys—sort of a filled-in bagel, topped with baked onion—are 35¢ apiece. Onion bread, a larger flat disc almost the size of a record album, goes for $1.25; and long rolls are 90¢. That's all, folks. But hey, when you only make four things, you probably make them well. Kossar's does.

Moishe's Homemade Kosher Bakery—181 East Houston St., Manhattan; 212/475-9624, and 115 Second Ave. (6th St.), Manhattan; 212/505-8555. The East Village is such a wonderful melting pot. Yuppies and artsy types mingle freely with the remainders of the old-world life that started here, and that refuses to leave. Such a business is Moishe's, with two locations offering the real Jewish stuff—wonderful loaves of rye and pumpernickel,

Mr. Cheap's Picks

✔ **Addeo's Bakery**—On Arthur Avenue in the Bronx, a.k.a. Little Italy North, this old-world storefront makes about four kinds of bread—and they are fantastic.

✔ **Jumbo Bagels and Bialys**—A neighborhood discovery that definitely lives up to its name.

✔ **Poseidon Bakery**—You never knew there were this many kinds of Greek pies—unless you're Greek, of course. Cheap and delicious.

challah (even whole wheat?), rugelach, and other pastries. The prices are no more modern than the setting. Closed on Friday afternoons and all day Saturday.

Poseidon Bakery—629 Ninth Ave. (44th St.), Manhattan; 212/757-6173. Since 1925, Poseidon has been baking a wide variety of Greek specialties that make it a must-stop on the ethnic parade of Ninth Avenue. The Anagnostou family has raised several traditional pastries to a new art form; sure, you can get a great piece of *baklava* but among their desserts, you should also try some *trigona* , a triangle of the same phyllo dough filled with a filling of almond paste, *afali* , which does the same with chopped pistachios, and a selection of nut cookies and fruit-filled strudels. Most of these are in a range from about $1.30 to $2.25.

Meat and cheese pies are wonderful here too, from the basic spinach and feta to something called a *menina* mash—not the Halloween hit song, but a vegetable pie filled with spinach, potatoes, cabbage, onion, and spices. And the *tiropita* contains ricotta, cream cheese, feta, and mint. These are all $2.00 to $3.00. Poseidon also offers party-sized quantities, as well as catering and nationwide shipping.

A. Zito and Sons—259 Bleecker St., Manhattan; 212/929-6139. Of the many bakeries along this bustling Greenwich Village strip, Zito's is perhaps the best—in both quality and value. Try a loaf of their fresh, crusty Italian bread, or a loaf filled with layers of prosciutto and provolone cheese; see for yourself why they'll continue to outlast everyone on the block. The prices are great, too. Don't miss Murray's Cheese Shop, right next door, for something to put on the bread. A perfect (and cheap!) one-two combination.

CANDY AND NUTS

Bazzini Importers—339 Greenwich St., Manhattan; 212/334-1280. Since 1885, Bazzini has been the top of the New York heap in peanuts, dried fruits, and candies. A wholesaler that sells to the public as well, this is your chance to shop where the buyers for Dean & Deluca get *their* stuff. Would you believe honey-roasted peanuts for $2.50 a pound? Get five pounds or more and the price drops to $1.90. How about salted cashews for $4.35 a pound, or a five-pound bag of pistachios for $22.00....plus all kinds of mixed assortments and gift baskets.

Mr. Cheap's Pick

✔ **Bazzini Candy**—An elegant-looking store with wholesale prices on candy, roasted nuts and dried fruits.

Dried jumbo apricots from California are $10.00 for a five-pounder, while Bing cherries (no, not the guy who sang "White Christmas"—he's into orange juice) are just $12.50 per pound. These prices are unreal. Bazzini also has candy jars in a palette of colors, along with imported specialties, condiments, and cookies. The bustling shop looks like an oasis of gourmet treats in the midst of a dilapidated old warehouse. Once inside, you'll be amazed at how fancy it is—and yet, with the warehouse prices. Open weeknights until 7:00.

Economy Candy—108 Rivington St., Manhattan; 212/254-1531. The old-time shops of the Lower East Side aren't just for clothing bargains, y'know. Economy Candy takes the same approach to sweets and snacks of all kinds, which they sell wholesale and retail (at near-wholesale prices). As a result, this place can be just as jammed on a Sunday as Orchard Street around the corner.

It's already jammed, of course, with treats from around the world. They're stacked in the aisles, packed into glass counters, and shelved up to the ceiling. From Baby Ruths to "Baci," if it's sweet, you'll find it here somewhere. Fresh halvah, cut to order, is just $2.29 a pound, in several flavors. Chocolates of every conceivable kind, also sold by the pound, are delectable. There are dried apricots, pears, and other fruits; cashews, peanuts, and the rest. Boxes of Perugina assortments are here at good prices, as well as store-made gift baskets for that basket-case of a sweet tooth. And for the sweet tooth who can't or shouldn't, there are sugar-free varieties too. Also, loose teas and fresh-ground coffees from around the world, all sold by the pound.

Speaking of which, owners Jerry and Ilene Cohen will ship gifts—or personal reserves—anywhere you want. Don't forget, all stores in this neighborhood close early on Friday and all day Saturday.

J. Wolsk and Company—811 Ludlow St., Manhattan; 212/475-0704. Not far from Economy Candy is Wolsk, a similar operation with yet another vast assortment of fresh chocolate candies, dried apricots and other fruits, halvah, nuts, and everything else for people who are sweet on candy. The prices are comparable to those at Economy; try 'em both and choose your personal favorite. These folks, too, close up on Friday afternoon and Saturday.

CHEESE

Ben's Cheese Shop—181 East Houston St., Manhattan; 212/254-8290. Down at the bottom of the East Village, there's this cluster of great food shops. The area landmark, of course, is Katz's Delicatessen, at the corner of Houston and Ludlow Streets; on the next block west, you'll find Ben's Cheese. It's a no-frills place where you can get all kinds of simple dairy products, from the freshest butter to farmer's cheeses and other basic varieties. The prices make Ben's a perfect complement to the bargain clothing stores for which the area is so well known. It's open seven days a week. Right next door, by the way, get some fresh bread to go with the cheese at Moishe's Homemade Kosher Bakery.

Calandra & Sons—2314 Arthur Ave., Belmont, Bronx; 718/365-7572. Arthur Avenue is known as the "Little Italy" of the Bronx, and places like Calandra's are perfect examples. It's like a trip to the old country as soon as you walk in—simple but old-fashioned. The prices seem to be from a bygone era as well. Stop in for a hunk of fresh, authentic mozzarella, provolone, ricotta, or gorgonzola. You'll want to eat it right then and there.

East Village Cheese Store—34 Third Ave. (10th St.), Manhattan; 212/477-2601. It was while he was prowling the estimable Gryphon Bookshop on the Upper West Side that someone told Mr. C about this store down in the East Village. "I forget the name, but they always have lots of signs in the window," he said. It is a generic enough name; and indeed, you can barely see into the place for all the signs listing the weekly cheese bargains to be had. Each week, over a dozen varieties are designated "Superspecials," selling for just $2.79 per pound. Double Gloucester and smoked gouda were among the tasty comestibles on this list during Mr. C's visit.

But there's so much more here—a veritable smorgasbord of culinary delights. Pates, such as green peppercorn with cognac, or duck liver mousse, sell for $5.99 a pound; that same price will also get you a thirty-four-ounce container of extra-virgin olive oil; and there are several types of fresh coffee beans at great prices, such as French roast for $3.99 a pound. They have fresh-baked breads and imported goods, too.

Murray's Cheese Shop—257 Bleecker St., Manhattan; 212/243-3289. With the East Village so well represented in this category, Mr. C had to find you something comparable in Greenwich Village—and this is it. Recently moved around the corner from the dingy location it held for many years, Murray's has expanded its selection, but not its prices. This makes it, of course, more popular than ever; hang in there, and you'll get some great deals. Certain cheeses are specially discounted each day. They also have a limited variety of fresh pastas and breads; but save your dough for Zito's Bakery, right next door (see above).

Ninth Avenue Cheese Market—525 Ninth Ave. (39th St.), Manhattan; 212/564-7127. Mr. C's cooking expert calls this one of his favorite shops. Among the gourmet foods from around the world, at very good prices, you'll find such cheeses as Swiss Emmenthal for $4.95 a pound, and a sharp Iberico from Spain at $6.95. A handful of these are always on special sale, and the

Mr. Cheap's Pick

✔ **East Village Cheese and Murray's Cheese**—One for each side of downtown. Big selections of the tasty blocks, at prices that won't leave your budget looking like a piece of Swiss.

nice folks will let you sample a taste of something exotic. They also have such items as duck mousse pate ($9.95 a pound), and flavored coffees all priced at $3.95 a pound (decafs $4.95). These include flavors like maple walnut and peaches and cream, plus at least half-a-dozen special in-store blends.

Just up the street, these folks recently opened a second shop, **Natura**, at 615 Ninth Avenue (212/397-4700). In addition to more cheeses and coffees, this shop specializes in soups, baked goods and prepared foods ready to take home that are made with natural and light ingredients. Unlike its parent store, which is closed Sundays, Natura is open seven days a week, including weeknights until 8 p.m.

Zabar's—2245 Broadway (80th St.), Manhattan; 212/787-2000.

See listing under "General Markets," below.

COFFEES AND TEAS

Ninth Avenue Cheese Market—525 Ninth Ave. (39th St.), Manhattan; 212/564-7127. See listing under "Cheese Shops," above.

Ninth Avenue International Foods—543 Ninth Ave. (41st St.), Manhattan; 212/279-1000. See listing under "General Markets," below.

The Open Pantry—184 Second Ave. (10th St.), Manhattan; 212/677-2640. A relaxed, folksy neighborhood grocery store, the Open Pantry is a fine place to stock up on your favorite gourmet coffees and teas. They have a good variety of blends to choose from. Many flavors of coffee beans are priced at $4.99 a pound, such as chocolate hazelnut and good ol' Columbian Supremo; and there are always weekly specials for just $3.99. Doesn't get much better than that. The Pantry is open until 11:00 p.m. seven nights a week.

Porto Rico Importing Company—201 Bleecker St., Manhattan; 212/477-5421, 107 Thompson St., Manhattan; 212/966-5758, and 40 1/2 St. Mark's Place, Manhattan; 212/533-1982. Walk into this shop and pause. Take a deep breath. Sure, it'll probably put caffeine into your veins simply by osmosis, but if you're part of the "coffee generation," it's pure heaven. Porto Rico's floor is dominated by sacks and sacks of beans—dozens of flavors from around the world. Brazil, Costa Rica, Venezuela, Santo Domingo....all of these tropical places have contributed beans that you can buy here for just $3.99 a pound. The folks at Porto Rico will, of course, grind these for you. A handful of blends are usually on special sale; when Mr. C wafted through, it was French roast from Nicaragua for $3.29 a pound. During special sales, the price can go down to $2.99. Why, that's just *beans* .

PR also sells loose teas from India, Russia, and the Far East. Huge glass jars of these line the walls. Most sell around $7.50 per pound, but again, look for flavors on sale—like English Breakfast or Earl Grey for just $5.00. And they have exotic spices, as well as chocolate-covered espresso beans, honeys, jams, and other condiments to enjoy with your beverages.

Ten Ren Tea Company—176 Canal St., Manhattan; 212/925-9822, 75 Mott St., Manhattan; 212/349-2286, and 135-18 Roosevelt Ave., Flushing, Queens; 718/461-9305. If you enjoy not only great teas but the entire culture surrounding tea, you should pay a visit to Chinatown's Ten Ren Tea and Ginseng Company. They grow their own tea in Asia and import it directly to these three outlets, where you can select from a bewildering array of teas, both loose and in

Mr. Cheap's Picks

✔ **Porto Rico Importing Company**—A dazzling array of coffee beans—if you can see through the aroma.

✔ **Ten Ren Tea Company**—A relaxing find amidst the crazy carnival of Chinatown. The most exotic teas (which you can sample), no more expensive than at the supermarket.

bags. The friendly folks here will be happy to explain what each variety is like, and you can even sample their exotic brew of the day. In fact, Ten Ren holds a traditional tea service daily, held at an ornate mahogany table in the store. Stop in to find out the schedule; there is no charge to participate.

While some teas can be as exotically priced as $116.00 for a ten-ounce cannister of loose tea leaves (the more expensive way to buy), most are as inexpensive as any old box of Lipton. A basic box of black tea, with twenty bags, is just $2.10; dozens of other varieties sell between $2.00 to $5.00 a box—including lemon, oolong, jasmine, plum and ginger. Each kind of tea sold is touted for various health benefits, which they have carefully researched—one kind of tea is made specifically to relax you; another is good for dieters; Japanese green tea has even been linked to lower rates of stomach cancer in the Far East. Whether or not that's really true, the world of tea is a pleasant one to explore.

GENERAL MARKETS

Arthur Avenue Market—2344 Arthur Ave., Belmont, Bronx; various phones. This large, enclosed version of an outdoor bazaar is like a stroll through some old-world Italian village. Each merchant has something different; walk along and you'll pass fruits and vegetables, meats, fish, cheeses, flowers, prepared foods, and even housewares and cooking utensils for all of the above. And everything is priced at market rates. Way at the back is the "Cafe al Mercato," a take-out counter with small tables, allowing you to take a breather from shopping over an espresso or a hot sausage sandwich. It's all been going on since 1940.

Cost Less Meats—3400 Fort Hamilton Pkwy., Borough Park, Brooklyn; 718/871-6217. Despite the name, there's more that meets the eye here than just meat. It's like a discount mini-supermarket. Easy to get to, and with a nice big parking lot, the store opened at the end of '92. Examples of their prices include Grade A whole chickens for 59¢ per pound; pork chops for 99¢ a pound; shell steak for $1.99 a pound; and extra-lean ground chuck for $1.39 a pound. Some deals are in quantities, like a ten-pound pack of baby pork spare ribs for $13.90. And there are similar savings in their deli department, such as sliced turkey breast for $2.99 a pound.

But again, this isn't just about meats. How about two dozen extra-large eggs for $1.49? Or cole slaw for 59¢ a pound? Milk, $1.79 a gallon? You can really do almost all of your shopping here. Get Entenmann's cakes for 50¢ below the printed prices (don't worry, they haven't expired), or a six-pack of Coke, in eight-ounce bottles, for $2.99. The store is open daily until 7:00 p.m., 8:00 p.m. on Fridays, and from 8:00 a.m. to 4:00 p.m. on Sundays.

Eagle Provisions—628 Fifth Ave. (18th St.), Park Slope, Brooklyn; 718/499-0026. Working your way along Fifth Avenue toward the Greenwood Cemetery area, in the midst of a largely Hispanic neighborhood, you suddenly come across a pocket of Polish restaurants and businesses. And they all shop at Eagle Provisions, a rambling food store in which the shelves are packed with both the familiar and unfamiliar—at least, to American shoppers. A full supermarket, with deli, butcher and bakery counters, Eagle specializes in European delicacies like kielbasa, fresh-baked hearty breads and *Polski* jelly doughnuts. Yet you may also find Middle Eastern foods, coffees and teas, polenta and other Italian ingredients, and more. They even sell newspapers from these various corners of the world. Packaged foods are often imported, without a word of English to tell you what they are. The delightful aspect of all this is that here the exotic is also inexpensive. Be open-minded—and daring!

East Village Cheese Store—34 Third Ave. (10th St.), Manhattan; 212/477-2601. See listing under "Cheese Shops," above.

Fairway—2127 Broadway (74th St.), Manhattan; 212/595-1888. Along with Zabar's up the street, Fairway is the supermarket of choice for good food, good prices, and shoving crowds. Look at it this way: It's not just food shopping, it's an adventure. Fairway has great values in fresh foods, like breads and cheeses. West Side residents also swear by the price and vast selection of fruits and vegetables, brought in daily from metro-area farms. And you can grind your own coffee beans, starting at just $2.99 a pound, with enough varieties to get your buzz a different way every morning for at least a month.

Gourmet Garage—47 Wooster St., Manhattan; 212/941-5850. Boy, SoHo doesn't have too many bargains like this. Gourmet Garage *looks* expensive, with white-washed walls and an espresso bar up front; but in fact, the fancy food they sell can cost as much as half that of nearby produce markets. That's because these guys have been wholesaling to New York's best restaurants for over ten years, and just recently decided to spend part of their day selling to the general public.

So once the morning rounds have been done, about noon or so, they open up and offer you the same tremendous prices, like shiitake mushrooms for $6.00 a pound, or $7.00 for a liter of extra virgin olive oil; plus meats and fish, like smoked salmon for just $17.00 a pound (compare it to deli prices of $35.00 or more). And you'll find similar savings on free-range chicken, venison, fennel, several varieties of tomatoes, white asparagus, and other delicacies; plus cheeses, prepared salads, and breads. Deals like a five-pound bag of Columbian, decaf, or espresso coffee beans for $14.00 (just $2.80 per pound!) can't be beaten anywhere in Mr. C's travels.

Everything is displayed as beautifully as in any market, and the coffee bar (hot espresso for $1.00) makes shopping all the more pleasurable. And since these folks are wholesalers in the food business, they really know their stuff. The store is open seven days a week from noon to 6:00 p.m.

International Groceries and Meat Market—529 Ninth Ave. (40th St.), Manhattan; 212/279-5514. One of the many shops up and down Ninth Avenue, near the

Port Authority Bus Terminal, that specialize in foods imported from around the world. International is one of the biggest, and walking in is like a trip to the old country. All kinds of foods, both familiar and exotic, are displayed in open barrels or behind glass counters, and sawdust covers the wooden floor. Many of the foods here are raw ingredients, enough for any recipe known to man: Dried beans in a dozen varieties, flours, spices, dried pastas, and more. Mr. C saw a one-liter can of virgin olive oil for $4.95. Most of the foreign products come from Greece, Italy, and Spain. There is, of course, a well-stocked butcher's counter, which also includes some fish and cheeses. Whatever you need, chances are it's here.

And yet there are several shops just like it within a few blocks; this probably helps you, the smart shopper, by keeping prices down. For example, the separately owned **Ninth Avenue International Foods** at 543 Ninth Avenue (212/279-1000) has many of the same items. Check out their eye-catching display of spices, like an artist's palette of reds, golds and browns. Paprika, turmeric, cayenne pepper, and dozens more are as low as 75¢ for a quarter-pound. This shop also has lots of coffees, like raspberry chocolate, all $3.49 a pound, and several flavors of halvah. Each of the shops in the area may have a better selection in one kind of food or another; it's helpful and fun to wander through them all.

Italian Food Center—186 Grand St., Manhattan; 212/925-2954. File this one under the category of insider's discovery. Tucked away in the heart of Little Italy, the IFC is like heaven for fans of Italian cooking. Stock up on your supplies of extra-virgin olive oil, imported tomato paste, dried pastas, freshly stuffed sausages and other meats, breads, and all the rest. At these prices, you can afford to do it easily. The store also makes fresh, wonderful sandwiches, as well as cooked specialties you can heat up at home. Take a friend along, and brag that you know *the* authentic places to shop in this hyped-up area.

Kam Man Grocery—200 Canal St., Manhattan; 212/571-0330. What the Italian Food Center is to Little Italy, Kam Man is for Chinatown. With only about a zillion shops that all look pretty much the same, you can come here and know that the quality is consistent and the prices great—even if you're not quite sure what it is you're buying. Rest assured that folks who *do* know Chinese products and ingredients (like dried shrimps and ginseng roots) often recommend Kam Man. Check out their hot prepared foods, too—roast duck, barbecued pork. Unfortunately, like so much of Chinatown, language can be a problem. Be patient, it's worth it. Open every day of the week.

Nader International Foods—1 East 28th St., Manhattan; 212/686-5793. No, Ralph Nader hasn't gone into the consumer-friendly food business. But Nader Aboutalebi has, right in the heart of the Garment District. This cozy shop is a smaller version of the Ninth Avenue stores, but no less serviceable; it has a bit of everything, particularly in foods from the Middle East and the Orient. There are cooking ingredients from bulgur wheat ($1.00 a pound) to lentils and various spices; imported pistachio nuts and several kinds of halvah (each $3.99 a pound); dried fruits and candies, and more. The shop is open into the early evening, if you want to grab something for a special recipe on your way home from the office.

Park Slope Food Co-op—782 Union St., Park Slope, Brooklyn; 718/622-0560. Well, this is probably only an option for those who live in or near the Park Slope neighborhood, since you do have to become a member to shop here. But Mr. C was so impressed with this unique opportunity to save money on everyday groceries that he wanted to pass it along to anyone who might be interested in joining.

The Co-Op offers everything you'd find in an ordinary supermarket, along with many specialty items, at a markup of only 16 percent above wholesale cost. Compare this with the markups of 20 to 30 percent or more at the big chains; you can save yourself hundreds of dollars a year on groceries. You'll find fresh-baked breads, organically grown produce (a three-pound bag of Macintosh apples for 95¢!), and lots of grains, nuts, dried fruits, spices, and similar items sold by the pound at "generic" prices.

So you have to work for your savings, right? Sure—all of three hours per month. That, plus a $10.00 fee twice a year, gets you in. There is also a $100.00 deposit, which you can pay over time and which is returned if you cancel your membership. Considering the amount of foods they have (much of it health-oriented), and the amount of money you're going to save overall, it's still quite a bargain. Stop in for membership info and a look around.

Ralph's Thrift Store—93 Chambers St., Manhattan; 212/267-5567. In the downtown discount district, Ralph's Discount City is probably the king of the heap. A couple of doors along, Ralph's Thrift Store takes the same closeout approach to packaged foods, like Pepperidge Farm and Oreo cookies, Cracker Jacks, breads and pastas, and beverages. Several varieties of Wise snack foods were seen here for 99¢ a bag, and three bottles of Appia mineral water were just a dollar. Much of the stuff in here is junk food, sorry to say; but then, maybe it's not so bad for you if you've paid less than retail prices for it....

Sahadi Imports—187-89 Atlantic Ave., Brooklyn; 718/624-4550. Larger and more elaborately laid-out than its Manhattan counterparts, Sahadi has an excellent stock of imported meats, cheeses, baked goods, prepared foods, candies, and the rest—mostly, but not exclusively, with a Middle Eastern touch. At the take-out counter you can get a falafel sandwich for $2.50; in

Mr. Cheap's Picks

- ✔ **Eagle Provisions**—Just your average Polish-Middle Eastern supermarket, that's all. See 'em all the time.
- ✔ **Fairway**—You can do all your food shopping here, if you can stand the crowds, and get exotic foods at everyday prices.
- ✔ **Gourmet Garage**—A wholesaler who opens up to the public—that's always music to Mr. C's ears. In SoHo, yet!
- ✔ **Italian Food Center**—The insider's place to shop in Little Italy.
- ✔ **Sahadi Imports**—Some call it the Dean and Deluca of Brooklyn; a winding maze of fresh foods and cooking ingredients, cheap.

the bakery area, grab a fresh baguette for a dollar, or an onion baguette for $1.75. Plus a cook's encyclopedia of spices, oils, dried beans, coffees, loose teas....the list goes on and on. Wind your way through; it's like a reasonably-priced Balducci's!

In fact, like the Ninth Avenue district, this section of Atlantic Avenue in Cobble Hill has several other Mediterranean food shops nearby. Stop in at **El Asmar Foods**, 197 Atlantic Avenue (718/855-2455), with a good, if smaller, range of general imported foods and cooking ingredients. Gourmet coffees here start at $4.25 a pound. Also, try the **Damascus Pastry Shop**, 195 Atlantic Avenue (718/625-7070) for freshly baked pita breads at 55¢ per bag (day-old, 45¢).

Teitel Brothers—2349 Arthur Ave., Belmont, Bronx; 718/733-9400. How guys with this name found their way into this heavily Italian neighborhood is of little consequence. They know what they're doing, and if you know what's good for you, you'll shop here for all your cooking needs. Get a gallon of extra-virgin olive oil, imported from the old country (that would be Italy, of course) for just $13.99. They also have cheeses, sliced meats, fresh and bottled olives, and all the other delicacies for your most special recipes.

Western Beef—403 West 14th St., Manhattan; 212/989-6572, 197 Fort Green Place, Brooklyn; 718/638-5400, 402 East 83rd St., Bay Ridge, Brooklyn; 718/241-5500, and other stores in Brooklyn, Bronx, Queens and Staten Island. Despite its name, Western Beef is like a complete discount supermarket. To be sure, this is a great place to buy all kinds of meats, especially if you can buy in quantity. That's where you'll get the best deals. Sirloin steaks, for example, may cost as little as $1.98 a pound—if you can buy ten pounds at a time (they will cut them for you). Beef spare ribs may be as low as 98¢ a pound. Or, you may find whole Perdue chickens for just 58¢ a pound, in a bag of two.

Everything's super-fresh; the main Manhattan location is side-by-side with the meat wholesalers near the river on 14th Street. This is one of the few places along that strip, in fact, which sells to the public (don't miss Basior-Schwartz, a few doors down), and you generally get the same wholesale prices. WB also has a deli department, where you can get sliced turkey breast as low as $1.89 a pound, and Swiss cheese for $2.69 a pound.

Meanwhile, Western Beef also has bargains on other supermarket items. Produce is nice and cheap, like four pounds of bananas for a dollar: Same price for a deal on two one-pound blocks of Dew Fresh margarine; Celentano frozen ravioli, just $1.29 for a thirteen-ounce package; and much more. It's a no-frills setting, and probably not as convenient as the corner store, but it's definitely worth the trip.

Zabar's—2245 Broadway (80th St.), Manhattan; 212/787-2000. Though perhaps not as inexpensive as they once were—success breeds excess—Zabar's is still *the* New York food market to many. For sheer selection, of course, they're hard to beat. And when they have specials, they're *really* special—like their sales on cheeses from around the world. One recent feature included French aged Emmenthaler for just $3.98 a pound, and Old Amsterdam cheese, reduced from $8.98 a pound to $5.98. Coffee beans, chocolates, caviar, smoked whitefish, fresh-baked loaves of bread, and other delicacies are all here at quite reasonable prices. Open daily, including evenings—and no matter when you go, be prepared for the crowds.

HEALTH FOODS AND VITAMINS

Bell Bates Company—101-107 West Broadway (Reade St.), Manhattan; 212/267-4300. A health and gourmet food store with even more: Coffees, herb teas, spices, dried fruits and nuts, you name it. And bargains abound! Some of the best Mr. C came across included loose Earl Grey tea, $6.75 a pound; B-complex vitamins, almost $6.00 below retail price; a four-ounce package of catnip for only $3.49 (pets can be healthy bargain shoppers too); and After the Fall fruit juices in thirty-two-ounce bottles for $1.89. For those who seek healthy alternatives for an insatiable sweet tooth, BB has fat-free chocolate as well as oatmeal-raisin cookies, made with whole-wheat flour and no refined sugar, at about 50¢ below the supermarket prices (if you can find them there).

Grab a flyer advertising their monthly sales. These have several pages of savings, such as organic peanut butter marked down from $5.49 to $3.29, Nasoya tofu at 50¢ off, and Ener-G brown rice bread reduced from $3.49 to $2.59 for a loaf. The store is open weekdays, 9:30 a.m. to 6:00 p.m., and Saturdays from 11:00 a.m. to 5:00 p.m.

Eva's Natural Foods—11 West 8th St., Manhattan; 212/982-2500. If you're trying to get lean, stay lean, or just live on a lean budget, Eva's is the place to visit. Its dual existence as both a health food store and a restaurant makes it perfect when you can't decide whether to eat a good meal at home or out (you can take out from the restaurant, too).

The store's selection is impressive. Prices are generally quite good, and regular sales may offer Santa Cruz Apple Juice at almost 50 percent off retail price; Kwai garlic tablets, $5.00 off a two-hundred-tablet package; a four-pound bag of Lick Your Chops all-natural dry cat food, retail price $8.00, here just $5.89; and personal care products like Tom's of Maine and Nature's Gate for far below what you'd pay in local supermarkets. Also, plenty of frozen foods and ready-to-prepare dinners. Whatever your nutritional and health food needs may be, you'll find them here. They're open weekdays 10 a.m. to 11:30 p.m., and weekends 11:00 a.m. to 11:00 p.m.

Good Health—324 East 86th St., Manhattan; 212/439-9682.

Another store within a restaurant, Good Health offers some great deals on foods like Jaclyn's fat-free pizza mix, usually $7.00, here just $4.99; two-for-the-price-of-one sales on Knudsen Organic Apple Juices; and Barbara's shredded wheat cereal for a dollar less than in supermarkets.

Aloe and apricot bath oils by Jason, retail price $8.00, were seen here for $4.99. Many of the vitamins and supplements carry the same sort of price reduction—such as evening primrose oil, $6.00 below retail, and Twinlab "Gainer's Fuel 1000" at $23.99 for a four-pound bottle, a savings of $8.00. The store is open seven days a week.

The Health Nuts—835 Second Ave. (45th St.), Manhattan; 212/490-2979, 1208 Second Ave. (63rd St.), Manhattan; 212/593-0116, 2141 Broadway (75th St.), Manhattan; 724-1972, 2611 Broadway (99th St.), Manhattan; 678-0054, Bay Terrace Shopping Center, Bayside, Queens; 718/225-8164, and 253-34 Northern Blvd., Little Neck, Queens; 718/423-1065. Nothing nuts about this. These stores have good prices on organic foods (with discounts on everything from muesli to mozzarella) and on dietary supplements and personal care products. If you

Mr. Cheap's Picks

✔ **Bell Bates Company**—A health food supermarket in TriBeCa with a terrific selection.

✔ **Nature Food Centres**—Help yourself and help the planet at this environmentally conscious chain.

✔ **The Vitamin Shoppe**—Big savings on every kind of pill imaginable—and some that are not. At least the prices are easy to swallow.

partake of Super Enzymall Tabs, Mr. C found them on sale here for $11.00 below the retail price; Allerdophilus caps, $9.00 off retail; and Milk Creek Natural Elastin Creme for almost half-price. The stores also carry the Traditional Medicinal line of products whose discounts and product names are sure to make you smile. Perhaps you could use some "Throat Coat," "Nighty Night Tea," "Eater's Digest Tea" or the aptly named "Smooth Move Laxative Tea." All can be found at about a dollar below retail. You can also get lots of books and printed information about health products, vitamins, and alternative medicine. Health Nuts stores stay open late, and you can even fax your orders in.

National Wholesale Liquidators—632 Broadway (Bleecker St.), Manhattan; 212/979-2400, and 71-01 Kissena Boulevard, Flushing, Queens; 718/591-3900. See listing under "Department Stores."

Nature Food Centres—28 West 57th St., Manhattan; 212/757-1539, 2119 Broadway (74th St.), Manhattan; 212/874-9128, 41 Union Square (17th St.), Manhattan; 212/627-0787, and over two dozen other locations throughout New York City.

Not only can you improve your own health by shopping at Nature Food Centres, but you'll be helping the planet as well. NFC supports nonprofit organizations working to save tropical rainforests by marketing products, like Brazil nuts and banana chips, from these groups. They're also big on recycling (return your empty vitamin bottles here and get a nickel back!) and animal rights (their "Cruelty-Free Policy" ensures that none of their products are tested on animals).

Oftentimes, such efforts can mean higher prices passed on to the consumer; not at NFC. Just about everything in the store is discounted. Everyday prices on bodybuilding supplements and sports nutrition products are 25 percent off retail; a variety of low-fat snack foods, like Hain rice cakes and Frookie cookies, are always on sale; and you'll find great prices on trail mix and organically grown nuts—raw, roasted or no-salt.

Save on DeBoles egg-free pastas; Health Valley vegetarian foods; Kiss My Face and Camo-Care beauty products; and vitamins from many national brands. During special sales, which seem to be on constantly, many items are reduced (no pun intended) to half-price. At Nature's, Mr. C can easily afford to change his name to "Mr. PC."

Prescriptions Limited—1151 Madison Ave. (82nd St.), Manhattan; 212/628-3210. This pharmacy carries the full catalog of Nat-Rul Health products, a discount mail-order brand that claims to be comparable to major national brands of vitamins and dietary supplements. These are made without additives like yeast, sugar, starch, and preservatives. The prices are among the lowest Mr. C has found yet. Examples of the many bargains include a hundred-caplet jar of vitamin E (200 i.u.) for $3.85; B-complex "stress-fighter" formulas, as low as $7.50 for one hundred tablets; and cold-fighting zinc lozenges, 100 tabs for an amazing $2.50. They also have garlic and wheat germ oil pills, sports nutrition powders, beauty products to strengthen hair and nails, fiber supplements, and facial cleansers, all at "generic" prices.

The Vitamin Shoppe—375 Sixth Ave. (Waverly Pl.), Manhattan; 212/929-6553, 295 Park Ave. South (23rd St.), Manhattan; 212/777-0060, 460 Seventh Ave. (35th St.), Manhattan; 212/736-6137, 666 Lexington Ave. (56th St.), Manhattan; 212/421-0250, 120 West 57th St., Manhattan; 212/664-0048, 139 East 57th St., Manhattan; 212/371-3850, 2086A Broadway (72nd St.), Manhattan; 212/580-0622, 203 East 86th St., Manhattan; 212/534-0622, and 215 West 92nd St., Manhattan; 212/724-2430. Bigger may not always mean better, but in the case of the Vitamin Shoppe, it does indeed mean better prices. Save up to 20 percent on hundreds of national brands, and as much as 40 percent on selected "super savers" throughout the store. VS also markets its own line of vitamins, at very low prices. Vitamin C pills start at $3.95 for a hundred-count jar of 500mg rose hips; natural vitamin E-400 complex starts at $6.90 for the same size. Herbs, from aloe to yucca, are available in capsule form; save also on body-building supplements, homeopathic medicines, and thousands of personal care items like natural hair colors and shampoos, skin masques, natural dental floss, blood pressure monitors, massagers, back pillows, foot care items, and much, much more. Best of all, if you're not satisfied with any product, you can return the unused portion within two months for a refund (think this includes the back pillows?).

It's too much to take in, really, but don't worry—Vitamin Shoppe has a 110-page catalog, from which you can also order by mail. It's very informative, with articles and descriptions carefully explaining the benefits of each item; this is clearly a company that cares about its customers. They even have a "Vitamin Shopper Plus" program which rewards loyal catalog customers with points that add up to dollars-off certificates for future purchases. And if you really love these guys, visit their factory outlet across the river in North Bergen, New Jersey for further bargains. It's only open on Saturdays; the New York stores are open weekdays 8:00 a.m. to 8:00 p.m. and Saturdays 9:00 a.m. to 5:00 p.m.

MEAT AND FISH

Abruscato Meat Market—534 Ninth Ave. (40th St.), Manhattan; 212/563-0391. This is one of a whole menagerie of butcher shops up and down a few blocks of Ninth Avenue, packed closer together than the links in their plump homemade sausages. At any one you're sure to find great prices on various cuts of beef, lamb, veal, poultry, pork, and even goat. Recent specials seen here have included short beef ribs for $2.98 a pound and spare rib tips for just 89¢ a pound. It's all fresh and top quality, as the steady flow of customers attests.

Right across the street are several more, such as **Joe's Ninth Avenue Meat Market** at 533 Ninth Avenue (212/947-

8090), which offers several options of "Family Specials." For example, you can get three pounds each of ground beef, chuck steak, beef liver, chicken legs, and turkey wings, all for $23.99—and they'll even toss in a pound of hot dogs at no extra charge. Such a deal!

Other merchants in this midtown meat mecca include **Cuzin's Meat Market**, 520 Ninth Avenue (212/736-5737), specializing in ham and pork; the **Esposito Pork Shop**, 500 Ninth Avenue (212/279-3298), another great place for bringing home the bacon; and **Michael's Meat Market**, 516 Ninth Avenue (212/279-2324). In fact, though some may specialize, each of these stores has just about any kind of meat you could want—including venison, rabbit, quail, Bush (oops, sorry), partridge, and squab.

Basior-Schwartz Meats—421 West 14th St., Manhattan; 212/929-5368. If you've ever seen the West Village's meat district, packed with trailer trucks loading and unloading into vast warehouses, you probably figured the area is off-limits to the average shopper. Yes, most of these dealers are wholesale-only; but a couple are open to the general public as well, so you can buy from the same places the restaurants do. Basior-Schwartz is a real find.

Mr. C had a pleasant chat with Barry Basior, one of several family members who run the operation. He's proud of their assortment of not only meats but gourmet foods such as patés, cheeses, condiments and seafood. The range is extraordinary. Planning a big bash? Pick up five pounds of filet mignon—or, for that matter, kosher frankfurters. Fresh veal stew is just $1.90 a pound. A whole oven-roasted boneless turkey breast was seen for $2.49 a pound, and a one-pound package of Nova Scotia salmon was just $16.50—about half the price of fancy shops. There are plenty of well-known brand names, like paté by Les Trois Petits Couchons (that's The Three Little Pigs, folks). You may even find whole cakes for dessert, sliced into sixteen pieces, for $15.00.

The exterior of this shop is non-existent; basically, it's a door amidst the trucks and loading docks. Have no fear, and venture in—the shop is all the way at the back. Once you see it, you'll find your way back again and again. Get there bright and early, though; store hours are weekdays only, from 5:00 a.m. (that's the wholesale business) to noon. The early bird catches the wurst, eh?

Biancardi's—2340 Arthur Ave., Belmont, Bronx; 718/733-4058. One

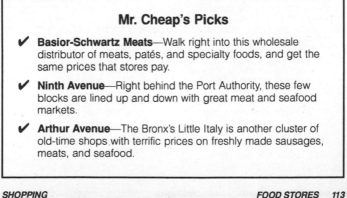

Mr. Cheap's Picks

✔ **Basior-Schwartz Meats**—Walk right into this wholesale distributor of meats, patés, and specialty foods, and get the same prices that stores pay.

✔ **Ninth Avenue**—Right behind the Port Authority, these few blocks are lined up and down with great meat and seafood markets.

✔ **Arthur Avenue**—The Bronx's Little Italy is another cluster of old-time shops with terrific prices on freshly made sausages, meats, and seafood.

of the many food shops in this Italian neighborhood in this "Little Italy" section of Belmont in the Bronx, Biancardi's specializes in pork sausages that are absolutely fresh and homemade. You can tell just by looking. There are so many varieties to choose from: Pork, veal, lamb, spicy, sweet, fresh, dried....you name it. In fact, they have all kinds of meats, from beef to veal to poultry, and these cost far less than you'll find at many other butcher's shops around town. Oh, and Biancardi's also has rabbit—be prepared to see several of these hairless hares stripped and hanging in the window.

Cost Less Meats—3400 Ft. Hamilton Pkwy., Borough Park, Brooklyn; 718/871-6217. See listing under "General Markets," above.

Randazzo's Fish Market—2327 Arthur Ave., Belmont, Bronx; 718/367-4139. Randazzo's is a crazy carnival of a seafood shop, bustling with shoppers and brimming with fish and snellfish. After eighty years across the street, they recently moved into more spacious, attractive quarters at their present address. "We wanted to be on the sunny side of the street," says the cheerful, talkative owner. It sure is a clean, bright place, with white tile and track lighting. But you'll go, of course, for the fish. Whether you want live lobster ($3.99 per pound), or their other specialties of clams, mussels, and crabs, you'll get excellent prices. They also feature baccala, the salt-dried cod that's considered a delicacy in these parts. Buy a whole fish or just the center cut.

Across the street from Randazzo's is **Cosenza's Fish Market**, 2354 Arthur Avenue (718/364-8510). Here the fish are so neatly arranged, they seem to be color-coded—from bluefish to red snappers. Mr. C found high-quality, fresh swordfish here for $9.99 a pound, a fraction of the price at fancier shops. Service is quick and attentive, with a less frenetic atmosphere than its competitor.

Sea Breeze Seafood—541 Ninth Ave. (40th St.), Manhattan; 212/563-7537. One of the many wholesale/retail food shops along Midtown's Ninth Avenue, Sea Breeze has that real "just off the boats" feel to it. Live lobsters roam around in bubbling tanks; a recent special offered three live one-pounders for $14.95. Swordfish was also seen at that time for $5.99 a pound, and $3.99 a pound for whole, small salmon. Of course, prices are seasonal, rising in winter and falling in the summertime, when the fishin' is easy. But you'll definitely find bargains here anytime.

Another nearby fish market to check is the **Central Fish Company**, 527 Ninth Avenue (212/279-2317). They also specialize in live lobsters, along with tuna steaks and things like smoked Norwegian salmon.

United Meat Market—84 Mulberry St., Manhattan; 212/962-6440. Again, if you want to look like a real Chinatown insider, buy your meats here. United has fresh steaks, poultry (especially duck, of course), sausages, and more, all at bargain prices. They don't speak much English, though, so take your time and make sure you get what you want. Open seven days a week.

Western Beef—403 West 14th St., Manhattan; 212/989-6572, 197 Fort Green Place, Brooklyn; 718/638-5400, 402 East 83rd St., Bay Ridge, Brooklyn; 718/241-5500, and other stores in Brooklyn, Bronx, Queens and Staten Island.

See listing under "General Markets" above.

PASTA

Borgatti Ravioli—632 East 187th St., Belmont, Bronx; 718/367-3799. Another gem in the Arthur Avenue area, Borgatti's is a bustling shop selling homemade pasta creations to an eager throng of customers. The line frequently runs out the door of this tiny storefront. Fresh, soft, pasta noodles are literally cut to order; just name your thickness.

Among the other items on their simple menu are the fresh ravioli, filled with your choice of spinach, meat, or ricotta cheese. Whichever you choose, it'll cost just $8.00 for a box of 110 ravioli. Can you beat it?

Bruno Ravioli—653 Ninth Ave. (45th St.), Manhattan; 212/246-8456, 1093 Lexington Ave. (77th St.), Manhattan; 212/988-9610, and 2204 Broadway (78th St.), Manhattan; 212/580-8150. "The King of Ravioli," they proclaim, and Bruno's has been at the top since 1905. This shop uses all natural ingredients, with no preservatives for its fresh pastas and sauces; and they're so concerned about your enjoyment of same that they offer up emphatically precise cooking instructions to get you the best results. Many of their pastas are actually made without eggs, for health-conscious diners.

A box of fifty ravioli, enough to serve four people, starts at just $4.50 for a low-sodium ricotta filling, and $5.75 for beef. But, whoa, Bruno's doesn't stop there. How about pumpkin ravioli ($5.95), or Florentine ravioli ($6.75), filled with spinach, carrots, mushrooms, shallots, and onions, all ground and stuffed into a spinach pasta shell? Or shiitake mushroom, same price, made with marsala wine? Talk about an inexpensive gourmet meal—bring some home and impress your friends.

Bruno's also has manicotti with the same basic and exotic fillings, tortellini, gnocchi, fresh pasta noodles, and all kinds of sauces to go on top of these. Try a pint of spicy *fra diavlo* sauce for $3.99. You can even get complete dinners to take home, from $4.95 a pound. And they have all the imported fixings to help you whip up a festive meal or party. The midtown branch is closed on Sundays; the others are open seven days a week.

Morisi's Pasta—647 Fifth Ave., Park Slope, Brooklyn; 718/788-2299. Mr. C has never seen so many unusual kinds of pasta as he did in this unique shop, and it's all so reasonably priced! Morisi's makes over two hundred varieties of dried pastas, in an artist's palette of colors, shapes, and sizes. The basics of spinach and tomato are here, but don't stop there. How about avocado pasta? Chili pepper fettucine? Lobster capellini? Goat cheese and walnut linguine? Or bright red strawberry pasta? These are some of the fifty flavors available, all priced from $1.49 to $9.00 per pound.

Morisi's also has soft, fresh noodles, cut to your order, like fettucine for $1.59 a pound. And a box of fifty meat ravioli, made on the premises and frozen, is $4.19. They also do a major mail-order business. Hours are Monday-Saturday, from 8:00 a.m. to 6:00 p.m. Check 'em out; you'll never look like such a gourmet for so little.

Raffetto's Pasta—144 West Houston St., Manhattan; 212/777-1261. A major supplier of pasta to many New York restaurants, Raffetto's is a longtime fixture at the southern tip of Greenwich Village. Here you can buy for yourself their freshly made pesto ravioli, just $5.50 for a box of fifty; vegetable ravioli, in a spinach dough, is $4.00 for the same-size box. Dried pastas are 95¢ per pound, in a wall-full of shapes and colors. Raffetto's

Mr. Cheap's Picks

✔ **Borgatti Ravioli**—Once more to Arthur Avenue, for this tiny but always crowded fresh pasta maker.

✔ **Morisi's Pasta**—A list of pastas grows in Brooklyn—this ever-expanding selection of dried pastas made from fruit, cheese, and even fish.

also has all the other items you'll need, such as sauces, oils, spices, breadsticks, and more. A recent special, for example, was a 101-ounce can of Filippo Berio olive oil for $13.95.

PRODUCE

Arthur Avenue Market—2344 Arthur Ave., Belmont, Bronx; various phones. See listing under "General Markets," above.

Fairway—2127 Broadway (74th St.), Manhattan; 212/595-1888. See listing under "General Markets," above.

Number 1 Farmer's Market—1800 Second Ave. (93rd St.), Manhattan; 212/289-8910. For lots of good produce cheap, check this place out. Here, depending on what's in season, you can find all kinds of fruits and vegetables for far less than in supermarkets. "Number 1" must mean their favorite price; everything seems to be some kind of deal for a dollar. Whether it's seven lemons for $1.00, or three pounds of potatoes for $1.00, or three pounds of bananas for $1.00....you get the picture. And when you get the food at these prices, you won't believe you're on the Upper East Side. Not that Zabar's, Fairway and the rest should get nervous; this place is tiny by comparison, and it can't match their quality. The address does not actually appear over the door, and the phone number is to a pay phone. But a bargain is a bargain, and customers regularly pack the store tighter than peas in a pod.

Stiles Farmer's Market—472 Ninth Ave. (41st St.), Manhattan; 212/967-4918. The zillions of bargain food shops running down Ninth Avenue from the Port Authority don't end with the station itself; just on t'other side, in the shadow of the bus ramps, is Stiles Farmer's Market. Despite its carnival-tent architecture, Stiles is a year-round operation, doing a brisk business in all kinds of fruits and vegetables. Buying in quantity makes for the best bargains: Recent specials included two pounds of fresh green beans, or three pounds of carrots, or three pounds of bananas—each priced at one dollar. Gourmet coffee beans are sold here too, starting at $3.49 a pound for French roast, decaf, or the house blend.

Zabar's—2245 Broadway (80th St.), Manhattan; 212/787-2000. See listing under "General Markets" above.

FURNITURE

NEW FURNITURE

Bella Furniture—107-08 Atlantic Ave., Ozone Park, Brooklyn; 718/441-6602. Bella features complete furniture sets for the bedroom, living room and dining room. They come in a variety of European and American styles, from old fashioned to contemporary. A recent sale offered an ornate Italian bedroom set of lacquered wood; the set included a queen-size bed, two night tables, a six-drawer dresser, and a vanity table topped with a large round mirror, all for $2,899.00. In their furniture warehouse you can get further savings, like a cloth-upholstered matching sofa and loveseat for $499.00. You may also find mattress sets in here, not big names, but priced as low as $80.00 per piece. Open seven days a week.

Bloom & Krup—202-6 First Ave. (12th St.), Manhattan; 212/673-2760. See listing under "Appliances."

Chairs and Stools Etc.—222 Bowery, Manhattan; 212/925-9191. Downtown, in the midst of the restaurant supplier's district, this store sells about half of its lines to the public at near-wholesale prices. They have the city's largest selection of, you guessed it, chairs and stools; everything from 1950s style kitchen counter stools to the latest European fashions. Country-style oak chairs for the dining room range from $69.00 to $99.00 apiece; this is about half the prices of many uptown stores. Counter stools in good ol' black vinyl and chrome go for $30.00, again, half of retail store prices. They also have resin/marble composite tables and tabletops, about $100.00 below retail. C & S prefers to do business with the public on Saturdays from 10:00 a.m. to 3:00 p.m., but they're also open Monday-Friday from 9:00 a.m. to 5:00 p.m.; call ahead if you want to stop in on a weekday, and they'll probably say "yes."

The Couch Potato—5113 New Utrecht Ave., Borough Park, Brooklyn; 718/972-7632. Underneath the elevated train along the northern end of New Utrecht Avenue there is a whole district of bargain shops much like Manhattan's Lower East Side. Many are owned by orthodox Jews, meaning two things: Good prices and odd hours. They close on Friday afternoons and reopen all day Sunday, in observance of the Sabbath.

This new store specializes in sofas of all kinds, from loveseats to modular sets to recliners and convertible beds. They sell between 30 to 50 percent below list prices. There are good names to be found here, including Sealy, Lane, Berkline, and Flexsteel. Basic models start around $299.00; sleep sofas start about $100.00 higher. All mattresses, by the way, are proper inner-spring mattresses, not foam rubber. The prices are cheap, not the quality.

Just down the street is

CP's parent store, **Loeffler Furniture**, 5127 New Utrecht Ave. (718/436-8989). Loeffler takes the idea of high quality at discount to a new extreme; you can easily spend $10,000 on a dining room set—no, not a typo—and believe it or not, still be saving money. The place is really a design center, where consultants will work with you on creating entire rooms. Even though it's still expensive here, you do get near-wholesale prices.

Furniture Gallery—581 Sixth Ave. (17th St.), Manhattan; 212/924-8802. For discounts on contemporary, good-quality living room and bedroom furniture, check out this place. Everything sold here is made with solid wood and other quality materials, and carries a lifetime guarantee. Yet you can find some excellent prices here. The main-floor showroom features lots of futons as couches and beds. Get a full-size futon bed with a hardwood frame—none of your soft pine on this baby—for $325.00, including a choice of splashy futon covers. It can be delivered in twenty-four to forty-eight hours, or they'll pay the fee.

Take a look upstairs, too, for further-reduced prices on clearance items. Most of these are slightly damaged in some way, but you may not mind when you can get a shiny black lacquer platform bed, originally $350.00, for $195.00. Or 20 percent off on a tall, solid-oak, six-drawer dresser. These pieces are, of course, sold "as is" and are not returnable. Furniture Gallery is open seven days a week.

Furniture Land—1224 Liberty Ave., Ozone Park, Queens; 718/235-2759. Right on the border between Queens and Brooklyn, Furniture Land is a large dealer with very low prices on individual pieces, room sets and bedding. Furnish your living room for as little as $298.00—for a contemporary-style sofa, loveseat, and chair. Get a dinette table with four chairs for just $99.00. At such prices, of course, these lines are made with inexpensive materials; they're good for student dorms, short-term situations or super-tight budgets. Furniture Land also has high-quality brands, like a six-piece Bassett bedroom set for $1,499.00, about $400.00 below list price. As the owner says, they have "everything for the home." Mattresses, again, come in budget and major-brand names. Sets start from just $78.00 in twin-size, $148.00 queen; Sealy Posturepedic twin sets start at $269.00. They have futons, too. Same-day delivery is available. The store is open Monday-Saturday from 10:00 a.m. to 6:30 p.m.

Gothic Cabinet Craft—360 Sixth Ave. (Waverly Pl.), Manhattan; 212/982-8539, 1601 Second Ave. (83rd St.), Manhattan; 212/472-7359, 1655 Second Ave. (86th St.), Manhattan; 212/288-2999, 2543 Broadway (95th St.). Manhattan; 212/749-2020, 27-50 First St., Astoria, Queens; 718/626-1480, 36-09 Main St., Flushing, Queens; 718/762-6246, 147-44 Jamaica Ave., Jamaica, Queens; 718/297-1109, 258-01 Union Turnpike, Glen Oaks, Queens; 718/347-5201, 31 Smith St. (Fulton St.), Brooklyn; 718/625-2333, 6929 Fifth Ave. (Ovington St.), Bay Ridge, Brooklyn; 718/745-0715, 2163 White Plains Rd., Bronx; 718/863-7440, and 2366 University Ave., Bronx; 718/365-9333.

Unfinished furniture is one of the great ways to save money. Gothic Cabinet Craft makes a wide variety of functional pieces for every room in the house, with plenty of styles and solid woods to choose from. A colonial-style hardwood rocking chair can cost as little as $39.00, and a four-drawer writing desk is just $189.00. Contemporary styles include solid-pine platform beds from just $99.00; or choose a birch model that includes headboard, drawers, and nightstands complete for $399.00. They can complete the outfit for you with discount prices on mattress sets by Serta and Sealy, as well as futons. There are also butcher-block tables, loft beds, computer desks, entertainment centers, bookcases, folding screens, and much more. It's all made in the good ol' U.S. of A.

MB Discount Furniture—2311 Avenue U (23rd St.), Sheepshead Bay, Brooklyn; 718/332-1500. MB is a large operation that offers substantial discounts on children's furniture. They have everything you'll need for infants to teenagers; from cribs and high chairs to bunk beds, traditional-style desks and dressers, and ultra-modern indestructible stuff. Service is a big part of their approach; they offer layaway plans, delivery, and even free consultations on the overall design of your kids' room. They know what they're talking about—they've been at it a good, long time.

Nationwide Warehouse & Storage—115 Allen St., Manhattan; 212/420-8590, 1991 Third Ave. (109th St.), Manhattan; 212/410-0707, 2102 Utica Ave., Flatlands, Brooklyn; 718/253-4200, and 152-65 Rockaway Blvd., Queens; 718/525-8700. If you're looking to furnish a room or an apartment super-quick and super-cheap, this place may be for you. Nationwide sells buyouts from manufacturers around the country. The furniture is brand-new, though not of premium quality materials; it looks nice enough, though, and the price is right. You can get a bedroom set in an ebony black veneer finish for as little as $298.00. This includes a headboard and bedframe, matching mirror and dresser. Three-piece coffee and end table sets may be as low as $89.00; again, these are made from inexpensive wood with a veneer finish. Other bargains here include leather-look vinyl sofas and loveseats from $225.00 and up; student desks from $19.00; dinette tables, with four chairs, from $148.00; recliner chairs from $89.00, and more in their constantly changing stock. They also have inexpensive mattress sets at bargain prices (wouldya believe $48.00 for a twin set?). Everything is out on display; free layaway and immediate delivery are available.

Oriental Porcelain And Furniture Outlet—255 Canal St., Manhattan; 212/941-5632. If the Far East is your taste around the house, you need go no further than (of course) Canal Street. Down a flight of stairs from the street, you come into a narrow store that is filled with tables and

Mr. Cheap's Picks

✔ **Chairs and Stools Etc.**—Buy with the wholesalers—chairs and tabletops for your kitchen and dining room, in a great variety of styles.

✔ **Gothic Cabinet Craft**—Unfinished furniture is a great way to save money, if you don't mind shellacking it yourself. This chain has good prices for every room in the house, with locations all around the city.

✔ **Weissman-Heller Furniture**—A family-owned business with great deals on pieces for the bedroom and living room.

chairs, tea chests, cabinets, and porcelain decorative items. Everything here is sold at discounted prices. A black lacquer cabinet, embellished with mother of pearl designs, was recently seen marked down from $499.00 to $299.00. Sculpted rosewood chairs, originally $299.00, were $199.00; and a six-panel folding screen, again in traditional black lacquer, was reduced from $650.00 to $399.00. There are also decorative pieces, like a floor-size porcelain flower pot, half its original price at $75.00.

Sofa Works—48 West 8th St., Manhattan; 212/473-3023. Looking for an inexpensive alternative for furnishing your living room or bedroom? Consider Sofa Works, a factory-direct showroom with a different kind of sofa. These products are made entirely of high-density polyurethane—that's foam to you and me. These modular pieces can be rearranged in your home to function as a couch, loveseat or bed, simply by the way you fold the base and drape the pad. And there's not a bit of wood, metal, or springs to be found. Both pieces, top and bottom, are made from foam, yet the base is rock-solid and the mattress is definitely comfy. These are covered in your choice of designer fabrics, which can be waterproofed at no extra charge; and the whole thing carries a six-month warranty. There are several configurations, from $199.00 for the simplest sofa bed to $800.00 for a seven-piece "L"-shaped set that's nine feet long on both sides. Delivery is available in all boroughs; and, after that, think how easy they'll always be to move!

Weisman Furniture Liquidators—4930 20th Ave., Borough Park, Brooklyn; 718/258-0202, and 119-17 Atlantic Ave., Richmond Hill, Queens; 718/441-0600. No relation to the estimable Weissman-Heller (see below) this Weisman sells fancy imported living room furniture at significant discounts. An all-leather-Italian sofa and loveseat pair was recently on sale for $1,899.00, and an L-shaped two-piece sectional couch, upholstered in a cotton print was $555.00. Specials also included a variety of sofabeds in twin, full, or queen size, each $369.00. There is a lot more to see here, and it is well worth the trip. Both stores are open seven days a week and offer free delivery to all five boroughs.

Weissman-Heller Furniture—129 Fifth Ave. (19th St.), Manhattan; 212/673-2880. Forty is the only number you need to know at this great store. That's how many years Weissman-Heller has been around. And Larry Weissman sells both residential and commercial furniture and bedding, with big-brand names like Hickory-White, Lane, and Sealy—at about 40 percent below the prices in major department stores. Anyone, whether in business or the general public, can walk in and get the same great deals.

The store does not advertise; word-of-mouth, and lots of regular customers, are what keep the prices so low. A recent sale featured a complete bedroom set in solid oak—a triple dresser, two nighttables, mirror, chest, and queen-size headboard, with a value of $2,100.00—selling for $1,370.00. There are lots of sofabeds, starting from $499.00, with real inner-spring mattresses—none of that cheap, back-aching foam rubber! And good prices on mattress sets by Simmons and Sealy. They'll ship and install anywhere in the tri-state area; personal service is a big plus here.

USED FURNITURE

Be sure to read through the "Flea Markets and Emporia" section for lots of other used furniture ideas!

Calvary/St. George's Furniture Thrift Shop—277 Park Ave. South (21st St.),Manhattan; 212/979-0420. For a thrift store with thrifty prices, Calvary/St. George's has a lot of great furniture in very good condition. Many of these pieces could easily show up in an antique store. Mr. C admired himself in a 1930s art-deco oak mirror and dresser set priced at $295.00. A mohair couch from the same period, for $925.00, would look just right beside it. If these are still out of your price range, there are plenty of smaller and more recent items, like a mahogany end table finished with a leather top, just $50.00, as well as lots of chairs, dining tables, bookcases, and more. To go with these, the store also has great prices on lamps, vases, teapots, and china. They even had a Philco tabletop radio from the 1940s for $135.00—and yes, it still works.

Many items, marked with a red dot, are on further sale for 10 to 30 percent off. Not only that, but the friendly folks are often willing to make you a deal on certain pieces. The store is open Tuesdays through Saturdays from 11:00 a.m. to 5:30 p.m., and until 9:00 p.m. on Thursday evenings.

The Garage Sale—2200 Broadway (78th St.), Manhattan; 212/721-8497. This rambling, cluttered shop looks like more than just its name; it looks like every garage sale you've ever seen all rolled up into one. Used and antique furniture is stacked up to the ceilings, leaving just enough aisle space for you to wind your way through. There is a seemingly endless supply of tables and chairs, dressers, lamps, picture frames, mirrors, and sets of dishes. Oh, and what would a garage sale be without the ever-popular "Bric-a-Brac"? Just what is "Bric-a-Brac," anyway? Whatever it is, there's a lot of it here. Much of the merchandise has seen better days, and given the condition, prices seem a tad high. Individual chairs, for instance, start at $15.00, and range up to $85.00 or more. Sets of chairs begin around $125.00. You may even find a cheap but working TV here. Stuff changes all the time. Open seven days a week until 7:00 p.m.

The Small Furniture Store—363 Lafayette St., Manhattan; 212/475-4396. Yes, it's small, and it's barely a store. Someone set up shop on a busy street corner in the East Village and began refinishing old furniture. He knew that if he built it they would come, and they did. Folks wander in and out of this shack and canvas tent looking at such pieces such as a maple-frame mirror for $35.00, or a four-drawer pine dresser for $165.00, as well as chairs, tables, bookshelves, and whatever else the crew happens to be working on.

Mr. Cheap's Pick

✔ **Calvary/St. George Thrift Shop**—Biggest selection and best condition make used furniture a real option for you at this cozy shop.

There are also some proper antiques priced somewhat higher. The store stays open well into the evening, with flood lights that make it resemble a used car lot more than a furniture shop, but don't be fooled. Squeeze in.

OFFICE FURNITURE (NEW AND USED)

Affordable Used Office Furniture—480 Canal St., Manhattan; 212/274-0500. Wayyyyyyy over at the end of Canal Street, near the Holland Tunnel entrance (don't try to drive to *this* place around rush hour), AUOF is like a used-furniture mega-store. As a contract dealer, they are ready to sell you one chair or a whole office. Their warehouse holds four floors of furniture and accessories, grabbed up from many of the city's biggest and best firms. They try to get the best-quality stuff, such brands as Steelcase, Knoll, Herman Miller, and others.

In the main-floor showroom, Mr. C noticed a handsome oak executive's desk by Kimball, in good shape, selling for $425.00; new, it would list for $1,500.00. There are also some "artsy" designs here. Lots of floor samples are available for 50 percent off their original prices. Conference tables as large as eighteen to twenty feet long are sold at $100.00 per linear foot; and you can get cubicle panels, with built-in electrical outlets, by the foot as well.

In the warehouse there seem to be acres and acres of chairs stacked up, as well as desks, tables, and the rest, ready for quantity sales. Often, these are scratched or are missing parts; the folks here will do their best to match everything up, and they do offer a recovering service at an additional charge. Even so, you can save a lot of money over the original prices. A Steelcase "454" executive's chair, for instance, was seen for $160.00, as is—but the retail price for this popular model was once $900.00. You could fix it up and still get a bargain.

Curtis Discount Office Furniture—35 East 19th St., Manhattan; 212/505-2660. Since 1920, Curtis has been quietly selling all kinds of high-quality office furniture at considerable savings—as much as 50 percent below retail prices. They have a wide range of items in stock, available on the spot—chairs, desks, credenzas, file cabinets, computer stands and much more. One recent sale featured a $699.00 leather executive's chair, marked down to just $299.00. Curtis designs and manufactures its own products; so you're getting factory-direct prices here. The showroom is open seven days a week, including Mondays and Thursdays until 8:00 in the evening.

David's Office Equipment—327 Canal St., Manhattan; 212/966-5418. David sells office furniture from a tiny storefront—in fact, you can't miss him, since his merchandise spills out onto the sidewalk. Most of the stuff he deals in is used, like the drafting tables Mr. C saw for $125.00, or the four-drawer file cabinets for $85.00 and up. He does carry several lines of catalog merchandise, which he can order for you; and, there are the occasional closeout deals, like some unused computer system tables for $99.00. David is there Monday through Saturday from 9:00 a.m. to 6:00 p.m.

Discount Office Furniture—147 West 24th St., Manhattan; 212/691-5625. Although this small but serviceable storefront sells both new and used office furniture, owner Howard Diamond says he moves more of the used goods these days. However, you can find budget-priced new pieces, at about 30 percent below list prices. Mr. C saw an ergonomic steno chair with a retail price of $229.00 selling here for $159.00. Toward the rear of the store are the used items, such as chairs from $25.00 to $75.00 and vertical file cabinets from $25.00 to $125.00. Yes, they may be a bit scuffed here and there, but at these prices, it's such a bargain. One lateral file cabinet was selling for $275.00; it's original list price had been $800.00. And Diamond has a good network around the city—if he doesn't have something you need, he'll locate it for you. Meanwhile, he crams a lot of stock into a tiny store. He's also willing to negotiate prices if you're buying in quantity.

Fileworks—95 Vandam St., Manhattan; 212/989-5687. Charlie Kessler runs a very impressive one-man operation catering to the needs of artists, architects, photographers, and anyone else who needs to furnish an office on the cheap. As he puts it, "You can set up any kind of studio from this one place—overnight!" He scavenges a huge stock of top-quality brands from offices around town and resells them, by his estimate, at about half the price of the city's best *discounters*. He's got Hamilton drafting tables—around $700.00 new—for $175.00. Steelcase file cabinets, originally $400.00, for $70.00. And dozens of those nifty ergonomic office chairs, once $600.00 each, now $125.00. He'll knock that down to $100 if you buy in quantity.

Not to mention flat files, light tables, art supplies, typewriters, and more. Almost all of it is used, and some items need refinishing if you want them to look their best—but at these prices you can afford to redo them and still save a bundle over retail. These are pieces that will last. And if there's something you need that's not here, Charlie will put you on his computerized waiting list and keep a sharp lookout—no charge, and no obligation to buy. He just figures it's good business, and his repeat customers prove it. Hours are flexible, but by appointment only.

Frank Eastern Company—599 Broadway (Houston St.), Manhattan; 212/219-0007. This is a major downtown showroom offering brand names in new office furniture at discount. Save as much as 50 percent off of list prices on chairs for everyone from secretaries to the president. These start as low as $89.95, with further discounts through quantities of three or more. Leather executives' chairs start around $189.00. Frank Eastern also has a wide variety of computer workstations for every application

Mr. Cheap's Picks

✔ **Affordable Used Office Furniture**—A vast warehouse, the place where all offices go to die. You could set up a whole building here, really cheap.

✔ **Fileworks**—A one-man operation with a surprisingly deep selection of used file cabinets, rolling chairs, drafting tables, and more.

✔ **Office Furniture Heaven**—For bargains in new office furniture, look no further. Like a fancy showroom, with great service.

and amount of space. Many of these are made of inexpensive wood with veneer finishes; assembly required. However, you can get a genuine oak executive desk for $499.00—a smart executive decision. And there are filing cabinets aplenty in wood and in steel, from such companies as Oxford and Hamilton. These are all very welll priced, and again, offer quantity discounts. The store is open six days a week, closed on Sundays and open on Thursdays until 7:00 p.m.

Office Furniture Heaven—22 West 19th St., Manhattan; 212/989-8600. You may well believe you've gone to heaven when you enter this store—that is, if you need to furnish any kind of office on a budget. Two big, bright floors with twelve thousand square feet of showroom space are filled with first-quality contemporary pieces, all selling at hundreds of dollars off. The stuff is gorgeous; this looks more like a fancy "regular" full-price store. One recent example seen was an executive's desk made of cherry wood, which originally retailed for $2,300.00; it was on sale here for $775.00. These are manufacturer's closeouts and discontinued items, never used. As soon as they come into the store, they are instantly marked at 50 percent below retail price. Many go down further until they sell.

All the big names are here—Knoll, Bernhardt, Herman Miller, Oxford, and more—in conference tables, chairs, bookcases, file cabinets, and accessories. There are some used items, only if they are in very good condition; wood furniture is completely refurbished. Whatever you see is immediately available, allowing you to furnish a room or an entire office right away. The sales staff is friendly and laid-back; they know, as you will see, that they've got a good thing going.

Staples—1075 Sixth Ave. (40th St.), Manhattan; 212/944-6744, and 205 East 42nd St., Manhattan; 212/697-6049.

See listing under "Stationery, Office and Art Supplies."

HOME FURNISHINGS

A Repeat Performance—156 First Ave. (9th St.), Manhattan; 212/529-0832. This cozy, if cluttered, shop specializes in stylish older pieces in small furniture and home decor at prices way below those at antique stores. Make your way (carefully!) through the narrow aisle and you may pass anything from a brass candelabra to a Hohner accordion. There are plenty of old wooden chairs and tables, too—but the best thing about Repeat Performance is the lamps. If you're looking for something old and unusual to become the conversation piece of your living room, you can find it here. If you need to replace a lampshade, look no further; all of these items range in price from $10.00 to $85.00 or thereabouts. RP also has lots of vintage hats and costume jewelry, along with a few racks of clothing. The folks here are very friendly, as so many East Village shopowners seem to be. Stop in just to chat.

Bernie's Discount Center—821 Sixth Ave. (28th St.), Manhattan; 212/564-8582. See listing under "Appliances."

Broadway Panhandler—520 Broadway (Spring St.), Manhattan; 212/966-3434. For anything and everything to do with the kitchen, Broadway Panhandler will allow you to create delectable works of culinary art on any budget. From the simplest paring knife to entire sets of designer pots and pans, the selection here is immense, and it's all at discount. Stainless steel cookware by All Clad, for example, includes things like a three-quart casserole dish with lid, list price $100.00, here $76.00. A thirteen-inch *paella* pan sells not for $130.00, but for $98.00. Mr. C also saw a five-quart French oven by Le Creuset, in that famous speckled orange finish, reduced from $160.00 to just $102.00.

And the same discounts apply to the world of appliances. A Kitchen Aid 300-watt mixer, with stainless steel bowls and beaters and a retail price of $300.00, sells here for $212.00; a Krups four-cup coffeemaker was marked down from $45.00 to $30.00. You get the idea. It's rare, even in New York, to find such discounted prices in what is essentially a specialty store.

Buddy Gallery—523 Hudson St., Manhattan; 212/929-4251. For something really unusual for your home, check out the Americana at this cluttered shop. You'll think you've stopped at a roadside antique barn somewhere in New England. Buddy Gallery claims to be the nation's largest seller of "recycled" farm and barn windows, which they sell quite inexpensively. Many of these are turned into stylish rustic mirrors, with the wood cross-frames intact. Most sell for $25.00 to $75.00, in a variety of sizes and natural wood finishes. You'll also find chairs, hand-carved wooden ducks, and carnival items. A most interesting store.

Eastside China—5002 Twelfth Ave. (50th St.), Borough Park, Brooklyn; 718/633-8672. In the New Utrecht Avenue area of Brooklyn, a district identical to Manhattan's Lower East Side, is another "east side"—this china shop. Like its downtown counterparts, such as Kaufman Electric (see listing below), Eastside offers discounts of 25 percent and more on hundreds of patterns in china and crystal from Noritake, Wedgewood, Spode, Royal Doulton, Lenox, and many others. They'll spruce up the decor of your home, but the decor in the shop itself is minimal. Some patterns are on display, but if you don't see what you're after, they have all the catalogs and can order just about anything at the same low prices. The store is closed on Saturdays, open on Sundays.

The Elegant John—812 Lexington Ave., (63rd St.), Manhattan; 212/935-5800. It certainly is. But that's not the only room they cover. Along with great prices on bathroom fixtures, towel rods, and mirrors, this East Side boutique has dressers, chairs, trunks, and hampers (in sparkling white wicker) for about 30 percent less than other stores in the area. A five-drawer lingerie dresser was seen here reduced from $289.00 to $239.00. And nowhere else will you find *très elegant* mirrors by French Reflection at 20 percent off. The store also has competitive prices on linens and other accessories.

H. & G. Cohen—306 Grand St., Manhattan; 212/226-0818. For linens, this small but packed store can fulfill all your needs. Like so many places on the Lower East Side, that's all they do—and they've been doing it forever. The walls are stacked floor to ceiling with comforters, blankets, sheets, pillows, and towels; all are guaranteed first quality and are sold from 35 to 50 percent below department store prices. You'll find such brands as Wamsutta, Martex, Stevens, and more.

Cohen's also "creates" comforters and pillows for custom orders, for another great way to save on top quality. Maybe you'd like a comforter made from designer fabrics, or one that's double-filled for extra warmth. These folks can do it all; from polyester to down, they really know their stuff—and stuffing.

Fishs Eddy—889 Broadway (19th St.), Manhattan; 212/420-9020. 551 Hudson St., Manhattan; 212/627-3956. The spelling isn't the only unique thing about these two shops. Fishs Eddy specializes in china, glassware, and food-related accessories that are collected from stores, manufacturers and restaurants around the country. This enables you, merely by going to Greenwich Village, to acquire a coffee mug emblazoned with the logo of "Krispy Kreme Donuts," found somewhere deep in the nation's heartland. Lots of all-American diners are represented here, some of their coffee mugs going for as little as 95¢. Country clubs and snooty restaurants too, though these are more expensive; sugar bowl and creamer sets, ashtrays, beer mugs, and shot glasses in the shape of cowboy boots ($1.95) are just some of the ever-changing repertoire to be discovered here.

Fishs Eddy also sells industrial china by such restaurant mainstays as Fiesta and Fire King. They even offer bridal registry, and will ship orders of $50.00 and up to anywhere in the country. Don't laugh, people do it! Fishs Eddy has raised salvage to an art form, as evidenced by such visitors as Spike Lee and Donna Karan. The Broadway store is the main location; the West Village shop is tiny, so be careful as you walk through. Both are open seven days a week, into the evening.

Harris Levy—278 Grand St., Manhattan; 212/226-3102. Here's another of the Lower East Side's great stores for bargains on all kinds of domestics (except servants, that is). Harris Levy boasts one of the largest selections in the *country*, and does mail-order business far and wide. Even the most expensive of tastes can save money here; many of the fabrics are imported from Europe and the Far East, but sell for 20 to 60 percent off list prices. Thus, a complete set of bed linens from Italy, which would retail uptown for as much as $700.00, are discounted to $500.00 here. Among the names found here are Laura Ashley, Bill Blass, Adrienne Vittadini, and many others.

Of course, with a selection ranging from the fancy to the everyday, there is plenty to choose from at far more reasonable prices too. And the folks at Harris Levy don't stop at the bedroom—there are big savings on kitchen towels and cutesy pot holders, bathroom rugs, shower curtains, laundry hampers, and lots more. The store is spacious and comfortable, with display areas that make it more boutiquey than most in the area; service is relaxed and shopper-friendly.

Jonas Department Store—62 West 14th St., Manhattan; 212/242-8253. Along the parade of junk stores for which 14th Street is famous, you'll find several stores like this one—filled with inexpensive housewares of varying quality. They have lots of domestics, kitchen gadgets and the like. If you need simple stuff for your apartment, these may do: Hand towels for 99¢, tweed-style luggage at $18.99 (half its original price), touch-activated table lamps for $19.99, and more. There are some name brands mixed in, so it's worth a look. You may see a Proctor-Silex two-slice toaster for $13.99, or a cast-iron Dutch oven with a glass top for $19.99.

Downstairs in the basement, Jonas has clothing closeouts, including inexpensive dress-up wear for children—boys' suits from $33.00 to $60.00, and girls' dresses from $22.00 to $40.00. Also, men's and women's shoes for $10.00 to $30.00; and, for some reason, cheap (and cheap-looking) wigs. You can get *anything* cheap in New York, if you know where to look....

Not far away, the **B & G Bargain Store** at 148 West 14th Street (212/929-7607) is another of the area's many similar markets with a good selection of kitchen items. Mr. C found a seven-piece set of stainless-steel pots and pans for $69.99 there, along with lots of small appliances.

Kaufman Electric—365 Grand St., Manhattan; 212/475-8313. For over thirty years this tiny shop on the Lower East Side has been quietly serving up some of the city's best deals on china, silver, and kitchen appliances. You can get fine place settings and stainless steel flatware by some of the world's best manufacturers, including Noritake, Yamazaki, and Mikasa, at just above wholesale prices. With many flatware designs plated in twenty-four-karat gold, you can live like royalty without mortgaging the castle.

Kaufman's also sells small appliances by Sunbeam, Regal, and Farberware, as well as larger items like Frigidaire refrigerators and Hotpoint ranges—again, at substantial discounts. They will also make free deliveries to anywhere in the five boroughs. What could be easier? And you thought the only bargains down here were in clothes.

A few doors down, check out **Eastside Gifts and Dinnerware** at 351 Grand Street (212/982-7200). Here too you will find fine-quality china, flatware, and crystal by such makers as Royal Doulton, Noritake, Wedgewood, and Limoges, at up to 50 percent below retail prices. Remember, all stores in this area close at 2:00 on Friday, and all day Saturday.

Martin Paint—387 Park Ave. South (27th St.), Manhattan; 212/684-8119, 588 Ninth Ave. (42nd St.), Manhattan; 212/ 664-8158, 1489 Third Ave. (84th St.), Manhattan;

Mr. Cheap's Picks

✔ **Broadway Panhandler**—Like a resource center for your kitchen. Cookware, appliances and utensils, all at discount.

✔ **Harris Levy**—Fantastic prices on first-quality designer fashions for your bedroom, kitchen and bathroom—just what you'd expect on the Lower East Side.

✔ **SoHo Mill Outlet**—More bargains on linens, as well as some clothing items, direct from the manufacturers.

✔ **Williams-Sonoma Outlet Center**—Four famous houseware stores in one, selling overstocks and second-quality items at big savings.

212/650-9563, 308 West 125th St., Manhattan; 212/ 864-9712, and 521 West 181st St., Manhattan; 212/928-6645. As the commercials tell us so often, "It Ain't Just Paint." Martin has a wide variety of things for your home—everything from ceiling-fan lamps for $45.00 to vinyl mini-blinds for $2.99 to 4' x 6' oriental rugs for $29.00 (synthetic, of course). They have electric and oil-filled portable heaters as low as $25.00, table lamps in all shapes and styles from just $9.99, and lots of cheap, assemble-it-yourself furniture. A walnut veneer student writing desk is $35.00, and was recently on sale for $19.99. Martin is great for home hardware needs, from lightbulbs and tools to (of course) paint, wall coverings, and tile.

Oriental Porcelain And Furniture Outlet—255 Canal St., Manhattan; 212/941-5632. See listing under "Furniture—New."

Pearl River Mart—277 Canal St., Manhattan; 212/431-4770, and 200 Grand St., Manhattan; 212/966-1010.

See listing under "Discount Department Stores."

The Second Coming—72 Greene St., Manhattan; 212/431-4424. See listing under "Clothing—Used; Vintage Clothing."

SoHo Mill Outlet—490 Broadway (Broome St.), Manhattan; 212/226-8040. What a find this is. If you want to save money on bed linens, towels, tablecloths, and even hosiery—in other words, just about anything woven—you've got to see the SoHo Mill Outlet. They have a big selection, including many name brands, at factory-direct prices. These include both first quality and irregulars. One recent sale offered goose-down comforters for $79.99, in all sizes from twin to king size. Get the sheets, pillows, blankets, and everything else you need for your bed too, while you're at it. The SoHo Mill Outlet is open seven days a week; look for the giant banner overhead, flying from this great old turn-of-the-century industrial building.

Just up a few blocks are some similar, if smaller, linen stores; none is as good as SoHo Mill, but one of the better of these is the **Home Fashion Outlet**, 515 Broadway at Spring Street, where you can find bath towels at two for $10.00 and comforters from $20.00 and up.

Straight From The Crate—342A West 57th St., Manhattan; 212/541-4350. You wouldn't expect to find a great discounter in this area, and you'd be right.

However, these two shops next door to each other do have good prices on furniture, appliances, and decorative items for the home. A 500-watt halogen torch lamp, in a black enamel finish, goes for $59.99; you can also get a regular-bulb version for $35.00. A five-foot-tall Scandinavian white dresser with eight drawers was seen for $140.00. You'll also find things like coffee makers and food processors at decent prices, along with glassware and china and decorative items for the kitchen and bathroom.

In their other store, two doors to the west, you'll find more furniture—like a twin-size futon that folds up into a chair for $159.00. This is a real futon, not one of those foam-rubber cheapies they have at Woolworth's. Mr. C also saw several handsome coffee tables, including one with a round glass top for $69.00.

Williams-Sonoma Outlet Center—231 Tenth Ave. (24th St.), Manhattan; 212/206-8118. On the fringe of Chelsea lies one of the best discoveries in town for every kind of houseware. This, in fact, is the clearance center for several related retail chains: Williams-Sonoma, Pottery Barn, Hold Everything, and Gardener's Eden. Three floors of closeouts cover everything for inside and outside your home.

The main level features china, glass, and cookware. Fiesta teapots in several colors were recently seen for half-price at $6.95. A five-piece Basic White pasta bowl set was $22.99. Individual pieces of fancy French cutlery were marked down from $7.50 to $1.50 each. You'll also find lots of large glossy cookbooks at half-price.

On the second floor, it's things for other rooms in the house. Decorative woven baskets, closet space-savers, flannel sheet sets, and other linen items are all at drastically reduced prices. Most of these, again, are like-new closeouts and leftover stock. Moving up to the top floor, we come to gift items and outdoor furnishings. Bag a canvas-twill backpack for $30.00, half its original price. There are unique items, like a wrought-iron side table with a marble top, also half-price at $140.00. Plus rag-wool rugs, hurricane lamps, picture frames, outdoor mats, and even a variety of brass door numbers.

The stock changes all the time; whenever you stop in, you're sure to find wonderful bargains and delightful treasures. The store is open seven days a week.

Zabar's—2245 Broadway (80th St.), Manhattan; 212/787-2000. Manhattan's mecca of mackerel (and other smoked fish) is, in fact, a vast emporium selling *everything* for the kitchen. Upstairs from the food market is a cluttered bazaar of pots and pans, utensils, appliances and, for some reason, vacuum cleaners. A clean kitchen is a happy kitchen! All of these are at very good prices. Find a ten-piece Calphalon cooking set including an eight-quart stock pot, a ten-inch frying pan and several sauce pans for $260.00. A Chef's Choice diamond-hone knife sharpener, retail price $80.00, was recently on sale here for $44.98, and a deluxe hot tray by Salton was reduced from $100.00 to $60.00. If juice extractors are still all the rage as you read this, you may find one here for as little as $20.00 (If the fad has faded, maybe less!). There are lots of bargains on china, silverware, woven placemats, and serving bowls too. And you thought all Zabar's sold was the food.

JEWELRY AND CRAFTS

See listings in the "Flea Markets and Emporia" section also.

African Art Gallery—305 West Broadway, Manhattan; 212/925-8018. Situated on the outskirts of SoHo near Canal Street, this store imports handcrafted African jewelry that is both inexpensive and beautiful. A pair of drop earrings with wavy green Malachite stones is just $8.00; hammered copper bracelets in a variety of shapes and widths are $10.00. You'll also find beautifully polished decorative shells for $15.00, along with other crafts.

All By Hand—7810 Third Ave. (78th St.), Bay Ridge, Brooklyn; 718/745-8904. This lovely shop specializes in handmade jewelry of all kinds, as well as crafts from candlesticks to pottery to stained glass and more. Each one is a unique piece, created by a virtual gallery of artists. Prices are very reasonable; many items are in the $5.00 to $10.00 range, including lots of little knickknacks, like artsy refrigerator magnets. The store is open seven days a week.

Bargain Jewelry Exchange—510 Fulton St., Brooklyn; 718-875-5895. Part of the Bargain Bazaar along Fulton Street's pedestrian mall (see listing under "Department Stores"), this counter sells lots of stuff from the cheap to the flashy, at near-wholesale prices. Look carefully, and make sure you know what you're getting. Gold-plated earrings go for $5.99 a pair and up, while ten-karat gold anklets start at $11.99. Fourteen-karat chains begin at $59.00, available in any length. They also have lots of inexpensive bronze bracelets, rings and the like.

Fermata Craft Gallery—437 East 9th St., Manhattan; 212/228-6831. Here's a cute little find in the East Village. "Fermata" is a musical term meaning to "hold" a note for a long time; and you'll want to behold the jewelry in this narrow storefront for just as long. Among the eclectic paraphernalia here, you'll find handcrafted bead necklaces priced from $6.00 to $15.00, peace sign earrings of tooled brass for $7.00, and many more items made in styles from all around the world.

Fortunoff—681 Fifth Ave. (51st St.), Manhattan; 212/758-6660. Huh? Have you *lost* it, Mr. C? Fortunoff—the place where Lauren Bacall does the commercials, dahling? Well, sure, "Fortunoff, The Source" (always beware of businesses that put a pretentious "the" in the middle of their names) is mostly expensive. But take a tip from Mr. C—savvy shoppers know that this glitzy store can sometimes yield up a bargain treasure. Don't go for the big items, but check out smaller jewelry like earrings, chains, and bracelets. Often these are very well priced, meant to lure you into the store so you'll buy something else. Meanwhile, you know that they'll match the quality found throughout the store.

Golden Empire Jewelry Center—241 Canal St., Manhattan; various phones. Canal Street is lined with jewelry shops, selling everything from gold chains to diamonds. In many cases (no pun intended), several dealers have joined together into mini-malls at a single storefront. These offer you a chance to compare merchandise and prices from different retailers easily. And since the overhead costs are shared, these businesses can offer some great prices. One of the better malls is Golden Empire, at the corner of Canal and Centre Streets. Inside, Mr. C spoke with some very friendly salespeople at various counters. At Uno Diamond Jewelry, for example, he saw 14-karat gold chains for as little as $15.00 to $20.00, almost half the price of fancier stores. They also have a good selection of diamond rings, most about 30 percent below retail. Always shop around carefully, of course, when it comes to jewelry; make sure you know what you're getting. Check out retail stores first, if you can, so that you'll know how much certain items *should* cost before you buy at one of these malls.

Leekan Designs—93 Mercer St., Manhattan; 212/226-7226.

See listing under "Unusual Gifts."

Max Nass Jewelry—118 East 28th St., Manhattan; 212/679-8154. There may not be too many jewelry shops as distinctive (and affordable) as this one. Perry Shah, who took over from founder Nass, keeps this narrow shop filled with trinkets of every conceivable kind, old and new. He can repair jewelry or make items new again by putting old pieces onto new chains or settings. These stones may be your own, or something from his collection of turquoise, onyx, ivory, coral, and more. Shah also replaces watch batteries, pierces ears—you name it.

There is a large collection of antique jewelry pieces, many of which are genuine gold and silver, at low prices: Silver rings for $6.00, $7.50, $10.00, and up, earrings from $5.00, and 14-karat gold earrings from $30.00. Some have semiprecious stones; some are plain. If they are faded and tarnished, you may have them restored, or kept as is. The options are nearly endless!

Shah also buys up closeouts from department stores, like splashy decorated watches that once sold for $30.00 to $200.00, all sold here for $20.00 each. And, twice a year, everything in the place goes on extra sale: 25 percent off all prices for two weeks in July, and 33 percent off for three weeks in January. And it's fun just to look at the variety of unique items.

Savage Unique Jewelry—59 West 8th St., Manhattan; 212/473-8171, 267 Columbus Ave. (73rd St.), Manhattan; 212/724-4662, and 1007 Madison Ave. (76th St.), Manhattan; 212/794-6463. Not a particularly inexpensive boutique, Savage does have a lot of contemporary jewelry and

Mr. Cheap's Picks

✔ **Max Nass Jewelry**—A wonderfully eclectic shop selling new and used jewelry, which they can refinish for you—or use it to create a new piece.

✔ **Ziggy Originals**—This is not a greeting card shop. Ziggy sells vast amounts of very cheap, very hip jewelry for the downtown crowd.

gifts at reasonable prices. Sterling silver earrings, for example, start around $16.00 and go up from there. But it's such a large selection that there's nearly always lots on sale; and these items can be as much as 50 percent off their regular prices. So have a look if you're in the area—and in the market for baubles made in the shapes of exotic animals, cartoon characters, or multicolored abstracts.

Seashell Boutique—208A Columbus Ave. (69th St.), Manhattan; no phone. Tucked into a narrow indoor space between two buildings, Dorothy Young's store is lined with more jewelry than you can shake an earlobe at. Young's stock ranges from kooky costume jewelry to sterling silver; the prices range accordingly. But there are lots to choose from at the inexpensive end. Semiprecious stone necklaces and pendants start around $12.00, with pins as low as $1.99; there are earrings of carved wood, brightly-painted, for $6.50, and some made from seashells from $4.00. Silver earrings are slightly higher. The store is open seven days a week from noon until 9:00 p.m.

Ziggy Originals—267 Bleecker St., Manhattan; 212/255-2762. Among the many, many stores hawking cheap jewelry in the Village, Ziggy stands out. They make most of their own unique pieces, wholesaling and selling to the public, with literally hundreds of fun, funky designs. It's almost impossible to describe the displays that line the walls, pegboards, and glass cases here: Rings, earrings, necklaces and more. Such a range of colors and shapes—hearts, flowers, hoops, beads....and the prices are low. Many earrings are $6.00, or two for $10.00; large, intricate Peruvian creations of metal and stones are $10.00. Sterling-silver hoops or studs, $3.00 each or two for $5.00. Silver-plated lockets for $12.00. Chokers from $8.00. You really have to see it all; it's a fun stop on the lively Bleecker Street circuit.

LIGHTING

Canal Electric and Lighting—369 Canal St., Manhattan; 212/274-8813. Canal Electric sells all kinds of lighting and supplies; halogen lamps, track lighting, and traditional fixtures. You can find torch lamps (conventional bulbs) from $30.00 and $40.00; and gooseneck desk lamps for as little as $9.00 and up. If you're looking for something bigger, their selection is not the biggest, but it's worth checking out. They are quite good for bulbs, wires, and other minutiae.

A few blocks away, check out **CL Lights** at 317 Canal Street; telephone 212/219-8076. In addition to lamps and track lighting, they specialize in bulbs and hard-to-find parts.

Lamp Warehouse—1073 39th St., Borough Park, Brooklyn; 718/436-2207. Wow. If you're hoping to see the light, you'll probably find it in one of Lamp Warehouse's six big showrooms. What's more, you'll find it for 10 to 50 percent less than at most other stores. LW claims to be New York's biggest; Mr. C wasn't about to start counting, but it's certainly right up there. They've got it all—halogen lamps, track lighting, crystal chandeliers, ceiling fan/lights, wall sconces—and, of course, bulbs for all.

Among the bargains recently spotted were a Strass crystal chandelier, reduced from $6,000.00 to $2,400.00 (also Waterford and Baccarat); halogen track lights, with transformers, reduced from $90.00 to $30.00 each; Casablanca ceiling fans, all 30 to 40 percent off; a Stiffel floor lamp, list price $540.00, on sale for $349.00; and a six-foot halogen torch lamp for $99.00. Some of these are closeouts, of which there are usually many; and some are copies of famous brands that LW makes in its own factory—another great way to save. Repairs and restoration can also be done in the store. Open every day but Wednesday.

Lee's Studio—1755 Broadway (56th St.), Manhattan; 212/581-4400, and 1069 Third Ave. (63rd St.), Manhattan; 212/371-1122. With branches on the East and West Sides of the island, Lee's Studio discounts many famous brands of contemporary and designer lighting. You'll find track and recessed lighting, halogen lamps, and outdoor landscape fixtures by such names as Koch & Lowy, Juno, Halo, Luxo (sounds like the Marx Brothers!), and lots more. Plenty of bulbs, dimmers, and spare parts, too. They offer installation and repair services, as well as rentals, and they're open seven days a week.

Lighting By Gregory—158 Bowery, Manhattan; 212/226-1276. Just off of Delancey Street, LBG is actually three stores in one location; what they call "The Other Store" next door at 160 Bowery (212/966-1965) specializes in traditional styles, while "Lighting by Gregory East" across the street at 171 Bowery (212/941-8277) mixes traditional with contemporary. And that doesn't include their 'burb branches in Scarsdale and Englewood.

Anyway, what goes on in this bustling complex is nothing

Mr. Cheap's Picks

✔ **Lamp Warehouse**—Paris comes to Brooklyn—this store is like an indoor city of lights. Great discounts on everything.

✔ **Lighting by Gregory**—Another hands-down winner, on the Lower East Side. Three separate but related stores on one block offer you wholesale prices on every illumination device known to humankind.

less than the sale of 126 lines of lighting—in stock—at "contractor" prices. LBG is the largest in-stock distributor of Lightolier and Halo in the eastern United States, doing a substantial mail-order business nationally. And if there's a brand you want that they've somehow missed, they can literally get it for you wholesale.

They have Tizio lamps, considered the "grandaddy of halogens," Casablanca ceiling fans, Stiffel and Lenox traditional lamps, and ultra-contemporary designs by Artemide, George Kovacs, Flos, and many more. Stained-glass lamps can be custom-made to order. They even have theatrical stage lighting. For any room in the house, not to mention outside the house, they've got it. The helpful salespeople will consult with you and figure out just what you need. Open seven days a week from 8:30 a.m. to 5:30 p.m.

This neighborhood, meanwhile, is sort of a lighting/home furnishing district. While you're in the area, you may also want to stop in at **Lite Elite**, with locations at 150 Bowery (212/226-3063) and 153 Bowery (212/966-2214); and, further down the street, **Sovereign Lighting** at 138 Bowery (212/966-5644), which also discounts designer lighting. These stores have their work cut out for them, though, next to the big kid on the block—but a comparison shopper is a money-saving buyer.

Tudor Electrical Supply—222 East 46th St., Manhattan; 212/867-7550. Surprisingly enough on the East Side of midtown, Tudor Electric offers good prices—if not rock bottom—on lots of classic and modern lighting fixtures and lamps. The tiny showroom is cluttered, but it displays a good variety of floor lamps, desk lamps, halogen lighting, track lighting, ceiling fixtures, and more. The rear half of the store is given over to bulbs of seemingly every size and shape, as well as other hardware and accessories. Service can be minimal; just finding the salesmen behind stacks of boxes is a good start.

LIQUOR AND BEVERAGES

Buying liquor, inexpensively or not, can always be a tricky business. Most people feel that wine merchants are similar to car dealers; they've all ganged up to make their products so complicated that you cannot help but be at their mercy. Mr. C has often found this to be the case (sorry, no pun intended). No expert oenophile himself, he can only hope to steer you in the direction of reputable shops with good prices. Beyond that, you're on your own.

Astor Wines And Spirits—12 Astor Place, Manhattan; 212/674-7500. Located between NYU and the Cooper Square area of the East Village, Astor Wines and Spirits has a longtime reputation for value. "They put an emphasis on good wines that are not expensive," says Mr. C's professional wine expert. In a neighborhood mainly populated by students and artists, that should not be surprising—and you should go have a look.

B & E Quality Beverage—511 West 23rd St., Manhattan; 212/243-6559. Just off Tenth Avenue, B & E's location looks industrial and foreboding, but this warehouse-style operation is open to the public. They have some of the best prices around on beers from all over the world, mineral water, soda, and fruit juices; yet you can shop here as though it were your corner liquor store or supermarket. A twelve-pack of Michelob goes for just $7.99, and a full case of Molson, in bottles, is $14.99. Heineken cans are $20.99 per case. You can also buy by the keg at great prices.

San Pellegrino mineral water is $1.39 for a twenty-five-ounce bottle; but you can get a case of twelve for $13.95. A six-pack of Coke goes for just $2.29, or $8.99 for a case of twenty-four. They also have mixer-sized bottles of orange, cranberry, and grapefruit juices. Bruce, the B of B & E, is a friendly guy, and he makes sure that his staff is just as friendly and very helpful. If you find this kind of shopping at all intimidating, you're in for a pleasant surprise here.

Brill's Wine And Spirits—150 Chambers St., Manhattan; 212/227-3390. Jerry Tannen runs this good-sized TriBeCa shop with a sharp eye for bargains, and customers with the same desire flock here for them. Tannen believes that there are alternatives to pricey French wines; namely, smaller vineyards that turn out the same quality under less famous names. He carefully evaluates and selects his wines, bringing you a savings of as much as $5.00 per bottle. Of course, no two wines can be exactly the same, but Tannen feels he comes very close. Try it for yourself. He has many good wines to choose from under $10.00, including varieties from Spain and California.

Crossroads—55 West 14th St., Manhattan; 212/924-3060. Many folks swear by this Greenwich Village shop, which is usually crowded with both bottles and buyers. But Crossroads is filled with interesting wines from all over the world, and has lots of good values tucked away on its racks. If you're confident about wines and know what's good (and not so good), you'll be able to find yourself a genuine bargain or two.

Ehrlich Wines And Liquors—222 Amsterdam Ave. (70th St.), Manhattan; 212/877-6090. Just above Lincoln Center, this family-owned store has reasonable prices on wines and other liquor, with a fairly large selection. But it's on wine in particular that you can save here, if you buy in quantity; Ehrlich offers a 10 percent discount on all wines purchased by the case. It's a wholesaler's kind of bargain, available to the general public. Mr. C, of course, always encourages moderation. Make it last!

Garnet Liquor—929 Lexington Ave. (68th St.), Manhattan; 212/772-3211. Near Hunter College, Garnet is a large and bustling shop offering what many shoppers consider the best wine prices in the city. There is a good selection of wines from Italy, France, and Calfornia. The quality of their service can sometimes be as low as the prices, but look at it this way: The discounts are worth the aggravation, and the wine will relax you once you get it home.

Gotham Wines and Liquors—2519 Broadway (95th St.), Manhattan; 212/932-0990. The West Side's discount complement to Garnet, Gotham has been a favorite wine emporium for over fifteen years. Low markup and friendly service also make it a more pleasant experience than Garnet. Good deals found here recently included a 1989 Bordeaux Chateau Margaux for $68.00, as low a price as you'll find in the city. For more everyday wines, they had a 1986 Taltarni cabernet sauvignon for $7.99, and good prices on wines from France, Spain, and Italy. Everything is neatly laid out and well labeled; the staff is very knowledgeable and will be happy to answer any questions about their wines.

Nancy's Wines—313 Columbus Ave. (75th St.), Manhattan; 212/877-4040. A new, year-old entry on the West Side, Nancy's is fast becoming known for good values in wines designed to be matched with certain foods. This approach to wine buying has gotten to be all the rage lately; it's more than a matter of etiquette; it's a real art of matching the tastes of particular wines and foods. It makes a difference, and Nancy's can help you with it—at good prices.

Scotto's Wine Cellar—318 Court St., Cobble Hill, Brooklyn; 718/875-5530. Serving the general area from Brooklyn Heights

Mr. Cheap's Picks

✔ **B & E Quality Beverage**—Good prices on a huge selection of beers and sodas, with real service in a warehouse atmosphere.

✔ **Brill's Wine and Spirits**—A friendly, relaxed downtown shop where lesser-known labels mean better values.

✔ **Garnet and Gotham**—Remember the two G's and you'll never go wrong.

to Park Slope, Scotto's has a good selection of basic wines and liquors. Of course, not all wine cellars are necessarily bargain basements; but Mr. C found the prices here to be quite reasonable, and special sales make for even better deals. Among the recent sale items were Glen Ellen Cabernet Sauvignon for $4.49 a bottle (or $4.00 a bottle for a case of twelve), Korbel Brut champagne for $8.99, and good ol' Sutter Home Zinfandel for $3.99.

On the liquor side of things, a 750 ml bottle of Amaretto di Saronno was $14.99; Emmet's Irish Cream, at $9.99, offered a substantial savings over the better-known Baileys; and Bacardi light rum was just $9.99 for a 750 ml bottle. The shop also offers a delivery service.

Warehouse Wines and Spirits—735 Broadway (Waverly Pl.), Manhattan; 212/982-7770. Just around the corner from Astor Wines and Spirits is this rather spirited competitor—and no doubt, they keep a watchful eye on each other's prices. Who benefits? You, of course. Here, you'll find such bargains as Glenlivet 12 Year single-malt scotch for just $19.99, a liter of Seagram's dry gin for $8.99, and Stolichnaya pepper vodka at $2.99 for a 375 ml bottle. Jose Cuervo Gold tequila in the 750 ml bottle is $10.99, and the same size for Martel V.S. cognac goes for $16.99.

Warehouse also works to take a lot of the guesswork out of wine shopping, listing their "Top Twenty Everyday Whites" and such. These ranged from a 1991 Sutter Home Sauvignon Blanc ($3.99) up to a 1988 chardonnay from a French vineyard called Henri Meurgey ($14.99). They also specialize in little-known wines from Australia, which make even better bargains.

LUGGAGE

A to Z Luggage—26 Broadway (Beaver St.), Manhattan; 212/344-0900, 6 East 23rd St., Manhattan; 212/228-0180, 425 Fifth Ave. (38th St.), Manhattan; 212/686-6905, 1113 Sixth Ave. (42nd St.), Manhattan; 212/768-0097, 708 Third Ave. (44th St.), Manhattan; 212/ 867-5556, 420 Madison Ave. (48th St.), Manhattan; 212/ 688-1944, 1193 Third Ave. (69th St.), Manhattan; 212/ 249-1866, 2468 Broadway (91st St.), Manhattan; 212/ 787-6897, and 4627 New Utrecht Ave. (47th St.), Brooklyn; 718/435-2880. A to Z Luggage is a citywide chain discounting not only luggage but all kinds of travel and home accessories. The stores are big and well stocked with such lines as Samsonite, Perry Ellis, and Diane von Furstenberg. In fact, a recent sale featured Miss Di's Lisbon collection at up to 50 percent off. These floral-print softsiders included a carry-on tote reduced from $125.00 to $75.00 and a twenty-six-inch Pullman, with wheels, marked down from $140.00 to $85.00. A Samsonite "Focus" attache case was recently on sale for $89.99, a savings of $40.00.

The store also discounts leather carry bags and luggage carts as well as address books, closet organizers, CD racks, shaving kits, and even golf and ski accessories. They clearly cater to the person who not only travels but has many important things to do at the other end. Stop in to browse or to grab a catalog.

Altman Luggage—135 Orchard St., Manhattan; 212/254-7275. The Lower East Side's luggage discounter, Altman carries all major brands (no pun intended) at 30 to 50 percent off list prices. American Tourister, Perry Ellis, Le Sportsac, and more. How do they do it? Volume! The aisles are packed (sorry, really...) with suitcases, briefcases, garment bags, overnight totes, army duffels, backpacks—and shoppers. The salespeople are hard to get to sometimes, since the store is so popular; be patient. Another thing to check for clearance markdowns; anything that hasn't sold after a few months is sold at cost, to keep the stock moving. Altman also sells all kinds of supplies for the business person, such as pens by Cross and Parker. They have a toll-free shopping number, 1-800-372-3377. Note the location; Altman is closed Friday afternoon through Saturday, open Sunday.

Ambassador Luggage—371 Madison Ave. (46th St.), Manhattan; 212/972-0965. Unlikely as it seems on the east side of midtown, Ambassador Luggage sells fine brand-name bags at discounts of up to 40 percent below list prices. Of course, as Mr. C often notes, "list price" can sometimes be a fictitious number that no one ever really pays. Nevertheless, with such a substantial discount, you can be sure that the prices are good even with a little padding. Speaking of which, the high-quality names you'll find here include Hartman,

Mr. Cheap's Picks

✔ **Altman Luggage**—Carry your Lower East Side clothing bargains in a travel bag from this place in the same neighborhood.

✔ **Romino Boutique**—Similar bargains and a big selection in an unlikely locale—in midtown, facing the Hudson River. Try it.

Lark, Delsey, and Andiamo. Ambassador also offers free delivery in Manhattan.

Jobson Discounts—666 Lexington Ave. (55th St.), Manhattan; 212/355-6846. Jobson has everything for the traveler who's really on the move. All the famous names are here, such as Andiamo, Halliburton, American Tourister, Lark, Ciao, and many more—all at major discounts from retail prices. They also have a very complete selection of business needs, like portfolios and brief cases, as well as pens by Mont Blanc and Shaeffer. They have a toll-free service (1-800-221-5238), fax line, and immediate delivery.

Lexington Luggage Limited—793 Lexington Ave. (61st St.), Manhattan; 212/223-0698. Across the street and up a few blocks, LLL makes this area something of a luggage district. Like Jobson's, they offer a vast array of suitcases, garment bags, and attaches; plus business accessories like pens, day planners, wallets, and more. The brands, again, include all the big boys, and the store claims it will not be undersold. Take them up on the offer: Compare the two dealers and see how well you can do. Lexington has its own toll-free number, 1-800-822-0404.

Pioneer Novelty—295 Canal St., Manhattan; 212/966-5907. Along with electronics, clothing, and jewelry (and food!), Chinatown seems to have an endless supply of luggage stores, selling every kind of bag, tote, and suitcase. For a wide selection of inexpensive brands, check out Pioneer Novelty. It's more packed than your carry-on after the duty-free store. Merchandise is stacked on the floor, pinned to the walls, hanging from the ceiling. Among the stuff you'll find here are nylon garment bags from $25.00, attache cases for $20.00 and up, and suitcases from $40.00. There can be a bit of a language barrier, so negotiating can be tough, but it's worth a try.

Romino Boutique—588 Twelfth Ave. (44th St.), Manhattan; 212/977-7751. All the way over at the Hudson River, across from the Circle Line and other docks, Romino is a tiny and cluttered shop that clearly caters to tourists—especially international ones. They carry an eclectic array of luggage, designer sunglasses, electronics and other small appliances, all at good discounts. The luggage, by such makers as Samsonite and American Tourister, is sold at 40 to 50 percent off list; there are several other brands at similar savings. Ray-Ban sunglasses start around $40.00, a good $15.00 to $20.00 below boutique prices.

A word of warning: Romino's video equipment, kitchen appliances, and such are geared toward the many foreign residents who come here to stock up on these items—meaning that, anything that plugs in probably runs at the higher voltage used in every country but the USA. So you may not be able to take advantage of everything in the store. Conversely, if you're a traveler yourself and need an electric razor that'll shave in Sri Lanka, this is the place.

The store is closed Saturdays, and open Sundays. Next door, **Triest Export** at 560 Twelfth Avenue (212/246-1548) is another version of the same kind of shop, with more discounts on luggage and electronics.

MUSICAL INSTRUMENTS

J & R Music World—23 Park Row, Manhattan; 212/732-8600.

See listing under "Electronics."

King James Music—2352 Flatbush Ave., Marine Park, Brooklyn; 718/377-8532. Not far from Kings Plaza, King James is one of the city's longtime landmarks in the guitar biz, although they also offer discount prices on a few lines of keyboards, drums, and recording equipment. Student-model guitars start at just $50.00 to $60.00; name brands, like Ibanez and Epiphone, are around $200.00 and up. Other makes of guitars and basses here include Gibson, Fender, Ovation, Rickenbacker, and all the biggies. Amplifiers too, by Peavey, Ampeg, and more. Servicing is done in the shop, under full manufacturers' warranties. Open Mondays through Saturdays from 10:00 a.m. to 6:00 p.m., and until 8:00 p.m. on Mondays and Thursdays.

The Piano Store—158 Ludlow St., Manhattan; 212/674-5555.

What began as a small moving company on St. Mark's Place has grown into a serious reseller of antique and used pianos. This no-frills shop on the Lower East Side can save you a lot of money without necessarily compromising on quality. The outsides may not always look ready for Carnegie Hall, but you can be sure that the insides have been rehabbed with plenty of care and attention. "What would you rather have," asked Ernie, who runs the store, "an old mink or a new rabbit?"

And that's what counts. Used pianos start at $650.00 to $700.00 here, most of which are upright styles. A Gulbransen spinet was recently on sale for $900.00. The prices include free delivery and one free tuning in your home. Although they sell some new pianos, these start around $3,000.00 and carry no guarantee."We've priced them to move," said Ernie.

Royal Music Center—1966 Rockaway Pkwy., Canarsie, Brooklyn; 718/241-3330. For over twenty-five years, Royal Music Center has been offering very competitive prices on a full range of band instruments, keyboards, guitars, and drums. They carry the big brand names, like Peavey amplifiers, Rickenbacker guitars, Selmer woodwinds, Ludwig drums, and much more. And service is a big emphasis here, too. For further bargains, ask whether any used instruments are currently available.

Sam Ash—160 West 48th St., Manhattan; 212/719-2625, 1669 East 13th St., Sheepshead Bay, Brooklyn; 718/645-3886, 113-25 Queens Blvd., Forest Hills, Queens; 718/793-7983.

With its empire based in the heart of the midtown Manhattan music district, just above Times Square, Sam Ash is the undisputed king of musical instruments and related products. Four different storefronts are spread out around the block, selling everything you've ever heard tooted or strummed (and several things you may *not* have heard of). Almost all items are new, sold at discount, though there are occasionally some deals on used instruments. The company is perhaps best known for guitars, most of which sell for 30 to 40 percent below list price; you can get a new Fender Stratocaster for $199.00. But they also sell brass, woodwinds, drums, and all the accessories. You can find a set of D'Addario guitar strings here for $3.75, about half the price of other stores.

Across the street from the guitar shop is their electronics branch, where they have all manner of keyboards and MIDI computers. A Kawai electric piano was recently on sale for $430.00, reduced from $650.00; and a Macintosh "Mac Classic II", complete with keyboard, monitor, and mouse, was on sale for $990.00. This same branch also sells stereo equipment, like a set of JBL oak cabinet speakers, marked down from $360.00 to just $199.00 for the pair. The mega-store continues to expand and rearrange its empire, so the various departments may have played musical chairs since this was written; but the bargains will always make you the winner. Their outposts in the boroughs offer the same vast selection.

Second Hand Guitars—220 West 23rd St., Manhattan; 212/675—4993. Owner Les Leiva runs this small, faded Chelsea shop clearly out of love for the guitar—selling them, trading them, repairing them. It must be love, because even he admits there isn't much profit to be made in the secondhand guitar biz. But he'll poke around and find you a Fender, Gretch or Hondo for as little as $100.00. Maybe a Yamaha twelve-string acoustic for $125.00, or a Gibson "Flying V"—just like the late blues master Albert King's—for $325.00. Leiva sells amplifiers too, in the $100.00-to-$200.00 range, plus strings and any accessories you may need. All sales are final, but the store does offer on-site repair.

United Music—168 West 48th St., Manhattan; 212/575-2286. Next to Sam Ash, this tiny shop is a different kind of bargain option. Along with top-line brands like Yamaha and Casio, they sell lesser-known brands, which tend to be lesser-priced as well. Guitars are the primary instruments here starting for as little as $100.00 and up. They also have keyboards, horns, and drums. If you or your band are working on a really tight budget, this may be worth looking into.

We Buy Guitars—159 West 48th St., Manhattan; 212/869-3985. And so they do. Brashly doing business amidst the Sam Ash empire, WBG offers fine used guitars at low prices. Brands like Hondo and Kramer, which cost $200.00 to $300.00 new, sell here for as low as $100.00. They

Mr. Cheap's Picks

✔ **The Piano Store**—Secondhand pianos, the real wood kind, are lovingly restored and sold here for hundreds of dollars less than new.

✔ **Sam Ash**—For new instruments and related electronics of every kind, Sam Ash is the reigning king, with several storefronts on the same Times Square block. High volume (no pun intended) makes for low prices.

go way up from there, right on up to special items like a Gibson "Birdland" jazz model for $3,500.00. New, the same guitar can sell for almost twice the price. Acoustic guitars, by such makers as Fender, may sell for $175.00, and there are lots of vintage styles from the 1950s and 1960s. Plus a few each of most other stringed instruments: banjos, violins, mandolins, again starting around $100.00.

All instruments carry a one-month warranty, in case you find any rehab need that's been overlooked—though that seems unlikely. When you buy your guitar, the shop will set it up, tune it, and adjust it for you. The spacious workshop has a quietly dedicated feel to it, as opposed to the frenetic atmosphere across the street at Sam Ash. During his visit, Mr. C even spotted G.E. Smith, the band leader from "Saturday Night Live", checking out a few axes.

PETS AND SUPPLIES

PETS

When it comes to buying pets themselves, don't expect to go on the cheap. Owning a pet is a serious, ongoing proposition, and there are constant expenses for food and health care. Still, one way to save some money initially is to adopt a pet rather than to buy one in a pet store. Adoption is not free; there are many up-front fees. But these are usually less than prices at a store, and you also get the satisfaction of giving a home to a pet that really needs one. Here is the best-known example.

American Society For The Prevention Of Cruelty To Animals—424 East 92nd St., Manhattan; 212/876-7700, and 2336 Linden Blvd., East New York, Brooklyn; 718/272-7200. Established in 1866, the ASPCA is America's oldest humane society—and one of the world's biggest. They're known for having the best selection of puppies of any shelter in the city. When you apply for adoption, you'll be scrutinized almost as much as the pets they show you. You may even be turned down. Of course, there's a reason for such a careful process; the ASPCA is dedicated to quality matchups that work out for both pet and owner.

The fees they charge are lower than the prices you'd pay at stores: $55.00 for a dog and $45.00 for a cat (and senior citizens may even be exempt). The animals have had all the required initial shots; follow-up shots may be needed, for an extra charge. But the basic fees include veterinary care at the shelter, should you find your new pet has a health problem that's gone undetected; they also have a "Behavior Help Line" you can call if it's having trouble adjusting to your home. And they offer free neutering and spaying as well. The Society is truly committed to the happiness of both you and your pet.

There are other shelters you may want to check out, for variety of selection and fees. These include the **Bide-A-Wee Home Association**, 410 East 38th St., Manhattan (212/532-4455), and the **Humane Society of New York**, 306 East 59th St., Manhattan (212/752-4840).

PET SUPPLIES

The Beastly Bite—140 Court St., Cobble Hill, Brooklyn; 718/522-5133.

It was a very friendly New Yorker who told Mr. C that he must check out "that pet food store in Cobble Hill." She didn't even remember the name of it, but she said it had the best prices in New York. In spite of its name, the prices at Beastly Bite are indeed remarkably tame. They stock one of the largest varieties of dog and cat food that Mr. C has found, from the ordinary to the gourmet. B.B. of-

Mr. Cheap's Picks

✔ **The Beastly Bite**—The name indicates the offbeat sense of fun at this Brooklyn shop. Low, low prices won't take a bite out of your wallet.

✔ **Petland Discounts**—The buying power of this big chain keeps a leash on the prices of all kinds of basic items.

fers good prices on individual packages, and even better prices by the case. You and your cat will sing over a case of Figaro, forty-eight six-ounce cans for $16.25. You'll also find Science Diet, Pro-Plan, Old Mother Hubbard, Eukanuba, Neura, Max, Mighty Dog, and lots more. Not to mention cat litter, scented clay, cedar chips and all the accessories.

Beastly Bite prints a flyer regularly detailing whatever is new in the store, as well as products whose prices have increased or decreased lately. They also make deliveries for a small charge in the local Brooklyn areas, as well as Lower Manhattan for a slightly higher charge. The store is open seven days a week into the early evening.

Little Creatures—126 St. Mark's Place, Manhattan; 212/473-2857, and 770 Amsterdam Ave. (97th St.), Manhattan; 212/932-8610. Here's a pair of small but well-stocked neighborhood pet supply stores that'll make it easy for you to keep Fido fed. High-volume buying makes it possible for Little Creatures to keep prices low on a good selection of dog and cat foods—in such quality brands as Iams, Cornucopia and Science Diet. If you like to buy in volume yourself, you can do very well; a recent example seen was Lick Your Chops cat food, a case of twenty-four tins, for just $17.79. They also have a good variety of accessories, from dog leashes to cat condos. The stores are open into the early evening seven days a week, and they even offer free delivery.

Pet Deli—340 East 92nd St., Manhattan; 212/831-8645.

This tiny neighborhood shop is just the thing for basics, mainly for dogs and cats. Even with its Upper East Side location, the store discounts prices on a good range of foods and accessories. They don't have absolutely everything, but they stock as many major brands as they can fit on the shelves. Get a good price on Eukanuba dry dog food, just $10.30 for an eight-pound bag. Iams dog biscuits are $2.29 for a one-pound bag; and a four-pounder of Iams cat food is $6.95. And a recent special offered C-9 cat litter at just $1.77 for an eight-pound sack. Pet Deli has thick nylon dog leashes for $9.95; good prices on Science Diet cans, too. According to Mr. C's animals expert, all these prices are reined in quite obediently. The store is quiet and the folks behind the counter are friendly and helpful. They're open until 7:00 on weeknights, for those of you rushing home from work to a hungry critter. Delivery is also available.

Pet Shed—209 West 96th St., 2nd Floor, Manhattan; 212/663-4265. Pet Shed is in a large Upper West Side complex (which also includes a store called Plant Shed; see that listing in the "Plants" section). They not only cater to dogs and cats but specialize in fish, birds, and small reptiles. A recent sale offered iguanas, regularly $60.00, reduced to $20.00. Just the thing for a small Manhattan apartment.

Back to more conventional pets. The store has good deals on aquarium starter sets and tropical fish, parakeets, and cages, and food for all. Get an eight-pound bag of Iams dog food for $8.99, or a five-ounce tin of Science Diet cat food for 79¢. The staff is pleasant and ready to help you with any advice you may need; Pet Shed is open seven days a week until 8:00 p.m., except Sundays until 6:00 p.m.

Petland Discounts—132 Nassau St., Manhattan; 212/964-1621, 7 East 14th St., Manhattan; 212/675-6102, 404 Third Ave., (29th St.) Manhattan; 212/447-0739, 304 East 86th St., Manhattan; 212/472-1655, 2675 Broadway (102nd St.) Manhattan; 212/222-8851, and many locations in the outer boroughs.

Petland is a huge chain whose volume sales allow them to keep prices very low. An eight-pound bag of Eukanuba dog food goes for $9.99—perhaps the lowest Mr. C has seen in the city. A four-pound bag of Iams cat food is $6.79. And they have plenty of snack treats, rawhide bones and accessories for dogs and cats. They also have full lines of aquariums and fish, birds and cages, and other things for small animals.

Sweetie Pie—722 Second Ave. (39th St.), Manhattan; 212/986-4407. In the Murray Hill area, you can care for your sweetie pie at this small neighborhood shop. In spite of its miniature poodle size, the store is well stocked from floor to ceiling with all the basics. Dog and cat food from Iams, Science Diet, Friskies, and many others are very reasonably priced. You'll also find the occasional in-store special, like a two-gallon container of Ever-Clean cat litter for $13.99. Talk about cleaning up!

PLANTS AND FLOWERS

La Vie En Rose—82 Christopher St., Manhattan; 212/366-4010. Owner Isabelle Nataf runs this delightful Greenwich Village store with an eye on service as well as good prices. It's open seven days a week, with bouquets of roses from just $6.00 a dozen for short (ten-inch) stems. Longer stems range up to $16.99 for thirty-inch stems. These come in all kinds of colors—at least half a dozen shades of pink alone—including two-tone varieties. And just $30.00 will send a box of these long-stemmed beauties to just about any Manhattan address; for $35.00, they can be shipped anywhere in the country overnight.

La Vie en Rose also specializes in floral displays, artfully designed to suit any decorative need. They have a scrapbook filled with snapshots of previous creations, starting at $50.00 for tabletop bouquets to around $150.00 for floor-standing displays. These can cost up to $200.00 at many other florists around town.

Park Plants—774-776 Sixth Ave. (26th St.), Manhattan; 212/696-9222. The neighborhood between Sixth and Seventh Avenues, from about 25th to 28th Streets, is the city's Flower District; unfortunately, most are wholesalers who do not sell to the general public. There are a few, though—especially in these tough times—who'll sell to just about anyone. After all, they have huge amounts of plants and flowers, and they have to keep things moving. Danny at Park Plants is a nice fellow who keeps a vast store filled with ficus trees, palms, cacti and lots of other lush, tropical plants. Walking around in here is like exploring the Brazilian rainforest; everything is big, green and healthy, climbing up toward the suitably high ceilings.

A four-foot tall ficus tree is just $15.00; the six-foot ones are $45.00, and ten-footers are $75.00. If you're buying in any quantity, you'll get a further discount. Park also has a large selection of baskets and clay pots at wholesale prices. Some plants come with special, self-watering pots that can last up to five months with a single filling. Rentals and delivery are available; the store is open seven days a week.

Another great place to look is **International Garden**, 807 Sixth Avenue (212/929-9418), which specializes in silk, dried, and fresh flowers. A dozen long-stemmed roses are $24.00, boxed, about half the price of "presentation-style" roses elsewhere around town. They have similar savings on carnations and other cut flowers. More unusual are their gardenia plants, selling for just $15.00 to $25.00 each. Plants of this size could cost as much as $50.00 uptown. International also does citywide deliveries.

There are only a few other stores in the district that sell to the public. **Bill's Flower Market**, 816 Sixth Avenue (212/889-8154) also sells real and silk plants at near-wholesale prices. Look for Bill's sidewalk sale items, like silk azaleas reduced from $24.00 to $5.99. Further down the street, **Stanley Saul Associates** at 777 Sixth Avenue (212/243-8555) has good deals on tall plants and trees as well as hanging plants, like a nice, big philodendron for $12.00.

Plant Shed—209 West 96th St., Manhattan; 212/662-4400.

Just a few steps east of Broadway, this Upper West Side shop is more than a shed; they call themselves "your house plant supermarket," and that seems more appropriate. Wandering up and down the lush green aisles, you'll find anything from cute little cacti, $2.99 each, to a big, strapping, yucca plant in a ten-inch pot for $14.99. Leafy, green scheflera plants for $9.99 will add a healthy look to your apartment; same price for pretty cyclamens, with bright pink and red blossoms, in a woven basket planter. The store is open daily from 9:00 a.m. to 8:00 p.m., and Sundays from 10:00 a.m. to 6 p.m.

Princess Flowers—142 Chambers St., Manhattan; 212/587-3130. The woman who runs this lovely little shop has good prices, like roses for $11.95 a dozen, or twenty-five carnations for $5.99. But since this is the Financial District, which gets pretty quiet on the weekends, you can find yourself a super bargain on Fridays after about 3:00 and all day on Saturdays. Then her prices come down to $9.95 for that dozen roses, along with such other specials as ten gladiolas for $2.00. If you're in SoHo, TriBeCa or Battery Park City, or if you're just passing through the neighborhood, take a look—you can save some real money.

Rosa Rosa—831-A Lexington Ave. (63rd St.), Manhattan; 212/935-4706, and 140 West 72nd St., Manhattan; 212/769-3900.

Guess what they specialize in here? These popular stores have bouquets of roses starting as low as $6.00 per dozen. That price is for short stems, ten to fourteen inches in length. Medium, long, and extra-long stems increase by about four inches with each size. Yet each is only a dollar more, making extra long-stemmed roses just $9.00 a dozen. Unlike the flowers sold at every corner grocery, these can be wrapped or boxed; and the store also delivers. The roses come in a wide variety of colors, and in spite of the name, there are other kinds of flowers here as well.

Roses Only—1040 Sixth Ave. (39th St.), Manhattan; 212/869-7673, 803 Lexington Ave. (62nd St.), Manhattan; 212/751-7673, and 142 East 86th St., Manhattan; 212/360-7673. She's only what? Seriously folks, they specialize in just one thing here, and thus they can do it cheaply. A bouquet of roses starts at just $7.00

Mr. Cheap's Picks

✔ **La Vie en Rose**—Mr. Cheap picks his flowers here, for the most variety at budget prices. Excellent service, too.

✔ **Park Plants**—For potted plants, right on up to full-size indoor trees, thrash your way through the jungle at this Flower District shop—one of the few wholesalers who sells to the public as well.

a dozen for flowers with twelve-inch stems. The menu ranges up to $18.00 for extra-long, thirty-two-inch stems. The quality, meanwhile, is better than what you might expect at these prices. Oh, and don't ask them for anything else—it really is "roses only."

Rose Valley—140 Montague St., Brooklyn Heights, Brooklyn; 718/625-7673. Half a flight down from the sidewalk along this pleasant row of shops, Rose Valley specializes in bouquets of roses fresh from the farm. These start at just $6.00 for a dozen roses with short twelve-inch stems. The prices range slightly upward through five more sizes; $9.00 for twenty-inch stems on up to a top price of $15.00 for thirty-two-inch stems. These are fine-quality flowers at prices that are only slightly higher than at your corner grocery. The shop is clean and attractive, with a relaxed atmosphere and careful personal attention.

RUGS AND CARPETS

Carpet Factory Outlet—1492 First Ave. (79th St.), Manhattan; 212/988-5326. Don't be fooled! The terms used to indicate discount stores around town are sometimes used very loosely. Carpet Factory Outlet *sounds* great; however, it's not really a factory-direct outlet at all. But they do have a substantial selection for a tiny storefront, with some good prices. A bound 9' x 12' remnant in grey wool was seen here recently for $259.00; a nylon remnant, same size, for $198.00. And again, the same size in a tight-weave industrial/office remnant was just $98.00. They also have some orientals, including runners as well as tile and linoleum by the foot. Service is minimal, but if this is your neighborhood, stop in for a look.

Kalfaian & Son—475 Atlantic Ave., Brooklyn; 718/875-2222. Here's a great American story. This huge operation began around the turn of the century as a rug cleaning service in a backyard. It's now one of New York's largest dealers of rugs and carpeting, yet it's still in the same family. Current owners George and Edwin Kalfaian keep that family atmosphere going today, offering great prices *and* full service.

The store has recently expanded to three floors of orientals, residential and commercial broadloom, and remnants. The warehouse building is nevertheless bright and comfortable inside. On the main floor, you'll find all-wool berber rugs at up to half the cost of many other stores; a 12' x 19' rug, list price $920.00, sells here for $459.00. Wool blends and synthetics are much lower still, as little as $14.00 per square yard—including padding and installation. They also have such new innovations as "Kangaback" carpeting, which has the padding sewn in underneath; Mr. C saw a 12' x 9' rug for $99.00.

Tightly woven commercial broadloom, suitable for offices, starts around $12.00 a square yard installed; remnants are as low as $8.00 to $10.00 a yard. Upstairs showrooms include the orientals and country-style rugs, also well-priced. They even have oriental runners: a 2' x 8' size will make your hallway dazzling for just $49.00.

Every item is clearly marked. Kalfaian claims to be the first major store in New York, way back when, to display each piece, tagged with the size, style and price. The name brands show that these guys have nothing to hide; personal attention is their watchword here. The store is open seven days a week, from 10:00 a.m. to 5:00 p.m.

Redi-Cut Carpets—208 East 23rd St., Manhattan; 212/685-3626. You probably remember the old TV commercials for this chain: "It's like having an uncle in the carpet business!" Well, Uncle sold the business, and Redi-Cuts are now run independently. This East Side branch is one of the best carpeting stores in Manhattan. Joan Stanger and her son David have been running it as their own family business,

Mr. Cheap's Picks

✔ **Kalfaian and Son**—A family tree grows in downtown Brooklyn. Three floors of savings should mean something great for *your* floors.

✔ **Redi-Cut Carpet**—Two unrelated descendants of this one-time chain still offer great service and prices.

with an accent on personal service that you won't always find at stores large or small (and Mr. C has seen a lot of them).

This Redi-Cut is quite big, having just moved into new, larger quarters from a shop that was already substantial. The overall prices tend to be a bit lower here than the sales at many larger stores, with an equal emphasis on natural fibers and synthetics. Top-quality remnants, which would be as high as $30.00 to$40.00 per square yard in other stores, are $20.00 per yard here. In a recent sale, a 12' x 10' nylon remnant was further reduced from $420.00 to $259.00. Mr. C also saw a 5' x 8' all-wool Oriental for $499.00, and an 8' x 11' colonial-style rug for $239.00.

The store also has accessories, like decorative baskets and pillows, to spruce up your place even more. Installations can be done within two or three days, and they do offices too. Redi-Cut is open seven days a week.

Redi-Cut Carpets—1903 Bruckner Blvd., Bronx; 718/409-6300. Here's another of the Redi-Cut offspring, which also recently moved; they've left the pricy Upper East Side for a high-visibility location just off the Bruckner Expressway (take the White Plains Road exit). This means lower rent and more space, both of which help the customer when it comes to price and selection. They buy in bulk, passing discounts on to you by keeping a lot of stock on hand; a broadloom that retails for $25.00 a square yard may only cost you $18.00 per yard if it's in stock and ready to go. To keep things moving, the sales staff will inform you of these kinds of deals whenever possible.

Remnants offer even better bargains. Many of these are on huge rolls, which can be cut to your order like any broadloom. Mr. C saw a nylon "Khaddar" style by Masland, with stain-release protection; list price was $61.00 a square yard, but RC had it for $25.00. Genuine orientals are well priced at $500.00 and up; or, if you don't mind the difference, they have American machine-made versions for as little as $99.00. Even at these warehouse prices, installation is available within forty-eight hours.

The Rug Warehouse—220 West 80th St., 2nd Floor, Manhattan; 212/787-6665. Just around the corner from Broadway on the Upper West Side, The Rug Warehouse is one of Manhattan's largest dealers of area rugs with over a thousand on display. Unlike many stores, which run special sales, Rug Warehouse calls itself a "year-round discounter," keeping prices as low as possible on orientals, Persians, Dhurries, hook rugs, and contemporary designs. These are all about 20 percent to 25 percent below prices in many other stores. They do run an annual three-week anniversary sale, though, when prices are reduced by a further 10 percent to 15 percent. All-wool rugs start as low as $199.00, with a wide range of 8' x 11' and 9' x 12' rugs from $500.00 to $800.00.

Rug Warehouse has a few other ways to save money. They sell used rugs—mainly Persians—as well as copies of expensive hand-made rugs. Every rug is clearly labeled with its price, age, and country of origin, making it easy for you to browse without heavy pressure from salespeople. They even offer a seven-day return policy—clearly a reputable operation, as nearly fifteen years' worth of city and out-of-state customers will attest. The store is open daily; delivery is available.

SEWING AND FABRICS

First Avenue Fabrics—180 First Ave. (11th St.), Manhattan; 212/353-1355. Many people know about the yards and yards of fabric stores in and around the Garment District; fewer probably are aware that there is a similar, if smaller, gathering of stores down in the East Village. First Avenue Fabrics is just one of these, offering materials of all kinds at discount prices. Cottons, wools, velvet, spandex, and lots of exotic weaves are on display here. You'll also find a good selection of low-priced remnants, such as rayon pieces from just $1.99 a yard.

Another good place to check out in the neighborhood is **Pari's Fabric Mart**, 166 First Avenue at 10th Street (212/473-6506). In addition to the fabrics just mentioned, you'll find unusual tapestries, brocades, and even furs—real *and* fake. Both of these shops are open seven days a week.

Harry Zarin Company—292 Grand St., Manhattan; 212/925-6112. This may be the best place for discount fabrics in town. For over fifty years Zarin has been one of *the* wholesale sources for upholsterers; about a dozen years ago they decided to sell to the public as well, so now you can benefit from their vast selection and buying power. The main storefront, on Grand Street, offers complete upholstery services; but you don't have to use them to shop in the upstairs warehouse, around the corner at 72 Allen Street (telephone 212/226-3492).

Upstairs you'll find an incredible universe of fabrics, all first-quality current designs, most at about one-third the price you'd pay for the same materials at retail upholstery shops. Not only that, but everything is right there; no need to place an order from a book and wait a month. The stock moves quickly, new patterns are coming in all the time—and you can buy any amount, large or small. One of the best values is Zarin's collection of woven tapestries in ornate patterns. While these can cost up to $100.00 a square yard elsewhere, here they go for just $25.00 to $35.00 a yard for the very same fabric.

Occasionally you'll also find some closeouts and overruns, reduced even further. And there's another location across the street selling all the accessories—rods and other trimmings—to create your own draperies, slipcovers, bedspreads, etc., if you wish. The main store is open six days a week, but the warehouse (unlike everything else on the Lower East Side) is open every single day from 9:00 a.m. to 5:30 p.m.

M & J Trimming—1008 Sixth Ave. (38th St.), Manhattan; 212/391-9072. Right across the street from the Yarn Center (see listing below), there are several trimming stores catering to your every need in sewing accessories. M & J is one of the biggies, with wall displays stretching literally from floor to ceiling. Hundreds of designs are on view—lace trim, embroidered

Mr. Cheap's Pick

✔ **Harry Zarin Company**—Without doubt, they've got the fabric section all sewn up. Their warehouse is like a city within a city, at one-third the price of retail upholsterers.

trim, gold and silver trim, buttons, threads, and just about any other kind of bauble, bangle or bead you could possibly want. The prices are very good, and the folks here will help you find that *one* particular style you're looking for. Talk about finding a (sewing) needle in a haystack....

Paron Fabrics—239 West 39th St., Manhattan; 212/768-3266, and 60 West 57th St., Manhattan; 212/247-6451. Actually three stores, Paron's main branch is the 57th Street location. They sell a good variety of linens, wools, imported silk and other clothing fabrics, wholesale and retail. While their prices are good, you should also check out their clearance center a couple of doors down at 56 West 57th Street, on the second floor. Here, everything is reduced to 50 percent of its original retail price, and you can still find some nice stuff. Finally, there is a third shop in the fabric area of the garment district, just below the Port Authority.

While you're in that neighborhood, some other places to prowl include **Art Max Fabrics**, 250 West 40th Street (212/398-0755), for designer patterns; **B & J Fabrics**, 263 West 40th Street (212/354-8150), with three floors of European silks, suedes and lace; **Felsen Fabrics**, 264 West 40th Street (212/398-9010), specializing in bridal work; and **Rosen & Chadick**, 246 West 40th St. (212/869-0136), which has interesting designer fabrics for evening wear.

Silk Surplus—235 East 58th St., Manhattan; 212/753-6511, and 1147 Madison Ave. (84th St.), Manhattan; 212/794-9373. Silk Surplus has more than just silk, and at less than retail prices. In addition to bargains on imported silk fabrics, you'll find cottons and wools as well as linen wallpapers, draperies, and other home decor fabrics and trimmings. The selection is very good, and the prices are well worth checking out.

Somewhat near the midtown branch, **Poli Fabrics** at 132 West 57th Street (212/245-7589) has discounts on velvets, silks and brocades from European designers. Be sure to check it out.

Yarn Center—1011 Sixth Ave. (38th St.), Manhattan; 212/719-5648. The name says it all. Yarn Center has everything for all your knitting needs. They have a big selection of wools, and acrylics, including English mohair, textured Italian wools and many others. Large skeins of 100 percent wool start around $5.99; and you'll always find something on sale, like soft, fluffy Icelandic wool reduced to $3.99. There are also several "final sale" bins, where you can find a good selection for as low as $2.99. Of course, Yarn Center has needles, tools, patterns, and all the rest.

SHOES AND SNEAKERS

Ananias Leather—197 Bleecker St., Manhattan; 212/254-9540, 367 West Broadway, Manhattan; 212/274-9229, and A & S Plaza, Sixth Ave. (33rd St.), Fifth floor, Manhattan; 212/947-4814. For all sorts of leather accessories, Ananias is a great place to check out. "We only look expensive," say their ads, and they're right. These three small shops—in Greenwich Village, SoHo, and Herald Square—import brand-new natural leather goods directly from the Greek Isles. Sturdy-looking sandals, for men and women, range in price from $20.00 to $35.00; end of the summer is a particularly good time to buy, when remaining stocks are sold at 35 percent off regular prices. Ananias also sells knapsacks for about $15.00 to $20.00 less than many other stores: In brushed suede for $60.00, leather from $110.00 to $135.00.

Most items are sold untreated, in a light brown color, and will age naturally into a deeper brown. The salespeople can show you examples of "before and after."

Benedetti Custom Shoes—225 West 34th St., Manhattan; 212/594-6033, and 530 Seventh Ave. (38th St.), Manhattan; 212/719-5075. With two small stores in the Garment District, Benedetti specializes in men's dress shoes. They discount such brands as Dexter, Adolfo, Bostonian, Nunn-Bush, and others. Save about $15.00 to $20.00 on Rockport casual shoes and $40.00 to $70.00 on tassled loafers from Bally. They also have some athletic shoes, like Reeboks at about $10.00 to $20.00 below retail.

Bentley's Shoes—144 Montague St., Brooklyn Heights; 718/330-0275. Along the chic stretch of Montague Street, not far from the Promenade, Bentley's is one of those places that makes everyone say how good Brooklyn is for bargains. It's a tiny, no-frills shop, selling women's shoes at big discounts. Names like Anne Klein or Joan & David may go for as little as $19.00 to $39.00 a pair; Mr. C also saw leather shoe-boots, in a mock lizard-skin look, reduced from $75.00 to $50.00. It was hard to get near 'em. As a further incentive for quick bargains, the store offers a 10 percent overall discount on your purchase if you pay in cash. Hooray for those who don't worship the almighty plastic!

Broadway Sneakers—323 Canal St., Manhattan; 212/966-1125, 430 Broadway (Howard St.), Manhattan; 212/334-9488, 25 West 45th St., Manhattan; 212/944-9844, and 1351 Forest Ave., Staten Island; 718/876-7978. This lively store has only been around for about ten years, but it has carved out a good name for itself for prices and service. The guys who run it are young, personable, and know their stuff where athletics are concerned. The store carries a wide range of shoes for various sports, most at $10.00 to $15.00 below department store prices. Beyond that, there are always lots of closeout sales, where you can get a pair of Asics Gel running shoes, say, for $30.00—about half of their original price. Reebok "Pump" basketball shoes sell about $10.00 below list, at $85.00. There are also lots of children's sneakers, such as Nikes from $35.00. And the store sells hiking shoes from $45.00, rollerblades from $90.00, and other running wear, from socks to windbreakers, at modest discounts.

Cipriano Shoes—148 Orchard St., Manhattan; 212/477-5858. Cipriano's specializes in casual shoes, sneakers, and work shoes. They have men's and women's styles with brands like Dexter, Rockport, Nike, L.A. Gear, and Timberland. Most of these are priced at about 20 percent below retail, and sometimes more. The place is small but they have a good selection, and the folks are very friendly. It's a good stop on the Orchard Street discount mile.

Cooper's Shoe Outlet—5 East 33rd St., Manhattan; 212/686-0751. This tiny shop sells a pretty good selection of all-leather women's shoes at a single price of $20.90. At this price you're obviously not dealing with top brands, but there are a couple of recognizable names in the bunch. Gloria Vanderbilt suede pumps were seen there, for instance, in a variety of bold colors. Otherwise, poke around; you may find some good shoes for casual use. They have boots, too, including the styles that go all the way up to the knees. Everything is shelved in boxes, and you can serve yourself.

Fishkin Knitwear—314 Grand St., Manhattan; 212/226-6538. See listing under "New Clothing: Men's and Women's General Wear."

Frankel's Discount Store—3924 Third Ave. (39th St.), Sunset Park, Brooklyn; 718/768-9788.For discount prices on the ever-popular Doc Martens, Timberland hiking boots, Nike running shoes, and more, check out this Brooklyn institution located in the shadow of the BQE. Frankel's offers discounts of 25 percent

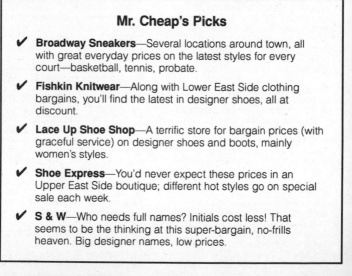

Mr. Cheap's Picks

- ✔ **Broadway Sneakers**—Several locations around town, all with great everyday prices on the latest styles for every court—basketball, tennis, probate.
- ✔ **Fishkin Knitwear**—Along with Lower East Side clothing bargains, you'll find the latest in designer shoes, all at discount.
- ✔ **Lace Up Shoe Shop**—A terrific store for bargain prices (with graceful service) on designer shoes and boots, mainly women's styles.
- ✔ **Shoe Express**—You'd never expect these prices in an Upper East Side boutique; different hot styles go on special sale each week.
- ✔ **S & W**—Who needs full names? Initials cost less! That seems to be the thinking at this super-bargain, no-frills heaven. Big designer names, low prices.

and up on closeouts and surplus of these very desirable brands. Cowboy boots by Justin, Dan Post, and Frye can be found here; also jogging suits, designer sunglasses, and all the other accoutrements. Closed Sundays and Mondays.

Moe Ginsburg—162 Fifth Ave. (21st St.), Manhattan; 212/242-3482. See listing under "Clothing—New: Men's and Women's General Wear."

Lace Up Shoe Shop—110 Orchard St., Manhattan; 212/475-8040. Ladies, if you like fancy shoes, get thee to this wonderful shop on the corner of Orchard and Delancey. You'll save lots of money on designer labels, with all the service and selection of an uptown store. Two floors of display areas cover just about anything from classy to casual, all at good discounts. Mr. C saw such shoes as Joan & David dress flats, retail price $320.00, here just $200.00. Colored suede loafers by Evan Picone were reduced from $110.00 to $87.00; and lizard-skin western boots by Dan Post were marked down from $380.00 to $230.00, in a variety of colors.

There are some shoes for men also, such as the entire Mephisto line of casual styles; these are not able to be discounted, but Lace Up will at least kick in the sales tax for you. The store is open Sunday through Friday, 9:30 a.m. to 5:30 p.m. Get on their mailing list to find out the latest sales; with shipping available all over the United States, Lace Up has made an industry of shoe bargains.

Leslie's Bootery—319 Grand St., Manhattan; 212/431-9196. Leslie's Bootery is another one of those great shops you've heard about on the Lower East Side. They offer a wide range of men's and women's shoes mostly around 20 percent below list prices. These include such designers as Cole-Haan, 9 West, Liz Claiborne, Clark's, Birkenstock, and many others. Mr. C was asked not to divulge the prices, in order to respect the store's relationships with these dealers—but trust him, they're good. The service here is just as good. The store is closed on Saturdays, but is open every other day, including Thursdays until 7.

Manhattan Sports—740 Seventh Ave. (49th St.), Manhattan; 212/664-1360, 2188 Broadway (78th St.), Manhattan; 212/580-4753, 151 East 86th St., Manhattan; 212/876-3200, and 2878 Broadway (112th St.), Manhattan; 212/932-0514. These small but well-stocked stores specialize in all kinds of athletic shoes. Prices are generally about 15 percent below retail, and they claim that they will beat the prices of many other similar stores. The best deals can be found on their closeout racks, where shoes by Avia, Prince, and Reebok go for $29.99 to $39.99. Further clearance sales reduce prices by 30 to 50 percent—and Mr. C noticed shoes by Reebok, Nike, and New Balance on these racks. Service is friendly and very helpful. The stores are open evenings.

Manufacturer's Shoe Outlet—537 Broadway (Prince St.), Manhattan; 212/966-4070. New York City is always full of little surprises. Like shoe bargains in snooty SoHo. For no-frills shopping, this store is hard to beat—nothing but racks and racks of shoes all out on display. Just find the aisle for your size, and start poking around for something to try on. There's lots of junk mixed in, and no doubt many irregulars and seconds; but there are some recognizable brands for men, women, and kids. A pair of men's Nunn-Bush dress loafers for half-price at $30.00, and women's short heels by Capezio marked down to $10.00, were among the deals seen here. Plus Jordache, John Weitz, and even Pappagallo. Give 'em a try.

Modell's Sporting Goods—200 Broadway (Fulton St.), Manhattan; 212/964-4007, 280 Broadway (Chambers St.), Manhattan; 212/267-2882, A&S Plaza, Sixth Ave. (33rd St.), Manhattan; 212/594-1830, 109 East 42nd St., Manhattan; 212/661-5966, 243 West 42nd St., Manhattan; 212/575-8111, 39-12 Main St., Flushing, Queens; 718/539-6100, 163-40 Jamaica Ave., Jamaica, Queens; 718/297-4402, 30-88 Steinway St., Astoria, Queens; 718/956-4526, Starrbrook Plaza, 1000 Penn Ave., New Lots, Brooklyn;718/345-9300, 360 Fulton St., Brooklyn; 718/855-1921, 31 East Fordham Rd., Bronx; 212/295-7800, 2929 Third Ave., Bronx; 212/993-1844, and 1801-B South Ave., West Shore Plaza, Staten Island; 718/698-8900. See listing under "Sporting Goods."

Moshell's—87 Nassau St., Manhattan; 212/349-6630. This long, narrow store along Nassau Street's pedestrian mall features a mix of shoes, handbags, and gold jewelry, all at discount prices. Shoes are the main deal; you'll find brands like 9West's Spa Collection, Zodiac, and Nickels. These tend to be in dressy contemporary styles. Texas Brand lizard-skin boots, in several popular colors, were recently seen for $79.00 a pair. There are sales clerks to assist you in finding the right size. Moshell's has another store across the street, at 80 Nassau, selling gifty trinkets and more inexpensive jewelry.

Natali's Shoes—30 Third Ave.(9th St.), Manhattan; 212/979-5816, and 460 Seventh Ave. (35th St.), Manhattan; 212/629-6044. Natali's discounts designer shoes, boots, and handbags in the latest styles. The Third Avenue shop is the larger of the two, offering men's shoes as well as women's. The Garment District outpost is smaller and focuses on ladies' styles. Both are packed with great bargains. One pair of dress heels by Via Spiga was reduced from its list price of $135.00 to a slender $79.00. Bandolinos range in price from $49.00 to $79.00; and you'll find similar savings on Amalfi, Paloma, and Vittorio Ricci. Not to mention suede boots by Jazz for $69.00 as well as good savings on deerskin boots by Dan Post. Leather handbags included a design by Pavia reduced from $250.00 to $110.00.

Plaza On Broadway—620 Broadway (Houston St.), Manhattan; 212/477-3826. This NoHo boutique, part of a larger fashion store, offers a few bargains worth checking out. Mr. C saw a pair of men's leather casual shoes from Pierre Cardin's Espace line, originally retailing for $125.00, here marked down to $60.00. Also, Dan Post's selection of lizard-skin cowboy boots at $40.00 off retail prices. Some of these deals are closeouts, but the selection on sale for both men and women is pretty good.

S & W—165 West 26th St., Manhattan; 212/924-6656, and 4217 Thirteenth Ave., Borough Park, Brooklyn; 718/438-9679. See listing under "New Clothing: Men's and Women's General Wear."

Shoe City/Sneaker City—133 Nassau St., Manhattan; 212/732-3889. For over fifty years this has been a great downtown spot to find dependable brand-name casual men's shoes, as well as sneakers for the entire family. Everything in the store is sold at discount—and they even put up ads and catalogs from other stores to show you the savings. Timberland waterproof hiking shoes, priced at $140.00 in Bloomie's, sell for $120.00 at Shoe City. Nike "Air Jordan" sneakers, selling for $125.00 elsewhere, are $105.00 here. You'll find similar savings on shoes by Rockport, Dexter, Nunn-Bush, and others, along with Totes overshoes. Service is relaxed and very outgoing.

Shoe Express—1420 Second Ave. (74th St.), Manhattan; 212/734-3967. Here is a terrific spot where women can save lots of money on all their casual and dress shoes. Joe Rotella, the manager, is especially proud of the store's quality and prices. Everything here is at least 10 to 15 percent below department stores. Beyond that, a different selection of shoes goes on special sale each week. On this table you may find designs by Via Spiga reduced from $110.00 to $50.00, or Vaneli reduced from $105.00 to $76.00. These are not irregulars or closeouts; they are current styles chosen at random. You'll want to stop in regularly to see what may be on sale.

Shoe Express does carry some men's lines, though these are somewhat less discounted. Still, Joe says he will beat any advertised price on Rockports. They are also exclusive dealers on the Upper East Side for a number of items, including Harley-Davidson motorcycle boots, Mephisto, and Peter Kaiser comfort shoes. And the store specializes in hard-to-find wide and narrow sizes. The store is open into the evening seven days a week.

$10 The Limit—15 Warren St., Manhattan; 212/227-0459, 71 Nassau St., Manhattan; 212/693-1188, 1620 Kings Hwy., Brooklyn; 718/627-0006, 384 Knickerbocker Ave., Brooklyn; 718/455-3688, 2167 86th St., Brooklyn; 718/372-2502, and 3029 Steinway St., Long Island City, Queens; 718/278-9084. Mr. C wants to cover the entire spectrum of savings, whether it's designer names at discount or just plain cheap stuff. At these stores, you'll find some recognizable brands, like Keds, Valenti, and Mootsies Tootsies, mixed in with the riff-raff. Hey, sometimes you just want something to play around in. In spite of the name, Mr. C didn't see anything for $10.00; but there were plenty of flats, pumps, and sneakers for around $20.00, which still ain't bad. Also (fake) suede boots for $29.00, as well as a selection of handbags. Come in at the end of the summer and you'll find sandals on sale for $11.88, or two pair for $20.00.

Vamps—1421 Second Ave. (74th St.), Manhattan; 212/744-0227. A sister store to Shoe Express across the street, Vamps has a good variety of the latest women's fashions. The discounts are not tremendous, but worth a look. Their sales are particularly good; you may find a pair of navy-colored lizard-skin boots by Nocona marked down from $285.00 to $199.00. In fact, boots are probably the best thing here. They carry the full line of Justins at discount. Styles that sell for $249.00 elsewhere are just $219.00 here.

V.I.M. Jeans—16 West 14th St., Manhattan; 212/255-2662, 15 West 34th St., Manhattan; 212/736-4989, 388 Fulton St., Brooklyn; 718/855-0112, and other locations around the city.

See listing under "New Clothing: Men's and Women's General Wear."

SPORTING GOODS

Better Health Fitness Center—5201 New Utrecht Ave., Borough Park, Brooklyn; 718/436-4693. Better Health is a small but well-stocked store selling all kinds of sports gear and exercise equipment. Their prices are not rock-bottom, but they are certainly trim. They have treadmills by Tunturi and Trotter, exercise bikes by Lifecycle, stair climbers, weight sets, floor mats, Everlast belts, and lots more. If your home or business takes you out this way, you should definitely check them out. Better Health also specializes in quantity price breaks for businesses and schools.

Gene's Bicycles & Fitness Store—242-244 East 79th St., Manhattan; 212/249-9344. Gene's is not really a discount store—note the neighborhood—but he does have competitive prices on all kinds of bikes. Mountain bikes, for instance, start at $225.00 for a Royce-Union twelve-speeder. The real bargains are in last year's models, which are reduced for clearance but every bit as good as a new bike; and there are usually some used bicycles to check out, too. The service staff has cleaned and tightened everything, and you can get a used ten-speed racing bike for as little as $90.00. The stock comes and goes on these, so you never know what they'll have, but if you're in the market, do stop in. The store is open seven days a week into the early evening.

Modell's Sporting Goods—200 Broadway (Fulton St.), Manhattan; 212/964-4007, 280 Broadway (Chambers St.), Manhattan; 212/267-2882, A&S Plaza, Sixth Ave. (33rd St.), Manhattan; 212/594-1830, 109 East 42nd St., Manhattan; 212/661-5966, 243 West 42nd St., Manhattan; 212/575-8111, 39-12 Main St., Flushing, Queens; 718/539-6100, 163-40 Jamaica Ave., Jamaica, Queens; 718/297-4402, 30-88 Steinway St., Astoria, Queens; 718/956-4526, Starrbrook Plaza, 1000 Penn Ave., New Lots, Brooklyn;718/345-9300, 360 Fulton St., Brooklyn; 718/855-1921, 31 East Fordham Rd., Bronx; 212/295-7800, 2929 Third Ave., Bronx; 212/993-1844, and 1801-B South Ave., West Shore Plaza, Staten Island; 718/698-8900. From humble beginnings as a small family-run shop, Modell's has become one of the city's largest retailers of sports gear and clothing. Just about everything is sold at very good prices. Find good deals on in-line skates by Bauer, Rollerblade, and California Pro. They have lots of exercise equipment; a monorail "Ski-Master" by Weider was recently seen for $129.00, along with weightlifting sets, stair climbers, and everything else to get you in shape before you go to the gym. Sneakers are another great reason to shop at Modell's, with high-tops, running shoes and walkers by Champion, Reebok, Etonic, Pony, and more at low prices.

Nylon warm-up suits by Spalding and Pony start as low

Mr. Cheap's Picks

✔ **Modell's**—Extensive selection of clothing and gear at everyday low prices make this a popular chain.

✔ **Paragon**—Who says bigger isn't better? Perhaps the largest single sporting goods store in the city. Regular prices are competitive (sorry, couldn't resist), but frequent sales make for great deals in every department on three floors.

✔ **Stuyvesant Bicycle**—Again, one of the city's largest stores—this time for bikes. Big volume means good values in every price range, from kiddie models to serious racing machines.

as $40.00, and women's lycra activewear separates as low as $10.00. Lots of stuff for kids, too, like football jerseys, sweats, and sneakers. You'll also find hiking boots, parkas, and plenty of camping and fishing gear. Modell's really covers all the bases.

New York Golf Center, Inc.—131 West 35th St., Manhattan; 212/564-2255. Tee off here for all your golfing needs. It's one of New York's most complete stores devoted entirely to duffers. It's not a discount store, but their prices are well under par. Save on clubs, bags, shoes, balls, and accessories. They have a wide selection of major brands, many of which are just below retail prices. Clearance sale items offer some further bargains. If golf is your game, this place will hit a hole-in-one.

Paragon Sporting Goods—871 Broadway (18th St.), Manhattan; 212/255-8036. Founded in 1908, Paragon has long been the crowned champ of sporting goods stores in New York. Recent expansions have created three full floors of departments covering every sport known to man (or woman). While this is not, strictly speaking, a discount store, Paragon's prices are as competitive as any gridiron match. Frequent sales afford you the chance of even better savings. Mr. C found a pair of Avia men's walking shoes for $40.00; a pair of Rossignol "Advantage AR" skis for $109.00; a Head "Atlantis" large-size tennis racquet reduced from $200.00 to $119.00; and Wilson footballs emblazoned with the logo of your favorite team for $15.00.

Clearance racks and off-season equipment offer further bargains. In any department you may find things like wood or aluminum baseball bats at 40 percent off their original prices, or Nike windbreakers at 50 percent off. Mr. C also saw ladies' Nordica ski jackets, a Burlington brand, reduced from $180.00 to $144.00.

On their top floor, Paragon also has an extensive selection of outdoor wear and equipment. You can find anything from a bow and arrow to binoculars, as well as down vests, hiking boots, sunglasses, and sailing gear. Again, being such a large store, most of these are very reasonably priced.

Spiegel's Sporting Goods—105 Nassau St., Manhattan; 212/227-8400. Spiegel's has been around since 1916, so they should know their way around a court, field, or diamond. They have good prices on a large selection of equipment for just about any sport or training, with most of their merchandise on the street level. Downstairs there is just as large a selling area for sneakers and clothing in all the same sports. Here you'll find some serious discounts: Reeboks for men and women may be on sale for as much as $10.00 to $15.00 below list prices, and there are always lots of running tops, shorts, and tights on Spiegel's 40 to 50 percent off rack. Mr. C saw a pair of Hind nylon/lycra running shorts, perfectly good, marked down from $25.00 to just $12.99. Other frequent sales may put the entire stock of running wear at 20 percent off. Sprint on over.

Stuyvesant Bicycle—349 West 14th St., Manhattan; 212/675-2160. Billing itself as the largest single bike shop in the city, Stuyvesant is certainly big—and its high-volume sales allow them to price new bicycles an average of $20.00 to $30.00 below many other stores. Find twelve-speed mountain bikes from $185.00 and up, and Fuji mountain/city hybrid styles for $275.00 to $300.00. Mr. C also saw a twelve-speed Raleigh racer for $179.00. And they have lots of children's bikes to choose from. All are backed by full on-premises repair service, seven days a week. Stuyvesant also sells Tunturi exercycles at competitive prices.

Triangle Sports—182 Flatbush Ave. (Fifth Ave.), Park Slope, Brooklyn; 718/638-5000, and 710 Grand St., Williamsburg, Brooklyn; 718/388-9101. This packed store (the downtown branch, that is) seems to take its name from the traffic formation that makes the store appear to be sitting out in the middle of the road. Once you get inside, though, you'll see that they definitely take the low road when it comes to prices on sporting goods and athletic wear. They have terrific discounts on shoes by Nike, Reebok, Adidas, and more; as well as Timberland hiking boots and other outdoor gear, all kinds of team sports equipment, swimming and tennis stuff, and exercise machines. With such a huge stock, Triangle can usually offer even better deals on last year's leftover models; be sure to check these out.

Triest Export—560 Twelfth Ave. (44th St.), Manhattan; 212/246-1548. See listing under "Appliances."

STATIONERY, OFFICE AND ART SUPPLIES

For business items like date planners and fancy mechanical pens, check out the stores in the "Luggage" section too. Many cater to the business person's every need.

Art Station—144 West 27th St., Manhattan; 212/807-8000. Art Station offers good prices on just about anything an artist may need—paints, paper, tools, canvas, tables and more. A recent sale offered three sheets of Letraset for $10.00, and large, heavy-stock manila envelopes in bright colors at three for 99¢.

Be sure to check the downstairs area, where you'll find clearance bargains like a four-post oak drawing table reduced from $709.00 to $499.00, an ergonomic chair marked down from $159.00 to $125.00, or a 36" x 60" chalkboard for $29.00. Plus lamps, light tables, and framing services.

The staff is helpful and knowledgeable; the store is open Monday through Friday from 8:00 a.m. to 6 p.m., and Saturday from 10:00 a.m. to 2:45 p.m.

Ciro Office Supplies—57 Warren St., Manhattan; 212/406-1323. This small, rather worn-looking shop is crammed from floor to ceiling with every kind of paper and stationery supply imaginable. Since the displays extend out to the sidewalk in front of the store, some of the stock looks worn-out too. But there is plenty of good stuff here, sometimes at incredible prices. You may find a five hundred-sheet ream of blank white three-hole paper, reduced from $8.95 to just $2.99. Or a box of ten large-size (5-1/4") floppy disks marked down from $25.00 to a mere $5.00. Other accessories recently spotted included a plastic stand for a computer printer, the kind that lifts it off the table at an angle, ten dollars off at $19.95. If you work downtown and you're into supplies (you know who you are, organization junkies), you may come to love this dingy little place.

Fileworks—95 Vandam St., Manhattan; 212/989-5687. See listing under "Furniture: Office."

Jam Paper And Envelope—111 Third Ave.(14th St.), Manhattan; 212/473-6666. 125 Fifth Ave. (20th St.), Manhattan; 212/388-9190, 621 Sixth Ave. (19th St.), Manhattan; 212/255-4593, and 1111 Second Ave. (59th St.), Manhattan; 212/980-1999. Jam is the undisputed king of discount paper supplies. They specialize in papers, from business to artsy, that have gone unsold at other stores—or that are left over from orders they've made up for clients. Find a five hundred-sheet ream of high-quality business stationery marked down from $54.00 to $35.00, in a variety of colors and thicknesses; even "Astrobright" neon bond paper with grooved texture. They also sell envelopes, note cards, packages of invitations, gift wrapping, notepads with funky designs, and loose note stationery. The selection is vast, with everything out on display—and helpful service to find what you need, or the next-best thing.

Jam does have new stock, also at discount; often a less expensive copy of name brands. These can save you half the price of the better-known, but same-quality, paper. The stores are open six days and accept cash or certified checks only.

Menash Office Products—462 Seventh Ave. (38th St.), Manhattan; 212/695-4900, and 2307 Broadway (84th St.), Manhattan; 212/877-2060. "Office supplies at warehouse prices," is the claim at Menash. Not everything here is rock-bottom, but you'll certainly find a huge selection at good prices. Please your boss and save money with the store's own brand of fax and computer paper, as well as desktop computer diskettes. They also have competitive prices on the Filofax line of products, and discounts of 20 to 40 percent on mechanical pens like Parker and Cross.

Pearl Paint—308 Canal St., Manhattan; 212/431-7932, and 42 Lispenard St., Manhattan; 212/431-7932. Pearl is the granddaddy of them all—a sort of art supply department store, now celebrating its sixtieth year. Five floors offer complete lines of paints, paper, portfolios, easels, canvas, tools, tables, lamps, chairs, storage systems, computer desks, and pretty much everything for the studio or office. They've even spread to a second store a block away on Lispenard Street, as well as national chain outposts.

Among the many sale items recently spotted (Pearl's everyday prices are great, but there are always special promotions for even better deals): An HP-B "Pro-Pak" airbrush kit, list price $185.00, here $100.00; leather briefcases reduced from $150.00 to just $44.00 (with lots of other briefcases and presentation cases on sale); a Gagne 16" x 18" lightbox reduced from $170.00 to $75.00; a sixty-piece Rembrandt soft pastel set, half-price at $70.00; a Rover portable office storage system, marked down from $295.00 to $140.00; and the comprehensive *Artist's Handbook*, with information on the latest techniques and technologies, reduced from a cover price of $30.00 to $19.99. Lots of package deals, too—grab a flyer when you come in the front door.

The store offers national and international mail-order service. The store is open from 9:00 a.m. to 6:00 p.m., Mondays through Saturdays, and from 10:00 a.m. 5:30 p.m. on Sundays.

Mr. Cheap's Picks

- ✔ **Jam Paper and Envelope**—These stores collect overstocks of quality business stationery and resell them at greatly reduced rates. Talk about paper recycling.
- ✔ **Pearl Paint**—The city's biggest and best art supply store, bar none.
- ✔ **Staples**—Everything for the office, under one roof. They'll probably even sell you the roof.

Staples—1075 Sixth Ave. (40th St.), Manhattan; 212/944-6744, and 205 East 42nd St., Manhattan; 212/697-6049. This fast-expanding national chain calls itself "The Office Superstore," and it's easy to see why. They've brought the mega-warehouse approach to office supplies—including everything from paper clips to computers to furniture. They stock several thousand items, making them pretty hard to beat. Now, Mr. C tries not to spend too much time telling you about places like this; not because they aren't bargains, but because they do enough advertising for you to know about them already. He prefers to bring the smaller, less celebrated stores to your attention—they are often more interesting anyway, with character that can't be Xeroxed into some chain, and yield their own unique bargains.

Still, Staples has deals that have to be passed along. Especially if you run an office—home or Fortune 500—which needs lots of supplies on a regular basis. Many of the best bargains, you see, are available in large quantities. You can get a six-pack of Bellwether fax paper, for example, at a savings of 70 percent off retail—just $12.88. A dozen bottles of Liquid Paper correction fluid for $7.89, or a dozen pads of Post-It Notes for as low as $2.99.

Then, things get bigger. Copying and fax machines from $399.00, personal computers at competitive (if ever-changing) prices, workstations on which to put those computers from about $100.00, filing cabinets for as low as $85.00, and just about everything else to set up an office but the potted ferns. Maybe they'll get those in, too.

Is there any reason to shop anywhere else? Sure there is. Even megastores can't have everything. Ironically, in trying to stock every *kind* of item, they can never fit every variety of the item. So, you may not find a particular brand that you like, or as wide a selection as smaller stores can offer. For basic stuff, though, Staples is pretty darn good. And popular. By the time you read this, no doubt more branches will have opened around town—including the smaller Staples Express stores, focusing more on those things you need for the office right away—like, well, staples.

Utrecht Art & Drafting Supplies—111 Fourth Ave. (12th St.), Manhattan; 212/777-5353. From its base in New York, Utrecht has become one of the country's largest art supply houses, manufacturing its own line of paint, canvas and related products—along with low prices on other brands. The store boasts over twenty thousand items at discount. A hundred-sheet pad of Utrecht newsprint drawing paper sells as low as $2.75; and their permanent acrylic Gesso colors are just $2.95 a pint. Save money on Rembrandt oils and pastel sticks, Chartpak lettering, Pelikan inks, Neilsen frames, Rapidograph pens, a variety of guide books, and much, much more. In addition to their regular low prices, Utrecht has periodic sales offering discounts of up to 60 percent on many items. The staff is friendly and very professional.

TOYS AND GAMES

The world of retail toys is a very competitive one; fun 'n games is serious business to such stores. The result is that there aren't many ways to save money beyond shopping the retail giants, a couple of which are listed here. Mr. C recommends, also, that you check many of the stores listed in the "Discount Department Stores" section of this book, where you can save money on closeouts and surplus. These can sometimes be as extensive as the retailers themselves. He has pointed out the best examples for you below.

Conway—111 Fulton St., Manhattan; 212/374-1072, 37 Broad St., Manhattan; 212/943-8900,450 Seventh Ave., Manhattan; 212/967-1371,1333 Broadway (Herald Sq.), Manhattan; 212/967-3460, 11 West 34th St., Manhattan; 212/967-1370, 49 West 34th St., Manhattan; 212/967-6454, 225 West 34th St., Manhattan; 212/967-7390, 201 East 42nd St., Manhattan; 212/922-5030, 505 Fulton St., Brooklyn; 718/522-9200. See listing under "Department Stores."

Dapy—431 West Broadway (Prince St.), Manhattan; 212/925-5082, and 232 Columbus Ave. (71st St.), Manhattan; 212/877-4710. See listing under "Unusual Gifts."

Job Lot Pushcart—140 Church St., Manhattan; 212/962-4142, 80 Nassau St., Manhattan; 212/619-6868, and 1633 Broadway (50th St.), Manhattan; 212/245-0921. See listing under "Department Stores."

Kiddie City—24-32 Union Square East, Manhattan; 212/353-0215, 35 West 34th St., Manhattan; 212/629-3070, and 2220 Broadway (79th St.), Manhattan; 212/877-4252. Kiddie City (it's just fun to say out loud, isn't it?) is one of New York's most complete toy stores; each branch has two huge floors with everything from dolls, toys, and games to novelty clothing and tricycles. The selection is vast and the prices are very low, whether it's the latest rage or a classic we all grew up with. KC also specializes in Lionel train sets and accessories. Geared toward volume purchasing, they even offer a "Frequent Shopper's Club" which allows you to save up extra discounts.

National Wholesale Liquidators—632 Broadway (Bleecker St.), Manhattan; 212/979-2400, and 71-01 Kissena Blvd., Flushing, Queens; 718/591-3900. See listing under "Department Stores."

NYC Liquidators—158 West 27th St., Manhattan; 212/675-7400. See listing under "Department Stores."

Odd-Job Trading—10 Cortlandt St., Manhattan; 212/571-0959, 149 West 32nd St., Manhattan; 212/564-7370, 7 East 40th St., Manhattan; 212/686-6825, and 66 West 48th St., Manhattan; 212/575-0477. See listing under "Department Stores."

Penny Whistle Toys—132 Spring St., Manhattan; 212/925-2088, 448 Columbus Ave. (81st St.),

Mr. Cheap's Pick

✔ **Toys "R" Us** and **Kiddie City**—Two mega-stores with every plaything under the sun, all at low-markup prices.

Manhattan; 212/873-9090, and 1283 Madison Ave. (91st St.), Manhattan; 212/369-3868. Don't be too quick to judge Penny Whistle. Yes, it's an upscale toy store for upscale parents who see toys as quality-time learning activities; yes, most of the items in here are expensive. But if you look around, you can find lots of stuff in the $5.00 to $10.00 range, like unique jigsaw puzzles, toy cars and trucks, and dolls.

Star Magic—743 Broadway (Astor Place), Manhattan; 212/228-7770, 275 Amsterdam Ave. (73rd St.), Manhattan; 212/769-2020, and 1256 Lexington Ave. (85th St.), Manhattan; 212/988-0300. See listing under "Unusual Gifts."

Toys "R" Us—1293 Broadway (34th St.), Manhattan; 212/594-8697, 1880 Bartow Ave., Bronx; 718/320-0722, 87-93 Bay Pkwy. (87th St.), Bensonhurst, Brooklyn; 718/372-4646, 2875 Flatbush Ave., Mill Basin, Brooklyn; 718/258-2061, 66-26 Metropolitan Ave., Middle Village, Queens; 718/326-2038, Douglaston Pkwy. (61st Ave.), Little Neck, Queens; 718/224-2800, and 2845 Richmond Ave., Staten Island; 718/698-8821.

Perhaps the country's biggest retail toy chain, Toys "R" Us is also the premier discounter on aisle after aisle of toys, games, bikes, kids' clothing—and even diapers. The place is huge, and the prices are likely to be the lowest in town for the latest in toys. They even offer to match the advertised prices from any other store. How do they do it? Volume! They've got Barbie, they've got roller skates, they've got radio-powered cars. If your game boys and girls are screaming for the very latest Nintendo technology, get it here. But do yourself a favor—go on a weekday if you can, and leave the kiddies at home. That way, you're *sure* to spend less money.

Weber's Closeouts—132 Church St., Manhattan; 212/571-3283, 475 Fifth Ave. (41st St.), Manhattan; 212/251-0613, 45 West 45th St., Manhattan; 212/819-9780, and 2064 Broadway (72nd St.), Manhattan; 212/787-1644. See listing under "Department Stores."

West Side Kids—498 Amsterdam Ave. (84th St.), Manhattan; 212/496-7282. An all-purpose store for young children with books and educational toys, WSK has a fun section up front with bins and bins of tiny, colorful, cheap toys. They range in price from 25¢ to about $3.00, and include the ever-popular Silly Putty, super balls, wind-up robots, kazoos, and much more. Take a kid with you, so you won't look *too* foolish while you're playing.

UNUSUAL GIFTS

Abracadabra—10 Christopher St., Manhattan; 212/627-5745. In addition to selling all kinds of professional magicians supplies, Abracadabra has enough wacky costumes and gag gifts to make lots of fun appear in your life. They have all the novelty items you've ever groaned at, like the ever-popular dribble glass and the shocking cigarette lighter. A set of wind-up chattering teeth is $7.00, and a can of peanuts with snakes that spring out when you open it is $3.50. As many times as we've all seen this, it never fails to liven up the party. And, of course, Abracadabra is fully prepared to meet all your "Groucho glasses" needs. If more elaborate get-ups are your style, they have wigs, mustaches, and theatrical makeup as well as full costumes and accessories for sale or for rentals. During the holiday season, which for these guys means Halloween through Christmas, the store is open seven days a week; otherwise, Monday through Saturday from 11:00 a.m. to 9:00 p.m.

Brooklyn Women's Exchange—55 Pierrepont St., Brooklyn Heights, Brooklyn; 718/624-3435. Not far from the popular shops of Montague Street, this beautiful store sells all sorts of lovely handmade clothing, toys, and things for the home, much of it in classic American and country styles. Find all sorts of soaps and candles, stationery, educational toys and clothing for children and infants, hand-knit scarves and afghan blankets, and more. Not everything is particularly cheap, but many items are quite reasonable, and all proceeds benefit this nonprofit organization, which was begun in the nineteenth century as an outlet for poor women to sell handicrafts in order to support themselves. That work continues today. The store is open Tuesdays through Saturdays from 10:00 a.m. to 4:30 p.m.

Dapy—431 West Broadway (Prince St.), Manhattan; 212/925-5082, and 232 Columbus Ave. (71st St.), Manhattan; 212/877-4710. Perhaps the king of the kooky gift stores, Dapy sits comfortably amidst the art galleries of SoHo (and the trendy boutiques on Columbus) and basically thumbs its nose at them. This Paris-based shop has made it possible for crowds of grownups to play with the silliest of toys, as well as the very latest modern-day electronic gadgets. There is a seemingly harmless hand mirror, for example, that emits a piercing scream when you pick it up and look at your reflection. At $12.00, it's a fun and affordable gift—or something to leave around the bathroom for unsuspecting guests. A pair of glasses made from one long, winding straw, allows you to sip a drink and send it on a roller-coaster ride around your face, for just $3.00. Use these next to your dancing Coke bottle, just $10.00. And Dapy has those little tin cans that "moo" when you turn them upside down. Technology is fine, but some things will never go away.

DOM—577 Broadway (Prince St.), Manhattan; 212/966-5226. Not to be outdone by the French Dapy, DOM is Germany's entry into the crazy knickknacks Olympics. The first thing you'll notice here, perhaps before you even go in, is the decor. It's, um, pink. *Really* pink. If you can stand that, though, the place is a lot of fun. Ultra-hip Eurotrash items range from the practical to the trivial, with lots of unusual items for $5.00 to $10.00 and less. Cocktail stirrers, pencils, key rings, napkin rings, silverware, compact disc racks, and decorative things are among the crafted merchandise in this large, long store They have clothing items too, though these tend not to be cheap.

Fishs Eddy—889 Broadway (19th St.), Manhattan; 212/420-9020, 551 Hudson St., Manhattan; 212/627-3956. See listing under "Home Furnishings."

Leekan Designs—93 Mercer St., Manhattan; 212/226-7226. This large, beautiful SoHo shop specializes in Asian folk art, making for lots of unique gift options from the elaborate and expensive to the small and simple. Mr. C, of course, will focus on the latter. His visit to this Orient revealed such treasures as enameled porcelain bracelets from $8.00 to $12.00, jade earrings from $16.00, and myriad tiny cases and decorative boxes ranging from $8.00 to $16.00.

Get that special someone a notebook with a heavy cover done over in brightly-colored silk, for just $6.00; add a caligraphy brush for $10.00, and see if it gets any creative juices flowing. Or look at all the little handmade toys, from paper fans for 50¢ to a Noh character hand puppet for $8.50. These are gifts that should certainly make a unique impression.

Little Rickie—49 1/2 First Ave. (3rd St.), Manhattan; 212/505-6467. Little Rickie is one of those great, fun, wacky shops for which the Village is well known. It's packed with the hippest of the hip in toys, trinkets, and gag gifts—many of which, of course, are too naughty to describe here. But don't worry, you can steer away from these if you wish, into the safer realms of sparkler guns, postcards, and refrigerator magnets of your favorite old rock groups and TV shows. There are plenty of ideas to brighten up your day, or someone else's, for just a coupla bucks—and it's fun just to look around. You'd never guess how much cutesy junk is being made out there!

Love Saves The Day—119 Second Ave. (7th St.), Manhattan; 212/228-3802. See listing under "Clothing—Used: Vintage Stores."

Marco's Art Gallery—37 Orchard St., Manhattan; 212/219-2738. Local artist and tireless self-promoter Marco has moved in from the streets of SoHo to a gallery/factory among the clothing wholesalers of Orchard Street. He describes himself as "an unschooled, self-taught artist who paints in an expressionistic style, influenced by Picasso, Matisse, Van Gogh and Modigliani." His canvases have decorated the walls of Limelight, and now they can grace your walls as well. In what Marco likens to an "art restaurant," you simply choose a design from several hundred sketches, specify one of five sizes, and leave the rest to him. Within a few days you'll have a unique oil on canvas at a price you won't find in any art gallery. Prices start at just $50.00 for a 12" x 18" painting, going up to $250.00 for a 36" x 54". If you'd like something that isn't quite so mass-produced, Marco will work from your suggestion to create a custom design or portrait at slightly higher prices. The gallery is open from 8:00 a.m. to 8:00 p.m. daily.

Maxilla & Mandible, Ltd.—451 Columbus Ave. (81st St.), Manhattan; 212/724-6173. Mr. C has this friend. She's absolutely crazy about anything that has to do with dinosaurs. Judging by the popularity of the species in countless museum exhibits, television shows, and movies, she's just one of zillions of kids and adults these days. Maxilla & Mandible is the place for any such person. Smartly enough, it's right around the corner from the Museum of Natural History.

The store sells actual dinosaur fossils, bones, and other artifacts. Many of these are on display in their glass cases, making M & M as much fun to walk through as any exhibit. It's a hip joint in more ways than one. Most of the objects are quite expensive, out of Mr. C's price range; but many of the smaller fossils are priced from about $10.00 to $30.00. They make a way-out gift for that special bone hunter in the family. There are also exotic shells from $2.00 to $9.00, and baskets of semi-precious stones, polished and colorful: Turquoise, amethyst, agates, and such, all just $2.00 to $4.00.

Star Magic—743 Broadway (Astor Place), Manhattan; 212/228-7770, 275 Amsterdam Ave. (73rd St.), Manhattan; 212/769-2020, and 1256 Lexington Ave. (85th St.), Manhattan; 212/988-0300.

With its glistening gems and minerals, space-age music, and dramatic lighting, Star truly is a magical store to browse in. They also specialize in the latest way-out toys and trinkets, not all of which are as expensive as they may look. Digital watches with hologram faces—one has an eye that seems to look back at you—are just $15.00. There are lots of hologram stickers too, just $1.95 each. Official NASA shoulder patches from various space missions are $5.00 each, and there is a bewildering array of cube, maze, and puzzle toys and doodads, most between $3.00 to $10.00. And *you* thought there was no life beyond Rubik!

Stick Stone & Bone—111 Christopher St., Manhattan; 212/807-7024. This delightful shop specializes in primitive crafts and jewelry, primarily from the American Southwest and Latin America. It's filled with unique and affordable gift ideas. Among the more eclectic items: A Brazilian samba whistle ($5.00), miniature turtles that look amazingly like the actual endangered species ($6.00), Native-American incense in such varieties as sage

Mr. Cheap's Picks

✔ **Dapy**—Replace the "p" with "ff" and you get a better idea of the wacky fun of this toy boutique.

✔ **Marco's Art Gallery**—Check out the menu, place your order, and get some take-out; not food, but paintings. Also, wildly funny T-shirts, printed while you wait.

✔ **Maxilla & Mandible, Ltd.**—Where else but New York could you come across a store selling real dinosaur fossils and animal bones?

✔ **Star Magic**—This place is a magical experience, with space-age toys, decorative items, gems, and other gifts—not to mention the spacey music playing in the background.

and sweetgrass (under $5.00) and handmade leather pouches for crystals and minerals ($10.00). Don't have any minerals? You'll find a nice selection of these, too—whether in their raw form, most around $10.00, or smaller polished stones, just $1.00 to $3.00. Plus lots of "Day of the Dead" crafts—for that Mexican holiday with the morbid sense of humor. The salespeople are very knowledgeable about everything in the store, which is open seven days a week—including Fridays and Saturdays until midnight. Viva La Village!

Van Win—331 Canal St., Manhattan; 212/334-0378. Canal Street is like Import City—shop after shop of electronic gadgetry from the ever-more-efficient factories of the Far East. These stores, mostly identical, carry a wide variety of both practical and amusing products. Among Mr. C's favorites, for selection, is Van Win. Whether you want a 35mm camera, like a Yashica Auto-Focus with case ($48.00), or a talking digital clock that literally tells you the time ($11.99), Van Win probably has something for you. There is a huge stock of cheap (in every sense of the word) but fun watches in brightly-colored plastic designs, for $10.00; a solar-powered calculator for $2.25; and lots of other automated toys. It used to be true that "Made in Japan" meant junk; nowadays it's the entire Pacific rim, and the junk does some pretty amazing things.

Another well-stocked shop nearby is **Broadway and Canal Merchandise**, 424 Broadway (at the corner of Canal—where else?); 212/941-6299. In addition to the kinds of items mentioned above, this store carries a wider selection of small appliances, such as coffee grinders and food processors, at good prices. Both of these stores—as well as their many clones—are also good places to stock up on brand-name blank videotape and audiotape. Mr. C found BASF brand T-160 video cassettes, which allow up to eight hours of recording, for $3.49.

ENTERTAINMENT

ART GALLERIES

Any good New Yorker knows that browsing the galleries is one of the city's enlightening, civilized—and *free*—cultural activities. Many places will have to buzz you in, for security purposes; but don't worry that you're being kept out for reasons of, say, annual income below that of Ross Perot. Go on in! After all, the richer people are, the less they have to care about their appearance, right? For all the gallery owners know, someone in torn jeans may be an eccentric millionaire. (Be sure to sneer at one or two paintings, as though you *could* buy one if it were any good.)

Many of the city's art galleries are concentrated into a few major centers. The traditional areas include 57th Street, just east and west of Fifth Avenue, and Madison Avenue in the 60s and 70s. Many of these are closed on Sundays and Mondays. In more recent years, SoHo and TriBeCa have become havens for more contemporary styles. A cruise along West Broadway, from Houston Street down to Spring Street—and then along Spring to Broadway—can easily fill an afternoon (including weekends), costing you no more than pastry and a cup of espresso at a nearby cafe.

Here are just a few of the many well-known galleries in these and other areas. Bear in mind that art galleries move around quicker than the proverbial bunny; but, while addresses may change, you'll always find plenty to see in the main areas.

Alternative Museum—594 Broadway (Houston St.), Manhattan; 212/966-4444. True to its name, this gallery is like a small, informal museum. It presents contemporary shows around themes like "Artists of Conscience."

Also at 594 Broadway is **Humphrey Fine Art** (212/226-5360), which recently offered a group show of works by Latin American female artists.

American Indian Community House—708 Broadway (4th St.), Manhattan; 212/598-0100. Shouldn't they change their name? Anyway, this gallery showcases works by Native American artists, usually in group shows.

Art in the Anchorage—Cadman Plaza West at Old Fulton St., Brooklyn Heights, Brooklyn; 718/206-6674. If you're having nothing to do with SoHo or Madison Avenue, a great place to see art on a grand scale is in the Anchorage of the Brooklyn Bridge. On the Brooklyn side, the very base of this hundred-year-old bridge (first to span the East River) has been turned into an outdoor art exhibition area. From spring into the fall, you can see the work of many different New York artists, in both conventional works and site-specific installations. This is also the site of a series called "Fiction in the Anchorage," with authors reading aloud from their works. It's all free, of course; call for more info.

Artists Space—223 West Broadway, Manhattan; 212/226-3970. This TriBeCa gallery combines the latest in multimedia art environments with performance by such avant-garde artists as Ping Chong. They even have fun par-

Mr. Cheap's Picks

✔ **Artists Space**—In this TriBeCa gallery, artists create (and sometimes perform in) complete art "environments."

✔ **DAI Center for the Arts**—Another haven for downtown's lively visual/performance art scene.

✔ **Fashion Institute of Technology**—When this school puts together an exhibition, like its recent Versace costumes mega-show, get to it. More like a museum, and free.

✔ **Findlay Galleries**—Renowned for late nineteenth- and twentieth-century masters.

✔ **The Fuller Building**—Two dozen different galleries under one roof, for a concentrated gallery cruise.

✔ **Meisner SoHo**—A bright new entry showcasing New York's rising young stars.

✔ **Studio 53**—For American early masters, such as Andrew Wyeth.

ticipatory art—like a recent exhibit of miniature golf, with each hole created by a different artist, which you could actually play.

Asian American Arts Center—26 Bowery, Manhattan; 212/233-2154. Near Canal Street in Chinatown, AAAC specializes in works by Asian-American artists (what would you expect?).

Benedetti Gallery—52 Prince St., Manhattan; 212/226-2238. Focusing primarily on twentieth-century European art, this SoHo house has an especially large collection of sculptures by Erte.

CDS Gallery—76 East 79th St., Manhattan; 212/772-9555. CDS primarily presents the work of Latin American and North American artists—paintings, sculpture, drawings, and more. Also at this address is the **Thompson Gallery** (212/249-0242), focusing more on European works.

Children's Museum of the Arts—72 Spring St., Manhattan; 212/941-9198. See listing under "Children's Activities."

DIA Center for the Arts—548 West 22nd St., Manhattan; 212/431-9232. There are actually several locations around the downtown area for this visual and performance art haven. In addition to a gallery at the above address, you'll find DIA at 141 Wooster Street and 155 Mercer Street, as well as at 393 West Broadway—locations all in SoHo. The installations found here can range from art "environments" to exhibits of artists like Joseph Beuys. Often these include inexpensive lectures on the featured artists.

Fashion Institute of Technology—Seventh Ave. at 27th St., Manhattan; 212/760-7760. The galleries at FIT may be well off the beaten path, but they are worth finding. It's more like a museum here, with exhibits that can take up several rooms on each of two levels. A big hit last year was the Versace show, displaying the fashion creations and theatrical costumes by this racy Italian designer. Admission to the galleries is free.

Findlay Galleries—17 East 57th St., Manhattan; 212/421-5390. This longtime gallery founded in 1870 specializes in post-Impressionists and other early twentieth-century masters. Marc Chagall, Jean Dufy, and Henri-Martin are among the artists on display here.

Franklin Furnace—112 Franklin St., Manhattan; 212/925-4671. A good example of the burgeoning TriBeCa arts scene, Franklin Furnace presents the latest works by happening downtown artists.

French Embassy—972 Fifth Ave. (79th St.), Manhattan; 212/439-1400. This is not just another gallery—it really is the French Embassy! Inside, though, they present exhibitions relating to *la belle France*. What else? On display recently were landscape photographs commissioned by the Belfort Arts Center of that northern province. Admission is free, open Mondays through Fridays.

The Fuller Building—41 East 57th St., Manhattan; 212/644-8300. About twenty-five separate galleries are found at this address, including **ACA** (212/644-8300); **Cavaliero/Navarra Gallery** (212/223-2828); **Andre Emmerich Gallery** (212/752-0124); **Krugier Gallery** (212/755-7288); **Littlejohn/Sternau Gallery** (212/980-2323); **Jason McCoy Gallery** (212/319-1996); **Robert Miller Gallery** (212/980-5454); **Schmidt-Bingham Gallery** (212/888-1122); and **Washburn Gallery** (212/753-0546). These frequently have impressive exhibitions, from late-nineteenth-century European works to early prints by Picasso to steel sculptures by today's leading American artists.

Gagosian Gallery—136 Wooster St., Manhattan; 212/228-2828, 980 Madison Ave. (77th St.), Manhattan; 212/744-2313. These folks have both of the art centers covered. Both galleries, uptown and down, present major exhibitions by modernists like Richard Serra and Yves Klein.

Galerie St. Etienne—24 West 57th St., Manhattan; 212/245-6734. This gallery puts on group exhibits and theme shows, like its recent "The Dance of Death," with works by Holbein, Durer, Grosz, and many others.

Again, this building houses several other galleries, including the **Arras Gallery** (212/265-2222); **Fischbach Gallery** (212/759-2345); **Galeria Joan Prats/Poligrafa** (212/315-3680); **Marian Goodman Gallery** (212/977-7160); **Grand Central Galleries** (212/867-3344); **Reece Galleries** (212/333-5830); **Suzuki Graphics** (212/582-0373); and **Jack Tilton Gallery** (212/247-7480).

Graham Galleries—1014 Madison Ave. (80th St.), Manhattan; 212/535-5767. This is actually two galleries, a traditional (nineteenth and twentieth century) and a modern, both under the same roof.

Greenwich House—27 Barrow St., Manhattan; 212/242-4140. Located in the heart of Greenwich Village, this gallery boasts an extensive permanent collection of ceramics and pottery.

Hirschl & Adler Galleries—851 Madison Ave. (70th St.), Manhattan; 212/744-6700, and 21 East 70th St., Manhattan; 212/535-8810. The Madison Avenue branch of H & A, "Modern," features contemporary artists, while the post around the corner on 70th Street, "Folk," exhibits older American works—such as its recent selection of New England landscapes done in the 1850s.

851 Madison is also the brand-new home of the **Barry Friedman Gallery** (212/794-8950), known for its fine exhibits of early-twentieth-century avant-garde artists.

Illustration Gallery—330 East 11th St., Manhattan; 212/979-1014. Over in the East Village, this gallery—as you might guess—specializes in drawings and lithographs, mainly focusing on contemporary artists.

International Center of Photography—1133 Sixth Ave. (43rd St.), Manhattan; 212/768-4680, and 1130 Fifth Ave. (94th St.), Manhattan; 212/860-1778. See listing under "Museums."

Jane Kahan Gallery—922 Madison Ave. (74th St.), Manhattan; 212/744-1490. The Kahan Gallery hosts shows of major twentieth-century artists, both European and American. These have included Picasso, Arp, Chagall, and Miro.

Kool Art Gallery—375 West Broadway, Manhattan; 212/966-9277. It sure is. Kool presents art from all media, as in its recent show "The New Art Scene," featuring sculpture, paintings, video, and performance art.

Marlborough Gallery—40 West 57th St., Manhattan; 212/541-4900. A longtime favorite, Marlborough recently held a major retrospective of works by Larry Rivers. Also at this address is the **Kennedy Gallery** (212/541-9600), featuring American paintings from the late eighteenth century to the present, such as works by Edward Hopper.

Marymount Manhattan College—221 East 71st St., Manhattan; 212/517-0475. See listing under "Colleges."

Meisner Soho—96 Greene St., Manhattan; 212/431-9589. One of SoHo's newest major galleries, Meisner represents and shows the works of a handful of rising young artists on the New York scene.

Metro Pictures—150 Greene St., Manhattan; 212/925-8335. Cute name for a serious SoHo gallery; they recently presented a retrospective of photographs by Cindy Sherman, along with her latest works.

New York Public Library—Central Branch, 455 Fifth Ave. (42nd St.), Manhattan; recorded info, 212/869-8089. Don't forget the library for art! In addition to its busy slate of films, lectures, poetry readings, and music (oh yes, and books), the NYPL galleries have regular exhibits throughout the year. Often the subject matter relates somehow to rare texts or the written word. Some local branches show art, too; call the above number for a tape of upcoming events.

NoHo Gallery—168 Mercer St., Manhattan; 212/219-2210. The SoHo art scene has been spreading north of Houston Street for some time; thus was NoHo born, and this gallery shows a variety of works by current New York artists similar to the galleries on the other side of the street.

Pace Gallery—142 Greene St., Manhattan; 212/431-9224, and 32 East 57th St., Manhattan; 212/421-3292. Another company hitting both the uptown and downtown scenes. Each gallery runs separate exhibitions, focusing on new works by major modern artists like Andy Warhol. The uptown branch also has a print gallery, which recently held a showing of lithographs by Matisse.

SoHo Photo Gallery—15 White St., Manhattan; 212/260-8571. Guess where this place is and what they show there? The name says it all—but then, a picture's worth a thousand words, so you should absolutely go and see for yourself. Recent exhibits included "Irish Eyes: Children of West Belfast," photographs by Michael Schwartz.

Studio 53—424 Park Ave. (55th St.), Manhattan; 212/755-6650. Norman Rockwell and Andrew Wyeth are among the American masters seen at this midtown gallery.

Wimmer Gallery—560 Broadway (Spring St.), Manhattan; 212/274-0274. This gallery of contemporary art features paintings and sculpture by today's emerging artists.

In the midst of this eclectic neighborhood, as well known for Canal Jeans as for art galleries, 560 Broadway also houses many other salons. These include the **Paula Allen Gallery**

(212/334-9710); **Diane Brown Gallery** (212/219-1060); **David Nolan Gallery** (212/925-6190); and the **Wolff Gallery** (212/431-7833).

Meanwhile, just a few doors up at 568 Broadway, there's yet another cluster of galleries—two dozen in all, under the same roof. You can pass an entire day without leaving the block.

CHILDREN'S ACTIVITIES

See the "Museums" and "Outdoors" chapters for listings on zoos and other activities suitable for children.

Brooklyn Academy of Music/ "Family Fun" Series—30 Lafayette Ave., Brooklyn; 718/636-4100. During the winter and spring months, usually from January through May, BAM offers this series of shows specially geared toward children and families. These are fully professional shows, ranging from plays and musicals to concerts. You may see *Hansel and Gretel*, Shakespeare's *A Midsummer Night's Dream*, performed by the London Ballet Theatre, or pop bands from around the world. Tickets are $12.00 for adults, and $7.00 for kids. And, if you buy tix in advance for three or more shows, you can save up to 30 percent. Call to see what's coming up next.

Brooklyn Children's Museum—145 Brooklyn Ave. (St. Mark's Ave.), Crown Heights, Brooklyn; 718/735-4400. Tucked away in the heart of Brooklyn, this is one of the nation's first—and foremost—children's museums. Yes, it's in Crown Heights, but it's a large, safe location in Brower Park—and the museum even takes racial issues as a point of departure for many of its exhibits. Kids can learn about the many cultures of people in the city, and perhaps gain a better understanding through participation in hands-on workshops and play areas. This was one of the first museums, in fact, to develop the hands-on approach to learning. It's a modern facility, in which an old-fashioned subway entrance leads into neon-lit tunnels—the history of the city in symbols. Special programs, free with admission, may focus on plant life, animal survival, or even body movement workshops. The museum is open Wednesdays through Fridays from 2:00 to 5:00 p.m., Saturdays and Sundays from noon to 5:00 p.m.; closed Mondays and Tuesdays. Admission is a $2.00 suggested donation.

Children's Museum of the Arts—72 Spring St., Manhattan; 212/941-9198. Families who enjoy browsing SoHo art galleries can get their kids right into the scene without leaving the neighborhood. This museum/learning center offers exhibits as well as active participation for children; it's recommended for toddlers of eighteen months up to kids of about ten years old. Among their programs are afterschool art classes and weekend workshops, in which children can really "express themselves" and just have fun. Hours are Tuesdays through Sundays from 11:00 a.m. to 5:00 p.m. (Thursday evenings until 7:00); admission is $4.00, and free to anyone under eighteen months or over sixty-five years. Family memberships are also available, reducing the costs for regular visitors.

Children's Museum of Manhattan—212 West 83rd St., Manhattan; 212/721-1234. Recently moved into expanded quarters,

CMOM is a hands-on haven for youngsters—bright, big, and lively. Everything is geared toward activities that make learning painless and just plain fun. What else would you expect from a gallery called the Brainatarium, or the Urban Tree House? There's a media laboratory where kids can make their own effects-laden videos, and lots of workshops in which they can design flags or stamps, musical instruments, or pottery. Add live music and theater performances, and you've got what amounts to an indoor carnival. Great, creative toys in the gift shop, too. Admission is $5.00, $2.50 for senior citizens, and kids under two get in free. There may be a $1.00 or $2.00 additional fee for workshops and performances. The museum is open every day but Tuesday; hours are 10:00 a.m. to 5:00 p.m. during the summer, though it's closed on weekday mornings during the school year.

IBM Gallery of Science and Art—590 Madison Ave. (56th St.), Manhattan; 212/745-6100. This popular hall features a variety of fun exhibits geared toward family visitors. Their permanent shows highlight, of course, the Itty Bitty Machine Company's contributions to the world of technology; temporary art exhibits may show paintings from various American periods and ethnic groups, like the recent show of African-American artists. Daily films and lectures accompany these exhibits. Best of all, it's all free; hours are Tuesdays through Saturdays from 11:00 a.m. to 6:00 p.m.

Another great reason to stop here on any day of activities is the Garden Plaza, one of midtown's best indoor atriums. It's a peaceful place to cool your jets—and they have clean, free restrooms.

Mostly Magic—55 Carmine St., Manhattan; 212/924-1472. Remember growing up with that Sunday morning TV show, "Wonderama"? Remember its affable host, magician Bob McAlister? He's still around, looking about the same; still performing magic for young audiences, and still singing his signature "Kids Are People Too." He's just one of the many entertainers who's delighted families during the "Children's Magic Matinees," held on Saturday afternoons at this Greenwich Village nightclub. Tickets are usually $10.00; call to see who's "appearing" next (excuse the pun), and to make reservations.

Mulberry Street Theater—70 Mulberry St., Manhattan; 212/349-0126. See listing under "Dance."

Mr. Cheap's Picks

- ✔ **Brooklyn Academy of Music**—BAM's "Family Fun" series hosts big-time professional companies doing everything from Shakespeare to world music.
- ✔ **Children's Museums**—Manhattan, Brooklyn, and Staten Island all boast wonderful play-worlds where kids really have fun while learning.
- ✔ **IBM Gallery of Science and Art**—High-tech dazzles you with the past, present and future of the computer age.
- ✔ **Mostly Magic**—And entirely delightful.

Pips Comedy Club—2005 Emmons Ave., Sheepshead Bay, Brooklyn; 718/646-9433. Tickets are only $6.50 per person for Sunday afternoon shows at this neighborhood nightclub. The admission price even includes one soda, and a snack menu is also available. Performances start at 1:30 and 3:30 p.m. These extravaganzas are filled with comedy, magic, ventriloquism, and lots of audience participation; recommended for ages three to twelve. Reservations are recommended too.

Puppetworks—338 Sixth Ave. (4th St.), Park Slope, Brooklyn; 718/965-3391. Though they perform all over the city, this cozy, climate-controlled theater is the home base for one of New York's longtime, popular puppetry troupes. These folks make their own marionettes, presenting them in forty-five-minute shows every Saturday and Sunday afternoon. Fairy tales and other children's stories make up most of the repertoire, good especially for the younger kiddies. Tickets are $5.00 for adults and $4.00 for children.

Queens Museum of Art—New York City Building, Flushing Meadow Park, Queens; 718/592-9700. See listing under "Museums."

Spoke The Hub—295 Douglass St., Park Slope, Brooklyn; 718/596-5250. See listing under "Dance."

Stand-Up New York—236 West 78th St., Manhattan; 212/595-0850. Just off of Broadway, here's a comedy club with a difference—a family-run place with careful attention to your comfort and enjoyment. In addition to their regular night-time comedy shows for grownups, Stand-Up NY offers children's shows every Sunday at 2:00 p.m. No, they haven't found a way to clean up the comics' acts. Instead, the comedy in these shows comes from magicians, clowns, storytellers and other performers. The family fun is best suited for ages two to ten or so. Admission is $7.00 to $8.00, depending on the show; call for more info.

Staten Island Children's Museum—1000 Richmond Terrace, Snug Harbor, Staten Island; 718/273-2060. It may not be huge, but this museum is a goldmine for active children—with lots of hands-on exhibits and special activities. Taking a cue from the most famous thing about Staten Island, for example, there is a large workshop area where kids can pretend to build their own ferry boat—complete with passing skyline! A five-minute ride on the "Snug Harbor Trolley" takes you from the ferry (the real one, that is) to the museum. All programs and workshops are free with admission, which is just $3.00 for all ages (under two, free). Hours are Tuesdays through Saturdays from noon to 5:00 p.m.; the museum is closed on Mondays.

Storytelling Hours—Various locations and times. Many bookstores around the city, especially those that cater to children, offer free storytelling sessions—often with authors reading from their own latest works. The times and places change, but here are a few well-established offerings that Mr. C found in his travels. Call the stores to confirm their current schedules.

Barnes & Noble Jr., 120 East 86th St., Manhattan; 212/427-0686. Tuesdays, 10:30 a.m., and Thursdays, 7:30 p.m. This store also has a regular schedule of puppet shows, short plays, and live book character appearances. Stop in for a calendar.

Books of Wonder, 464 Hudson St., Manhattan; 212/645-8006., 132 Seventh Ave. (18th St.), Manhattan; 212/989-3270. Sundays, 11:30 a.m., at both stores.

Eeyore's Books, 2212 Broadway (79th St.), Manhattan; 212/362-0634. Sundays, 11:00 a.m.; and 25 East 83rd St., Manhattan; 212/988-3404. Sundays, 12:30 p.m.

Shakespeare & Co., 2259 Broadway (81st St.), Manhattan; 212/580-7800. Sundays, 10:00 a.m.

Storyland, 1369 Third Ave. (78th St.), Manhattan; 212/517-6951. Wednesdays, 12:30 p.m., and Sundays, 1:30 p.m.

West Side Kids, 498 Amsterdam Ave. (84th St.), Manhattan; 212/496-7282. Wednesdays, 11:00 a.m.

Another well-known place to hear stories, during the summer months, is by the **Hans Christian Andersen Statue** in Central Park (on the Fifth Avenue side, near the 72nd Street entrance). For years, this has been a gathering place for practiced talespinners from around the country. It all takes place from early June through late September, every day at 11:00 a.m.

While storytelling takes place in many branches of the New York Public Library citywide, the **Donnell Library Center** at 20 West 53rd Street in Manhattan (212/621-0618) houses the city's largest collection of children's books—over 100,000 of them! They also offer regular programs of storytelling, films, workshops, and evening programs for parents. Call for upcoming events.

Other branches that frequently offer activities for kids include the **Tompkins Square Branch**, 331 East 10th St., Manhattan (212/228-4747); the **Kips Bay Branch**, 446 Third Ave., Manhattan (212-683-2520); the **Library for the Performing Arts**, 40 Lincoln Center Plaza, Manhattan (212/870-1630); and the **96th Street Branch**, 112 East 96th St., Manhattan (212/289-0908). To find out what's on at the other libraries, call: Bronx, 718/220-6565. Brooklyn, 718/780-7700. Manhattan, 212/869-8089. Queens, 718/990-0700 or 718/291-ARTS. Staten Island, 718/442-8562.

West End Gate—2911 Broadway (113th St.), Manhattan; 212/662-8830. This Columbia-area restaurant, which features fine jazz at night, also offers children's theater every Saturday at 1:00 p.m. The recommended age range is three to nine. Performers include real circus clowns, magicians, and ventriloquists, as well as musicians, comedians—and everything in between. The restaurant even serves up a specially priced children's lunch before or after the show. Tickets for most performances are $7.00, with discounts for groups of seven or more. Call or drop in any time for the season's lineup.

COLLEGE ARTS

New York City's many college campuses offer a wealth of music, dance, theater, films, and lectures that don't require much personal wealth to attend. These include both student and professional performances. Many events are free to students, of course (don't forget your ID card!), but some also to the general public. It's a great way to put culture into your life on a regular basis.

City University of New York—Office of Community Relations: 535 East 80th St., Room 710, New York, NY 10021. True to its name, these guys are everywhere—and so, therefore, is inexpensive entertainment of all kinds. CUNY has twenty-one separate campuses throughout all five boroughs. Opera in Flatbush? Sure. Take in an aria by the Brooklyn College Opera Theater, at BC's Walt Whitman Hall. Tickets are usually around $10.00, and $7.00 for students, senior citizens, and children. Crave a bit of comedy instead? Actor Frank Ferrante recently brought his off-Broadway rendition of *Groucho* to the Whitman, with tickets just $10.00.

Other recent events included the Hunter College Dance Company in Manhattan (recital tix, $8.00 and $6.00); the Copland Contemporary Ensemble, free at Queens College in Flushing; the hot rhythms of the Mario Bauza Big Band, featured in *The Mambo Kings* , at Kingsborough Community College in Brooklyn; an all-Rossini concert, free, at the College of Staten Island; Moliere's *The Misanthrope* at Queensborough C.C. in Bayside ($10.00 and $5.00); tenor Robert Merrill in a recital for only $18.00 and $15.00; plus Mummenschanz, the Tokyo Festival Ballet, jazz guitarist Al DiMeola, comedian Alan King, The Flying Karamazov Brothers, and so much more.

And that doesn't even cover lecture series, most of which are free to all, with such novelists as E.L. Doctorow or subjects like, "How the IRS Selects Individuals for Audits"; special events, like the Langston Hughes Festival; classic and modern films; photography and art exhibits from around the world, free and open to all; and lots of activities for parents and children. Write to get on the mailing list for CUNY's free quarterly calendar, twenty pages packed with events, prices, and addresses.

Columbia University—Kathryn Bache Miller Theatre, Dodge Hall, Broadway at 116th St., Manhattan; 212/854-7799. Columbia's Miller Theatre hosts a number of different music and performance series from October through April. The past year's "Distinguished String Quartet" series, for example, presented such groups as the Juilliard String Quartet and France's Ysaye Quartet. Ticket prices were $16.00 and $18.00 per concert, with a set of three for just $39.00; student rates were half-price. Tickets to their

Mr. Cheap's Picks

✔ **City University of New York**—Get CUNY's huge monthly catalogue of free and low-cost performances taking place at branches all over the city.

✔ **The Julliard School**—You can enjoy a steady diet of all the performing arts, without ever leaving this campus.

✔ **Manhattan School of Music**—Wonderful, inexpensive classical concerts for free (or close to it) in four different-sized halls.

"Music Uptown" series, four concerts of contemporary classical ensembles from around the country, were just $5.00 each for the public and free to students.

The season also includes jazz, from the likes of Mose Allison, Jimmy Heath, and Windham Hill pianist Billy Childs. "Literary Evenings" may consist of readings by anyone from Susan Sontag to Irish poet Seamus Heaney—tix $8.00, students $5.00. And Columbia's theatre department offers an ongoing series of student-written and -directed plays, also for $5.00 per ticket (the department chair is the award-winning playwright Romulus Linney).

Fordham University—Lincoln Center Campus: 113 West 60th St., Manhattan; 212/636-6340. Rose Hill Campus: 441 East Fordham Rd., Bronx; 718/579-2000. Fordham's theater department presents plays several times a year; productions have included the ambitious *Our Country's Good* , a recent Broadway hit. These generally take place at the Lincoln Center location. At Rose Hill's Collins Auditorium, you can hear music from the likes of the Bronx Arts Ensemble Chamber Orchestra (see listing under "Live Music: Classical"); tickets to concerts are often free, or around $5.00. Also, the philosophy department's lectures are free and open to the public.

The Juilliard School—144 West 66th St., Manhattan; 212/769-7406. Juilliard can't be beat for inexpensive, high-quality classical music— as well as dance and theater. Julliard being one of the top arts schools anywhere, it's a fair bet that some of these young musicians will soon be playing concert halls around the world; likewise for the dancers, and the actors can practically write their own tickets to Broadway stages. Performances take place from late September through May, and best of all, most of them are free!

Located at the northern edge of Lincoln Center, Juilliard has several locations in which performances take place. Alice Tully Hall is the main site, hosting everything from informal lunchtime concerts to the Juilliard Symphony; but in the Juilliard building there is Paul Hall, a cozy and handsome three-hundred-seat recital hall with good sightlines and acoustics; and the Juilliard Theater, an intimate thrust-stage auditorium for drama and opera.

There are so many kinds of shows to see here. Tuesday and Friday evenings at 8:00 p.m., hear the Symphony or one of the many chamber ensembles in Alice Tully Hall, all for free. Same place for "Wednesdays at One," with freebies like "Music for Winds, Harp and Guitar" or

"Arias and Scenes." In Paul Hall you can check out the finalists of the Vaughn Williams Violin Competition, again free. Juilliard Theater offers operas twice a year, as well as fall and spring drama and dance repertories. Tickets for each of these are $10.00. And at the impressive Avery Fisher Hall, major concerts by the Juilliard Orchestra are given four times a year, tix $5.00 and $10.00.

Tickets are available through the box office for just a few weeks in advance; even most free concerts do require tickets. One exception is "Wednesdays at One," for which you simply show up at Tully Hall from 12:30 on. Needless to say, the major series are extremely hot tix; to take full advantage of this treasure trove, Mr. C recommends getting on the mailing list for Juilliard's monthly calendar of all events.

Manhattan School of Music—120 Claremont Ave., Manhattan; 212/749-2802. Near the Riverside Church, MSM is one of the city's foremost training schools for classical musicians. Four different halls—from a hundred seats to a thousand—present the Manhattan Symphony Orchestra, myriad chamber ensembles, opera, and more. Though not as fancy as the auditoriums at Juilliard, these are serviceable nevertheless—and with so many of the concerts free, who can complain? The program choices are not always daring, but they offer a nice mix of traditional warhorses and modern challenges. The students, meanwhile, are known for their dedication and budding talent. The Manhattan Symphony and the Manhattan Philharmonic, the school's two major groups, play more than a dozen free concerts through the academic year.

Marymount Manhattan College—221 East 71st St., Manhattan; 212/517-0475. This Upper East Side college space is, in fact, frequently rented by small professional companies. Most of these are "homeless" dance troupes—those without a theater of their own. So you can often see innovative modern dance performances here; drop by to sort through the flyers advertising upcoming events. Ticket prices vary, depending on the company, but they're sure to be cheap.

Marymount also has an art gallery, with shows of paintings, murals and multimedia works. These change over once or twice a month; admission is free.

New York University—Loeb Student Center, 566 LaGuardia Place, Manhattan; 212/998-5424. The Loeb is the heart of NYU's many performance spaces, with its "Ticket Central" box office in the lobby. Stop in for information about the many kinds of arts events taking place around the area. These include performances by the NYU Symphony Orchestra, the Chamber Music Society, the Graduate Acting Program, and many other groups—the quality of which can be quite good.

The phone number above is for information about music concerts. For theater, call 998-1921, and for dance, 998-1980. Other NYU venues include the Abe Burrows Theater at 721 Broadway, near Washington Place; faculty and student dance recitals are often presented at another theater, located at 111 Second Avenue, between East 6th and East 7th Streets. Many events are open to the public, with prices ranging from $10.00 or so down to freebies.

And don't forget NYU's Grey Gallery and Study Center, at 33 Washington Place (212/998-6780), with its wide variety of art exhibits in all media. Also, free lectures and poetry readings take place from time to time at the Loeb.

School of Visual Arts—209 East 23rd St., Manhattan; 212/679-7350. This downtown school may be small, but it's one of the city's most vibrant for artists. They run two main galleries, showing work by students and professionals. The Visual Arts Museum, at the above address, presents exhibitions of graphics, crafts, photography, video installations and more, mostly by professional artists. Once a year, their "Masters Series" highlights the work of major stars in these fields.

The Visual Arts Gallery, at 137 Wooster Street in SoHo (212/598-0221), shows the school's best thesis work in fine arts. Both galleries are open year-round and are free. There are also smaller student galleries in the 23rd Street building.

COMEDY

As you'll see in some of these descriptions, many of the big-name (and big-price) comedy clubs host "Open Mike" nights, when younger comedians get to strut their stuff. These may include amateurs getting their first break in front of a crowd—which can make for some unintentional humor—or seasoned vets from around the country who are ready to take a bite of the Big Apple. Occasionally big stars also drop in, unannounced, to try out new material on an adventurous audience. Open mike nights can come and go, but they're generally found in the first half of the week. If your favorite club is not listed below, call them to see if they currently have such an offering.

Catch A Rising Star—1487 First Ave. (77th St.), Manhattan; 212/794-1906. This most famous of comedy clubs, with locations around the country, can also be one of New York's more expensive; prices here can go as high as $12.00, plus two drinks, for their weekend shows. Is there a way around this, Mr. C? Of course there is! Catch the *really* rising stars who perform on Mondays at 9:00 p.m. You'll see about ten different performers who are making their way up the comedy ladder, MC'd by a well-known headliner (so you're still guaranteed to get plenty of laughs). The cover is reduced to $4.00; there is the same two-drink minimum, but all drinks are priced at $3.00 on Mondays. So it's possible to have a big evening here for around $10.00 per person—or $1.00 per comedian.

Chicago City Limits—351 East 74th St., Manhattan; 212/772-8707. Comedy in a church? Yes, this performance space is in the basement of Yorkville's Jan Hus Church, a friendly, relaxed kind of place. It's also the current home of this longtime improv comedy troupe, which does sketches and songs based largely on audience suggestions. Top prices here are $20.00; but again, you can save dough by going on Monday nights. That's when "CCL Unlimited," the touring version of this fast-moving show, performs for just $10.00. The rest of the week they're working at corporate seminars and colleges throughout the region. One of the earliest groups to present this kind of humor in New York, at the beginning of the comedy wave, Chicago City Limits is consistently funny and innovative.

It's also worth noting that this is the only top-line comedy show in town at which no alcohol is served. This makes a great alternative for teens, or anyone who prefers to avoid the drinking scene at other comedy clubs.

Gladys's Comedy Room—988 Second Ave. (52nd St.), Manhattan; 212/832-1762. Upstairs at Coldwater's Restaurant is this intimate club, with perhaps one of the best comedy bargains in town. Every Thursday, Friday, and Saturday night at 9:30, nationally known comics perform.

Many have appeared on MTV, Showtime, and the like. The regular cover price is $8.00; but if you make reservations and mention the name of this book, you'll get in for $5.00. They also have a Wednesday night "Open Mike" show, from 6:00 to 10:30, with a cover price of just $3.00.

But in fact the deal gets even sweeter: Dinner/show packages are available, with dinners starting at just $7.95. Add that reduced cover price upstairs, and you can have an entire evening out for around $15.00 per person. Just tell Gladys you saw her in *Mr. Cheap's New York*. Don't say Mr. C never did any favors for ya.

Gotham City Improv—At Duplex, 61 Christopher St., Manhattan; 212/714-1477. This cabaret at the corner of Seventh Avenue South in the heart of Greenwich Village is the current home for this wacky troupe, who perform a mix of written sketches and comedy improvised on the spot. They've also been a training ground for many famous comics, in both New York and Los Angeles. They perform every Saturday night at 8:00; it's not the lowest-priced comedy show around, but $10.00 (plus a two-drink minimum) on a weekend in this hopping part of town is really not bad at all.

"House Comedy" at Westbeth Theater Center—151 Bank St., Manhattan; 212/741-0391. Way over in the West Village, by the banks of the briny Hudson, this group offers a weekly parade of terrific comedy sketches and parodies every Thursday evening. Showtime is at 10:00 p.m. The admission price is just $7.00, and there is no drink minimum.

Mostly Magic—55 Carmine St., Manhattan; 212/924-1472. Here's something different in the world of entertainment. Mostly Magic is a Greenwich Village restaurant/nightclub featuring the country's finest magicians five nights a week. With everything from close-up coin magic to full-stage spectacles, artful to outrageously funny, it would be quite a trick *not* to be entertained here. The restaurant has a menu of continental and American entrees and desserts. Dinner and show packages are just $22.50 per person, Tuesday through Thursday evenings; Fridays and Saturdays it's $25.00—not bad, considering all you get. The most magical deal of all is on Tuesdays and Wednesdays from 6:00 to 9:00 p.m., when you can

Mr. Cheap's Picks

- ✔ **Catch a Rising Star**—'Open Mike' nights at one of the city's best-known clubs offer a reduced cover charge and reduced drink prices.
- ✔ **Chicago City Limits**—A longtime favorite for sketches and improvisational comedy.
- ✔ **Gladys's Comedy Room**—Perhaps the lowest-priced standup comedy you'll ever find on prime weekend nights . . .
- ✔ **New York Comedy Club**— . . . unless it's the second show at this club, which actually has a lower cover charge than the early show.

enjoy close-up magic in the bar (right at your table!) with no cover or drink minimum.

NADA—167 Ludlow St., Manhattan; 212/420-1466. More of a performance art space than a comedy club, Nada has an ever-changing schedule of comedians, comedy troupes, and other wild productions. Admission prices are always $10.00 or under, with many shows just $5.00, and no drink minimum. There's a real "underground" feel to the place, both in the style of the up-and-coming performers and in the atmosphere of the theater. In fact, make sure you arrive on time, or the door—which leads from the street directly onto the stage area—may be locked. To find out just what's there and when, call for a recorded message.

National Improvisational Theatre—223 Eighth Ave. (21st St.), Manhattan; 212/243-7224. This ten year-old Chelsea theater/school trains actors in both the serious and comic uses of "improv," or theater with no script. Weekends feature professional performances by its resident troupes. Thursdays through Saturdays at 8:00 p.m., catch "Split-Second Theatre": The audience suggests the plot and characters, and these talented (not to mention brave!) actors spin out one-act plays on the spot. Monday evenings feature a different group, "Interplay," billed as New York's longest-running improv ensemble. Their curtain is also at 8:00. All admission prices are $15.00, and with only seventy-five seats, reservations are suggested. It's a wacky, different kind of theater—one where you can literally get in on the act.

New York Comedy Club—915 Second Ave. (48th St.), 2nd Floor, Manhattan; 212/888-1696. Here's a way to save money for you night owls. The second, late-night show at NYCC actually costs *less* than the early set. On weekends, for example, the 9:00 p.m. set has a cover charge of $10.00, but the 11:30 p.m. set is just $5.00. Both shows have a two-drink minimum, which does add to the overall cost, but your total cost for the second show can still be lower than many other clubs in town. Better yet, their "Open Mike" night—held on Mondays—has free admission. Now, *there's* a bargain!

"No Shame"—Public Theater, 425 Lafayette St., Manhattan; 212/598-7150. "No Shame" takes a comic approach to performance art. It's part of the vast slate of theater, poetry readings, films, and other events that take place at the late Joseph Papp's theater complex (see listing under "Theater"). As the title suggests, material can get pretty adventurous—so bring an open mind. You won't have to bring too much cash, though, since the admission price is $10.00 and there is no drink minimum. Showtime is 10:30 p.m. on Saturday night; call in advance to get the upcoming schedule.

DANCE

American Ballet Theater—Metropolitan Opera House, Lincoln Center, Columbus Ave. (64th St.), Manhattan; 212/799-3100. Like the Met itself, with whom ABT shares a home, tickets can be outrageously expensive for this traditional company. But also like the Met, you can buy standing room tickets for just $13.00 behind the orchestra section and $9.00 behind the family circle. The *one* major difference is that while the Met sells these tickets a week at a time, ABT only sells on the day of performance. Call them for more info.

American Museum of Natural History—Central Park West at 79th St., Manhattan; 212/769-5304. The Museum has four separate auditoriums of varying sizes (from a thousand seats to under a hundred). Periodically through the year, they present dance performances of groups from the United States and around the world. Many of these are traditional folk dance troupes. Tickets are usually around $10.00, but some shows are free—with many geared to children. Call to see what's coming up!

Blue Door Studio—463 Broome St., Manhattan; 212/431-8102. If you want to stay in tune with the experimental dance world, here's a good (and cheap) place to do it. Blue Door Studio is the classic kind of space you'd envision: SoHo loft location, natural wood floors—you know. Performances are a mix of music and dance, by both a resident company and others who rent the place out. Admission to most of these shows is around $5.00; call to see what's coming up.

Bryant Park Ticket Booth—Sixth Ave. (42nd St.), Manhattan; 212/382-2323. Broadway has its half-price ticket booth in Times Square; a few blocks away, behind the New York Public Library in Bryant Park, you'll find the dance and classical music version of the same thing. As with "tkts.," tickets are sold here at half of their box office prices, plus a $2.00 fee per ticket, only on the day of performance if available. Programs often found here include those at Lincoln Center (sometimes even the Metropolitan Opera!), Carnegie Hall, the Joyce Theater, Symphony Space, the Brooklyn Academy of Music, the City Center, and many other smaller houses. The booth is open Tuesday through Saturday from 12:00 noon to 2:00 p.m. and 3:00 to 7:00 p.m. (Wednesday and Saturday matinee days from 11:00 a.m.), as well as Sundays from noon to six. Cash only.

Merce Cunningham Studio—55 Bethune St., 11th Floor, Manhattan; 212/691-9751. Considered the elder statesman of modern dance, Merce Cunningham runs his company from these West Village studios, part of the vibrant Westbeth Artists' Complex. Eleven stories up, looking out over the Hudson River, the Cunningham loft space seats 125 and is host to workshops by this world-famous troupe as well as performances by other companies that rent the space out. Tickets are usually in the $10.00 range. Call for current info.

Mr. Cheap's Picks

✔ **Bryant Park Ticket Booth**—Check the booth daily for the possibility of half-price tix to the day's dance performances around town.

✔ **Dance Theater Workshop**—More than the sum of its parts, dance and theater—this is where many big name performance artists got their first big breaks.

✔ **Danspace Project**—See the work of the city's vital and adventurous choreographers, in this lovely downtown church space.

✔ **Spoke The Hub**—Brooklyn's own haven for experimental dance is another great place to visit regularly; so spoke Mr. C.

✔ STANDING ROOM BALLET TICKETS—Both the **American Ballet Theater** and the **New York City Ballet** offer cheap standing room tickets, when available, at their box offices.

Dance Space—622-626 Broadway (Bleecker St.), Manhattan; 212/777-8067. Another one of New York's many informal, inexpensive studios in which you can see a variety of local dance (and theater) troupes performing on a regular basis. Dance Space, in fact, has two different flexible spaces, both with limited seating—which means you'll see everything up close and personal. Tickets are generally in the $8.00 to $10.00 range. DS is also known for its monthly showcases featuring short works by several choreographers, a sort of Whitman sampler of modern dance. Call for schedules.

Dance Theater Workshop—Bessie Schonberg Theater, 219 West 19th St., 2nd Floor, Manhattan; 212/924-0077. One of New York's most renowned avant-garde performance spaces for almost thirty years, DTW has been a "birthplace" for such current celebs as Mark Morris, Bill T. Jones, Bill Irwin, and Whoopi Goldberg. This organization also sponsors the "Bessie" Awards, dance's version of the Tonys. Discover the stars of tomorrow for yourself, *before* their ticket prices become as big as their names. The packed schedule features performers from all over the country, developing serious works in dance, music, and performance art. These have recently included choreographer John Malashock, formerly a dancer with Twyla Tharp; Douglas Dunn & Dancers, accompanied in person by jazz musician Steve Lacy; and award-winning performance artist Linda Mancini, whose "Economy Tires Theater" blends words, music, movement, sound effects, and visual imagery. All of the artists presented at DTW are in some way funded by its many supportive programs, making this a sort of farm club for the major leagues of performance art. Tickets to most shows are $10.00 to $12.00; DTW also offers "Cheap$eats," a design-your-own subscription: Tickets to any four events in one season for just $36.00. There are dozens to choose from. With a name like that, how could Mr. C fail to recommend it?

DTW also recruits box office volunteers; this is a great way to see lots of shows here and save big money. Just work at least two dates per month, and you'll be admitted to other performances for free!

Danspace Project—St. Mark's Church, 131 East 10th St., Manhattan; 212/674-8112. This renovated church, with its large, open interior, is home to many dance and theater troupes. It's one of "the" places to see the latest in avant-garde dance, with an active year-round schedule. See the work of creators like Bebe Miller, Ralph Lemon, and the Urban Bush Women; or check out the New York Improvisation Festival. Many of the people who come to these showings are dancers and choreographers themselves, keeping up with each other's work—and performances are sometimes followed by audience-performer discussions. Tickets to most shows are $10.00; some are free of charge. There are tables inside stacked with flyers and brochures about all the upcoming performances.

DIA Center for the Arts—155 Mercer St., Manhattan; 212/431-9232. Owned by the Demenil family, longtime patrons of the arts, the DIA Center offers a variety of performances in its intimate one-hundred-seat space. These include modern dance, of course; but also poetry and literary readings, as well as art exhibitions in its galleries. Admission for most events is around $10.00. All of this is tucked into an industrial building in SoHo; look carefully and you'll find it. Hey, sometimes bargain hunting really *means* a hunt.

Dixon Place—258 Bowery (East Houston St.) , Manhattan; 212/219-3088. See listing under "Theater."

The Juilliard School—144 West 66th St., Manhattan; 212/769-7406. See listing under "Colleges."

The Kitchen—512 West 19th St., Manhattan; 212/255-5793. See listing under "Theater."

The Knitting Factory—47 East Houston St., Manhattan; 212/219-3055. See listing under "Live Music: Rock/Pop."

Laziza Space—123 Smith St., 2nd Floor, Brooklyn; 718/797-3116. Downtown Brooklyn's answer to the Blue Door Studio (see above), Laziza is another cozy upstairs loft featuring rising young choreographers along with its own resident troupe, the Laziza Light and Dance Company. This group is known for its mix of multimedia elements, such as lighting and video, with dance. Four times a year they host the "Spontaneous Combustion Festival," in which visual artists and dancers go wild. Be adventurous. Admission to most shows at Laziza are free, but it's a small space, so reservations are recommended.

Lincoln Center/Damrosch Park—Amsterdam Ave. at 62nd St., Manhattan; 212/877-2011. See listing under "Live Music: Free Summer Performances."

Marymount Manhattan College—221 East 71st St., Manhattan; 212/517-0475. See listing under "Colleges."

Mulberry Street Theater—70 Mulberry St., Manhattan; 212/349-0126. Located on the border (if there really is one anymore) of Chinatown and Little Italy, the Mulberry Street Theater specializes in Asian-American dance performances of all kinds. These often include children's shows as well. Ticket prices are well under $10.00—leaving enough cash for the inevitable dinner nearby.

New York City Ballet—Lincoln Center, Columbus Ave. (63rd St.), Manhattan; 212/870-5500. As the New York City Opera (see listing under "Live Music: Classical") presents an affordable option for opera lovers, the New York City Ballet does the same for balletomanes. Both perform at Lincoln Center's New York State Theater. NYCB ticket prices start at just $9.00, for the topmost circle; a limited number of standing room tickets are usually available for $8.00, for a place at the rear of the fourth balcony.

A related option is the "Fourth Ring Society." Join this group for $10.00, and then you can purchase tix in the fourth ring for $10.00 each. Go as often as you like, and buy in advance for any performance. Membership also includes access to pre-show lectures by the company, a free cup of cappuccino, discount coupons for area restaurants, and a NYCB T-shirt. Talk about friends in high places.

P.S. 122—150 First Ave. (9th St.), Manhattan; 212/477-5288. See listing under "Theater."

The Performing Garage—33 Wooster St., Manhattan; 212/966-9796. See listing under "Theater."

Spoke the Hub—295 Douglass St., Park Slope, Brooklyn; 718/596-5250. Part of the Gowanus Arts Exchange studios in this hip section of Brooklyn, Spoke the Hub's seventy-five-seat loft space is ideal for the range of modern and experimental dance performances you'll see here on a regular basis. A number of different series take place throughout the year; and since this is where so many artists, forced out of pricey Manhattan, are coming to live and work, the quality is often among the best in New York. Tickets for most shows cost $8.00 to $10.00.

Spoke the Hub also presents shows for children, mixing dance, puppetry, storytelling, and lots of audience participation. Some programs even help young kids develop their own performances.

Oh, and you adults can get in on the act, too; about once a month, Spoke throws open its doors for a live dance party, where you can strut your stuff to pulsing sounds from around the world—making for a rather artsy disco. Call to find out the next date.

Summerstage—Rumsey Playfield, Central Park, Manhattan; 212/360-CPSS(2777). See listing under "Live Music: Free Summer Performances."

Theater Development Fund—1501 Broadway, Suite 2110, New York, NY, 10036. See listing under "Theater."

Theater of the Riverside Church—91 Claremont Ave. (120th St.) , Manhattan; 212/864-2929. This landmark church, looking out majestically over the Hudson, actually boasts four different performance halls of varying sizes. These are rented out by an equal variety of dance troupes, for which ticket prices are generally in the $10.00-to-$15.00-range. Call to see what's coming up next.

Warren Street Performance Loft—46 Warren St., 2nd Floor, Manhattan; 212/732-3149. Smack in the heart of one of New York's craziest bargain shopping areas, the Warren Street Loft is just as much of a bargain for the dance world. Most performances here are around $10.00 per ticket, for high-quality dance in an up-close setting. The resident troupe, Richard Bull Dance Theatre, is known for experimental interaction between dancers and video; other groups perform here as well. Call for schedules.

World Financial Center/World Trade Center—West St. (between Liberty and Vesey Sts.), Manhattan; 212/945-0505, 212/466-4170. See listing under "Live Music: Free Summer Performances."

LECTURES

Art In General—79 Walker St., Manhattan; 212/219-0473.

That's actually the name of an art gallery in the TriBeCa section, very much a part of the hip world downtown. Along with its exhibitions, AIG often presents free talks about the arts scene in New York. Call to see what's coming up.

Bernard Shaw Society—991 Fifth Ave. (80th St.), Manhattan; 212/288-2263. See listing under "Poetry and Literary Readings."

Cooper Union—Cooper Square, Third Ave. (7th St.), Manhattan; 212/353-4195. In 1858 Peter Cooper founded a school of art and science, with an ornate "Great Hall," dedicated to freedom of speech and affordable learning. To this day the free exchange of ideas is fostered by a distinguished slate of authors, poets, scientists, and performers who share their wisdom with the general public. These programs are often free and seldom more than $10.00 per ticket. Recent freebies have included noted physicist Dr. Gerald Holton on "What Einstein Really Meant"; "Parallel Bass Views", in which two bassist/composers—one German, one American—compared their approaches by playing solos and duets; and Irene Worth, one of theater's most respected actresses, tracing "The Hero as Lover" through Greek drama and Shakespeare.

Other programs, with admission fees, have presented authors Gloria Steinem, Joyce Carol Oates, and Allen Ginsberg; a concert by the American Jazz Orchestra; and more. Stop in for a brochure.

DIA Center for the Arts—548 West 22nd St., Manhattan; 212/431-9232. See listing under "Art Galleries."

Fraunces Tavern Museum—54 Pearl St., Manhattan; 212/425-1778. See listing under "Museums."

Judith's Room/Books for Women & Their Friends—681 Washington St., Manhattan; 212/727-7330. This West Village bookshop offers free readings and discussions by authors working in various fields of women's issues. A recent speaker was Elizabeth Reba Weise, reading from her book *Closer to Home: Bisexuality and Feminism*. These generally take place on weekday evenings; call about upcoming events.

The Municipal Art Society—457 Madison Ave. (50th St.), Manhattan; 212/935-3960. This organization runs Sunday afternoon lecture series like "Voices and Visions," in which artists talk about their work. Admission is $3.00.

New York City Audubon Society—71 West 23rd St., Manhattan; 212/691-7483. See listing under "Outdoors."

New York Historical Society—170 Central Park West, Manhattan; 212/873-3400. As you might expect, this organization presents regular talks on subjects of social and political interest. As a recent example, take "Why Bother Putting Humpty Dumpty Together Again? Regions, Ethnicity and the Fragmentation of American History." Presumably, the lecture itself was only slightly longer than the title. Admission to these lectures is usually $7.00.

New York Public Library—Mid-Manhattan Branch, 455 Fifth Ave. (42nd St.), Manhattan; recorded info, 212/869-8089. Where else to hear the written word spoken but the grand marble hall of the library's Celeste Bartos Forum, at the main branch? NYPL's Public Education Program brings a full slate of authors and lecturers to the auditorium. Recent guests have included Stuart Curran, expert on the poet Shelley; author E.L. Doctorow; and urban sociologist Robert Coles. These begin at 6:00 p.m.; call the above number to get on the mailing list. Tickets are $6.00, available in advance at the Library Shop (room 116) or at the door if seats are still available. Many talks sell out; you can try the standby line, but success is not guaranteed.

This branch also sponsors book discussion groups, currently meeting on Tuesday afternoons from 1:00 to 2:00 p.m. These focus on literary classics from Dickens to Stendhal, and are free of course; but space is limited, so you must register in advance.

Among the many activities at NYPL's branch libraries, the **Donnell Library Center** at 20 West 53rd Street (212/621-0618) is another location for regular lectures and readings, as well as children's storytelling.

92nd Street "Y"—1395 Lexington Ave. (92nd St.), Manhattan; 212/415-5440. See listing under "Poetry and Literary Readings."

Poets Circle—Various locations; 718/651-1664. Based in Queens, Poets Circle holds lectures on different facets of poetry, followed by readings and discussions of participants' work. Kind of like an open class for poetry. These usually take place on weeknights at the Wine Gallery Restaurant, 70-20 Austin St., Forest Hills, Queens. Call for more info.

Poets House—72 Spring St., Manhattan; 212/431-7920. Poets House takes a slightly different approach to poetry, focusing on discussions of well-known writers or ethnic cultures. Recent talks have included "Strange Courage: The Spanish American Roots of William Carlos Williams" and "Oral Traditions: Caribbean Discourse, Creole and Creolization," as well as talks on Sylvia Plath and others. The programs

Mr. Cheap's Picks

✔ **Cooper Union**—The city's longtime champion of free speech, literally and figuratively. You may have to pay a small admission charge nowadays, but many lectures are still free—and the ideas *always* are.

✔ **Judith's Room**—A bookstore offering a free weekly series in which authors discuss women's issues.

✔ **New York Public Library**—Who says there's no talking in the library? While free lectures and readings are offered at many branches around town, the main branch has the most active program.

✔ **Poets House**—Lectures and discussions on the significance of famous poets throughout literature.

begin at 7:00 in the evening. Admission is $3.00 to $5.00, depending on the event.

The Public Theater/New York Shakespeare Festival—425 Lafayette St., Manhattan; 212/598-7150. See listing under "Theater."

South Street Seaport Museum—207 Front St., Manhattan; 212/669-9400. Along with all that there is to see and do here, the museum frequently offers free lectures on subjects related to maritime history. Call to see what's on next.

LIVE MUSIC

CLASSICAL

Amato Opera—319 Bowery (Bleecker St.) , Manhattan; 212/228-8200. Opera has to be *big*, right? Big theater, big sets, big prices. Not true! For forty-five years now the Amato Opera has been producing operas that are up-close-and-personal. This tiny East Village auditorium only holds about a hundred people, and the neighborhood has seen better days; but oh, do they flock here. (Crowds in fur coats, mingling along the Bowery before going in, is quite a sight—only in New York!) The atmosphere inside is very homey, presided over by Anthony Amato and his wife Sally. He directs the cast, conducts the orchestra, and makes the fundraising curtain speech. Given his name, it's no surprise that the repertoire leans toward the Italians: Rossini's *Barber of Seville*, Verdi's *Otello*. Yet their season of half a dozen productions may also yield a Mozart, or an unusual work rarely heard at all. Many of the operas are sung in English.

Since New York is the center of the American opera world, you can rest assured that the singers are well qualified indeed. You may catch the occasional weak voice, but these are all serious professionals, and they've got the reviews to prove it. Talented too are the set designers and costumers, who seem to create just as much spectacle as the Met with a fraction of the space—and budget. Speaking of which, how much does all this cost? A mere $16.00 per ticket. Sure, you can get into the Met for that much, but you'll never hear the music so intimately.

There are several other small opera companies around the city. These often feature talented younger singers and musicians who are making their way up the ladder, but you're not likely to be disappointed. Especially at prices mostly in the low, baritone range of $10.00 to $20.00. Places to check out include the **Bronx Opera Company** (718/365-4209), performing at locations in both the Bronx and Manhattan; **Brooklyn Lyric Opera** (718/837-1176), which performs at various locations around town; the **Brooklyn Opera Theatre** (718/638-6563), heard at the Brooklyn Conservatory of Music, 58 Seventh Ave., Park Slope, Brooklyn; **Il Piccolo Teatro dell'Opera** (718/643-7775), which performs at the Brooklyn Academy of Music and, in summer, at Prospect Park; and the **Regina Opera Company** (718/232-3555), which has performed at Regina Hall in Bensonhurst for over twenty years. Call these companies for further info about their current seasons. Also, during the summer, you can often hear free opera in Central Park, presented by the New York Grand Opera (see "Summer" listings below).

Bargemusic—Fulton Ferry Landing, Brooklyn Heights, Brooklyn;

718/624-4061. Great, inexpensive music in New York is often going on right under your nose—or, in this case, right under the Brooklyn Bridge. Begun by Olga Bloom, a concert violininst who still runs the program, this is a chamber music series that actually takes place in an old barge, converted into an informal concert hall. The performers include soloists from the international circuit, working in intimate ensembles—or larger groupings, when the program (Bach's *Brandenburg Concerti*, for example) requires it. Concerts are presented throughout the year, on Thursday evenings at 7:30 (tickets $15.00) and Sunday afternoons at 4:00 (tickets $18.00). For senior citizens and students, tix are $13.00 at all times; further discounts are available with subscriptions. It's one of the city's great and unique bargains.

Before or after the concert, Mr. C recommends dinner just up the hill at Patsy's (see listing under "Restaurants: Outer Boroughs"), for a lively atmosphere and some of the best pizza you'll ever taste.

Bronx Arts Ensemble—c/o Golf House, Van Cortlandt Park, Bronx, NY, 10471; 718/601-7399. The Bronx's fully professional resident company, BAE presents a wide variety of concerts in an equally wide variety of settings—from outdoor orchestral shows in parks around the borough to chamber ensembles performing in private homes. They are frequently found at the Rose Hill Campus of Fordham University, the Riverdale "Y," the Bronx Zoo, and other such places. To best keep up with this lively company, write to the address above and get on their mailing list. Tickets for these concerts are usually in the $10.00 range, with discounts for students and senior citizens; many summer family performances are free.

Bronx Symphony Orchestra—Lehman College, Bedford Park Blvd. West, Bronx; 718/960-8232. For almost fifty years the

Mr. Cheap's Picks

- ✔ **Amato Opera**—Small-scale operas (but big on love) are always popular at this cultural oasis on the Bowery.
- ✔ **Bargemusic**—At the base of the Brooklyn Bridge, world-class chamber concerts hit the waterfront on a converted barge.
- ✔ **Bruno Walter Auditorium**—The New York Library for the Performing Arts has a lovely hall offering free concerts.
- ✔ **Open Rehearsals at the Philharmonic**—Another Lincoln Center bargain—the New York Philharmonic Orchestra for just $5.00. Tux definitely optional.
- ✔ **St. Paul's Chapel/Trinity Church**—Take in a free lunchtime concert at either of these historic Financial District churches.
- ✔ STANDING ROOM TICKETS—Both the **Metropolitan Opera** and the **New York City Opera** offer standing room tix (if you've got the feet for it).

Bronx Symphony Orchestra has been presenting concerts of traditional symphonic fare. The orchestra blends serious nonprofessional musicians with younger players on the rise. Don't go in expecting the New York Philharmonic, and you'll enjoy yourself. Especially when you consider the price; these concerts are free and open to all.

Brooklyn Museum Court—200 Eastern Pkwy. (Washington Ave.), Park Slope, Brooklyn; 718/638-5000. The Museum Court of this elegant turn-of-the-century building is host to weekly classical music and dance performances that are free with regular museum admission. The concerts, sponsored by the Brooklyn Arts Council, take place on Sunday afternoons at 2:00. Admission to the museum is $4.00 for adults, $1.50 for senior citizens, and free for kids under age twelve.

Bruno Walter Auditorium—111 Amsterdam Ave. (65th St.), Manhattan; 212/870-1630. At the "back" of Lincoln Center, the New York Public Library for the Performing Arts includes this comfortable performance hall. It's home to concerts, lectures, and films throughout the year, all free. Also, a series of free classical recitals takes place on weekdays at 4:00 p.m. and Saturdays at 2:30 p.m., through the summer. For tickets, just show up at the door ahead of time on the day of performance. Stop in any time for a schedule of upcoming events.

By the way, don't forget that this branch of the NYPL is the city's main collection of recorded music, on LP, cassette tape, and compact disc. These number in the thousands, with a tremendous array of classical music as well as Broadway musicals, jazz, and pop. You can don a set of headphones and listen right there, or take them out for two weeks if you have a library card.

Bryant Park Ticket Booth—Sixth Ave. (42nd St.), Manhattan; 212/382-2323. See listing under "Dance."

The Frick Collection—1 East 70th St., Manhattan; 212/288-0700. This fabulous art museum also presents free chamber music concerts on Sunday afternoons. During the warm-weather months, these take place by the fountain in the glass-topped Garden Court; otherwise, they're given in the Music Room. Either way, the concerts are high quality, high class, and as low-priced as any can be. The schedule can be irregular, so call ahead to find out what's on.

The Juilliard School—144 West 66th St., Manhattan; 212/769-7406. See listing under "Colleges."

Metropolitan Opera House—Lincoln Center, Columbus Ave. (64th St.), Manhattan; 212/362-6000. Whoa! What's the Met doing in Mr. Cheap's book? Their tickets cost more than the gross national product of most countries! Well, hang on to your binoculars. You *can* get into the Met cheaply, if you know how. Each and every performance offers a limited number of standing room tickets, at $13.00 for the orchestra section and $9.00 for the family circle. These are sold in advance at the box office, only for the week ahead, on Saturday mornings from 10:00 a.m.; get in line early, because they're almost always gone after just an hour or two. And you must pay in cash.

If you love opera, many say there's none better in the world; it's sure to be worth the effort. And just think—at the finale, you'll already be poised to give a standing ovation!

New York City Opera—Lincoln Center, Columbus Ave. (63rd St.), Manhattan; 212/870-5570. Next door at the New York State Theater, the troupe founded by Beverly Sills to bring opera to the people does so by undercutting the Met's prices substantially.

The quality of performance, meanwhile, is consistently good. NYCO even looks to alternative, "pop" sources of operas, such as its recent hit revival of Stephen Sondheim's *Sweeney Todd*—bridging the gap between opera and Broadway operetta. The City Opera season runs from July through November only; ticket prices start at $10.00 for the top circle. They offer standing room as well, at the rear of the fourth balcony, for $7.00; and there are rush tickets for students and senior citizens (with ID!) for $10.00, if any regular seats are still available on the day of the performance. These are sold at the box office only, from 10:00 a.m.

New York Philharmonic Orchestra—Lincoln Center, Columbus Ave. (64th St.), Manhattan; 212/875-5000. Continuing our roam around Lincoln Center, we come to Avery Fisher Hall. Here the New York Philharmonic sells rush tickets—if the concert is not sold out already—from 6:00 p.m. on the evening of a performance. For their Friday afternoon concerts, rush tix go on sale at noon. These are sold at half-price, which can still mean over $20.00 apiece, but it *is* a substantial discount; and they're available to anyone, not just students—first come, first served.

The Philharmonic also holds open rehearsals, another way to hear their delightful music at greatly reduced rates (would you believe $5.00 each?). These usually take place on weekday mornings, and tickets may be purchased in advance—in fact, it's recommended that you do.

People's Symphony Concerts—Various locations; 212/586-4680. This may be the ultimate in low-priced classical music—apart from summer freebies, of course. The People's Symphony is dedicated to providing music to those who can't afford tickets to the big concert halls, yet who don't want to miss out on high-quality delights. It was founded at the turn of the century by just such a person; a poor music student who vowed to make things better for future generations of students and other music lovers. That's you. The top PS price is usually—get ready—a mere $7.50. Most tix, in fact, are in the $3.00-to-$5.00 range. And with a subscription, you can actually pay as little as $2.00 per concert to hear some of the city's top musicians! Concerts take place at the Washington Irving High School Auditorium (40 Irving Place, at 16th Street), and at Town Hall (123 West 43rd Street), both in Manhattan. Call for more details.

Queens Borough Public Library—89-11 Merrick Blvd., Jamaica, Queens; 718/990-0700. The Central Branch of the Queens Public Library hosts a series called "Sunday Concerts at Central," featuring a wide variety of music—not just classical chamber ensembles, but jazz and ethnic music as well. They happen on Sundays, of course, at 2:00 p.m.; call for upcoming events.

St. Paul's Chapel—Broadway at Fulton St., Manhattan; 212/602-0747. New York's oldest surviving church is the site for wonderful free lunchtime concerts every Monday and Thursday at noon. Chamber groups, chorales, and soloists are among the delightful performers heard here. St. Paul's is related to another historic church, **Trinity Church** (74 Trinity Place at Wall Street), which holds its own series of lunchtime concerts on Tuesdays. These times and places may be subject to change, but the concerts take place year-round, except on holidays.

Symphony Space—2537 Broadway (95th St.), Manhattan; 212/864-5400. This large Upper West Side hall is a musical landmark for New York City. A non-profit institution, they offer a full schedule of concerts, theater, spoken word, and childrens' performances at reasonable ticket prices. Take in some Indian music (both American and Asian), Irish theater, or the New York Gilbert and Sullivan Players. There are also free concerts by such groups as the Mannes College Orchestra. Garrison Keillor's American Radio Company shows are broadcast from here, as is the "Selected Shorts" series on WNYC radio, short stories read by Broadway actors. And then there are the free marathons, all-day presentations focusing on one composer or author. Very few events are priced above $15.00 or $20.00, and many shows start under $10.00. Become a member for as little as $35.00 a year, and among other benefits, you'll save $3.00 to $5.00 on most tix.

Theater Development Fund—1501 Broadway, Suite 2110, New York, NY, 10036. See listing under "Theater."

Town Hall—123 West 43rd St., Manhattan; 212/840-2824. Built during the 1920s, Town Hall has fallen somewhat into disrepair but is still regarded as one of the city's finest concert halls. With 1,500 seats and excellent acoustics, the auditorium hosts classical, jazz, and popular music concerts at very reasonable prices. You can hear piano soloists and string quartets, big bands and experimental modern jazz, rock stars and international sounds from Africa or Brazil. Ticket prices vary, but many start as low as $10.00—and they have discount books of tickets that can bring prices even lower. Call for details.

Whitney Museum at Philip Morris—120 Park Ave. (42nd St.), Manhattan; 212/878-2453. The Sculpture Court at the Whitney's midtown branch doubles as a comfortably sized concert hall. It hosts free concerts of all kinds of music, including classical, jazz, and country. Currently these are held on Wednesday evenings at 7:30 p.m.; seating is first come, first served, so get there early or you may be disappointed.

World Financial Center/World Trade Center—West St. (between Liberty and Vesey Sts.), Manhattan; 212/945-0505, 212/466-4170. See listing under "Free Summer Performances," below.

FOLK

For up-to-the-minute info on folk performances all around the city, dial the **Folk Fone** at 212/666-9605 for a recorded message packed with listings. Also, you can call **Country Dance New York** at 212/459-4080 for information about participatory dances around town.

Advent Lutheran Church—Broadway at 93rd St., Manhattan; 212/874-3423. This Upper West Side church hosts a folk coffeehouse every Monday night. Call them to find out what kinds of performances are coming up.

Bell Caffe—310 Spring St., Manhattan; 212/334-2355.

What a find *this* is. Bell offers live music Tuesdays through Saturdays, with a different ethnic sound each night. One evening it may be native American music, the next night experimental jazz; then on to blues, Brazilian jazz, or even sitar music. There is never a cover charge. Unlike its Spring Street neighbors, the Ear Inn and McGovern's Bar, the Bell Caffe is more of a coffeehouse, though international beers are available; the inexpensive food leans toward vegetarian, though not exclusively. It's a very "sixties" kind of place.

Centerfold Coffeehouse—Church of St. Paul and St. Andrew, West End Ave. at 86th St., Manhattan; 212/866-4454. On Fridays, this very progressive and welcoming

Mr. Cheap's Picks

✔ **Bell Caffe**—Folk and ethnic music almost every night of the week in a cool, coffeehouse atmosphere. No cover charge.

✔ **Ryan's Irish Pub**—This rowdy East Village tavern hosts a free Irish music "jam session" every Sunday evening.

✔ **World Music Institute**—A terrific lineup of international sounds with low ticket prices, at venues around the city.

church hosts the Centerfold Coffeehouse, with an ever-changing series of folk and other live performance. A recent Friday offered two different shows: A poetry reading at 5:45 p.m., and then at 8:00, something called "The Hocus Pocus Variety Revue," with folk music and other acts. Call to see what's lined up for this week.

Eagle Tavern—355 West 14th St., Manhattan; 212/924-0275. Eagle is one of the zillion places to hear Irish and folk music in New York. Every Monday evening from 9:00 p.m. until about 12:30 a.m., hear lilting Irish sounds with no cover charge. At other times during the week there is a $5.00-to-$10.00 cover, depending on the night, but no drink minimum. You may hear bluegrass music or a "Singer-Songwriter Night." The atmosphere here is as laid-back and friendly as you'll find in the big city.

Peter Hilary's—174 Montague St., Brooklyn Heights, Brooklyn; 718/875-7900. Every Tuesday night, this hip Brooklyn restaurant and club hosts an Irish *sesiun*—that's the Gaelic term for an open jam session. It's traditional Celtic music, all acoustic, the way it was meant to be heard. There is no cover charge for the music.

Ludlow Street Cafe—165 Ludlow St., Lower East Side; 212/353-0536. See listing under "Rock/Pop."

Ryan's Irish Pub—151 Second Ave. (9th St.), Manhattan; 212/979-9511. Every Sunday starting around 8:00 in the evening, Ryan's makes good on its name by sponsoring another of the city's Irish *sesiuns*—an open jam session on classic Celtic instruments. If you feel, as Mr. C does, that many great Irish bands have become over-amplified and rock-oriented, you'll enjoy this primarily acoustic music. And if you play, of course, feel free to join in. It's an open-mike arrangement, and there is no cover charge. While there, you can also enjoy hearty food, from burgers to full dinners, at reasonable prices. Ryan's has great beers, naturally, as well as the rare and wonderful Woodpecker Cider.

Siné—122 St. Mark's Place, Manhattan; 212/982-0370. It's pronounced "sheenay." An Irish-style coffeehouse with music seven nights a week starting at 8:00 p.m. Mostly Irish folk bands and singer-songwriters. If you're into celebrities, they do drop by here occasionally. (Sinead O'Connor, whose manager runs the place, is said to have come here after being booed at the Dylan tribute. She was given a standing ovation by the crowd at Siné.) No cover charge; they just pass the hat.

Skep—527 Broome St., Manhattan; 212/219-2626. Folk music, poetry, and play readings are the fare at this SoHo club. The cover is just $5.00 or $6.00. Another place where the big names sometimes drop in to try out new material.

World Music Institute—49 West 27th St., Manhattan; 212/545-7536. This organization puts together a busy schedule of great concerts at various halls around town, all at reasonable prices. You may hear "Celtic Fiddles" at Symphony Space, avant-garde jazzman Anthony Braxton at the Merkin Concert Hall, or a Caribbean festival at Brooklyn College. Tickets to most events are $10.00 to $20.00; become a member for $30.00 and up and you'll save 15 to 30 percent on two tickets to each WMI event. Their monthly calendar is not only an interesting read but also lists lots of non-WMI concerts around town that are also inexpensive.

JAZZ AND CABARET

Birdland—2745 Broadway (106th St.), Manhattan; 212/749-2228. The original Birdland, Charlie Parker's famous hangout, is long gone; this Columbia-area club admirably keeps up the name. Performers heard here have included the legendary James Moody, the David Amram Quartet, and Bill Lee (Spike's father, a longtime jazzman). In fact, live jazz is played here seven nights a week. Sunday through Thursday evenings there is no music charge for those having dinner in this handsome restaurant; there is a $10.00 cover on weekends, but it's only $5.00 if you sit at the bar. Birdland has a Sunday brunch from noon to four, at which the music is free. And the food, which features lots of down home cookin', is very reasonably priced.

Blue Note—131 West 3rd St., Manhattan; 212/475-8592. One of the most famous jazz spots in the country, Blue Note is also one of the city's more expensive night clubs. Considering the top-name stars who shine here, it's no wonder. But wait—there are ways around this! If you're a night owl, drop in after hours—from 2:00 to 4:00 a.m., when the players hang out and jam. You never know who, after "working" for the evening, may drop in to wail just for fun. There's only a $5.00 cover charge, less than half the prime-time rates, and no minimum. For an inexpensive option at more "normal" hours, try the weekend brunches, where you get live music, a variety of breakfasts, and one drink—all for $14.50 per person. These take place every Saturday and Sunday from noon to 6:00 p.m., with sets at 1:00 and 3:30 p.m. You may catch headliners like Houston Person and Etta Jones—in what finer fashion to while away a lazy afternoon?

Cameos—169 Columbus Ave. (67th St.), 2nd Floor, Manhattan; 212/874-2280. Very elegant and cozy, this chic Upper West Side restaurant features jazz with no music charge, every night. There is a $10.00 minimum if you want to sit at one of the linen-covered tables, but none if you sit at the bar. The stage is small, limited to solos and duos; the players are serious, if not well-known, names—guys like John Bunch, Rufus Reid and Walter Booker. Cameos also has Sunday jazz brunches and Monday night jam sessions.

CBGB Gallery—313 Bowery (Bleecker St.), Manhattan; 212/677-0455. See listing under "Rock/Pop," below.

Don't Tell Mama—343 West 46th St., Manhattan; 212/757-0788. The piano bar at this very popular theater district hangout features singing waiters and waitresses, waiting, of course, for that big break to land them at a nearby Broadway theater. Customers are invited to join in as well—many of whom turn out (big surprise!) to be aspiring actors too. No problem; that just gives you high-quality entertainment for the cost of a couple of, well, high-priced drinks. Still works out to be quite inexpensive overall. The music starts at 9:00 every night, with no cover charge or drink minimum.

Eighty-Eight's—228 West 10th St., Manhattan; 212/924-0088. Answer to trivia question: It's the number of keys found on a piano. Deep in Greenwich Village, Eighty-Eight's is another of the city's great cabarets (a bit pricey), which also boasts a cozy sing-along piano bar. Here you can sing or dance the night away with no cover charge—just a two-drink minimum. The music starts at 9:00 each night, going on until 3:00 or 4:00 in the morning.

Hors d'Oeuvrerie—1 World Trade Center, 107th Floor, Manhattan; 212/938-1111. Sure, you won't be coming in for the music—but it's there, along with the best view in town, all for a cover charge that seems as small as the cars seen from this height. Actually, solo piano starts around 4:00 p.m., with no cover or minimum at all; what a way to enjoy the sunset. From 7:30 on a jazz trio takes over and the cover goes up to a mere $4.00, still with no minimum. There's dining and dancing too, if you're so inspired.

Hotel Lobby Jazz—Various locations; see below. Hotel music (not the kind found in their elevators) has traditionally been the ultimate cosmopolitan experience for the well-heeled. A smart lobby, a crystal chandelier or three, plush couches, and elegant jazz—now *that's* New York. So, why should this be enjoyed only by people in town for the annual widget salesmen's convention? Fact is, many of these places ask no cover charge and no drink minimum—though they do request that you order *something*. So order one drink (expensive, yes) and nurse it along. This also makes a great alternative to the clubs, especially if you want to be able to have a relaxed conversation and less cigarette smoke. Here are some of the hostelries around town that regularly offer live music; call them to find out current schedules. Also, ask whether they require men to wear jackets, as some do even in these casual times.

Mr. Cheap's Picks

✔ **Blue Note**—Stop in to this world-famous jazz club after hours, and there's no cover charge. Hey, jazz is *meant* to be heard at two in the morning.

✔ HOTEL LOBBIES AND PIANO BARS—Fun and elegant ways to hear music free—hotels such as the **Parker Meridien**, and sing-along cabarets like **Rose's Turn**.

✔ **Rathbone's**—A cozy Upper East Side tavern, with top-notch free jazz several nights a week.

✔ **Village Corner**—Hip, low-key Greenwich Village hangout, with free piano jazz every night, as well as during Sunday brunch.

Embassy Suites Hotel, 1568 Broadway (47th St.), Manhattan; 212/719-1600. Above the Palace Theater, Fosse's piano bar is located on the fifth floor; you may need to ask at the lobby (third floor) for the best route. No minimum, but you are requested to order food or a drink.

Grand Hyatt Hotel, Park Ave. and 42nd St., Manhattan; 212/883-1234. One of New York's truly beautiful hotels, above Grand Central Station. Jazz trios begin during the dinner hour and play until midnight every weekend. No drink minimum.

Helmsley Palace Hotel, 455 Madison Ave. (50th St.), Manhattan; 212/888-7000, ext. 6731. A piano bar on the street level offers show tunes and popular jazz favorites every evening. There's no minimum, but you must order something to eat or drink. If Leona walks in, better make sure she sees you do it, too.

Marriott Marquis Hotel, 1535 Broadway (45th St.), Manhattan; 212/398-1900, ext. 6610. Like the Embassy Suites, above, this is part of the new generation of glitzy hotels lining Times Square. The Broadway Lounge, on the eighth floor (the Marriott's lobby), is one of those rooms that rotate—slowly, don't worry—so your view overlooking the street and the performers is ever-changing. There is a one-drink minimum.

Parker Meridien Hotel, 118 West 57th St., Manhattan; 212/245-5000. World-famous as an elegant hotel, the Parker Meridien's "Bar Montparnasse" is done up in light natural wood paneling and features solo piano jazz every night from 5:00 to 9:00 p.m. (except Sunday from 1:00 to 3:00 p.m.). There is a one-drink minimum; make it last. The bar is also well known for the big-name jazz players who drop in, unannounced, to jam. Among these have been guitarist Bucky Pizzarelli and singer Bobby McFerrin.

Waldorf Astoria Hotel, 301 Park Ave. (50th St.), Manhattan; 212/872-4895. Didn't think the Waldorf would show up in this book, did you? Well, they have two wonderful piano bars, Peacock Alley (street level) and Cocktail Terrace (second floor), both of which offer quiet, elegant piano music. Cole Porter himself hung out at the Peacock, and you can see his own piano there. Neither room has a minimum, but you must order something to eat or drink.

J's—2581 Broadway (97th St.), 2nd Floor, Manhattan; 212/666-3600. You'd hardly expect it from the graffiti-splattered door, which is all you see from the street; but hidden away upstairs is a spacious, elegant jazz club. Large windows look out over Broadway. There's music every night of the week; the bookings here lean toward piano, small jazz combos, and cabaret singers. Dick Hyman, Joel Forrester, and Richard Rodney Bennett are just a couple of the folks who've performed in this intimate setting. There is never a cover charge, just a $12.00 food minimum at the white-linen-covered tables and a two-drink minimum ($7.00) at the bar—which has an unobstructed view of the stage.

The Knitting Factory—47 East Houston St., Manhattan; 212/219-3055. See listing under "Rock/Pop," below.

Rathbone's—1702 Second Ave. (88th St.), Manhattan; 212-369-7361. In addition to being a fine old hangout of a restaurant and bar (see listing under the "Restaurants: Upper East Side"), Rathbone's presents great jazz several nights a week, with no cover charge and no minimum. Tuesdays and Wednesdays, bands start playing around 9:30; on Saturdays they start a bit later, at 10:30. And on Sunday evenings you can enjoy solo piano jazz from 8:30. All go well into the evening. Among the names who've recently played here are trumpeter Roy Hargrove and electric violinist Michael Urbaniak. Enjoy good, inexpensive dinners or desserts, or just hang out over great beers from around the world.

Rose's Turn—55 Grove St., Manhattan; 212/366-5438. Longtime fans of the cabaret scene may still think of this Greenwich Village club as the Duplex (which more recently moved just across Seventh Avenue to 61 Christopher Street). Meanwhile, the current operation looks exactly the same as it always has. The downstairs piano bar is a popular hangout for lovers of show tunes and ribald comedy songs, sung by a parade of waiters, waitresses, bartenders (all aspiring singers and actors), and patrons who want to get in on the act. The pianist seems to know every song ever written, and many that were not; the audience sings along in a truly campy fashion.

All the entertainment is free, with no cover or minimum; "But we do expect you to drink heavily," says the bartender. Well, don't overdo it—but there certainly is a merry atmosphere. Get there early if you can, because the place really packs 'em in. Music starts at 9:00 every night of the week and plays on into the wee hours. If you've ever wanted to sing in front of a crowd, squeeze your way in and take your turn at Rose's.

The Sazerac House—533 Hudson St., Manhattan; 212/989-0313. Built in 1826, the Sazerac House is an historic West Village landmark that's made as much of a name for itself as a bar and grill. More recently, it's become known as a place for good jazz with no cover. What's the deal? You get free jazz, and students from the New School Jazz Program get a chance to strut their stuff in front of a real live audience. And the kids are all right. They play all varieties of traditional, straight-ahead jazz, with different ensembles playing for two weekends in a row. On the first night for each booking, the group is "introduced" by a name player, such as Junior Mance, Jim Hall or Lew Tabackin, who anchors the evening; many of these stars are on the New School faculty. Some of the students have gone on to major recognition, too, like Roy Hargrove and Christopher Hollyday. Sets begin at 9:30, 11:00, and 12:30 on Friday and Saturday nights; there is also a jazz brunch on Sundays from 12:30 to 4:30 p.m. Whenever you go, there is no cover and no minimum.

South Street Seaport, Pier 17—South St. at Fulton St., Manhattan; 212/SEA-PORT (732-7678). Upstairs in the atrium of these popular food and shopping halls, South Street Seaport sponsors free concerts each spring and fall. These midweek shows generally take place during the dinner hours. Jazz in all its forms is the mainstay, and some major names pass through. Some nights also feature rock and "oldies" tunes.

Tompkins Park Restaurant—141 Avenue A (9th St.), Manhattan; 212/260-4798. On the heels of the cultural revolution that has turned Tompkins Square Park from a haven for drug addicts into a truly pleasant area, this is a comfortable and moderately priced cafe with indoor and outdoor seating. They host live jazz, with no cover or minimum, on weekends; also special events, like a jazz gospel brunch. Call to see what's coming up.

Town Hall—123 West 43rd St., Manhattan; 212/840-2824. See listing under "Classical Music," above.

Village Corner—142 Bleecker St., Manhattan; 212/473-9762. Near NYU, this friendly establishment consists of a front bar/restaurant room, long and with a high ceiling, and another dining room toward the back. The kitchen serves up inexpensive food, like a burger and fries for $4.75, shepherd's pie for $5.75, and lots of early bird dinner specials; the bar offerings are extensive. And while you while away the hours over food or drink, you can listen to solo jazz piano from 9:30 p.m. nightly (8:30 p.m. on Sundays) with no cover charge. On weekend afternoons from 1:00 to 4:30, this expands to jazz trios over a big brunch menu. Again, the music is free—and very hip.

Visiones—125 MacDougal St., Manhattan; 212/673-5576. This restaurant, serving spicy Spanish food, doubles as one of Greenwich Village's lesser-known—and lower-priced—jazz clubs. The cover charge may be low, but the quality is consistently top-rate. Admission prices seldom top $10.00 and are often as little as $6.00, even on weekend evenings; there is also a two-drink minimum. On some weeknights there is no cover charge at all.

West Bank Cafe—407 West 42nd St., Manhattan; 212/695-6909. See listing under "Theater."

West End Gate—2911 Broadway (113th St.), Manhattan; 212/662-8830. This large, friendly neighborhood restaurant has not one but two big rooms offering jazz through the week. The acts include local and national groups, playing everything from straight jazz to salsa. Cover charge on most nights is a reasonable $6.00, with a two-drink minimum; but the cover is half-price for students with ID. And Monday is big band night, with a $3.00 cover for everyone. The menu, meanwhile, has burgers from $5.25, lots of appetizers, sandwiches, and salads, and entrees mostly in the $7.00-to-$10.00 range. Stop in or call to check the current schedule.

ROCK/POP

Bell Caffe—310 Spring St., Manhattan; 212/334-2355. See listing under "Folk Music," above.

The Bitter End—147 Bleecker St., Manhattan; 212/673-7030. One of the cluster of rock clubs at the "end" of Bleecker Street, near Houston, the Bitter End has three or four live bands every night of the week. You can hear them all for a $5.00 cover (sometimes a bit more). These groups, all clawing their way up the music biz ladder, tend to have names like "Flay of Soul," "Def Troop," and "Big Black Nun." You get the idea. If this rowdy scene is your speed, you'll love the End.

Other clubs along this boisterous strip (just try squeezing into any one on a hopping Saturday night) have very similar offerings. These include **Rock 'n Roll Cafe** (149 Bleecker St.; 212/677-7630), **Kenny's Castaways** (157 Bleecker St.; 212/473-9870), **Mondo Perso** (167 Bleecker St.; 212/477-3770), and, around the corner, **Lion's Den** (211 Sullivan St.; 212/477-2782).

CBGB/OMFUG—315 Bowery (Bleecker St.), Manhattan; 212/982-4052. For the terminally curious, it stands for "Country, Blue Grass, Blues, and Other Music for Uplifting Gourmandizers." Judging by the real range of music played here, you're better off with just the initials. After all, this is where Talking Heads got their New York start. Top up-and-coming bands play hardcore rock here on their way, they hope, to similar discovery. An average night consists of five or six different bands, with a cover charge no higher than $8.00. It's wild and loud; and shoulder pads (the football kind) are a good idea on the dance floor.

Next door at 313 Bowery, **CBGB Gallery** (212/677-0455) takes the same approach to cutting-edge jazz. Don't worry, the atmosphere's more refined—looks more like an art gallery, actually, than a music club. Hear

Mr. Cheap's Picks

✔ **The Bitter End**—Three or four loud bands for $5.00, every night.

✔ **Ear Inn**—Mondays through Wednesdays at 11:00 p.m., great rock and country with no cover.

✔ **The Knitting Factory**—Progressive rock, jazz, world beat, and anything else you can think of, with cover charges between $5.00 and $10.00.

✔ **Ludlow Street Cafe**—They just pass the hat at this comfortable tavern hidden away on the Lower East Side. Hear as many as three bands in an evening—rock, blues, folk.

✔ **Roulette**—Art rock from the U.S. and Europe, in a TriBeCa studio. Most concerts cost around $7.00.

three or four groups, with a variety of sounds, for a top cover of $7.00.

Desmond's Tavern—433 Park Ave. South (30th St.), Manhattan; 212/725-9864. A few blocks below the Murray Hill area, this neighborhood pub offers live local bands Wednesday through Saturday nights, with no cover charge. Often there are drink specials early in the evening, like dollar drafts.

Ear Inn—326 Spring St., Manhattan; 212/226-9060. At this cozy bar just west of SoHo, the neon sign out front has been surgically altered from "Bar" to "Ear"—and those two words tell it all. This is a very hip hangout, serving good beers and food at moderate prices; and on weeknights they have a mix of rock, country/western, and blues bands from 11:00 p.m. with no cover charge. Music generally happens on Monday, Tuesday, and Wednesday nights.

Katie O'Toole's—134 Reade St., Manhattan; 212/226-8928. Another old-style Irish tavern, improbably located in the heart of trendy TriBeCa, has good, cheap food—burgers, dinners, and beers—and live bands hold forth several nights a week. You may hear anything from traditional Irish music to rock & roll cover bands, often with no cover charge, even on weekends.

The Kitchen—512 West 19th St., Manhattan; 212/255-5793. See listing under "Theater."

The Knitting Factory—47 East Houston St., Manhattan; 212/219-3055. For the most progressive sounds in rock, jazz, world beat, and more, the Knitting Factory is a longtime fixture on the downtown music scene. Groove to the sounds of bluesman James Blood Ulmer, new wave country's Bela Fleck, and modern jazz artist John Zorn, as well as groups with names like "Drink Me," "101 Crustaceans" and "the Klezmatics." In one of the Factory's two listening rooms, you may hear "jazz rap," African drummers, or "industrial country." Cover prices start as low as $7.00 for two sets, and rarely top $10.00. Drinks are cheap here, too; at KF's "Progressive Happy Hour," Brooklyn Lager starts at just $1.00 from 5:30 to 6:00 and inches its way up to $2.00 by 7:00. Same scale for swell drinks, from $1.25 to $3.50. Or enjoy coffees and herbal teas instead.

Find out where the cutting edge lies *this* week. The Knitting Factory also presents poets and performance artists at various times through the middle of the week. Their new dance series costs just $4.00, Monday evenings at 7:30; "Thursday Night Videos" have a $5.00 admission. Even their weekend programs in the smaller space have tickets at $5.00 to $6.00 for live music. Entertainment here runs into the wee small hours of the morning.

Ludlow Street Cafe—165 Ludlow St., Lower East Side; 212/353-0536. The area looks deserted after 5:00 p.m., when all the wholesale/retail shops close up tight; and in fact, it's not one of the city's best areas to walk around in after dark. So should you stay away? *No* way! Take a big group of friends, or a cab, or the bus along East Houston Street, and walk a block south to the Ludlow Street Cafe. Inside, the friendly folks will make you feel very relaxed over terrific, inexpensive food (see listing under "Restaurants: Lower Manhattan") and good beers. Then, around ten o'clock, the place starts hopping.

Different bands every night, sometimes two or three in one night, play every kind of rock, folk, blues, and varieties thereof. The groups are local (including some open jam sessions), but the band Mr. C heard on his visit was very good indeed. Sounded like a blend of John Cougar Mellencamp and 10,000 Maniacs, a pleasant folk-rock sound with a marvelous female lead singer. Several hours of entertainment come at no cover charge; instead, they just pass the hat. Now, don't be cheap on *this*, readers, if you've been digging the sounds. Let 'em know!

The cafe gets pretty packed by about eleven or so, and the party tends to spill out onto the street before too long. If you want to get seats, arrive early and have something to eat or drink while you're hanging out.

Manny's Car Wash—1558 Third Ave. (86th St.), Manhattan; 212/369-2583. You'd hardly expect a down-home, rockin' blues joint on the refined Upper East Side, but here it is, folks. Texas bands, rockabilly, and a touch of soul are among the many variations that raise the roof of this barn, featuring national bands and big name solo players (Bo Diddley Jr., Charlie Musselwhite, Clarence "Gatemouth" Brown). Manny's Sunday Blues Jam is free every week. Otherwise, cover charges can be as little as $3.00 or as much as $12.00, depending on the bill and the night; but here's a tip from Mr. C—get there early. Arrive before 9:00 p.m., when the band is setting up and the bar is empty; no one will be at the door yet, and you can just walk in and grab yourself a seat. Then wait for the fun to begin. You'll be sitting (pretty) while people shove in tighter than chickens in the coop, *and* the music will be free.

McGovern's Bar—305 Spring St., Manhattan; 212/627-5037. Another of the many interesting rock clubs in the diverse (and less expensive) neighborhood just west of SoHo. McGovern's features two or three live rock bands just about every night of the week, with no cover charge. There's usually a warmup act at 9:00 p.m., with the "headliners" coming on around 10:00 p.m.

P.S. 122—150 First Ave. (9th St.), Manhattan; 212/477-5288. See listing under "Theater."

Roulette—228 West Broadway, Manhattan; 212/219-8242. This TriBeCa gallery offers a concert series of what it calls "Experimental and Adventurous Music," featuring artists from around the country and some from around the world. You may hear a duo from Switzerland, with music for drums and saxophone; a pianist who's modified his instrument to play twenty-four notes per octave; or a composer's version of Debussy for "three harps, record turntables, sampling keyboard, electric percussion, and trombone." Shows start at 9:00 p.m., mostly on Thursdays through Saturdays. Each series, fall and spring, consists of twenty-five different shows. Tickets are $7.00 for most concerts and free to members (join for $50.00 per year).

Teddy's Bar and Grill—96 Berry St., Williamsburg, Brooklyn; 718/384-9787. Williamsburg is the rising star of Brooklyn neighborhoods, as far as restaurants and the arts are concerned. Teddy's has already been a popular stop for many years. Live music on Thursdays and Saturdays alternates with evenings of DJ dance music. Whichever you take in, there's never a cover charge or drink minimum here. The live bands vary widely; you may hear straight jazz on a Thursday, blues on Saturday, and reggae the following week. Have dinner first in their restaurant, or just join the crowd at the bar.

World Music Institute—49 West 27th St., Manhattan; 212/545-7536. See listing under "Folk Music," above.

FREE SUMMERTIME PERFORMANCES

Summer in the city is a great time to enjoy music, dance, and theatre for free. It seems every park, atrium, and pier has something going on. These schedules, times, and venues change from year to year, but here are just a few of the possibilities. Keep an eye out for posters and advertisements for all the details.

Bryant Park—42nd St., between Fifth and Sixth Aves., Manhattan; 212/983-4143. This lovely park behind the main branch of the Public Library presents such free performances as the Young Artist Concert Series, as well as groups from the Manhattan School of Music, the St. Luke's Chamber Ensemble, and more—even stand-up comedy!

Lehman College—Bedford Park Blvd. West, Bronx; 718/960-8000. Like Manhattan's Central Park, the Bronx has a "SummerStage" series of its own on the campus of this CUNY branch. You'll find theater, children's activities, concerts, and much more.

Other places where you may find free performances around the Bronx include Pelham Bay Park and Van Cortland Park.

Museum of Modern Art—11 West 53rd St., Manhattan; 212/708-9400. See listing under "Museums."

New York Grand Opera—Central Park Band Shell, near 72nd St., Manhattan; 212/235-8837. What is more grand about these opera performances—the music or the price? Every summer NYGO presents classic works, with full staging, costumes, and orchestra, for free. It takes place under the stars at the main band shell in the center of the park. Call for details about this season's schedule.

"Out-of-Doors Festival" At Lincoln Center—Amsterdam Ave. at 62nd St., Manhattan; 212/877-2011. Lincoln Center's big annual extravaganza is always a highlight of the New York summer. At the large, outdoor Guggenheim Bandshell in Damrosch Park, you can enjoy dance troupes from around the world as they step through flamenco, pirouettes, and tap dance. Not to mention big bands, choral and gospel groups, comedy, and much more, all free.

Prospect Park Bandshell—Prospect Park, Brooklyn; 718/788-0055. There's something going on all year long in Prospect Park;

they also mount an annual summer series of free concerts, dance, and theater. You may see anything from the Kings County Shakespeare Company to jazz legend McCoy Tyner playing with the Brooklyn Philharmonic to the troupe known as "Il Piccolo Teatro dell'Opera." Call the above number for recorded info on what's coming up.

Among the many other Brooklyn sites offering freebie performances are Canarsie Pier, Bensonhurst Park, Park House of Sunset Park, Asser Levy/Seaside Park at Coney Island, Kings Plaza Mall, Marine Park, and, of course, the Brighton Beach Boardwalk. Check local newspapers for listings.

Seuffert Bandshell—Forest Park Music Grove, Woodhaven, Queens. Among the many events you'll enjoy here, the venerable Seuffert Band has been tooting its horns for over sixty years. They play concerts here and in other parks around Queens from June through October. When they're not playing a home game, you may instead hear anything from the Queens Symphony Orchestra (did you even know they had one?) to a show of Afro-Brazilian music and dance.

Elsewhere around Queens, look for free "Arts in the Parks" performances at such locations as Baisley Park in Jamaica and Astoria Park in Astoria.

Shakespeare In Central Park—Delacorte Theater, near Central Park West and 81st St., Manhattan; 212/598-7100. See listing under "Theater."

Snug Harbor Cultural Center—1000 Richmond Terrace, Staten Island; 718/447-8667. Continuing our cruise around the outer boroughs . . . . Try your hand, or rather feet, at square dancing; strike up the band—the U.S. Army Field Band and Soldiers' Chorus, that is; or just laze back with a little guitar music. All of these events take place at various locations around Snug Harbor; the gazebo, the South Meadow, and more.

South Street Seaport, Pier 16—South St. at Fulton St., Manhattan; 212/SEA-PORT (732-7678). Every summer means great outdoor "Summerpier" concerts under the stars. They put together a mixed bag, presenting the Tommy Dorsey Orchestra one week and top rock & roll bands the next. Concerts start around 7:30 on Saturdays in July and August.

Summerstage—Rumsey Playfield, Central Park, Manhattan; 212/360-CPSS(2777). This ambitious annual series presents dance, opera, international music, literary readings, and who knows what. It all takes place on

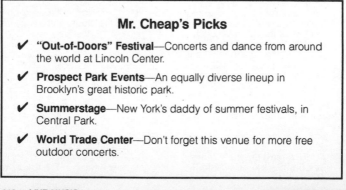

Mr. Cheap's Picks

✔ **"Out-of-Doors" Festival**—Concerts and dance from around the world at Lincoln Center.

✔ **Prospect Park Events**—An equally diverse lineup in Brooklyn's great historic park.

✔ **Summerstage**—New York's daddy of summer festivals, in Central Park.

✔ **World Trade Center**—Don't forget this venue for more free outdoor concerts.

the stage at this playground in the middle of Central Park near 72nd Street. Shows take place on Wednesday through Friday evenings at 8:30, and on Saturdays and Sundays at 3:00 p.m. Look for ads all over town, or check your newspapers for schedules.

Theatreworks/USA—Promenade Theatre, 2162 Broadway (72nd St.), Manhattan; 212/677-5959. See listing under "Theater."

Union Square Summer Series—Union Square Park, Broadway at 17th St., Manhattan; 212/614-2404. During the warm months from June through September you can hear a city's worth of musical variety every weekday afternoon at the northern end of Union Square Park. Everything from rock and jazz to folk, blues, and reggae. Programs usually start around noon and run for a couple of hours.

World Financial Center/World Trade Center—West St. (between Liberty and Vesey Sts.), Manhattan; 212/945-0505, 212/466-4170. Throughout the year, the various indoor and outdoor stages spread around these glitzy new mega-buildings present classical music, pop, jazz, dance, comedy, and more. The Austin J. Tobin Plaza, located along Church Street, is the main site at the World Trade Center. The newer World Financial Center, across West Street toward the river, boasts the glorious Winter Garden indoor atrium. A majestic three stories tall, the indoor space features dazzling architecture, cafes (alas, not cheap), and rows of real, living palm trees. Take the North Bridge from One World Trade Center to cross blissfully over West Street traffic into the Garden.

Performances include lunchtime shows from noon to 2:00 p.m.; in summer, there's a different kind of music each day of the week. Early evening shows usually start at 5:30 or 6:30. During the warmer months, outdoor performances also take place around the plazas. Needless to say, it's all free of charge. Call or visit to pick up a brochure.

MOVIES

American Museum of the Moving Image—35th Ave. at 36th St., Astoria, Queens; 718/784-0077. At this wonderful museum, converted from one of the earliest actual film studios in the country (the Marx Brothers made their first movies here!), you can see classic films from the United States and all around the world for free—with the price of admission to the museum. Film series here can cover anything from silent Russian cinema to an Al Pacino retrospective. The films may be old, but the theater is state-of-the-art, ready for both silent nitrate films and the latest Dolby wide-screen spectaculars. The museum also features the "Tuts Fever Picture Palace," a reproduction of an ornate Roaring Twenties movie theater, showing newsreels and Saturday afternoon adventure serials; and there's a small screening room too, showing the latest in experimental videos. Not to mention the exhibits themselves, with lots of genuine Hollywood props, costumes, and sets on display. You love the movies? You'll love this place! Admission is $5.00 for adults, $4.00 for senior citizens, $2.50 for students and children, and free to museum members. Open every day but Monday; call for movie schedules.

Brooklyn Center Cinema—Whitman Hall, Brooklyn College, Campus Road, Midwood, Brooklyn; 718/951-5295. Repertory cinema is alive and well and living in Brooklyn. And what a way to see a movie! The screen is a glorious forty feet wide and two stories high (take *that*, multiplexes), big enough for wide-screen epics from gladiator movies to the latest sci-fi space sagas. The auditorium has 2,500 seats in a room gilded with grand Art Deco ornamentation. The sound surrounds you in state-of-the-art THX stereo. And what is the price of admission to this old-fashioned movie palace? A mere $5.00. And discount ticket books are available, knocking the price down to about $3.50—that's not a typo, folks.

BCC shows classic films like *Casablanca, Gone With the Wind*, and great old MGM musicals from the 1940s and 1950s. "We show movies that look good on a large screen," says one of the programmers. These also include foreign films, recent Oscar winners, and Disney classics for the kids. Because the film people share this theater with other campus events, though, they don't play every day; so Mr. C advises calling to get on their mailing list. This will also keep you informed on one of the best secret freebies in all of New York: Sneak previews of new Hollywood films, about to be released, shown *absolutely free*.

Brooklyn Heights Cinema—70 Henry St., Brooklyn Heights, Brooklyn; 718/596-7070. If you want to avoid the long lines and high prices of commercial movies nowadays, you have to avoid Manhattan as well. But a short hop away in Brooklyn Heights, this old moviehouse (in the process of renovation) shows current Hollywood hits on two screens.

Mr. Cheap's Picks

✔ **American Museum of the Moving Image**—Not just a whole wonderful museum about the movies, in a real studio, but three different cinemas are included with admission.

✔ **Brooklyn Center Cinema**—A classic, grand old movie palace, lovingly restored and programmed with movies *made* for big screens.

✔ **Museum of Modern Art**—One of the best art repertory schedules in the world, included with admission to a museum that's no slouch, either.

✔ **New York Public Library**—Free movies! What more could you want? Check to see what's at the branches near you.

Regular price, as of this writing, is $6.50—about a dollar below many others in the city. Better still, catch the first show of the day (usually a matinee) for just $3.00, any day of the week. Yep, that's for the very latest releases, less than half-price.

Cobble Hill Cinema—265 Court St., Cobble Hill, Brooklyn; 718/596-9113. Another fine old neighborhood moviehouse, showing five different current hits at a time. Tickets are regularly $6.75, but the first showing of the day is just $3.75—on all five screens, every day of the week. These showtimes are usually around 1:00 or 1:30 p.m.

The French Institute—55 East 59th St., Manhattan; 212/355-6160. Guess what you can see here? Yep, French films, shown on Wednesday afternoons and evenings. All the great movies and directors are represented throughout the year; these are shown in French, *naturellement*, but don't worry—there are English subtitles for the rest of us. Admission is $6.00 for general, $4.00 for students, and free to members.

Goethe House—1014 Fifth Ave. (82nd St.), Manhattan; 212/744-8310. See listing under "Museums."

Museum of Modern Art—11 West 53rd St., Manhattan; 212/708-9490. MOMA's two large, comfortable movie theaters show American and world classics, along with recent avant-garde works by current world directors. All of these are shown daily and are free with the price of admission to the museum. In addition to silent films, you may also see art-house hits from the last few years, like *A Sunday in the Country, The Night of Shooting Stars* and *Pretty Baby*. Regular admission to the museum is $7.00, but think of all you get for that price—can any other movie theater in town match it? Meanwhile, students and seniors get in for $4.00, and the entire museum is free on Thursday evenings.

The Museum of Television and Radio—25 West 52nd St., Manhattan; 212/621-6600. What you'll usually see in this modern, cozy screening room is not feature films but rather television classics from the museum's archives. You may see comedy from Ernie Kovacs to "Saturday Night Live," or live dramas from the golden age of TV. These can be lots of fun on a screen that's measured in feet instead of inches, and viewed with a crowd of fellow fans. Screenings, free with regular admission, take place during the lunch hour every day but Monday, and also at 6:00 p.m. on Thursdays and Fridays. Admission is $5.00 for adults, $4.00 for students, and $3.00 for seniors and kids under thirteen.

New York Public Library—Branches all over town; recorded info, 212/869-8089. Don't forget to check your local branch of the NYPL for showings of free films! These can include anything from foreign classics to cartoons for kids (well, try to bring some so you won't look out of place). Times, locations, and schedules are always changing, so call or stop in for a flyer.

The Public Theater/New York Shakespeare Festival—425 Lafayette St., Manhattan; 212/598-7150. See listing under "Theater."

Queens Museum of Art—New York City Building, Flushing Meadow Park, Queens; 718/592-5555. Like so many of the museums listed here, the Queens Museum shows art films from around the world for free with regular admission. Unlike such institutions as the Modern, that admission price is just $3.00 for adults and $1.50 for students, seniors, and kids over five (under five, free). Call to find out what's coming up.

MUSEUMS

Mr. C firmly believes that *all* museums are bargains. Consider how much treasure you can see at such places for less than the cost of a movie. Still, everything is relative, and here are several of the city's best deals—museums that are free or have low regular admission fees. Some of these are higher-priced places that offer special free hours (subject to change; call to confirm).

Tip from Mr. C: If you really enjoy a particular museum, consider becoming a member. This usually gets you free admission all year, along with (perhaps) your spouse and/or kids, for the price of a couple of visits. It's a money saver that helps out your favorite institution as well.

American Museum of the Moving Image—35th Ave. at 36th St., Astoria, Queens; 718/784-0077. See listing under "Movies."

American Museum of Natural History—Central Park West at 79th St., Manhattan; 212/769-5000. This is one of the few museums that still operates under the old-fashioned admission policy: The entrance fee ($5.00 for adults, $2.50 for kids) is called a "suggested contribution" rather than a set price. That means, officially, that you can pay less if you wish, which may be helpful if you're bringing in a large family. Well, don't stiff them, do give something—remember, Mr. Cheap wants you to save money, not be a cheapskate. Needless to say, even at full price the museum is a bargain, with room after room of science and nature exhibits—and, of course, all those dinosaur bones.

Bronx Museum of the Arts—1040 Grand Concourse (165th St.), Bronx; 718/681-6000. Not far from Yankee Stadium you'll find this small but impressive museum. Along with its permanent collection, the BMA usually has one or two special exhibits focusing on contemporary artists. Admission is just $1.50; $1.00 for students and senior citizens. Hours are Saturdays through Thursdays from 10 a.m. to 4:30 p.m.; Sundays they open at 11:00 a.m.

Brooklyn's History Museum—128 Pierrepont St., Brooklyn Heights, Brooklyn; 718/624-0890. Run by the Brooklyn Historical Society, this museum is a city landmark itself. Begun in 1863 as the Long Island Historical Society, back when Brooklyn was considered a city getaway, this organization grew into one of New York's foremost preservationists. Its library is one of the best nineteenth century rooms left in the city. The museum features lots of Brooklyniana (is that a word?) in photographs, art, and remnants of famous buildings. Hours are Wednesday through Sunday, noon to five. Admission is $2.50 for adults, $1.00 for kids under twelve. And on Wednesdays the museum is free to all.

The Cloisters—Fort Tryon Park, Manhattan; 212/923-3700. An outpost of the Metropolitan Museum of Art, the Cloisters is located wayyyyyyy up at the top of

Manhattan Island—above the George Washington Bridge looking out over the Hudson. It's a trek, but a grand one, with its collected sections of various European monasteries all put together into a peaceful museum and park. Some parts of the collection date as far back as the eleventh century—needless to say, among the very oldest structures you can see on this or any other continent. Visit the stained-glass gallery, the famous Unicorn Tapestries, and the outdoor garden. Entrance to all of it is by a donation of your choice; truly one of the best "bargains" in New York City. Open daily (except Mondays) from 9:30 a.m. to 5:15 p.m. There is a subway stop, on the "A" line, at 190th Street, though the ride becomes less desirable above the Columbia area. If you're driving, the Henry Hudson Parkway will take you all the way there.

Cooper-Hewitt Museum—2 East 91st St., Manhattan; 212/860-6868. It took four years for Andrew Carnegie to build his dream house, finished in 1903. Now owned by the Smithsonian Institution, this sixty-four-room marvel of Georgian architecture has become a museum dedicated to—architecture. Appropriate, huh? Its galleries display permanent design collections and special exhibits. Admission is $3.00 for adults, $1.50 for students and seniors. Hours are 10:00 a.m. to 5:00 p.m., except Sundays from noon and Tuesdays until 9:00 p.m.; and, Tuesdays from 5:00 to 9:00 p.m. offer free admission to all.

Ellis Island National Monument/ Statue of Liberty—See listing under "Outdoors."

El Museo Del Barrio—1230 Fifth Ave. (104th St.), Manhattan; 212/831-7272. Enjoy the rich culture of Puerto Rico and other Latin American countries through paintings, sculpture, and photography. Admission is $2.00 for adults, $1.00 for students and senior citizens. Hours are 11:00 a.m. to 5:00 p.m., Wednesday through Sunday.

Forbes Magazine Galleries—60 Fifth Ave. (12th St.), Manhattan; 212/206-5548. This brownstone townhouse shows off the collections of this late millionaire (and member of Liz Taylor's collection of husbands). His collection is best known for its dozen large eggs; not grade A, but bejeweled Faberge eggs. Only about fifty were ever made. Forbes, who was also a military fan, owned lots of intricate model ships and toy soldiers; and he amassed a considerable catalogue of presidential papers and memorabilia. Considering his vast wealth, it's fitting that you can see it all for free. Hours are 10:00 a.m. to 4:00 p.m., Tuesdays through Saturdays.

Fraunces Tavern Museum—54 Pearl St., Manhattan; 212/425-1778. Did you know that this isn't the actual tavern in which George Washington raised a farewell glass with his men? It's a replica on the same site, but it's still pretty neat. How can you dislike an exhibit called "Star Spangled Spirits," tying history and drinking together? The museum also gives lectures on a regular basis, relating to all sorts of eighteenth-century topics. These are free with museum admission, which is $2.50 for adults and $1.50 for children and senior citizens. Open Monday through Friday from 10:00 a.m. to 4:45 p.m., and noon to four on Saturdays.

Frick Collection—1 East 70th St., Manhattan; 212/288-0700. One of the foremost private art holdings in the world, the Frick Collection is yet another result of a late millionaire whose vaults have been opened for all to behold. The paintings featured are predominantly European; room after room is filled with major works by Turner, Fragonard, Boucher, Vermeer, and many others. Sculpture and period French furniture are also among the highlights. And there is a delightful interior courtyard, with flowery landscaping and a large fountain. Admission to it all is just $3.00 for adults, $1.50 for students and seniors. Hours are 10:00 a.m. to 6:00 p.m., Tuesdays through Saturdays; Sundays 1:00 to 6:00; closed Mondays.

Goethe House—1014 Fifth Ave. (82nd St.), Manhattan; 212/744-8310. Many cities around the world host a Goethe House, set up by the Republic of Germany to present its art and culture. Touring exhibitions include photography and paintings, classic and contemporary films, lectures, concerts, and more. Admission is free to all; hours are Wednesday, Friday, and Saturday from noon to 5:00 p.m., and Tuesday and Thursday from 11:00 a.m. to 7:00 p.m.

Guggenheim Museum—1071 Fifth Ave. (89th St.), Manhattan; 212/423-3500. This famous Frank Lloyd Wright design, with its spiral shape, symbolizes the modern art it houses—one of the world's premier collections. The building is meant to be walked from the top down—you'll be less tired that way! In addition to the works of pioneers from Impressionism on through Picasso to the artists of today, see special exhibits such as the recent "Russian and Soviet Avant-Garde, 1915-1932." After a lengthy closure, the museum has returned to the scene with a whole new wing added. Now, admission can be as lofty as the architecture, with a top price of $7.00 for adults; but children under twelve are always admitted free, and Tuesdays from 5:00 to 8:00 p.m. are "Pay What You Wish" evenings. Hours are 10:00 a.m. to 8:00 p.m. daily, except Thursdays.

International Center of Photography—1133 Sixth Ave. (43rd St.), Manhattan; 212/768-4680, and 1130 Fifth Ave. (94th St.), Manhattan; 212/860-1778. Long-time New Yorkers may still think of this as the Kodak Center, since Kodak used to run this mid-town gallery as a freebie; it always made a great lunch-hour activity. Well, it's still a great place, and it's cheap, if no longer free. Several rooms house a permanent collection of award-winning photos, printed up into large displays; there are also temporary traveling exhibits, as in any museum. Recent exhibitions covered such themes as "Small Town America: The Missouri Photo Workshops, 1949-1991" and "Karsh: American Legends," a showing of celebrity portraits by one of today's most noted photographers. ICP also has a video gallery, and sponsors lecture series and special events. Admission is $4.00 for adults, $2.50 for students and senior citizens, $1.00 for kids under twelve, and free for members. Open Tuesdays from 11:00 a.m. to 8:00 p.m., and Wednesdays through Sundays from 11:00 a.m. to 6:00 p.m. ICP also has an uptown branch along the Museum Mile, with the same hours.

Lower East Side Tenement Museum—97 Orchard St., Manhattan; 212/431-0233. And you thought Orchard Street was only good for shopping bargains? This museum preserves the culture of New York City's nineteenth-century merchant class, a perfect complement to Ellis Island. The building itself is a genuine tenement built in 1863, and its exhibits display artifacts and re-created storefronts tracing the experience of the Jews, Italians, Irish, African-Americans and Asians who successively found this neighborhood a "Gateway to America." Films, photographs, and live performances by the museum's own theatrical troupe bring it all to life; the museum also sponsors walking tours through the actual neighborhoods themselves. Admission is a suggested donation of $3.00 per person (separate fees for plays and tours). Hours are Tuesday through Friday, 11:00 a.m. to

4:00 p.m., and Sunday from 10:00 a.m. to 4:00 p.m. Closed Saturday and Monday.

Museum of American Folk Art—2 Lincoln Square (Columbus Ave. at 65th St.), Manhattan; 212/977-7298. This charming gallery focuses on the artwork of Native American cultures, with changing exhibitions like its recent "Visiones del Pueblo," showcasing folk art from Latin America. With seventeen countries represented, from the 1500s to the present, this was assembled by the museum and became the first major traveling exhibit of its kind. MAFA also offers free educational programs for children, such as mask-making workshops, and for families in both English and Spanish. Admission is free as well; hours are Tuesdays through Sundays from 11:30 a.m. to 7:30 p.m.

Museum of The City Of New York—Fifth Ave. at 103rd St., Manhattan; 212/534-1672. If you could really fit the entire city into one building, this might be it. Five floors house everything from actual rooms of the first Rockefeller mansion to furniture by NYC's own Duncan Phyfe to model ships and a fast-moving multimedia show giving the entire history of the city in twenty minutes. Photo galleries host special exhibits, like the recent "Songs of My People," with works by African-American photo journalists. Hours are Wednesdays through Saturdays, 10:00 a.m. to 5:00 p.m.; Sundays and holidays 1:00 to 5:00 p.m.. Admission is $5.00.

Mr. Cheap's Picks

✔ **The Cloisters**—Not only is this a fresh-air getaway without leaving Manhattan, you'll see gothic structures older than our country itself—all for a donation of your own choosing.

✔ **Frick Collection**—Perhaps the world's foremost private art collection, it rivals the Met at half the price.

✔ **Museum of American Folk Art**—One of New York's wonderful free museums, showcasing the culture of our two continents.

✔ **New York Transit Museum**—See a real working subway station! Once, just a token (now a bit more) admitted you to this underground palace dedicated to the underground.

✔ PAY WHAT YOU WISH/FREE HOURS—Many major museums offer special hours, once a week, when you can enter for free or by a donation of your choice. These include the **Modern**, the **Museum of Natural History**, the **Guggenheim**, and the **Whitney**.

✔ **Queens Museum of Art**—Don't just look at art, make some yourself at this low-priced, participatory museum.

✔ **Richmondtown Restoration**—Williamsburg in New York—a colonial restoration is grows on Staten Island.

Museum of Modern Art—11 West 53rd St., Manhattan; 212/708-9400. Well, you probably don't need Mr. C to tell you about this landmark on the artistic map of New York (and the world). Anyone who tried to get tickets to the "Matisse" exhibit knows how hot this place can get—and how expensive. But don't be deterred. Regular admission is $7.00 for adults and $4.00 for students/seniors, which is still a bargain when you consider all of the permanent and travelling exhibits on MOMA's many floors. What Mr. C *does* want to add is that, on Thursday evenings from 5:00 to 9:00 p.m., admission is simply "Pay What You Wish." Be a patron of the arts—or just look like one. Regular hours are 11:00 a.m. to 6:00 p.m. daily, and Thursdays until 9:00.

Also, MOMA offers free "Summergarden" concerts in its famous sculpture garden behind the museum. These take place on Friday and Saturday evenings at 7:30 during July and August.

National Academy of Design—1083 Fifth Ave. (90th St.), Manhattan; 212/369-4880. The National Academy of Design is perhaps one of the lesser-known stops along the Museum Mile, but no less respected—and well worth a visit. Dedicated to all aspects of design and aesthetics, NAD features special exhibits that often focus on lesser-known subjects themselves. One recent example was its retrospective on the Scandinavian painter Helene Schjerfbeck, "Finland's Modernist Rediscovered." The exhibit showed over seventy landscapes, still-lifes, and portraits from her long career. You may not have realized that they even have modernists in Finland! Anyway, the museum is open Tuesdays through Sundays from noon to 5:00 p.m., with admission just $2.50 for adults and $2.00 for children and seniors; but on Tuesdays from 5:00 to 8:00 p.m. in the evening, admission is free to all.

New York Aquarium—Surf Ave. (West 8th St.), Coney Island, Brooklyn; 718/265-FISH (3474). Given its location on the Coney Island boardwalk, the New York Aquarium is a rather odd blend of wildlife conservation center (its true mission) and Sea World. Daily dolphin, sea lion, and whale shows are mixed in with exhibits and demonstrations about life at the bottom. The Discovery Cove, NYA's new environmental display area, features recreations of coastal tidepools and habitats for a variety of fish, reptiles, and other animals. And don't miss the shark feeding sessions, always a dramatic event. The Aquarium is open daily from 10:00 a.m. to 5:00 p.m., weekends from 10:00 a.m. to 7:00 p.m.; admission is still a bargain at $5.75 for adults, $2.00 for seniors and kids aged twelve and under, and free for ages two and under.

New York Transit Museum—Boerum Place and Schermerhorn St., Brooklyn; 718/330-3060. The original idea was to charge adults the price of a subway token for admission, and kids even less. Well, token prices keep rising and the museum's price has gone up faster still; but even at $3.00 for adults and $1.50 for children and seniors, you'll have a lot of fun. Watch an actual subway control center in action and walk through a station from the 1930s. Some of the cars on display here date back even further, to the earliest days of mass transit. Open Tuesday through Friday from 10:00 a.m. to 4:00 p.m., Saturday and Sunday from 11:00 a.m. to 4:00 p.m.

North Wind Undersea Institute—610 City Island Ave., City Island, Bronx; 718/885-0701. What's this—Jacques Cousteau in New York? Well, yes, in a way. Up near Westchester, jutting out into the Long Island Sound, City Island is like a getaway to the Hamptons without leaving the Apple. Sure, it's a bit of a drive—take Route 95 North to the Orchard Beach/City Island exit—but it takes less than half an hour from many parts of town. And what a difference when you get there! The main avenue is dotted with seafood restaurants and saltbox inns. (For great water views and inexpensive food, Mr. C recommends Tony's Pier—see listing under "Restaurants: Outer Boroughs.")

Meanwhile, be sure to check out this small yet fascinating museum. Its hands-on exhibits include themes like, "The Undersea World of the Bronx" (listening, Jacques?), exotic sea shells, life-size whale bones (just as exciting as dinosaurs), and a real hundred-year-old tugboat. Watch films of whale rescues, and look at rescued marine animals, like seals and turtles, being cared for. Animal rescue is one of the charter missions of the institute. So is education against pollution, and the idea that "One person can make a difference." Admission is $3.00 for adults, $2.00 for children and seniors. Open Monday through Friday from 10:00 a.m. to 5:00 p.m., Saturday and Sunday from noon to 5:00 p.m.

P.S. 1 Museum—46-01 21st St., Long Island City, Queens; 718/784-2084. A division of the Institute for Contemporary Art, the vast P.S. 1 has three floors of galleries devoted to the latest in creative performance and displays. The artists shown here come from all over the country and around the world. See wild video art installations, sculptured "environments," and other avant-garde works. On weekends the galleries often become flexible performance spaces for actors, musicians, and movement artists of all kinds. Admission is a suggested donation of $2.00.

Hours are 12:00 noon to 6:00 p.m., Wednesdays through Sundays. Free parking too, by the way.

Pierpont Morgan Library and Annex—29-33 East 36th St., Manhattan; 212/685-0008. The Morgan Library is another turn-of-the-century millionaire's home—not even built as a home for ol' J.P., just his books! Based on ancient Roman architecture, the library is now a public museum dedicated to literature and design. You'll be entranced by its domed entrance hall, done up in marble and murals. Exhibits range from stately landscape drawings to the recent whimsical "Puss in Boots: Three Centuries of the Master Cat." Admission is $5.00 to all, but this is a suggested donation; so they can't frown if you offer a smaller sum. Don't be too stingy; after all, *he* wouldn't have been. Hours are 10:30 a.m. to 5:00 p.m. Tuesdays through Saturdays, and Sundays from 1:00 to 5:00 p.m.

Queens Museum of Art—New York City Building, Flushing Meadow Park, Queens; 718/592-9700. This museum is about making art as much as viewing it; they give you the chance to do both. Enjoy the ever-changing array of exhibits, usually leaning toward the work of contemporary artists; and on Sundays, join a "Drop-In Workshop" ($1.00 per person), where you can try your own hand at something inspired by the shows. These take place at 1:00 and 3:00 p.m., led by museum staff. Express yourself! Admission is just $3.00 for adults and $1.50 for students, seniors, and children over age five. Kids under five are admitted free. The museum is located near the Grand Central Parkway, part of the original 1939 World's Fair grounds. It's in the process of major renovations, which have so far created new galleries and a new auditorium as well. Hours are Tuesday through Friday from 10:00 a.m. to 5:00 p.m., Saturday and Sunday from noon to 5:30 p.m.

Richmondtown Restoration—441 Clarke Ave., Staten Island; 718/351-1611. This is a museum only in the broadest sense; it's really a living, working re-creation of one of New York's original settlements. Just as at Plymouth, Massachusetts, or Williamsburg, Virginia, actors and historians in full costume wander around the complex and demonstrate the crafts and daily tasks of colonial settlers. In fact, several periods are represented, including the Civil War era. See a one-room school, buy something in the general store, and even drink at the local tavern—where, on weekend evenings, singers perform sea chanties and other folk music. Hours are 1:00 to 5:00 p.m., Wednesdays through Sundays (closed weekends during winter). Admission is $4.00 for adults and $2.50 for students and senior citizens. If you aren't driving, there is a bus (#113) that will take you there from the ferry.

Abigail Adams Smith Museum—421 East 61st St., Manhattan; 212/838-6878. Another one for you architecture and history fans. Built in 1826, this building has led a varied and illustrious life. It was in 1798 that Abigail Adams Smith, daughter of President John Adams, and her husband designed an estate on the banks of the East River. They never occupied it. Before it was finished, they sold it off; all that remains is this stone carriage house, which later became a hotel, and finally a museum filled with one of New York's finest collections of early-nineteenth-century furnishings. How much to see all this? $3.00 for adults, $2.00 for children, and $1.00 for senior citizens. Open Monday through Friday, 10:00 a.m. to 4:00 p.m., Sundays 1:00 to 5:00 p.m.

Whitney Museum of American Art—945 Madison Ave. (75th St.), Manhattan; 212/570-3676. One of the city's great art museums, its popularity is due not only to its estimable collections but also to its manageable size. You can comfortably "do" the place in an afternoon. The exhibits are twentieth century; the sculptor Alexander Calder has long been associated with the Whitney, and his delightful mobiles are evident throughout the building and in the courtyard. The many exhibit halls change over regularly, showing the work of important modern American artists past and present. While admission is $5.00 for adults and $3.00 for students and seniors, the museum is free to all on Thursday evenings from 6:00 to 8:00 p.m. Regular hours are 1:00 to 8:00 p.m. on Thursdays and 11:00 a.m. to 6:00 p.m. on Wednesdays and Fridays through Sundays.

But wait, there's more. The Whitney has several branch locations around Manhattan, each with different temporary exhibits:

Whitney Museum at Equitable Center, 787 Seventh Ave. (51st St.), 212-554-1113, adds art to a lovely indoor atrium—a peaceful oasis in the heart of Midtown. Open Tuesday through Friday from 11:00 a.m. to 5:00 p.m. (Thursday to 7:30), Saturday noon to 5:00 p.m.

Whitney Museum at Federal Reserve Plaza, 33 Maiden Lane (Nassau St.), 212-943-5655, is the newest outpost. With the high prices art commands these days, it's right at home amidst the brokers shouting for pork bellies. Open Monday through Friday, 11:00 a.m. to 6:00 p.m.

Whitney Museum at Philip Morris, 120 Park Ave. (42nd St.), 212-878-2550, has two galleries, open Monday through Saturday from 11:00 a.m. to 6:00 p.m., and Thursday to 7:30 p.m.; and a sculpture garden, open daily from 7:30 a.m. to 9:30 p.m. (Sundays and holidays, 11:00 a.m. to 7:00 p.m.). The garden also hosts free concerts of classical and popular music, usually at lunchtime.

Best of all, each of these branch galleries is always free!

OUTDOORS

The Bronx Zoo—Southern Blvd. (185th St.), Bronx; 718/220-5100. In spite of the popular book, this does not refer to Yankee Stadium. The Bronx Zoo, of course, is one of the earliest and foremost zoos in the country, opened in 1899. It was also decades ahead of its time in recreating natural habitats for its animals, as so many zoos are doing nowadays. There are three different ways to tour the park, getting you acquainted with its 250 acres: The Safari Tour tractor train, the Skyfari aerial tram, and the Bengali Express monorail.

These should help you narrow down the sights you'd like to see up close, from the seal pool to the monkey house to the "World of Birds" aviary. And don't miss the "World of Darkness," where our nocturnal friends are awake during the daytime.

The bison range alone takes up a full three acres near the main entrance. And at the southern end of the zoo are the "African Plains" and "Wild Asia," two expansive habitats in which large animals roam freely (don't worry, it's perfectly safe). Speaking of animals roaming, the famous Children's Zoo gives kids a chance to feed and pet all sorts of furry critters. Admission is $5.75 for adults and $2.00 for children to age twelve. During the off-season, from October to April, the zoo remains open, although many of the outdoor exhibit areas are closed; this makes for real bargain rates, though—just $2.50 for adults and $1.00 for kids.

Brooklyn Botanic Garden—1000 Washington Ave., Crown Heights, Brooklyn; 718/622-4433. When New Yorkers refer to the "Botanical Garden," they usually mean the larger, more famous one in the Bronx. But don't overlook this sister park, with its fifty acres of gorgeous flower beds, the Japanese landscaped garden, and the Steinhardt Conservatory, which displays the flora of different temperate locales. Admission to it all is free. Guided walking tours are also available. Just "next door" is the Brooklyn Museum, too (see listing under "Museums"). The garden is closed from October through March.

Central Park Rowboats—Loeb Boathouse, Central Park, near 72nd St., Manhattan; 212/517-4723. For a refreshing pause amid city life, rent a rowboat for just a few bucks and paddle an hour or two away. It's a delightful, not to mention romantic pleasure—and you don't really have to row very far. Bridges, fountains, and trees pass as you drift along. The cost is $8.00 an hour; split it with a companion and you've got a fun, cheap outing that'll energize you anew for returning to the daily grind. Boating is available almost as soon as the lake defrosts in March, through the summer and fall.

Coney Island/Astroland Amusement Park—Surf Ave. (West 12th St.), Coney Island, Brooklyn; 718/372-0275. This is it, kids, the original—or what's left of it. Coney Island was one of the very first amusement parks in the country; a technological paradise meant to help people get comfortable with the Industrial Revolution. Today, though, we've gotten ahead of this kind of place, and it feels nostalgic. Also, rather rundown. Still, you can have lots of fun here, on the rides or just strolling the boardwalk. It is a good idea to go during the daytime and keep a hand (your own) on your wallet; but police do maintain a strong presence, so you can enjoy yourself. For old-fashioned thrill-seekers, don't miss the Cyclone, one of the few classic wooden roller coasters left in America.

Ellis Island National Monument/ Statue of Liberty—It goes without saying that every American should visit these landmarks. So have you been there? Not only are they of historic importance, they make great outdoor activities that are not expensive to do. For starters, of course, you have to get there by ferry. On a sunny day, this is a worthwhile outing in itself. Ferries depart from Battery Park, at the southernmost tip of Manhattan (and from Jersey City too), affording you dramatic views of the Financial District skyline. Good photo opps.

Climb up to Lady Liberty's crown, all 350 steps of it; or just walk around the quiet island haven. At Ellis Island, the building which probably "processed" someone in your family has been completely restored and made into a fascinating museum. Find out, in the flash of a computer, which states now have the highest concentration of your nationality. See actual artifacts from immigrants of all ethnic origins, films about the experience, and the stately Great Hall itself. In fact, the place is more beautiful inside than it probably ever was during its use.

The ferry boats head for the Statue first, then on to Ellis Island, and finally back to the Battery. With frequent sailings, you can get on and off and spend as much time as you wish at each destination. Round-trip fares are just $6.00 for adults, $5.00 for seniors, $3.00 for youths age three to seventeen, and free for kids under three. And since there are no admission charges at the monuments, these prices (well, plus some hot dogs or such) can be your only expenses for the whole day.

Gateway National Park—Shore Pkwy., Sheepshead Bay, Brooklyn; 718/338-3799. Did you know that Brooklyn has the largest urban park in the country? Gateway is as wide open a space as you're likely to find anywhere in the metro area. In fact, its twenty-six-thousand acres extend out across the marshes of Queens and onto Long Island. The park includes the **Gateway Sports Center** (718/253-6816), a popular spot for runners and bicyclists. For that matter, there are also golf courses, tennis courts, and baseball diamonds. And **Floyd Bennett Field**, New York City's first airport, features an exhibition hall in one of its original airplane hangars.

New York Botanical Garden—Southern Blvd. (200th St.), Bronx; 718/220-8700. You like flowers? *We've* got flowers! How about 250 acres—a living catalog of trees, flowers, vines, shrubs, and perhaps the occasional weed. There is a preserve of virgin hemlock trees, the original land cover for the metro area (somewhat pre-skyscrapers). There is the conservatory, a sprawling complex of greenhouses filled with plants typical of hotter climes. And, of course, the museum, with its own exhibits on the environment. The gardens are open Tuesdays through Sundays from 10:00 a.m. to 4:00 p.m. Admission is a suggested donation of $3.00 for adults and $2.00 for children and senior citizens. The Botanical Garden also hosts walking tours focusing on different parts of the grounds, for an additional $5.00 per person.

Mr. Cheap's Picks

✔ **Botanical Gardens**—Stroll amidst floral beauty and nearly-fresh air. Don't forget that there are two of these—in Bronx *and* in Brooklyn!

✔ **Central Park Rowboats**—Split a relaxing float on this lovely oasis in the city, and it hardly costs a thing. Similar deal in **Prospect Park** too, by the way.

✔ **Ellis Island/Statue of Liberty**—Now that Ellis Island is up and running, a single ticket gets you two national monuments for the price of one—plus ferry rides to and fro, no extra charge.

✔ **Roosevelt Island Tram**—Amusement park ride masquerading as public transit. The island is full of outdoor activities, too.

✔ **Sail Away New York**—Not your average boat ride—a large, comfortable *sailboat*, at incredibly cheap rates.

✔ **Staten Island Ferry**—What else can you say? The most fun you'll ever get for 50¢—well, outdoors, anyway.

New York City Audubon Society—71 West 23rd St., Manhattan; 212/691-7483. Go birding (yes, that's the word) with the best-known bird lovers in the world. Audubon Society adventures take place on the weekends to local sites, and occasionally to locations a day or overnight trip away. These are remarkably inexpensive. The society also offers slide lectures once a month, free and open to anyone interested. Call for details about upcoming events. These take place near the main office, on the campus of the Fashion Institute of Technology. So, you'll get to see what the well-dressed pigeon is wearing this season.

Prospect Park Boating—Park Slope, Brooklyn; recorded info, 718/788-0055. From the people who brought you Central Park—nineteenth-century civic planners Frederick Law Olmsted and company—Prospect Park has over five hundred acres and many of the same kinds of activities as its larger sibling. On Prospect Lake, for instance, you can rent pedal boats for just $7.00 an hour; it's located near the Parkside Avenue entrance, along the southern edge of the park.

The famous Prospect Park Carousel is a fully restored merry-go-round originally built in 1874, with a mighty Wurlitzer organ inside and fifty animals to ride on. It's like a magical time machine, and just 50¢ a ride.

Prospect Park is also full of great outdoor activities that are free or very inexpensive. In the winter you can skate in the **Wollman Rink** for $2.00 for adults, $1.00 for kids. And summer activities include extensive bicycling and walking paths, as well as live concerts and children's shows (see listing under "Live Music: Free Summer Concerts").

Tour the park's two historic homes, **Litchfield Villa** and **Lefferts Homestead**, dating back to the 1800s and 1700s, respectively. Litchfield now also serves as the park's headquarters, where you can pick up more information. And this doesn't even get us to the Brooklyn Botanic Garden, which is yet another part of this magnificent park (see listing above).

Roosevelt Island Tram and Parks—Second Avenue & 59th Street, Manhattan. This amusement park ride masquerading as public transit is one of New York's unique thrills. Cheap, too. A mere $2.80 books you a round-trip passage—in the completely enclosed gondola that glides up to a height of 250 feet above the East River, pulled along by giant gears. The trip is delightfully silent and gentle. Walk around from window to window: The majestic Queensboro Bridge rises alongside you to the south, while the Upper East Side stretches off to the north. Live the motorist's dream of floating above the traffic of First and York Avenues, a glittery sight at night. The ride lasts an all-too-short four minutes; once you arrive on Roosevelt, explore its many activities, or hang out just a bit for the return voyage.

On the island itself, climb aboard one of the red buses that link the Tramway Plaza with Octagon Park at the northern tip of the island. Geared as much to visitors as residents, it stops at several points of interest along the way. Or pick up a brochure at the bus stop for a self-guided walking tour of such features as Meditation Steps (photo-perfect views of passing ships, with Manhattan in the background). Nearby is the restored landmark **Blackwell House**, dating from 1796—this farmhouse is one of the oldest buildings left in New York City. To the north, Octagon Park's facilities include a soccer field, a baseball diamond, and six tennis courts, along with barbecue grills and community gardens. And further up is Lighthouse Park, built in 1872 from the island's own granite. Though it's no longer officially needed, the light still works. It's surrounded by more park area. Indeed, you can spend a whole day on Roosevelt Island—just four minutes to a getaway from the rat race.

Sail Away New York—Battery Park, Manhattan; 212/825-1976. Sail Away offers a variety of inexpensive boat trips in New York Harbor on its seventy-foot wooden sailboat, the *Petrel*. Perhaps their best deal of all is on weekdays, when you can have a forty-five-minute lunchtime sail for just $8.00 (or $10.00, if you buy in advance and want "rain insurance"). The course is to Governor's Island, up the Hudson or East River or wherever the wind takes you. Noon departures are from Battery Park, starting in May and running through September.

If there is enough demand, Sail Away adds a ninety-minute trip at 1:00 p.m. (tickets $15.00 and $20.00); they also have weekend and evening cruises, and are available for private charters. Now, the Staten Island Ferry is fine, and its price can't be beat; but there's nothing quite like the feeling of cutting across the waters without the sound and fumes of an engine.

Staten Island Ferry—Battery Park, Manhattan and St. George, Staten Island; 212/806-6940 or 718/390-5253. Maybe the most (clean) fun you can get in New York for fifty cents. It takes almost half an hour to ferry from Battery Park, at the bottom of Manhattan, to the St. George terminal on Staten Island. Along the way, you'll pass the Brooklyn Heights promenade; the Statue of Liberty; Castle William and Fort Jay on Governor's Island; and of course, scenic New Jersey. Not only that, but they won't even charge you for the return trip! What a great idea for whiling away a lunch hour, or as a cheap getaway from the hustle and bustle of the city. You can forget, sometimes, that Manhattan really is an island; sailing the open seas is a true joy, even if it's only New York Bay.

Staten Island Zoo—614 Broadway (Forrest Ave.), Staten Island; 718/442-3100. Hey, they've got one too! Much smaller than its famous Bronx counterpart, the SI Zoo nevertheless makes the most of its compact size. This zoo is nationally known for its reptile collection, as well as its aviary and aquarium displays. There is no separate fee for entering the Children's Zoo, which is almost like a farm, with pony rides for the kiddies and opportunities to feed the animals. The zoo is open daily all year round; admission is $3.00 for ages twelve and up, $2.00 for ages three to eleven, and free for kids under age three and zoo members. Wednesday afternoons from 2:00 to 5:00 p.m. are "Donation Days," when you can pay what you wish to enter. They've even got free parking—whether you've come by pony or Pontiac.

POETRY AND LITERARY READINGS

Poetry lovers should subscribe to the ***Poetry Calendar,*** a monthly publication that lists the schedules for hundreds of free and inexpensive poetry readings throughout the city. The public funds that subsidize it have been cut back (naturally), but as of this writing, it's hanging in there. You can find it free in libraries and bookstores, but a subscription is only $15.00 for the year—well worth it for this fountain of information. Write to NYC Poetry Calendar, 60 East 4th St., #21, New York, NY 10003.

The Academy of American Poets—177 East 87th St., Manhattan; 212/427-5665. This organization presents readings of both American works and those from around the world, such as the recent "A Splintered Mirror: Contemporary Chinese Poetry." These take place at various locations, such as NYU's Vanderbilt Hall, and are offered free; call the above number for upcoming events.

Art In The Anchorage—Cadman Plaza West at Old Fulton St., Brooklyn Heights, Brooklyn; 718/206-6674. See listing under "Art Galleries."

Bernard Shaw Society—991 Fifth Ave. (80th St.), Manhattan; 212/288-2263. No, not the guy from CNN. For almost fifty years, lovers of the Irish bard have gathered periodically to read out and listen to his many plays and essays. Afterwards there is much animated discussion of the philosophical ideas brought out. While membership only costs $15.00 a year, giving reduced-price admission to the readings, these are also open to the general public for $5.00 per person. For more details, best bet is to write to them at Box 1373, Grand Central Station, New York, NY 10163 and get on their mailing list.

Brentano's—597 Fifth Ave. (48th St.), Manhattan; 212/826-2450. One of midtown Manhattan's all-time great bookstores, Brentano's frequently has noted authors in to read from their latest releases. Call to see if any readings are coming up.

Cooper Union—Third Avenue (7th St.), Manhattan; 212/353-4195. See listing under "Lectures."

DIA Center for the Arts—155 Mercer St., Manhattan; 212/431-9232. See listing under "Dance."

Dixon Place—258 Bowery (East Houston St.), Manhattan; 212/219-3088. See listing under "Theater."

Endicott Booksellers—450 Columbus Ave. (81st St.), Manhattan; 212/787-6300. This popular Upper West Side book store is the setting for frequent, if irregularly scheduled, readings by major and rising authors. Call or stop in to see who'll be plugging—er, appearing in the near future.

Exoterica—Various locations, Bronx; 718/549-5192. The Bronx has not been left out of the poetry revolution. Exoterica sponsors regular poetry readings at two restaurant locations: **The An Beal Bocht Cafe**, 445 West 238th St., at Waldo Ave.; and **Sidekicks Cafe**, 6031 Broadway, near the 242nd St. subway station. Cover charges range from free to $3.00. Call the above number for schedules.

Free Theatre Project—311 West 80th St., Manhattan; 212/874-5935. See listing under "Theater."

The Knitting Factory—47 East Houston St., Manhattan; 212/219-3055. See listing under "Live Music: Rock/Pop."

La Galleria Second Classe—6 East 1st St., Manhattan; 212/505-2476. This homespun little place offers fiction and poetry readings by writers who are firmly fixed in the downtown arts world. These usually take place on Friday evenings; call for more info. Admission is by a suggested donation of $5.00.

Life Is Art Cafe—170 Avenue A (10th St.), Manhattan; 212/505-2502. Another part of the hopping East Village scene, Life Is Art is one of the many clubs down here hosting poetry readings. On Tuesday nights at 9:00, join in an "Open Mike for the Spoken Word"—or just listen in. There is no cover charge.

New Press Readings—Various locations. This organization sponsors regular poetry readings in restaurants and bars all over the city. These are full-evening affairs, complete with master of ceremonies and sometimes an Open Mike, just like the folk and comedy clubs. Most of the venues require you to purchase at least one drink or food item, along with cover charges ranging from $2.00 to $5.00. Listed below are the current city locations; call them for upcoming schedules.

Brooklyn: **Moroccan Star Restaurant**, 205 Atlantic Ave. (Court St.); 718/643-1370.

Manhattan: **Cornelia St. Cafe**, 29 Cornelia St. (Greenwich Village); 212/473-1897. **Phebe's**, 361 Bowery (East 4th St.), 212-860-7860.

Queens: **Queens Cozy Corner Tavern**, 60-01 70th Ave., Ridgewood; 718/386-2737. **Status Quo European Restaurant,** 108-02 72nd Ave., Forest Hills; 718/263-5700.

Staten Island: **Shore Acres Inn**, 1389 Bay St. (Cliff St.); 718/448-5564.

New York City Storytelling Center—28 East 39th St., Manhattan; 212/697-6430. Hey, storytelling isn't just for the kiddies, y'know. In recent years it

Mr. Cheap's Picks

✔ **Bernard Shaw Society**—Match Shavian wits with fellow admirers of the Irish bard.

✔ **New Press Readings**—Spreading poetry far and wide through the boroughs, at various local cafes.

✔ **92nd Street "Y"**—Always a classy series of readings by well-known authors.

✔ **Nuyorican Poets Cafe**—The sixties live on! Perhaps the city's most diverse and vital poetry scene. Don't miss the annual Poetry Slam competition.

✔ **Speakeasy Cafe**—An Open Mike night for poetry? You bet. Try your own muse out on the folks at this Greenwich Village cafe.

has really blossomed into an art form, spinning tales truly meant for grown-up ears. For an annual fee of $25.00, you can become a member of this distinguished organization and attend its twice-monthly gatherings. Take delight in the spoken word and find out how you can get in on the act yourself, if you wish. Call for more information.

New York Public Library—Mid-Manhattan Branch, 455 Fifth Ave. (42nd St.), Manhattan; recorded info, 212/869-8089. See listing under "Lectures."

New York University—Loeb Student Center, 566 LaGuardia Place, Manhattan; 212/998-5424. See listing under "Colleges."

92nd Street "Y"—1395 Lexington Ave. (92nd St.), Manhattan; 212/415-5440. This Upper East Side branch of the YM/YWHA is long famous for its concerts and literary readings. For over fifty years the "Y" has been presenting such eminent authors as Kurt Vonnegut and Susan Faludi, along with adventurous series like the Native American Literature Festival. These are generally held on Monday nights at 8:00, which also happens to be the usual price of admission (some readings go up to $12.00 to $15.00).

Nuyorican Poets Cafe—236 East 3rd St., Manhattan; 212/505-8183. This place embodies many of the best aspects of the revitalized East Village; it combines the beauty of words and music with the gritty realities of everyday life in a setting that is on the border of both. That border is the rough area of the alphabet avenues—a neighborhood that is catching up to the gentrification just across Tompkins Park. Here the barrio meets artists seeking lower rents, and they both meet the yuppies who flock to this exciting scene.

The Nuyorican Poets Cafe presents dedicated, hard-working poets who read their works to appreciative audiences. Musicians are often on the bill as well, and the whole evening generally has a touch of various ethnic cultures. That, after all, is the New York experience. Nuyorican has even been the "studio" for live radio drama broadcasts. The cover charge for most shows is usually $5.00 to $6.00, with no drink minimum. There can be two sets to an evening, which may mean an extra charge for the second show. And don't miss the annual Poetry Slam, a sort of competitive literary sport. The Nuyorican puts a modern twist on the coffeehouses of the 1960s; only back then, these were in the other Village.

P.S. 122—150 First Ave. (9th St.), Manhattan; 212/477-5288. See listing under "Theater."

The Poetry Project—St. Mark's Church, 131 East 10th St., Manhattan; 212/674-0910. Diagonally facing Second Avenue in the East Village, St. Mark's Church is well known among the arts community for its full schedule of theater, dance, and poetry readings. All of these take place in its large, airy theatrical space, with various performance times; but there seems to be something going on nearly every week. Call or stop by for flyers and schedules. Recent readings included Gideon D'Arcangelo and the Blissful Kissful, and Amiri Baraka. Admission is $5.00.

Poetry Society Of America—15 Gramercy Park, Manhattan; 212/254-9628. Since 1910 this organization has been presenting authors reading from their latest works as well as noted actors reading the classics. A recent program offered a "Tribute to Wallace Stevens." These are held on midweek evenings through the year. Admission is $8.00 to $12.00, depending on the event; but for an annual membership fee you can usually attend these readings for half that price.

Poets House—72 Spring St., Manhattan; 212/431-7920. See listing under "Lectures."

The Public Theater/New York Shakespeare Festival—425 Lafayette St., Manhattan; 212/598-7150. See listing under "Theater."

Shakespeare & Co.—716 Broadway (Washington Pl.), Manhattan; 212/529-1330, and 2259 Broadway (81st St.), Manhattan; 212/580-7800. One of New York's preeminent book stores, Shakespeare & Co. frequently presents free readings by noted writers at its two locations in Greenwich Village and the Upper West Side. These are often "hot" authors reading from their latest novels, poetry, and nonfiction. Call to find out if anyone will be dropping by soon.

Speakeasy Cafe—107 MacDougal St., Manhattan; 212/598-9670. In the heart of Greenwich Village, the Speakeasy hosts weekly "Hack Poets Recitals" and Open Mike nights. There is usually a $3.00 cover charge and a one-drink minimum.

The Writer's Voice—5 West 63rd St., Manhattan; 212/875-4124. The Writer's Voice series presents a wide range of readings by noted authors. Hear anyone from Tom Wolfe to the Fifteenth Anniversary Celebration of the Writers Community. Readings take place at the Universalist Church, 160 Central Park West, at 76th Street. Programs begin at 8:00 p.m., and admission is generally around $8.00. They also offer courses in everything from poetry to screenwriting; sit in on a class for free.

SPORTS AND PLAY

No, Mr. C can't get you into Knicks games for free—though don't forget that many of the big sports arenas and stadiums do have ticket prices that start under $10.00. One great alternative is college sports; there are highly competitive schools throughout the city, and many have very affordable prices for football, basketball, hockey, and more. Meanwhile, why not consider some other kinds of sports—the kind in which your participation means more than just raising a bottle of beer?

Billiard Clubs—Feel like a game of pool? More and more people do these days. Billiard parlors are no longer dingy, smoke-filled dens habituated by unsavory characters—they've become chic clubs where you can eat, drink (beer *or* espresso), and while away a few hours with good, clean fun. And if you never mastered the game, don't worry; the folks at the table next to you may be no better.

It can be a fairly cheap night out, especially if you're splitting the hourly rate with your opponent. Rates tend to be anywhere from $5.00 to $20.00 an hour, depending on the room and the night. Oh, and many of these places also have other kinds of amusements too, like video games, skee ball, air hockey, and good ol' Ping-Pong.

One romanticized fact about pool rooms remains true: Most of them stay open into the wee small hours of the morning. Here are just some of the city's many clubs:

Amsterdam Billiard Club: 344 Amsterdam Ave. (76th St.), Manhattan; 212/496-8180. **The Billiard Club**: 220 West 19th St., Manhattan; 212/206-7665. **Chelsea Billiards**: 54 West 21st St., Manhattan; 212/989-0096. **Julian Billiard Academy**: 138 East 14th St., Manhattan; 212/475-9338. **Klipper Klub**: 636 Sixth Ave. (19th St.), Manhattan; 212/924-5151. **Prime Time Billiard**s: 1610 East 19th St. (Ave. P), Kings Highway, Brooklyn; 718/382-6400. **Society Billiards**: 10 East 21st St., Manhattan; 212/529-8600. **SoHo Billiards**: 298 Mulberry St., Manhattan; 212/941-6570. **Steinway Billiards**: 35-25 Steinway St., Astoria, Queens; 718/472-2124. **West Side Billiard Club**: 601 West 50th St., Manhattan; 212/246-1060.

Gateway Sports Center—3200 Flatbush Ave., Sheepshead Bay, Brooklyn; 718/253-6816. Part of the Gateway National Park, near Floyd Bennett Field, Gateway Sports has a golf driving range with a hundred practice tees; also, a full eighteen-hole miniature golf course, tennis courts, and baseball batting cages, all at reasonable rates. Call them for more info.

The Mammoth Club—114 West 26th St., Manhattan; 212/675-2626. No, it's not a lounge for prehistoric elephants. It's one of New York's largest indoor sports facilities, offering pool, Ping-Pong, billiards, snooker, and golf. Yes, golf. They actually

Mr. Cheap's Picks

✔ **Gateway Sports Center**—Way out there in Brooklyn, a great place to stretch your wings and strut your stuff . . . whether it's bicycling, baseball, golf, or whatever.

✔ **Sky Rink**—Inexpensive ice skating with a tremendous view of heaven and earth.

✔ **The Mammoth Club**—It sure is. Play billiards, pool, table tennis, and golf—yes, a real indoor golf driving range—with a few thousand of your closest friends.

have an indoor driving range, and there are even lessons available to help you perfect your swing here in town so you'll look better the next time you get out onto the course. The cost? Just $5.00 per person for half an hour. Pool tables rent at $3.00 per person for one hour, while Ping-Pong tables are $5.00 per half-hour. Snooker is $5.00 for one full hour, and billiards are $6.00 an hour for the table. A bit confusing from one to the other, but one thing is certain—it's good, cheap fun. And best of all, the Mammoth Club is open twenty-four hours a day, seven days a week. It's also a great place for private parties, which can accommodate up to two hundred people. *That* should give you an idea of the size of this place.

Sky Rink—450 West 33rd St., Manhattan; 212/695-6555. They're not kidding—somehow, sixteen floors up, it seems as though you can skate right on into the heavens. Sky Rink is one of the city's largest indoor rinks, with public sessions year-round on weeknights and all day weekends. Admission prices are $7.50 for adults; $5.00 for kids under twelve, and senior kids over fifty-five. Got no skates? Rent a pair for $2.50. You can call the above number for automated recordings with the exact hours of skating sessions for any day of the week.

Tennis Courts—Various locations. There are hundreds of tennis courts in **Central Park**, **Prospect Park**, and other city parks all over town. These are much less expensive than private clubs. You'll need to buy a permit at the beginning of the season (usually in April), but these are tremendous bargains when you consider that you can then play all through spring, summer, and fall. In 1993 the fees are $50.00 for adults, $20.00 for seniors over sixty-two, and $10.00 for children under eighteen. Call these numbers for more info: Bronx: 718/430-1838. Brooklyn: 718/965-8993. Manhattan: 212/360-8133. Queens: 718/263-4121. Staten Island: 718/390-8023.

Wollman Memorial Rink—Central Park (East Drive, near 65th St. entrance), Manhattan; 212/517-4800. At the north end of "The Pond," this is the city's largest outdoor rink, used for ice skating in winter (roughly, October through March) and roller skating in summer. Admission fees are $6.00 for adults, $3:00 for kids under twelve and senior citizens. Skate rentals are available too, for $3.25. Open daily from 10:00 a.m., including most evenings.

There's another Wollman in the city park family—the **Kate Wollman Rink** in Prospect Park. It too is just above a pond, at the southern end of the park near Lincoln Road and Parkside Avenue. Call 718/965-6561 for information.

World's Fair Ice Skating Rink—Flushing Meadows-Corona Park, Queens; 718/271-1996. Queens borough is not to be left out in the cold when it comes to ice skating, either. This park, of course, is the direct descendant of the 1939 New York World's Fair. The eighteen-thousand-square-foot rink is open on weekends, with certain day and evening times during the week. Admission for all ages is $3.50 to $5.50, depending on the session; skate rentals cost $3.50. The rink requires children under eighteen to get parental permission forms signed before they can skate.

THEATER

Special tips from Mr. C: Be a volunteer usher! Many of the city's smaller theaters save money on staff by using regular folks like you to seat people at their shows. You'll save money too, because once you're done ripping tickets or handing out programs, you can just find an empty seat and enjoy the show.

Tip #2: You can't usher at Broadway theaters, but many of these houses offer standing room tickets for about $15.00 apiece. Even the hottest shows in town may have a space or two available at the back of the house. You'll at least have the ledge behind the last row of seats to lean against. And if the show's not a complete sellout, you may find an empty seat (which won't have cost $50.00). Be tasteful, though, and wait until the end of intermission to grab it. You don't want to be booted out by latecomers in the middle of act one.

Meanwhile, here are just some of New York's many fine, affordable theaters and ticket options:

Cafe Arielle—432 West 42nd St., Manhattan; 212/629-9100. Located among Theater Row's off-Broadway houses, Cafe Arielle is an informal (though not necessarily inexpensive) restaurant best known as a good place to get a snack during intermission at one of the shows on the block. What fewer people know is that Cafe Arielle has two performance spaces of its own, a cabaret theater upstairs and a smaller stage area in the restaurant downstairs. Both are available to singers, actors, and comedians at low rental rates; meaning that, for a few bucks, you can see young hopefuls strutting their stuff, yearning to be discovered. You never know what kinds of shows may turn up, from the simple singer and piano to outrageous comic sketches. A rack of flyers helps to tell you what's coming soon.

Jean Cocteau Repertory—330 Bowery (Bond St.), Manhattan; 212/677-0060. At the small but stately Bouwerie Lane Theater, the Cocteau Rep has been staging critically acclaimed productions of the world's classics for two decades. Last season included *Under Milk Wood* by Dylan Thomas, Pinter's *The Caretaker*, and an adaptation of Dostoevsky's novel *The Idiot*. Don't worry about the troupe's French name, or its international slate of authors; everything's done in English. Performances are Thursdays through Saturdays at 8:00 p.m., and Sundays at 3:00 p.m. Tickets are $18.00; seniors $15.00, students $10.00. The Rep's repertoire, in fact, makes it very popular with school groups, who also get discount rates.

Dance Theater Workshop—Bessie Schonberg Theater, 219 West 19th St., 2nd Floor, Manhattan; 212/924-0077. See listing under "Dance."

Dixon Place—258 Bowery (East Houston St.) , Manhattan; 212/219-3088. This is one of

Manhattan's many downtown arts houses, presenting very progressive entertainment at rock-bottom prices. See staged readings of new plays still in the works, and wild experimental dance; hear the latest in poetry and fiction. Instead of stand-up comedians you may see a "stand-up tragedian"; and a variety of creative artists under that vague umbrella of "performance art." And every Monday evening features "Doug and Mike's Adult Entertainment," described only as "The funniest puppet show in town." Yes, the subject matter here tends to be . . . er, very liberal and open-minded. You should be too! Tickets are generally $5.00 to $8.00, depending on the show.

Gene Frankel Theatre Workshop—24 Bond St., Manhattan; 212/777-1767. Looking for an unusual night of theater? This is one of New York's top teaching studios, located in the lower corner of the East Village. Frankel, who has been teaching the school's major classes in acting, directing and writing for many years, is considered one of the founding fathers of the Off-Broadway movement (he's directed on Broadway, too). Among his grads are Judd Hirsch, Loretta Swit, Raul Julia, and Walter Matthau.

Regularly throughout the year, his current classes present evenings of scenes and monologues in this unexpectedly lavish and professionally outfitted theater. Admission is free, but reservations are necessary. "Discover" one of tomorrow's stars; call for the next showcase dates.

Free Theatre Project—311 West 80th St., Manhattan; 212/874-5935. *Free* theater? Hey c'mon, this is New York—you don't get nuthin' free. Wrong! For ten years, Stanley Eugene Tannen has been on a mission: To bring Broadway (well, on a smaller scale) to the people. And he does it. Once a month, currently at the Fifth Avenue Presbyterian Church at 55th Street in midtown, a noted Broadway actor or actress gives an hourlong lunchtime performance, absolutely free.

The roster is most impressive. Over the years, Jeremy Irons, Whoopi Goldberg, Norman Mailer (the actor?), John Malkovich, and many others have performed in this popular series. Jason Robards has done Eugene O'Neill. Frances Sternhagen has read Emily Dickinson. These actors, usually appearing in a major play at night, do this as a labor of love—and it shows.

Tannen believes that "the arts are a gift of life to all, and that everyone should have the opportunity to enjoy their beauty and benefits." To find out when and where you can do the same, call or write to get on the mailing list.

The Juilliard School—144 West 66th St., Manhattan; 212/769-7406. See listing under "Colleges."

Kampo Cultural Center—31 Bond St., Manhattan; 212/228-3063. Across the street from the Frankel Studio is this handsome theater and multi-media facility with an Eastern touch. The performance space is rented by a variety of professional troupes, presenting everything from a musical biography of Eleonora Duse to "Rick and Marty's Lab Rat Revue," an evening of darkly humorous sketches. Tickets are usually $10.00 to $12.00. The Kampo center also offers its own seminars and movement classes in various Asian disciplines, from calligraphy to yoga.

The Kitchen—512 West 19th St., Manhattan; 212/255-5793. One of New York's most famous (or perhaps infamous) performance art houses, The Kitchen cooks up wild servings of theater, video, dance, and music—as well as shows that are tossed salads of several ingredients. These works are well-known for pushing the envelope of avant-garde. You never know who'll turn up next here, with its ever-changing lineup of big names on the art house circuit—and those who hope to rise to such dizzying heights. Tickets to most of these performances are in the $10.00 range, with standing room tix available at sellouts. At these prices, you can afford to take a chance.

La Mama E.T.C.—74A East 4th St., Manhattan; 212/475-7710. Over several decades, La Mama has consistently presented the most daring and successful of modern theater's experimental artists. Works by playwrights like Lanford Wilson and Sam Shepard have been developed here, as well as more avant-garde pieces by performance artists Meredith Monk, Ping Chong and more. A wide variety of troupes have been seen in La Mama's three different flexible theater spaces. Ticket prices vary but are seldom higher than $15.00—and many performances allow TDF discounts (see "Theatre Development Fund" listing elsewhere in this section). There is also an art gallery displaying the works of local painters and sculptors; the place is a real haven for the downtown arts community. Stop in sometime and pick up a schedule of upcoming shows.

National Improvisational Theatre—223 Eighth Ave. (21st St.), Manhattan; 212/243-7224. See listing under "Comedy."

New Dramatists—424 West 44th St., Manhattan; 212/757-6960. Dedicated, as you might guess,

Mr. Cheap's Picks

✔ DOWNTOWN PERFORMANCE ART HOUSES—See the wildest shows in the east at avant-garde theaters like **Dixon Place**, **The Kitchen**, **The Performing Garage**, and **P.S. 122**. A little money gets you a lot of adventure.

✔ **Free Theatre Project**—One of those gems that makes New York great. It's one man's mission to bring big Broadway stars to church spaces, giving readings of their favorite writers, and it really is free.

✔ **New Dramatists**—For theater insiders, and wannabees. See readings of possible future hits, with free admission.

✔ **Playwrights Horizons**—A little closer to Broadway, literally and figuratively, workshop versions of hits that are just about ready to move up can be seen here for as little as $5.00.

✔ **The Public Theater**—Joe Papp's dream come true. It's still one of the best values for high-quality, adventurous theater in New York. And of course, every summer they bring free Shakespeare to Central Park.

✔ **"tkts." Booths**—The now-legendary kiosk in Times Square is guaranteed to save you big bucks on those ridiculous Broadway (and even off-Broadway) prices. A lesser-known tip: There are other "tkts." booths in downtown Manhattan and Brooklyn. Same deals, without the hourlong lines.

to the development of original plays, New Dramatists is one of those insider's finds; a place to discover a hit play well before it reaches Broadway, and at no cost. Yes, tickets are free for most of their showcases (don't expect much in the way of sets, lighting, or costumes), because the playwrights are seeking honest audience reactions to their writing. For over forty years, New Dramatists has been a vital pipeline between emerging writers and the Great White Way. Needless to say, tix can be in great demand; best bet is to put your name on their mailing list.

Ohio Theatre—66 Wooster St., Manhattan; 212/966-4844. If you're into downtown, avant-garde, in-your-face theater, this is a great place to find it. Ohio presents a variety of theatrical troupes, like House of Borax (gaining a reputation of its own for performing innovative plays in unusual locales like bars and dance clubs); TWEED, or TheaterWorks: Emerging/Experimental Directions; and many other dance and performance art groups. They've been doing so for over ten years, a lifetime in these circles. The seventy-five-seat house is in a loft space inside an old industrial building in the heart of SoHo. Tickets here tend to be in the $10.00 range, a small price to pay for certain adventure.

The Performing Garage—33 Wooster St., Manhattan; 212/966-9796. Wait—before we leave this theatrical thoroughfare, this avenue of avant-garde, this seminal SoHo street, we must walk down a block from the Ohio to the Performing Garage. For it, too, is a breeding ground for great experimental theater and dance, one of the best-known in the city. It is home to, among other companies, the Wooster Group; Spalding Gray and Willem Dafoe performed here for years before gaining wider audiences for their work. As it has become one of the better-known downtown venues, it is now a bit pricier than it once was. Tickets start in the $10.00 range, but can go as high as $25.00 or so; standing room tickets are sometimes available.

Playwrights Horizons—416 West 42nd St., Manhattan; 212/279-4200. One of the most highly regarded residents of Off-Broadway's Theatre Row, Playwrights Horizons has a national reputation for developing new plays and musicals by the most important writers of the day. As a result, first-rate directors and actors are the ones presenting these works. Yet, because many of the plays here are brand-new and still in development, performances—especially those under their "New Theatre Wing" series—are very inexpensive. Some seats are as low as $5.00 each. And what may you see? This is where Stephen Sondheim developed the Tony Award-winning musical *Sunday in the Park with George*. Jay Tarses, writer/director of TV's "Mollly Dodd," has worked on many scripts here. PH was the first place in New York to show the acclaimed drama *Marvin's Room*. Playwrights such as Christopher Durang, Albert Innaurato and John Patrick Shanley have had works done here. If you want to be way out on the cutting edge of contemporary writing, call for their schedule. Several new works are presented, in full and workshop formats, every season.

P.S. 1 Museum—46-01 21st St., Long Island City, Queens; 718/784-2084. See listing under "Museums."

P.S. 122—150 First Ave. (9th St.), Manhattan; 212/477-5288. Once it meant Public School. Now it means Performance Space. On the outside, little has changed; but once you go in, you'll see things they never taught when you were growing up. Eric Bogosian played here in his early days, as did Spalding Gray. P.S. 122 specializes in the most outrageous of the avant-garde, simultaneously on two floors. In fact, you can buy a "hall pass" instead of tickets to individual shows, entitling you to wander freely back and forth between the evening's events without being told to stay after school.

Programs may range from new music to gay monologues to raucous dance performances. One recent offering was music for electronic cello, synthesized sound, and video; another presented an evening billed as a dance-rap jam. A major event of last fall was "Sunday Afternoon Tea with Quentin Crisp." A monthly feature is "Ninth Street Theatre," with a spaghetti dinner and a different performing group each time. And on Fridays and Saturdays after the shows, you can join the evening's artists in the "Performance Cantina" for refreshments, a chat about their works, and perhaps further informal presentations. Admission is free; regular shows are $6.00 to $8.00.

The Public Theater/New York Shakespeare Festival—425 Lafayette St., Manhattan; 212/598-7150. What the late Joseph Papp started, with a bunch of actors performing Shakespeare for free in Central Park, has grown into a huge, year-round operation. Perhaps the anchor of the downtown theater scene, the Public presents a full season of adventurous works by the world's leading artists. Shakespeare is still the main man here (NYSF is working its way through all of the Bard's plays, one or two each year); but this is also the place where *A Chorus Line* first kicked up its heels. In between you may see rare plays of Samuel Beckett, controversial and political performance artists, films, readings, and late-night cabaret. It's all at Off-Broadway prices; most shows are no higher than $25.00, about half of the top rates uptown.

But there are even better bargains here. The Public offers "Quiktix" to most of its shows, subject to availability, at prices of $10.00 to $15.00. These are sold on a first come, first served basis at the box office, from 6:00 p.m. for evening performances and from 1:00 p.m. for matinees. There are also late-evening "Public Fringe" and "No Shame" performances of experimental works for $10.00 to $12.00. Then you have behind-the-scenes discussions with the playwrights, actors and directors, as well as "Public Books," readings by noted authors (like Susan Sontag, Tama Janowitz, and Stephen Jay Gould), both $5.00 per ticket. "Public Poetry" readings are free and open to all. "Film at the Public" screens everything from foreign adaptations of Shakespeare to classic detective movies at $7.00 a ticket; get a film membership and these can be as cheap as $3.00.

And there's more! The Public is a fine place just to hang out, with a delightful cafe and bookstore in the large, spacious lobby. These are open to anyone from 4:00 p.m. to midnight on weekdays (closed Mondays), and from 1:00 p.m. to midnight on weekends. And, yes, they still do free Shakespeare in Central Park (see listing below).

Riverside Shakespeare Company—316 East 91st St., Manhattan; 212/369-BARD (2273). Be not confused by the name—this troupe began on the West Side and eventually moved in to share the Playhouse 91 space with other independent shows. The RSC bears more relation to its soundalike counterpart than just initials; there has been direct contact over the years between directors from Riverside and the Royal Shakespeare Company in London. Many top Broadway actors, too, had beginnings with this respected group. Riverside produces dozens of Shakespearean works each year, along with plays by other classical authors. Many of these are free, and prices may range up to just $10.00. They also tour city parks with free productions during the summer.

Shakespeare In Central Park—Delacorte Theater, near Central Park West and 81st St., Manhattan; 212/598-7100. As noted above, this is where it all began for Joseph Papp and the now-mighty Public Theater. They haven't forgotten their humble roots; free Shakespeare in the park remains one of New York City's most joyous treasures. The New York Shakespeare Festival presents two or three different plays each summer on this large outdoor stage, with its elaborate scenery and lighting; usually, at least one offering is by Shakespeare, with other, more modern plays mixed in. The performers are Broadway's best, often with a Kevin Kline or an F. Murray Abraham at the top of the bill.

Getting a ticket, alas, is almost as hard as getting a Broadway audition. The shows are regular sellouts. So how do you get in on the act? You wait. Curtain time is 8:00 p.m., and they start distributing the free tix—one to a person—from 6:15 p.m. for that evening only. In order to be near the front of the line, die-hard New Yorkers start camping out around lunchtime. That's taken literally; folks bring picnic baskets, set out blankets and lawn chairs, and have a jolly old time. It's all part of the whole experience. Oh, and don't forget to bring a parasol for the sun, or an umbrella for the rain.

Symphony Space—2537 Broadway (95th St.), Manhattan; 212/864-5400. See listing under "Live Music: Classical."

T. Schreiber Studio—83 East 4th St., Manhattan; 212/420-1249. Like the Gene Frankel Workshop nearby (see above), the Schreiber Studio allows you a peek into the creative processes by which actors and directors learn their craft. From January through June, the Director's Unit stages new and little-known plays for three-week runs; admission is just $5.00. The artists on both sides of the footlights are students with varying degrees of professional experience; yet the overall quality is quite strong. Go on opening night, usually the first Friday of the run, and you can attend the wine and cheese reception afterwards. It's included with admission, and you can rub elbows with the actors and talk about the work you've seen. Call for schedules.

Theater Development Fund—1501 Broadway, Suite 2110, New York, NY, 10036. If you covet a life in the theater—from the audience side, that is—but can't afford to go as often as you'd like, consider joining this nonprofit agency. TDF helps people in many low-paying professions save money on tickets to Broadway shows, Off-Broadway, and beyond. At the same time, of course, they're helping the theaters themselves by putting more fannies in their seats. To qualify you have to be in the arts yourself; or a teacher, student, senior citizen, union member, clergyperson or member of the armed forces. If you're eligible to join, a $5.00 membership fee will magically entitle you to see Broadway shows, dance, and concerts for as little as $10.00 to $15.00 per ticket. You can also purchase special TDF vouchers, just $15.00 per book of five, which can be presented for discounts or free tickets to many other shows. Write to the address above for information on how to join.

Theatreworks/USA—Promenade Theatre, 2162 Broadway (72nd St.), Manhattan; 212/677-5959. This professional company, which specializes in theater for family audiences, offers free plays during the summer. Last year's show was an original musical, *From Sea to Shining Sea*, about the building of the first transcontinental railroad in the 1860s as seen through the eyes of three immigrant laborers. Performances are usually matinees, at 11:00 a.m. and 1:00 p.m. Call for this year's info.

"tkts." Booths—Duffy Square, Broadway at 47th St., Manhattan; 2 World Trade Center, Mezzanine Level, Manhattan; and Borough Hall Park, Court and Montague Sts., Brooklyn Heights, Brooklyn; no phone. Not eligible to join the Theatre Development Fund? Don't despair. For everybody else, TDF runs the highly successful "tkts." booths at three locations around the city, offering half-price tickets for Broadway and Off-Broadway shows. If a show has lots of seats available for that afternoon or evening's performance, they may send a batch of tickets over to the booths, where they sell at half their face value, plus a service charge of $2.00 per ticket. With top B'way prices above $50.00, you can save a lot. Of course, you have to hope "your" show is listed on the daily boards at the front (*always* be armed with several choices).

Available tix are spread among the three outposts; but the Times Square branch is the most popular. Be not daunted by the long lines, which, during tourist seasons especially, often double back on themselves. Once the windows open for business, workers at the front always keep the lines moving very quickly. In the meantime, everyone seems to enjoy lots of showbiz chat. Another good tip from Mr. C: Consider waiting until the last minute. When there's about half an hour to go before curtain, there are usually no lines—but lots of shows are still available. Some actually release more tickets at this time, including hard-to-get seats up front; you may even find a mega-hit, which hadn't been "on the boards" all day, suddenly becoming available.

Hours of sale at Times Square are from 3:00 to 8:00 p.m. for Monday to Saturday evening performances, and from 10:00 a.m. to 2:00 p.m. for Wednesday and Saturday matinees (no evening tickets sold before 3:00!). Sunday hours are from noon until the latest curtain time for whatever's available. Hours at the World Trade Center branch are Monday to Friday, 11:00 a.m. to 5:00 p.m., and Saturday from 11:00 a.m. to 3:30 p.m. In Brooklyn, hours are Tuesday to Thursday, 11:00 a.m. to 2:00 p.m. and 2:30 to 5:30 p.m.; Friday, 11:00 a.m. to 5:30 p.m.; and Saturday, 11:00 a.m. to 3:30 p.m. This booth also sells full-price tickets, in advance, for shows at the Brooklyn Academy of Music and other area halls.

Oh, and be sure to bring enough cash (or traveler's checks); at "tkts." they *don't* take American Express—or Visa . . . or any credit cards at all, for that matter.

West Bank Cafe—407 West 42nd St., Manhattan; 212/695-6909. In its Downstairs Theatre Bar, this popular night spot presents an ever-changing variety of plays, cabaret, and comedy. On any given Wednesday through Sunday, you may find political dramas, risque comedy revues, or just plain music. These shows feature professional actors and singers, many of whom work regularly on Broadway and Off-Broadway stages; they can use this stage rent-free, and so it's become an "in" place to try out new material or original plays. Admission is usually $10.00 or less. And every Saturday at midnight there's "The Free Show," an even looser performance that's literally free for all. You never know *what* you may get then, but it's sure to be lively.

WALKS AND TOURS

Adventure on a Shoestring—300 West 53rd St., Manhattan; 212/265-2663. The name alone makes this one of Mr. C's favorites. Not only does Shoestring offer the least-expensive walking tours in town, they have a huge, ever-changing selection of standard and unusual tours. They're also one of the originals in this business; Howard Goldberg founded the company thirty years ago, and he maintains a personal approach.

Goldberg is clearly in love with New York. Along with the basic guided walks through areas like Little Italy, he's also taken people to the "Little Odessa" neighborhood at Brighton Beach. He's taken people across the Brooklyn Bridge on its birthday, backstage at the Met, and through a fortune cookie factory in Chinatown. And offbeat tours like "Big Apple Love Affairs" showcase the locations and lore behind gigolos from Diamond Jim Brady to Dandy Donald Trump.

Some tours have gone as far afield as New Hope, PA, but most take place in and around Manhattan. Often you'll meet with people who live in these areas, to get a personal flavor—many tours wind up in coffee shops, chatting over pastry. Most important of all, Goldberg knows the locations of just about every restroom on the island. Oh, and about the price: It's just $5.00 per person, virtually the same as it was thirty years ago. This is half-price (or better) than most other tours in town. Memberships are available for frequent walkers, reducing the prices even further. Call to get on the mailing list.

Brooklyn Botanic Garden—1000 Washington Ave., Crown Heights, Brooklyn; 718/622-4433. See listing under "Outdoors."

Brooklyn Center for the Urban Environment—Prospect Park, Brooklyn; 718/788-8500. This nonprofit organization runs inexpensive tours throughout the year, focusing on various neighborhoods around Brooklyn. In one recent offering, for example, an architect and a community activist led folks through the Hispanic section of Greenpoint. The average prices for tours are $6.00 for adults and $3.00 for teachers, students, and anyone over sixty-five. Call 718/788-8549 for recorded information.

City Hall—Broadway and Murray St., Manhattan; 212/788-7585. It's a nice place to visit, but you wouldn't want to work there. You can indeed tour this fine early-nineteenth-century building, free, from 10:00 a.m. to 4:00 p.m., Mondays through Fridays. See historic portraits, antique furniture, the magnificent central rotunda and perhaps some actual inner workings of city government. Who knows, you may even be inspired to run for one of the offices you've examined.

Empire State Building—350 Fifth Ave. (34th St.), Manhattan; 212/736-3100. Now that it's the number-two skyscraper in New York, it's only fitting that the Empire State Building should be the better bargain among mega-

Mr. Cheap's Picks

- ✔ **Adventure on a Shoestring**—Mr. C loves the tours as much as the name itself.
- ✔ **General Grant National Memorial**—Stroll through Grant's Tomb, Riverside Church, and along the old-fashioned boulevard of Riverside Drive. Not a guided tour, just a lovely and historic walk that doesn't cost a thing.
- ✔ **New York Stock Exchange**—Free tours are one way to buy low at the NYSE.
- ✔ **Urban Park Ranger Tours**—All year long the rangers lead fascinating explorations of the city's park system, and it's all free.

views. And anyway, once you're this high up, what's a few more floors? Visit the 86th-floor outdoor observatory, or the 102nd-floor indoor one; admission is just $3.50 for adults and $1.75 for senior citizens and children under twelve (under five, free). Open from 9:30 a.m. to 11:30 p.m., seven days a week.

General Grant National Memorial—Riverside Drive at 122nd St., Manhattan; 212/666-1640. Quick, who's buried in Grant's Tomb? Sorry, couldn't resist. If you're really not sure, here's the actual place, way up on the Upper West Side. Modeled after ancient Greek mausoleums, it celebrates the great hero of the Civil War. Interestingly enough for 1897, the monument was completely funded by private contributions—many of which came from African-Americans. Open Wednesdays through Sundays from 9:00 a.m. to 5:00 p.m.; admission is free.

While you're up in this beautiful, out-of-the-way part of town, take a stroll along Riverside Drive itself. In the process of being renovated, this is a gently curving stretch of boulevard, lined with trees, old-fashioned gas lamps, and benches. The view across to New Jersey's Palisades is spectacular, while the buildings behind you will make you feel like a time-traveler to the nineteenth century. Nearby, stop into the **Riverside Church** (490 Riverside Drive; 212/222-5900), whose bell tower boasts seventy-four booming bells—the world's largest carillon. That's New York, all right. The four-hundred-foot tower also affords an even more dramatic view. It's open daily from 8:00 a.m. to 10:00 p.m., and it's all free.

Greenwood Cemetery Tours—Greenwood Cemetery, Fifth Ave. (25th St.), Sunset Park, Brooklyn; 718/469-5277. Find out the fascinating history of this vast Brooklyn tract adjacent to Prospect Park. Its main gate, built in a gothic revival style during the time of the Civil War, is a New York City landmark. Sunday afternoon tours, led by historians, take you to selected parts of the cemetery to show you the graves of noted people who are interred here—from Boss Tweed to Leonard Bernstein to Currier and Ives (separately, of course). There are three separate walks, a different one given each week; call to find out the whole schedule. Tours cost $5.00, and are conducted from April through November.

Lincoln Center Backstage Tours—70 Lincoln Plaza, Columbus Ave. & 63rd St., Manhattan; 212/875-5350. Do you love the glamor of behind-the-scenes showbiz? Take the Lincoln Center tour and you'll see the world of backstage, all right—*three* stages, in fact. This one-hour adventure takes you through three of the four major music and theater halls on the grounds: Avery Fisher Hall, the Metropolitan Opera House, the Vivian Beaumont Theater, and the New York State Theater. You may even catch a glimpse of rehearsals, or the Met's famous revolving stage. All this for just $7.75, adults; $4.50 for ages four to twelve; under four, free. Tours depart from the desk at the concourse level downstairs; they run frequently between 10:00 a.m. and 5:00 p.m. daily. Call ahead for more info and to make reservations.

New York Botanical Garden—Southern Blvd. (200th St.), Bronx; 718/220-8700. See listing under "Outdoors."

New York Stock Exchange—20 Broad St., Manhattan; 212/656-5167. Tour the inside of the Stock Exchange and look out onto the floor—the craziest, most chaotic scene in the world. If you can actually figure out what's going on, and how any important work gets done at all, you're doing well. Meanwhile, the tour is absolutely free, which may be the best insider deal going.

Radio City Music Hall Tours—1260 Sixth Ave. (50th St.), Manhattan; 212/632-4041. Ever wondered what it's like to be a Rockette? What this vast, six-thousand-seat auditorium looks like from the stage? How the heck that gigantic organ works? Find out during an hour-long behind-the-scenes tour of this art deco palace. Tours run seven days a week, starting from the main lobby; the schedule is sometimes cut short, though, when a new show is being put in—so call ahead for last-minute info. Tours cost $8.00 per person.

Sidewalks of New York—320 East 65th St., Manhattan; 212/517-0201. Among the offbeat topics covered and shown by this company are "Ghosts After Sunset," "Ye Olde Tavern Tour," and "Beautiful Brooklyn Heights." Their "All in the Family" has nothing to do with the Bunkers, but rather the Corleone family—a tour of Little Italy. Each tour is given several times, making for a steady selection. These cost $10.00 on weekends—already a good price—and only $5.00 on weekdays, an even better price.

Urban Park Ranger Tours—Various city parks. Ranger Rick in New York City? You bet. The Urban Park Rangers offer a tremendous variety of walking tours throughout the five boroughs, all year long. Best of all, these are free—clearly the best deal in this category. Find out about the flora and fauna that, remarkably, manage to coexist with you in the urban jungle. And we're not just talking Central Park here—there really is a lot to see and learn about. Some hikes in the outer boroughs are like trips to the country, a great and easy mini-getaway. Call these numbers to find out about upcoming programs: Bronx (Crotona Park, Van Cortlandt Park): 718/548-7070. Brooklyn (Prospect Park): 718/287-3400. Manhattan (Central Park): 212/397-3080. Queens (Flushing Meadow/Corona Park): 718/699-4204. Staten Island (Cromwell Recreation Center): 718/667-6042.

Walking with a New Yorker—Fifth Avenue and 61st St., Manhattan; 212/861-1876. Okay, so you've done all those other tours. You're a true, jaded New Yorker who doesn't need to be introduced to Chinatown. Meet Mimi Dalva, a tour guide at the Metropolitan Museum of Art, who's ventured out with her own special brand of tour for insiders. Focusing on the Upper East Side, she meets you in front of the Pierre Hotel (at the above address) and walks you from that ritzy locale toward the East River.

The fancy homes soon give way to a fascinating and less-traveled neighborhood, rich with New York history. See unusual places like the New York Doll Hospital and the Abigail Adams Smith House (built in 1799; see listing under "Museums"). See the warehouse that still contains the valuables Imelda Marcos can't take out of the country. Dalva also takes you on the Roosevelt Island Tram (roundtrip fare included), to guide you around that area as well. All the while you'll be regaled with real New York stories.

Tours depart at 11:00 a.m. every Thursday and Friday; just show up at the hotel. At $15.00, this tour is pricier than the others in this chapter; but consider the offbeat stuff you'll get out of it. After all, insider information always comes at a dearer price, right?

Restaurants & Lodging

Mr. Cheap's Picks
Tip-free restaurants

The following fine establishments won't give you a dirty look if you head out the door without leaving a gratuity, God bless them.

Chelsea

- ☐ Albino's, 251

Greenwich Village

- ☐ Bagel Buffet, 268
- ☐ Dallas Jones Bar-B-Q, 270
- ☐ Eva's Natural Foods, 271
- ☐ Mamoun's Falafel, 273
- ☐ Marnie's Noodle Shop, 273
- ☐ Miami Subs, 274
- ☐ Pita Cuisine, 274
- ☐ Ray's Pizza, 275
- ☐ Temple in the Village, 277

Lower Manhattan

- ☐ Cafe Limor, 281
- ☐ Piccola, 288
- ☐ Pita Cuisine, 288
- ☐ White Horse Tavern, 289
- ☐ Yip's Restaurant, 290

Midtown East

- ☐ Lc Cafe, 294
- ☐ Shaheen, 297

Midtown West

- ☐ Bella Napoli, 300
- ☐ Cupcake Cafe, 301
- ☐ Cynthiya and Robert, 302
- ☐ Kosher Delight, 304
- ☐ Little Saigon Cafe, 305
- ☐ Mom's Bagels, 306
- ☐ Ngone, 307

Upper East Side

- ☐ Dino's Kitchen, 312

Upper West Side

- ☐ Cafe Bloom, 321
- ☐ Harriet's Kitchen, 325
- ☐ Indian Delhi, 327
- ☐ Zabar's Cafe, 331

Outer Boroughs

- ☐ Fountain Cafe, 333

CHELSEA

Albino's—12 West 18th St.; 212/929-3433. This Chelsea spot is a quick, simple, casual restaurant serving good Italian food at very low prices. The dining area is a simple counter-and-table affair, so no tip is required. Albino's specializes in custom-designed pizzas; the basic individual eight-inch pies start at $3.00, with toppings available for an additional 50¢ each.

Although the restaurant is open until eight in the evening on weekdays, this really is a lunch spot first and foremost. (Albino's is also open from 8:00 am to 6:00 pm on Saturdays.) Lunches include many basic pasta dishes, such as lasagna ($5.50), or baked ziti ($4.25); a large plate of spaghetti with clam sauce is only $5.75. Weekdays from 11:00 a.m. to 5:00 p.m. you can take advantage of the lunch specials, featuring such bargains as chicken cacciatore for $4.75, shrimp marinara for $6.00, and beef braciola with gnocci for $5.75. This last item, which consists of rolled beef filled with ham, prosciutto, eggs, and cheese, served with potato pasta, is well worth checking out. All the lunch specials include salad and a choice of ziti, spaghetti, rice, or mashed potato and bread.

As of this writing, Albino's has an offer Mr. C's fans will no doubt love: a "Beat the Recession" special. Fasten your seatbelts, because weekdays from 5:00 p.m. to 7:00 p.m., it's *all you can eat for just $5.00.* Take advantage of this quick; who knows how long the recession—or this special—will last?

The decor is strictly coffee-shop, with pseudo-wood-grain formica table tops and plenty of good fake brick around the counter. But Albino's has been satisfying customers in its humble, inimitable way for twenty years now. If you're in the area, perhaps surveying its many discount shopping opportunities, and you want a quick bite to eat that doesn't take too big a bite out of your budget, Albino's ought to do the trick.

Bendix Diner—219 Eighth Ave. (21st St.); 212/366-0560. The Bendix is a fine example of New York's many retro diners, places that tend to offer campy fun and good food at affordable prices. The look here is a sort of "Neo-Deco" in bright colors, with original canvases on the walls—fitting for the traditionally artistic neighborhood. Unlike some of the city's other diners, though, the menu here is as eclectic as Chelsea itself. Yes, there is authentic diner food, from omelettes (starting at $3.25) to meatloaf ($5.95, with potato and vegetable). Good, strong coffee too, by the way. But the description of the grilled half-chicken tips you off to the style here: "Marinated with Thai herbs and spices, Jewish style..." Hmmm. The menu goes on to such wide-ranging items as chili con carne, fried tofu with ginger, yaki soba (stir-fried noodles with chicken, bean sprouts, and veggies), all of which are priced from about $6.00 to $8.00. Not to mention po'boy sandwiches, turkey melts, soups, salads, and burgers.

Can they do so many different foods well? The answer appears to be "yes." The food is homemade, cooked to order, and colorful. Sandwiches are on thick-cut fresh bread; French fries are done in the style of home-fry wedges, brown and crispy; Oriental dishes are served over brown rice, with crunchy vegetables. In fact, each platter that goes by your table looks so delightful that you want to come back and try them all. Ditto the homemade desserts!

Chelsea Commons—242 Tenth Ave. (24th St.); 212/929-9424. Way up in the far reaches of Chelsea, this old-time neighborhood spot is as comfortable a hangout as you could want. Done up in dark wood decor, with ceiling fans, hanging plants and a fireplace, Chelsea Commons offers up good food and drink in a relaxed setting. The not-as-large-as-it-looks room is neatly divided into several areas by low wooden partitions, making each section more intimate—and good for quiet conversation. You can also sit at the large, old-fashioned bar up front. Beers available include Samuel Adams, Guinness and other stout names; they also serves wines by the glass.

The menu ranges from casual snacks to full meals. Among the appetizers, all in the $2.00-$5.00 range, are guacamole and chips, chili, nachos, chicken wings. Good, fresh hamburgers start at just $3.50, and various toppings only crank the price up to $4.50. Sandwiches, like the Philly cheese steak ($5.50) and the mesquite-grilled chicken ($7.50), are appetizing too.

For lighter appetites, there are omelettes from $4.25 and salads from $4.00-$6.00. On the other hand, there are great dinner specials after 6:00 p.m.—such as fettucine primavera, chicken cordon bleu and good ol' fish and chips. Most of these are $8.95 and $9.95, and they include a side vegetable. Service is friendly and laid back, in keeping with the general atmosphere of the place. Open nice and late, too, seven days a week. Speaking of atmosphere: When the weather's nice, they open up the garden courtyard in the back—a real oasis in the city.

Eighteenth & Eighth—159 Eighth Ave. (18th St.); 212/242-5000. Just up the street from the Bendix Diner is another funky coffee shop, taking a modern approach to old-fashioned cooking. Smaller (read: cramped) and more sparely decorated than the Bendix, Eighteenth & Eighth takes as its logo a steaming cup of coffee. Indeed, this is a fine place to hang out over a cup of fresh-brewed hazelnut (or whichever is the coffee of the day, same price as regular) and a piece of their extraordinary sour cream apple walnut pie ($3.95). Plenty of teas, espressos, and cappuccinos too, in regular and decaf. While on the subject of beverages, unusual milk shakes are another specialty of the house. "The Energizer" ($2.95) combines yogurt, brewer's yeast, wheat germ, honey, banana, soy milk, and spirulina protein. It'll keep you going . . . and going . . . and going . . . .

There are lots of other contemporary touches to the menu, interesting ingredients and garnishes. Sandwiches are a bit on the pricy side, most being $5.95 to $6.95; but they are served on big, fresh breads with red potato salad and pickles on the side. Egg dishes are more reasonable, with two eggs, crispy home fries, toast and a slice of melon for just $2.85. At the other end of the day, dinners are also a good deal. Try the curry-mango chicken and rice, stuffed roast pork or one of the daily specials, all served with potatoes, vegetables, and soup or salad, from $9.00 to $11.00. This is a true coffee shop for the nineties. Sidle into one of the few seats at the tall counter, or squeeze into a table seat next to someone trendy, and dig in.

Flight 151 Bar and Restaurant—151 Eighth Ave. (17th St.); 212/229-1868. After leading a successful bombing run behind enemy lines (or perhaps through the crowds at nearby Barney's), return to base by touching down at Flight 151. This fun Chelsea hangout is decorated with all sorts of World War I memorabilia; the folks here have even concocted an intricate story about the flight that purportedly gave the restaurant its name. Keen observers may conclude that the name would seem to have more to do with the address of the restaurant than anything you're likely to see in a Time-Life video series, but never mind. The place is lively and very casual, serving up burgers for $4.95 as well as tuna melts and chili dogs for the same price. These all come with crispy French fries. Step up to a grilled chicken sandwich ($6.95) or fog up your goggles over the soup of the day, which on Mr. C's visit was Manhattan clam chowder ($2.95). The bar features lots of great beers and good prices on mixed drinks. Adding to the fun atmosphere are bowls of popcorn, a rowdy jukebox, pinball machines, and all kinds of old-time posters and advertisements on the walls. In addition to booths and tables, the restaurant opens its front to the sidewalk during warm months for al fresco dining. Flight 151 is open for both lunch and dinner; on weekends, be sure to check out the All-U-Can-Eat Bagel Brunch. Just $4.95, Saturdays and Sundays from noon to 4:00 p.m.

Intermezzo—202 Eighth Ave. (20th St.); 212/254-2054. Like so many restaurants that have popped up in Chelsea, Intermezzo sports an elegant "uptown" look. The uptown prices, however, are nowhere to be found. The cuisine is Italian, and from the high-toned atmosphere, white linen tablecloths, and sparkling glassware, frugal diners can be forgiven for a moment of panic upon being led inside. Trust Mr. C, though: you'll get out of here without having to roll up your sleeves and wash the dishes. The menu, which includes pasta, meat, and seafood, is reasonably priced throughout; nevertheless, the pasta dishes present the greatest opportunity for bargain dining. Pasta entrees range from $7.00 to $10.00, with over a dozen enticing items to choose from. Three that are high on Mr. C's list: Rigatoni Siciliana, made with eggplant, tomato, and mozzarella; capellini primavera, made with fresh spring vegetables; and tortellini with four

Mr. Cheap's Picks

✔ **Bendix Diner**—Funky diner with a similarly updated menu offering ethnic foods from around the world.

✔ **Eighteenth & Eighth**—Ultra-hip coffee shop for the artsy crowd, with reasonable (considering the tone of the place) prices.

✔ **Pastapot**—This casual restaurant/bar offers big Italian dinners at good prices.

cheeses. Meat and seafood entrees run somewhat higher, though most are in the $10.00 to $12.00 range; you can get calamari sauteed with tomato, avocado, and fresh hot pepper for $9.00, or grilled chicken Paillard for $10.00. In addition you can find ten different varieties of antipasti, including a delicious cold roast veal in tuna sauce. Most of these items are $6.50. Nice price, but the best deal at Intermezzo is probably its $5.00 lunch, served daily between 11:00 a.m. and 4:00 p.m. You start off with soup or a mixed salad, and then move on to one of several main dishes—such as chicken sauteed with lemon and capers, a Sicilian salad made with string beans, potatoes, and olives, or pasta with fresh tomato and basil sauce. Not bad for a five-spot. Intermezzo is the kind of place Mr. C loves to discover: a restaurant that is both elegant and unashamedly inexpensive.

Joe Babbington's Joint—202 Ninth Ave. (at 23rd St.); 212/741-2148. Joe's is a cozy, neighborhood-style place with an atmosphere that is relaxed and just a bit playful. The food is an intriguing mix of nouvelle cuisine and straightforward down-home cookin'. On a recent visit, the dinner menu featured entrees all priced at $10.00 or lower: definitely Mr. C's kind of place.

The front half of the restaurant is an ornate yet casual bar fully stocked with great beers from around the country and around the world. If you're curious about Grant's Scottish Ale, Catamount Porter, or Sierra Nevada Stout, you can sample these or other exotic brews for a less-than-exotic price of $2.50 per bottle (although a few are higher). The other half of the restaurant, a separate dining room, is decorated with potted trees, backlit stained-glass windows, and crafts from around the world.

That $10.00-or-lower dinner menu is no copout; its focus is on substantial seafood and meat dishes. A sampling: red snapper filets grilled in olive oil and served over three-grain rice ($8.95); honey-glazed half chicken ($7.50), also seasoned with herbs, and served with sweet potato fries and grilled vegetables; and roast duckling with apple-walnut stuffing ($9.95), served with the same sides as the chicken. Keep an eye out as well for the daily specials, which are often even more unusual.

Entrees are served with a very fresh green salad and a whole bunch of wonderful home-style breads and spreads to which you can help yourself at the sideboard. Save some room for one of the desserts, though: pies, cobblers, and so on are also laid out on a side table, where can help yourself to a portion, at minimal cost (but note that *you pick the size!*)

And then there are the Early Bird dinner specials, which take care of the empties for $6.95, or the bounteous lunch specials, which work comparable miracles for under $5.00.

Mary Ann's Chelsea Mexican — 116 Eighth Ave. (16th St.); 212/633-0877, 1501 Second Ave. (78th St.); 212/249-6165, and 300 East Fifth St.; 212/475-5939. Here's a trio of popular Mexican restaurants spread around Manhattan; all have long-standing reputations for good food at good prices. Mr. C sampled several different items and found no cause for argument. Lunch plates are a particular bargain, with two dozen choices starting at just $4.95, going up to about $8.00. Salsa and chips start you off, complimentary for the table. For an appetizer, try the tomato and avocado salad ($3.95), a nice accompaniment for the chips.

For entrees, daily specials are often the best values. How about this one: Burritos filled with shrimp and scallops sauteed in garlic butter, topped with tomato sauce and served with rice and vegetables. All for $6.95. Most unusual—and all of the food is homemade, so it's hard to go wrong. Atmosphere is casual, and sometimes boisterous; the decor is just enough to be authentic without seeming to try too hard, as some competitors do.

Moonstruck Diner—400 West 23rd St.; 212/924-3709, and 449 Third Ave. (31st St.); 212/213-1100. See listing under "Midtown East."

Pastapot—160 Eighth Ave. (18th St.); 212/633-9800. Don't be fooled by exteriors! From the outside, Pastapot looks like some sort of chain coffee shop, a safe place to take Aunt Henrietta for spaghetti. Once you go inside, though, you'll see that this place is just as "happening" as any of the other restaurant/bars in this hip neighborhood. The interior is all dark, elegant wood, including the long, attractive bar at the front of the main room. The B-52's or Pretenders may be booming from the jukebox. And toward the rear is another dark, cozy dining room.

Over a dozen pasta dishes prevail on the menu, from angel hair to stuffed manicotti. These are all priced from $7.95 to $9.75, and they are served piping hot, tender, and delicious. Each dinner entree comes with lots of fresh, chewy bread and a fresh green salad.

There are several chicken dinners, most under $10.00, including chicken parmigiana and chicken funghetti (served with mushrooms). Burgers from $5.95 and various nightly specials also offer good values. Other entrees go over Mr. C's $10.00 limit in price; but don't worry, there is a lot to choose from under that limit, and it's fine stuff. Lots of good beers to choose from at the bar, and the kitchen stays open nice and late, too—until 4:00 a.m. on weekends!

San Francisco Plum—544 Sixth Ave. (15th St.); 212/924-9125. For almost twenty years San Francisco Plum has been a dependable neighborhood bar of the sort for which Chelsea is famous. Its interior is an intimate blend of, yes, plum-colored walls, white latticework, and natural-wood tables—very, like, California. Sit at the bar or in a cozy booth. In addition to a good selection of beers and cocktails, SF Plum serves up pleasant, cheap food for lunch and early dinner.

The menu is naturally pretty casual. Start off with a plateful of barbecued chicken wings for $4.25. Move right along to a pizza burger and French fries for a laid-back $4.95; or try one of their many other dinner options like chicken parmigiana with linguine for $6.95, London broil with fries and a salad for $9.25, or one of the many listings on the daily blackboard.

Service is friendly and relaxed. Don't wait too late for dinner, though; this kitchen closes, unfortunately, around 8:00 p.m.

EAST VILLAGE

Angelica Kitchen—300 East 12th St.; 212/228-2909. Angelica's has to be one of the nicest vegetarian restaurants in the city. Inside the atmosphere is warm, friendly, and handsomely decorated, with natural wood tables and an open kitchen. The food is all organically grown, and prepared fresh daily. In fact, the menu of main entrees changes every day, with such platters as nori maki ($7.75)—a combination of rice, teriyaki tempeh, carrots, broccoli, string beans, Japanese radishes, red cabbage, and mustard, all rolled up in an edible wrapper and served sliced, like sushi.

A popular specialty of the house is the "Dragon Bowl," a heaping salad of rice, beans, lettuce, tofu, hijiki (a sea vegetable), and steamed fresh vegetables ($7.25). For an extra $2.50, Angelica's will add a bowl of hot soup and cornbread; and both versions are available in half-portions ($4.25/$7.50). Furthermore, you may switch any one item—tempeh for tofu, let's say—at no charge. Salad dressings are wonderful creations, like poppyseed vinaigrette made with toasted sesame oil, apple butter, and cider; or creamy scallion parsley tahini. There is also a daily selection of desserts made with organic ingredients (no refined sugars or dairy products); try the tofu cheesecake with apricot orange sauce ($3.75).

If things sound complicated, or if you're not fluent in vegetarian, don't worry! Your waiter will practically join you at your table and explain as many items on the menu as you need, and even make recommendations, if you wish. Angelica Kitchen also has a take-out juice bar next door, and they make free deliveries to both sides of the Village. The amazing thing about all of this is that you'll leave just as full as from any carnivore's den—with healthier food in your gullet and more cash in your wallet.

Around the Clock—8 Stuyvesant St.; 212/598-0402. New York is truly the city that never sleeps, and this joint near Third Avenue is a fine example of that. Small, though not cramped, the room divides into a dark wooden bar near the door with a raised dining area beside it. In that great New York tradition, you can get breakfast here twenty-four hours a day: A stack of challah French toast for $3.00, a Mexican Eggs Benedict platter for $5.95, or omelettes from $3.25 with home fries, vegetables, and toast (as this is a Village joint, you can have brown rice instead of vegetables, and black beans instead of toast).

The rest of the menu is just as diverse, with everything from burgers (beef or turkey, starting at $3.95) to stir-fry veggies and brown rice ($5.50) to pastas (spinach and cheese ravioli, $6.95). Not to mention pita sandwiches, fajitas, fish 'n chips, desserts, and more. Can so many things be done well? Well, Mr. C brought in a party of eight people, who tried everything from pancakes to burritos. No one left hungry or dissatisfied. There are usually specials too; on this visit these included a chicken parmigiana dinner with pasta, garlic bread and salad—the whole thing for $5.95. Can't beat that!

The bar offers daily specials of its own, like two-for-one drafts during happy hour. And that means such beers as New Amsterdam—two mugs, $2.50, too cool. The atmosphere is lively and fun.

Benny's Burritos—89 Avenue A (at 6th St.); 212/254-2054. Benny's has to be one of the liveliest, hippest spots in the East Village, serving up great Californian- and Mexican-style food in full platters for low prices. Obviously burritos are the specialty of the house; they come wrapped in a fresh twelve-inch flour tortilla, making a burrito you shouldn't even try to pick up with your hands. Most are in the $5.00 to $6.00 range. These bargain meals include such exotic varieties as the Super Vegetarian, filled with vegetables, beans, rice, cheese, guacamole, and fresh salsa; and an interesting nondairy burrito made with a whole-wheat tortilla and filled with beans, brown rice, tofu, sour cream, and guacamole.

Lest you think Benny's caters exclusively to the vegetarian crowd, there's a magnificent grilled shrimp burrito that comes with cilantro and garlic sauce. At $8.50, it's a notch or two over some of the other entrees pricewise, but it is a wonderful change of pace. Benny's also features tacos, enchiladas, quesadillas, and chili—all of which come in beef, chicken, and vegetarian varieties. Most dishes include your choice of black beans or pinto beans. On all entrees, you may substitute brown rice or whole-wheat tortillas for the standard items if you wish. (As you have probably deduced by now, Benny's is very health-conscious.)

Whatever you do, check out the daily specials. Mr. C snagged the corn and cheese fritters—a melt-in-your-mouth delicacy—for only $2.75, and an intriguing chicken and lime soup for $1.50 a cup. Delicious! Desserts at Benny's are special, too; different homemade delicacies are offered daily. On this particular visit, it was orange flan.

If you like Benny's as much as Mr. C did, you may find yourself wishing you could buy ingredients from them in bulk so you can make your own versions of their dishes at home. Well, you can. The good folks at Benny's will be happy to sell larger quantities of their no-lard, no-preservatives, no-MSG fixings—but be warned that the people here have had a lot of practice, and you may find it tough to match their standards. And besides, if you make the stuff at home, you'll miss out on the glorious and unapologetic boisterousness that is a nightly attraction at Benny's.

Caravan of Dreams—405 East 6th St.; 212/315-4690. On his way to Benny's Burritos, Mr. C happened across this restaurant, which bills itself as a "gourmet organic vegetarian cafe." One could—and Mr. C now will—call the place overaggressively hip, given its low lighting, natural-wood decor, and studiously mellow vibes. It may just take a seasoned veteran of the vegetarian cuisine scene to make full use of the occasionally indecipherable menu, but Mr. C was able to ascertain that it offered a number of intriguing meat-free, dairy-free, sugar-free, wheat-free, and other-objectionable-edible-compound-free dishes that don't cost very much money.

Start off with a bowl of black-bean chili with corn chips ($4.50) or a plate of peanut sesame noodles with cucumber ($4.75). Or perhaps you'd prefer to nibble on some whole-wheat walnut bread with an olive oil,

Mr. Cheap's Picks

✔ **Angelica Kitchen**—One of the Village's landmarks for upscale vegetarian cuisine.

✔ **Around the Clock**—Cool, laid-back bar with a big menu at small prices. Open, of course, around the clock.

✔ **Benny's Burritos**—Stuff yourself with a stuffed burrito at *the* happening scene for Tex-Mex.

✔ **Cucina di Pesce/Frutti di Mare**—Two hip places, sister Italian spots located across the street from one another. Sibling rivalry serves you well.

✔ **Dojo**—The Village's landmark spots for the downscale vegetarian. One on each side of the Village, east and west.

✔ **Manila Garden**—An elegant, relaxed restaurant serving food of the Philippines; refined, but still inexpensive.

✔ POLISH DINERS—The East Village is packed with 'em: **Kiev**, **Veselka**, **Little Poland**, **Teresa's** and many more. Stuff yourself silly for under $10.

✔ **Two Boots**—Another popular downtown scene, with the unlikely mix of Italian and Cajun food. Who knew?

herb, and garlic dip ($1.50). Salads include such choices as an arame seaweed salad with carrots ($2.50 for a small bowl or $4.75 for a large bowl).

Caravan also offers several unusual sandwiches, one example being the open-faced mushroom and greens sandwich with parsley pesto ($6.75). Moving on to full dinners, a grilled marinated tofu plate, which includes greens, an arame seaweed salad, and the Grain of the Day, is $9.25. Another tasty option is the ginger curry stir-fry vegetable platter served over pasta (also $9.25). There are usually several daily specials that can be very inexpenseive; on Mr. C's visit this included a plate of polenta in a peanut sauce with sauteed greens ($3.50).

There are, of course, plenty of fruit drinks and herbal teas to go along with your meal—and yes, just in case you were worried about this, the water they serve *is* reverse-osmosis-filtered. If this sounds like the caravan of your dreams, check it out.

Cucina di Pesce—87 East 4th St.; 212/260-6800. This East Village establishment has a sister restaurant, **Frutti di Mare**, located across the street. The menus are virtually identical. Together, they have long been two of Manhattan's most popular and enjoyable Italian restaurants. The prices are extremely reasonable, with pasta dishes starting at just $5.95 for a large plate of vegetarian lasagna; and the same price for a plate of fusilli with sun-dried tomatoes and gorgonzola cheese, served up in a cream sauce. Other pasta dishes include linguine with fresh clams in white or red sauce ($8.95) and shells stuffed with calamari and anchovies in spicy red sauce ($6.95).

Main-course entrees start at $6.95 for such dishes as grilled breast of chicken with sauteed mushrooms and garlic, or eggplant parmigian. Going up the scale a little bit, you'll find veal picatta at $7.95, filet of bluefish topped with almonds, sun-dried tomatoes, and orange peel in a marsala wine sauce for $8.95, and seafood entrees in the $9.95 to $10.95 range. Even for these more expensive entrees, the prices are quite attractive indeed when you consider that each meal comes with spaghetti marinara. Appetizers are also a good deal: Most are priced between $3.95 and $4.95. There are a number of good choices when it comes to appetizers—try the broccoli sauteed in a garlic and marinara sauce and topped with mozzarella (just $3.95). Another good bet is the cold antipasta with provolone sopressata and sun-dried tomatoes ($4.95). As you may gather, these restaurants add a nouvelle twist to traditional Italian food.

They must be doing something right, because crowds flock to these two restaurants. Very often people who can't get into one can be seen running across the street to the other. The only substantial difference between the two establishments has to do with atmosphere: Frutti di Mare has a quiet, traditional ambience, while Cucina di Pesce offers a virtually identical menu in a much livelier, "urban hip" setting across the street. Both restaurants offer full bars and takeout service.

Dojo—24 St. Mark's Place; 212/674-9821, also 14 West 4th St.; 212/505-8934 (Dojo West). If you live in either Village and like inexpensive healthy foods, you probably know about the two Dojo restaurants. They take Japanese and other Eastern culinary methods as a point of departure, mixing them with more American-style dishes with intriguing results—and at super-cheap prices.

First and foremost, Dojo is home to the soy burger, served in a whole-wheat pita pocket with lettuce, tomato, and carrot—for just $1.95. The hijiki tofu sandwich is another interesting selection, combining seaweed with tofu to form a patty that is served burger-style in pita bread with a teriyaki sauce. It costs $2.50. There are lots of vegetable plates, most of which are under $5.00; these include vegetable curry, stir-fried vegetables over brown rice, and vegetable tempura. Salads are in the same price range, and offer a wide choice of Eastern and Western approaches.

By now, you may have concluded that Dojo is an exclusively vegetarian place, but actually carnivores should not feel excluded. Dojo does serve regular hamburgers (and turkey burgers, for that matter), all priced between $3.50 and $5.00. Also available: chicken or beef curry and a variety of seafood dishes. There is a wide selection of beverages here, including a number of fascinating imported juice and mineral water selections, wine, and good beer on tap (New Amsterdam, Bass, and Woodpecker Cider are each $2.50 per glass). Freshly made desserts can be had, too, in varieties both ennobling and as close to decadent as this crowd gets (e.g., frozen vanilla yogurt with granola and carob chips—$2.75).

In true New York style, Dojo serves up breakfast right up until the dinner hour, and again from 11:00 pm until closing. The raisin French toast with fresh strawberries is particularly good, and it's just $2.95. Whatever time of day or night you go, the place is likely to be crowded, so be prepared to grab a drink at the bar and wait for a table.

Ed Debevic's—661 Broadway (Bond St.); 212/982-6000. How to describe the scene at Ed Debevic's? It is perhaps the ultimate expression of the retro-diner-chic currently in vogue in the Big Apple, offering all your favorite comfort foods—burgers, sandwiches, hot dogs, barbecued ribs, chicken-fried steaks, meatloaf, et al.—in an atmosphere that combines a restaurant and a discotheque in one. Ed's has three large rooms, the first of which is a bar and dance floor area; with the pulsing thud of music and the flashings of a mirror-ball hastening your steps, walk through this area to the main dining rooms at the back. The food is plentiful and moderately priced, with burgers and sandwiches all in the $7.00 range and dinner plates all priced under $10.00.

Get your kicks with a Route 66 Burger, which comes served on sourdough bread and topped with Monterey jack cheese, bacon, guacamole, and raw onions. Or wrap your hands around Martha's Mama Barbecue Pork Sandwich ($6.50). You can get a bowl of chili or a jumbo hot dog for $3.95, or a chili dog for $4.75. If you're looking for something lighter, you may want to try the salad bar, although Mr. C defies you to come away from this mega-buffet with a plate that could be described as light. For $7.95, you're free to roam through a sea of greens, vegetables, fresh fruits, pastas, homemade soups, and breads. (You can add the salad bar to any entree order for just $2.95.)

All kinds of great down-home cooking can be had at Ed's: a chicken pot pie ($7.50), fried chicken served in a basket ($8.25), or a full rack of hickory-smoked barbecued baby back ribs ($9.95, the top price on the menu). You might also want to try the fresh salmon glazed in barbecue sauce (also $9.95). If you still have room, go for some of the homestyle desserts: several fine pies, like banana cream or Oreo chocolate, go for $2.95 a slice; the fountain specializes in thick malted milkshakes in a number of unusual flavors, also $2.95 each. If you came of age in diners during the 1950s, drinks likes phosphates and Black Cows will take you right back. If not, here's where you can learn. Ed Debevic's is a wild and raucous scene that makes a great place for group outings and parties. Those who seek a quiet, intimate spot, search elsewhere.

First Street Cafe—72 East First St.; 212/420-0710. First Street, at the corner of First Avenue in Manhattan, may be the last place you'd expect to find a hip little eatery like this, but here it is. The First Street Cafe seems to have been transplanted from the streets of Paris or Vienna. It's a tiny storefront with even tinier tables and an open kitchen at the rear. The atmosphere is dark, intimate, and actually a little moody; the menu combines a variety of European and American influences into a melange best described as "offbeat nouvelle."

Breakfast is served daily from 8:00 in the morning until 4:00 in the afternoon; have a scrambled egg soufflé with a bagel and coffee for just $2.50. On Saturdays and Sundays, brunch is served all morning and afternoon, combining eggs with a variety of fillings, fresh fruit salad, vanilla yogurt, a toasted bagel, a large cappucino, orange juice, and mineral water—all for $7.50. Lunches, which for some reason are also served from 8:00 am through the evening, include a variety of home-style soups and chili, just $3.50 a bowl, and fresh salads made with red-leaf lettuce and a variety of vegetables. You can also get sourdough baguette sandwiches, which are priced from $3.95 to $4.95. Just to keep things wacky, the menu lists a few sandwiches as "Elvis

Presley's Favorites." The King purportedly had/has a predeliction for peanut butter and banana on wheat bread; whether or not Elvis has been spotted here, the sandwich has—for $2.50). Dinners are all priced under $6.50, and for that you can get things like porcini mushroom lasagna made with spinach and zucchini, or a vegetarian ravioli made with spinach, pesto, mushrooms, and vegetables. There are also lots of daily specials, as well as a notable house special: the California Burrito, a whole-wheat tortilla filled with brown rice, black beans, chili, cheddar cheese, and guacamole. It's just $3.95 ($4.95 if you add chicken). To accompany all of this, you'll find cappucino, espresso, cafe au lait, and a bevy of herbal teas, fruit juices, and shakes. Beer and wine are also available. Try to save room for one of the home-style desserts, such as German chocolate cake, cheesecake with fresh fruit, or pecan pie with whipped cream, all $3.00 each. As if the First Street Cafe weren't funky (and crowded) enough, a live band is squeezed into the place Thursday, Friday, and Saturday nights from 10:00 pm onward. No extra charge.

Frutti di Mare—84 East 4th St.; 212/979-2034. See listing for Cucina di Pesce.

Great Jones Cafe—54 Great Jones St.; 212/674-9304. Way down below Cooper Square, just off the Bowery, you'll find this cozy little bar/cafe (look for the banner overhead, or you could miss it). That puts it near such diverse musical homes as the Amato Opera and the rock club CBGB's, as well as the Jean Cocteau Repertory Theater and La Mama ETC—all inexpensive entertainment options profiled in the appropriate sections of this book.

The cafe, meanwhile, is a great little hangout if you're in on the young art scene. The music in here is as different from one song to the next as the clubs outside, wandering from blues to zydeco to hard rock. The food takes its cue from that Cajun beat, though, and stays there; great jambalaya, spicy but not too, served with homemade jalapeno cornbread for $7.95. Blackened catfish ($10.95) comes with the jambalaya on the side (or your choice of two sides) and a big, fresh salad.

For simpler eats, rustle up some Creole wings ($3.95) or one of several varieties of big, thick burgers—from $5.25 for the basic to $6.95 for a bacon cheeseburger and $7.25 for a chiliburger. Nice, crispy French fries, too. There are plenty of good beers on hand, like Anchor Steam and other microbrews and imports. Great Jones also has a $7.95 brunch on Saturdays and Sundays.

Kiev—117 Second Ave. (7th St.); 212/674-4040. At first glance, Kiev appears drearier than a rainy Monday morning. But wait—walk all the way through to the back dining room. The nearby kitchen and brick walls lend a more homey atmosphere, enhanced by the thick European accents of the friendly waiters. The food shares that thick European accent, namely Russian and Polish dishes of gigantic proportions. The prices are the opposite. Search no more.

You should start out with some pierogi—$5.95 for a platter of eight meat- or cheese-filled dumplings, fried or boiled. For the same price you can have a sweet cheese blintz and four pierogies; or two blintzes with sour cream; or apple pancakes with sour cream; or.....the list goes on and on. Combination dinners, from $6.00 to $10.00, assemble many of these items for you. For $9.50 you can get a cup of soup, schnitzel, a stuffed cabbage, kasha varnishkes in mushroom sauce, and a side order of cooked vegetables.

It's all homemade; you can

see for yourself in the bustling kitchen. Huge corned-beef sandwiches ($4.75), chopped herring salad platters ($4.95), kielbasa dinners ($6.75) and mega-sized veal cutlets ($8.50) are among the many other old-world specialties that will leave you begging for less. Kiev is a hangout, a place to relax with friends over a long, hearty meal. It's also open twenty-four hours, with great breakfasts like kielbasa and eggs or thick-sliced challah French toast, each $4.00.

The Levee—76 East First St.; 212/505-9263. Here's another great hangout for down-home cooking. They have a long, intimate bar, plenty of jazz and soul on tap with the brews, and hickory-smoked chicken and ribs that are all priced around $10.00 and under. Atmosphere at the Levee is as mellow as a warm Mississippi evening.

This can be as simple as an appetizer of BBQ wings for just $3.95, a pulled-pork sandwich for $5.95, or a chicken-ribs combo for $9.95. Or stuff yourself with a Leveeburger ($5.75) topped with grilled onions and jalapeno peppers ($1.00 more for great fries). Dinners come with your choice of two side items: Cornbread, greens, red onion rings, and more. You even get to choose the barbecue sauce, either Southern or Kansas City (the latter is spiked with paprika and pepper). There are several daily specials on the chalkboard, such as a warm chicken breast salad, or peanut gumbo. C'mon in and set a spell.

Little Poland—200 Second Ave. (12th St.); 212/777-9728. One of the many old-world restaurants for which this area is famous, Little Poland—like Kiev, Veselka and the rest—serves up hearty (read: heavy) food in large portions at small prices. Huge breakfasts, like two eggs with kielbasa, home fries, toast, and juice, coffee or tea, are $3.25 all morning. For lunch, try one of their fabulous homemade soups, like black bean and sausage or potato lamb, for $2.50.

Other lunch and dinner entrees include such hefty treats as beef goulash over noodles, with salad, for $5.00; two fried pork chops with a pair of side vegetables, $6.00; and stuffed cabbage, same sides, $4.75. Of course, there are the ever-popular pierogies and blintzes, each $4.00 to $5.00, depending on the fillings. And filling is what it's all about here. The service is friendly and quick, usually with an accent as charming as the food.

Nearby you'll find similar deals and quality at **Leshko's Coffee Shop**, 111 Avenue A (7th St.), telephone 212/473-9208; at the **K & K Restaurant**, 192 First Ave. (9th St.), 212/777-4430; and at **Christine's**, 208 First Ave. (12th St.), 212/505-0376. Christine's has a second, more contemporary-styled location at 462 Second Ave. (26th St.); 212/779-2220.

Manila Gardens—325 East 14th St.; 212/777-6314. Tucked away in the East Village is this very elegant restaurant that looks for all the world as though it should cost far more than it does. Manila Gardens, as you may have guessed, specializes in Filipino food; it is intimate and cozy, with warm lighting, white linen tablecloths, and pink linen napkins. Although there are plenty of meat and vegetable dishes, the menu leans heavily toward seafood. Start off with pork and shrimp eggrolls for an appetizer ($4.50); you'll get half-a-dozen crisply deep-fried small rolls. There are also a number of enticing soups.

For entrees, the best bargains by far are the *pancit*, or Filipino pasta dishes. This is not your run-of-the-mill spaghetti and meatballs, but thin, transparent noodles that are sauteed and, in the case of the *sotanghon*, laced with green vegetables, mushrooms, shrimp, pork, sausage, and chicken, then splashed with soy sauce. All of this comes on a large plate and runs you just $4.95. Several of the other vegetarian dishes are worth checking out. Beef dishes, priced mostly in the $6.50 to $8.00 range, include such delicacies as morcon ($6.50), which is beef rolled up and stuffed with eggs, chopped ham, pickles, and sausage. There are plenty of reasonably priced pork and poultry dishes, as well; chicken dishes are all priced between $5.00 and $8.00.

Really, just about anything you get here other than the seafood will fit comfortably within the confines of a tight budget. When you consider the elegant service and the decor of the place, you'll agree that Manila Gardens is a good place to go for a very special dinner that won't cost a fortune.

Passage to India—308 East 6th St.; 212/529-5770. One of the best-loved Indian restaurants along the East Village's "Curry Row," Passage to India is just that—a brief trip to a far-off land. Its interior is quite pleasant, with natural wood decor and candlelit tables. Sitar music fills the room, but gently enough to permit conversation. The outstanding feature here is Passage's tandoor, a clay oven where a variety of breads are baked to golden perfection. The glassed-in kitchen reminds a friend of Mr. C's of the "Hall of Presidents" at Disneyland; inside, a stately, almost waxen figure works relentlessly throughout the evening—though any resemblance to Abe Lincoln ends there.

Those breads, here called "sundries," are terrific appetizers. There are a dozen kinds, from $1.25 to $3.25, each of which fills an entire plate, large as a record album. Other good apps include Mulligatawny Soup ($1.75), a large bowl of spicy lentils with a handful of vegetable fritters on the side. Main courses are many; ten or more choices each among chicken, seafood, vegetarian, or lamb and beef dinners. Curries start at just $5.25. Chicken Karahi ($7.50) is described on the menu as, "Server will explain"; in fact, it's a fairly mild stew of chicken, rice, onions, and vegetables. Beef Vindaloo ($6.50) offers a super-spicy sauce—choose your weapon from the waiter's selection.

Portions are ample; indeed, you may well have trouble finishing. Service, like the spices, runs hot and cold—but someone is always nearby to refill your tea. Passage also offers several complete dinner deals for $11.00 to $13.00, which gets you soup and fritters, one of several entrees, Indian pudding for dessert, and coffee. Good deal. The place fills up quickly, especially on weekends; call ahead.

Rectangle's—159 Second Ave. (10th St.); 212/677-8410. Mr. C recently met someone from Israel who has moved to New York and who claims that Rectangle's is one of the few truly authentic Israeli restaurants in the city. The menu is written in both English and Hebrew, and the tables full of diners speaking both tongues further attest to Rectangle's authenticity.

As with the politics of that region, it's not easy to define the boundaries—even of cuisine. The food is an eclectic mix of Israeli and Yemenite, or Arab; world peace may be elusive, but hey, everyone has to eat. Rectangle's starts with all the basics, like beef, lamb, and chicken kebabs, couscous and baba ghanoush. Their falafel ($3.75 for a half-dozen) is dark and intense, well spiced and crunchy. But beyond that, you'll find appetizers like *mlawach* ($4.50) , a sort of deep-dish layered bread that's sometimes known as a Yemenite pancake; and "Moroccan Cigars" ($5.00), ground beef rolled up in phyllo dough.

On weekends they add extra Yemenite delicacies, such as *jahnun* ($4.50), another rolled flour dough that is actually cooked slowly overnight. In the morning they add eggs for a unique brunch dish. Weekday lunch specials are a real bargain too; just $7.75 gets you the entree of the day, with a cup of soup to start, plus coffee or tea.

Rectangle's has a long wooden bar, with touches of pink neon and works by local artists on the walls above it. There are beers from over a dozen countries—not just Maccabee from Israel, but plenty from England, Ireland, and Germany, and even Red Stripe from Jamaica. And be sure to finish off your meal with a marvelously thick, grainy demi-tasse of Turkish coffee, just $1.00. The place is open seven days a week until midnight or 1:00 a.m.

Not far away is another Israeli/Yemenite gem, **Village Crown**, 96 Third Avenue (12th St.); 212/674-2061. If Rectangle's is the hip young hangout, this has a more traditional, family-oriented clientele—many of whom are, again, transplanted Middle Easterners. The owners themselves seat and serve you. Both restaurants are kosher, but Village Crown observes more strictly, closing Friday afternoon through Saturday. Whichever you choose, you can be sure you're getting the kind of rich ethnic experience that makes New York great.

Rono e Giorgio—65 St. Mark's Place; 212/777-4520. If you need a quick, super-cheap meal—more like a re-fueling—try Rono e Giorgio. The simple, no-frills decor is one-upped by the no-frills prices on a wide variety of food. You can go basic, with burgers from $4.00 and three-egg omelettes from $3.50; or be more adventurous with braised Creole mussels ($5.10), cold Thai roast beef and avocado ($7.00) or Iberian chili con carne ($6.20).

Picadillo, $7.80, is a spicy Cuban dish of ground beef sauteed in garlic, tomatoes, and raisins; it's served over rice pilaf with guacamole. And "Trinidad Rice" ($8.10) combines ground beef and sausage in a white wine and tamarind sauce, with green vegetables. Can all these be good, at these prices? Will Rono and Giorgio figure out which country their restaurant represents? Does it matter? Tune in tomorrow—or, better yet, stop in and find out for yourself.

Rumbul's—128 East 7th St., Manhattan; 212/473-8696. See listing under "Greenwich Village."

Sonali—326 East 6th St.; 212/505-7517. How to choose one from the many Indian restaurants lining this block of the East Village (known as "Curry Row")? Mr. C heartily recommends Sonali, a fine example of affordable Indian dining at its best. The extensive menu seldom exceeds $6.95 for any à la carte entree. Vegetarian specialties (and there are a lot to choose from) are all priced at $4.75. Bhindi masala, which is okra cooked with tomatoes and onions, is commendable. A dozen different chicken curry dishes are all in the $5.00-to-$6.00 range, and the same is true of beef and lamb dishes, like lamb dhan sak, which is lamb cooked with lentils and hot spices ($5.55).

Sonali also offers a great many seafood dishes, which is somewhat unusual for an Indian place: shrimp curry is $5.95, and a lobster-chili masala, cooked with onions and green peppers, tops out the basic menu at all of $8.95. All of the above-mentioned dishes, by the way, are served with rice and the obligatory spicy condiments. Sonali also has several special *prix fixe* dinners such as the tandoori dinner, which, for $9.95, offers soup, appetizer, bread, a main course such as tandoori chicken or lamb curry, vegetables, rice, a dessert, and tea or coffee. A very good deal.

Teresa's Restaurant—103 First Ave. (6th St.); 212/228-0604, and 80 Montague St., Brooklyn Heights; 718/797-3996. See listing under "Outer Boroughs."

Two Boots—37 Avenue A (2nd St.); 212/505-2276. What does "Two Boots" mean? It means that someone had the novel idea of combining food from Italy, a country shaped like a boot, with food from Louisiana, a state shaped like—you guessed it—a boot. The result is wild, wacky, and extremely popular. Where else can you order something like "Pasta Jambalaya" ($9.95), a spicy mix of shrimp, chicken, and sausage served over spaghetti? Or Linguine Dominique ($8.95), strips of blackened chicken and sauteed vegetables in a light cream sauce over pasta?

The "boot" motif even carries over into the shape of their frosted beer mugs, which gives an idea of the ambience here. The place is fairly raucous, painted in bright colors of red, yellow and blue. The clientele is that amazing East Village mix of artists, yuppies and families. Casual foods add to the fun for groups—especially those with kids. Po' Boy sandwiches, calzones, and pizzas with such toppings as barbecued shrimp, calamari, andouille sausage, or crawfish (mix and match your own). Not to mention lots of homemade desserts, like chocolate pecan pie.

Two Boots also has a take-out store, "Two Boots To Go," across the street at 36 Avenue A (212/505-5450), as well as a newer one at 74 Bleecker Street near Broadway (212/777-1033).

Veselka Coffee Shop—144 Second Ave. (9th St.); 212/228-9682. This is about as *hamish* as it gets, folks. For a dining experience that is truly New York and Old World, Veselka is one of the best. You can stuff yourself here for just a few rubles. The front of the joint is the coffee shop part, with lots of winding counter space. Cut through to the back and there are two rooms—up and down—with tables.

Like all the Russian/Polish restaurants in the neighborhood, the fare at Veselka consists of borscht, pirogies, blintzes, stuffed cabbage, and the rest. Various combination plates allow you to sample lots of these. The deluxe meal combo ($8.25) starts with a cup of soup (several choices daily), and moves on to salad, a stuffed cabbage, grilled kielbasa, and three pirogies (meat, potato, and cabbage). Hearty, to say the least. You can also have a vegetarian platter instead.

Daily specials are different each week; a recent Thursday offered up white turkey chili ($6.95, with salad), Polish tripe stew ($7.25, or $4.25 in a sandwich) and Ukranian meatballs ($6.95), oven-roasted in a creamy mushroom sauce. If you have room, try a Polish poppyseed danish or one of their many pies with some fresh-ground coffee. With or without dessert, you'll definitely want to linger awhile before getting up.

Next door, by the way, is another Russian restaurant that is less well known but just as much worth looking for. **The Ukranian East Village Restaurant** (140 Second Ave.; 212/529-5024) is actually inside a residence and business office building that caters to Ukranians in the city. Their dining room, at the rear through the lobby, is one of the more handsome of the Village's many such restaurants, and though it looks private, it is open to all. The food and prices are similar to Veselka, Kiev and the rest. Go ahead—walk in!

VG's Bar—Broadway at Bleecker Street, Manhattan. Near the East Village/NYU border, you'll find this funky, casual restaurant and bar. The atmosphere is spare and modern, with natural wood tabletops and warm lighting. There's a good-sized bar area that boasts a fine selection of foreign and domestic beers.

Start your meal off with fresh-made guacamole and chips ($3.00) or gazpacho (just $2.00). Move up to tacos, tortillas, and sandwiches, all in the $3.50-to-$5.50 range, or go for a selection from the extensive line of complete dinners, most of which run between $5.00 and $8.00. Mr. C loved a huge platter of barbecued beef ribs for just $6.95; there was plenty of meat on these bones, and the dinner included salad, cooked vegetables, and crusty rolls.

Other specials of the day offered were: an open-faced turkey sandwich with gravy and French fries for just $4.50; a huge bistro salad featuring lettuce, watercress, avocado, sliced apple, almonds, tomatoes, and cucumbers—all for $4.25; a plate of steamed fresh vegetables with tofu or cheese for $3.95; and a fried-chicken dinner with salad and brown rice for an extremely reasonable $4.75. The cuisine here leans toward nouvelle, but the portions don't. You'll get a big, fresh, satisfying meal for your money. The restaurant stays open late into the evening—for the benefit of those seeking fortification before or after checking out the local rock club scene.

Village East Restaurant—2 St. Mark's Place; 212/533-9898.See "Good Health Cafe" listing under "Upper East Side."

Yaffa Cafe—97 St. Mark's Place; 212/674-9302. Way cool. Yaffa is an East Village landmark, serving a wide variety of food in their dark, cozy restaurant/bar, or out back in their walled-in garden. The place is also "open all nite," as they put it. It's a scene just about any time of day, filled with artists, punkers, musicians, and the young professionals who have begun moving into the neighborhood in growing numbers.

The food is fine, whether you nibble on a Yaffa Salad for $4.95—Middle Eastern delicacies with pita bread on the side—or fettucine marinara for $5.25. A chicken teriyaki dinner ($8.00) includes a green salad and bread. Yaffa also serves up a mean weekend brunch for just $6.95. Whenever you go, one thing's certain—there will be plenty to look at and plenty to eat, and it won't take plenty of cash to enjoy it.

GREENWICH VILLAGE

Aggie's—146 West Houston St.; 212/673-8994. Right on the border between Greenwich Village and SoHo, Aggie's is a crowded little coffee shop serving up wonderful home-style food. It's long been known as an inexpensive, definitively hip place; though in recent years its hipness may have given rise to some prices that are not quite as congenial as they once were. True to its reputation, Aggie's boasts a quintessential New York scene, with brusque waitresses who will keep you waiting to secure a few square inches of counter space—or, if you're really lucky, an actual table. This place seems to be busy just about any time of day.

Once you have found a seat of some kind, order a big meatloaf sandwich for $5.25 or a grilled chicken sandwich stuffed with roasted peppers for $6.95. Homemade soups (ham and lentil, for instance) are priced aroud $2.50, and bacon and egg platters start from $4.25. Daily specials offer more creative fare at reasonable, if not particularly groundbreaking, prices: the warm vegetable salad and chevre, a mountainous platter, runs $7.95. The countertop is stacked high with the muffins and pastries of the day, all baked on the premises. Sounds of jazz waft across the room, part of that oh-so-funky atmosphere that keeps people coming back for more.

Atomic Wings—At Down the Hatch, 179 West 4th St.; 212/627-9500, Blondie's, 2180 Broadway (77th St.); 212/877-1010, Cannon's, Broadway and 108th St.; 212/316-2300, Name This Joint, 1644 Third Ave. (92nd St.); 212/410-3800, and Spanky's, 1446 First Ave. (75th St.); 212/772-8400. Here's something a little bit different—Atomic Wings is not a restaurant; it's a menu offered by several restaurant/bars all over town. This is convenient for fans of true Buffalo chicken wings, though not for Mr. C, who prefers to be as thrifty with his time at the typewriter as he is with his cash.

Anyway, at these establishments you can enjoy what are touted as the only "authentic" Buffalo wings in the city. They are actually shipped in daily from the jewel of upstate New York, where chickens presumably have ample room to stretch out and grow up big. A single order of the juicy nibbles costs $4.95; a double order is $9.20. Each comes with plenty of blue cheese, carrots, and celery. Sauces range from mild to hot to "nuclear" to "suicidal"; hence the nom de plumage.

There are plenty of other variations on hand, such as "Chicken Littles"—strips of skinless breast meat on a bed of lettuce with your choice of dips (BBQ, honey mustard, Atomic, etc.). A platter of eight goes for $5.50. A grilled breast of chicken sandwich is $4.95; add fries and slaw for a buck.

You can also get a hamburger platter for $5.95—but why would you want to with these flappers around? After all, when in Rome . . .

The atmosphere at most of the places mentioned above is much like the campus pub we so fondly remember from our college days. Adding to this raucous environment is the regular Monday night special—all the wings you can eat for just $8.50, plus dollar drafts with the deal. If you love the wings but not the crowd, each of the bars offers free delivery.

Bagel Buffet—406 Sixth Ave. (9th St.); 212/477-0448.

Talk about your Village institutions. Bagel Buffet is much more than that—a full-service deli in cafeteria style. The place is clean and bright, if nothing fancy, with lots of small tables; and best of all, it's open twenty-four hours a day. They hand-roll fifteen varieties of bagels on the premises, including all the basics, along with pumpernickel raisin, honey wheat, and even spinach.

Obviously, breakfast is a big deal here. From 6:00 to 11:00 a.m., you can choose one of half a dozen specials, like two eggs, potatoes, coffee—oh, and a bagel—for $1.95. Beat that with a stick. For $2.95 you can get a western omelette with all the above sides. Add a homemade all-natural muffin for $1.10.

Meanwhile, you can, of course, get just about anything on a bagel, from peanut butter and jelly ($2.15) to lox and cream cheese ($5.40) to hot corned beef ($4.50). How about a tuna melt bagel for $3.70, or hot chicken breast for $3.25? And this doesn't even begin to touch the other deli delicacies, like knishes, Hungarian goulash, homemade soups (in regular, large, and extra large), gefilte fish, and so much more. They have, in fact, just about everything under the sun—not just bagels.

It's like that old comedy routine, about the guy named Ray J. Johnson: "You don't have to just call me Ray. You can call me Ray, or you can call me Ray J., or you can call me...."

Barrow Street Ale House—15 Barrow St.; 212/206-7302. This is another one of those places where you can eat, drink, and be merry—all for very low prices. As Mr. C has always noticed bars are often terrific places to get cheap food. They make their money off the brews. Still, the drafts at Barrow Street are all priced at $1.75, and these include McSorley's Ale, Prior Double Dark Ale, and several other hearty mugs. The food is strictly pub-style; you can get a nice big bowl of Texas longhorn chili for $5.25, fish and chips for $5.75, or a plate of chicken fajitas for $7.50. The bar itself is a long, narrow affair with high ceilings and low lighting, and the atmosphere is at times, well, boisterous. Expect to be entertained, more or less simultaneously, by sports on the tube, music from the jukebox, and the clatter of people playing pool as you while away the evening.

Burritoville—148 West 4th St., Manhattan; 212/505-1212, 1489 First Ave. (77th St.); 212/472-8800, and 1606 Third Ave. (90th St.); 121/410-2255. Fast food, Mexican-style, is one of New York's latest rages. At Burritoville's three locations, you can really stuff your face for well under $10.00. Most of the menu items, in fact, are priced from $5.00 to $7.00. The ingredients for some of these are as unusual as their names: "Davey Crockett's Last Burrito" ($6.95) is filled with grilled marinated lamb, brown rice, beans, and cheese; the "French Quarter Burrito" ($7.50) is resplendent with sizzling shrimp; and the "Vegged Out in Santa Fe Burrito" ($5.95) contains—surprise—nondairy soy cheese, grilled vegetables, tofu sour cream, brown rice, and beans. (The Santa Fe may be one of the few things you can find in a fast-food restaurant that is both heavy and undeniably good for you.)

Burritoville also offers tacos from $2.50 apiece, fajitas for $7.95, and a bowl of good old chuckwagon chili for just $2.50. Burritoville prides itself on using no lard, no preservatives, and only fresh ingredients. There is no liquor license here, so if you want a beer, bring your own. There are also few tables at Burritoville; Mr. C. did not inquire as to whether diners could bring those, as well. It may be simpler to take out or have Burritoville deliver, which they do at no charge. The restaurants are open seven days a week from noon to midnight. Olé!

Chef Ramon's Steakhouse—147 Christopher St.; 212/929-0335. Chef Ramon's may not sound Italian, but boy, is it ever. Way over in the West Village, almost to the river, is where you'll find this cozy little place—and it is quite a discovery. The quiet and ornately decorated room sets the scene for a relaxed and elegant dining experience at a much more affordable price than you might think.

Everything is à la carte; there are half a dozen antipasti to choose from, including eggplant rollatini and Caesar salad, all priced around $4.00. Choose from over a dozen pasta dishes; Mr. C recommends the rigatoni prosciutto with peas and a tomato cream sauce ($6.95) or the penne with eggplant, goat cheese, and tomato sauce ($7.50). Another good choice is the spaghetti with broccoli ($6.00). Entrees, or second courses, as they are known in Italian restaurants, are mostly priced from $7.50 to $9.00. Several veal choices are $8.95, including veal parmigiana and veal marsala with mushrooms. Chicken franchese is $7.50, and baked clams oreganato are just $5.75.

Finish off your meal with espresso or cappucino, and something from the daily selection of desserts. The Italian ricotta cheesecake ($2.50) is definitely worth checking out. Service, like the restaurant itself, is quiet and polite. A very elegant evening out.

Chez Brigitte—77 Greenwich Ave.; 212/929-6736. Somebody had a brilliant idea for this tiny Greenwich Village coffee shop: Turn it into a French-style cafe and offer great food at low prices. You can sit at the lunch counter or find a stool by the window, but if you're visiting the place during the dinner hour, you may run into space problems, as the entire restaurant seats maybe a dozen. (You can, of course, get your food to go.) Among the specialties here are boeuf bourgignon, a fancy

Mr. Cheap's Picks

✔ **Bagel Buffet**—Great bagels and great stuff to put on them. Not just cream cheeses, mind you, but a full deli. And it's open 24 hours a day.

✔ **Corner Bistro**—Perhaps the biggest, cheapest, and, darn it, best burgers in town. Go, quick!

✔ **Cucina Stagionale**—Big, delicious Italian dinners starting as low as $5.95.

✔ **Dallas Jones Bar-B-Q**—Great ribs and chicken. Mainly for take-out, though.

dish for an unfancy $7.30; and gigot de mouton (lamb to you and me, bub), for just $7.95. Dinners come with vegetable and potato, rice, or macaroni. Also on the menu: omelettes ($4.00), a variety of sandwiches (the filet of sole is $4.60), and, for dessert, a nice slice of pie (only $1.90). Chez Brigitte offers cut-price rates to match the cut-price surroundings—that nevertheless add up to a very chic dining experience. If you can get a stool.

Corner Bistro—331 West 4th St.; 212/242-9502. Up at the top of the Village, the Corner Bistro serves up what are arguably some of the best burgers to be had in the Big Apple. Other establishments may claim their fair share of partisans but in Mr. C's opinion, said partisans couldn't have visited Corner Bistro yet. Monstrously sized burgers of freshly packed ground beef, served on an equally fresh roll, start at just $4.00. Nice. You can add an overflowing plate of crispy french fries for just two bucks more. Alternatively, you might choose to pick up a chili burger for $5.25 or the Bistro burger topped with cheese and fresh bacon, all for a mere $5.00.

If you don't want a burger, no problem: go for the grilled cheese and bacon sandwich, just $3.75. Add a bottle of Brooklyn Beer for $3.25, or a mug of Yuengling Dark for $2.00. Yes, the menu is simple and the atmosphere old-fashioned—the front tables near the bar are self-service, the back room is composed of quaint wooden booths—but if you like good cheap food in an unassuming (okay, down-and-dirty) environment, this is the place. Never mind the old-world decor, the worn wooden floors, or the tin ceiling. You're looking for great burgers that won't leave you bankrupt. Head for the Corner Bistro.

Cucina Stagionale—275 Bleecker St.; 212/924-2707. Mr. C has a friend of Italian descent who eats at this Village spot frequently. It's a cozy, casual restaurant, but not without a certain elegance; yet, the prices are fantastic. Almost nothing on the entire menu—which is not small—goes over $10.

Appetizers start at $2.95 for an escarole salad; or, for $3.95, try the unique strawberry pesto salad with endive, mozzarella and radicchio. Pasta dishes are all priced between $5.95-$7.95, with over a dozen options, all of which come in substantial portions. Mr. C very much enjoyed his linguine with wild mushrooms in cream sauce ($6.95); another good bet, same price, is spinach penne with asparagus, sun-dried tomatoes and Fontina cheese.

Meat dishes, again, are terrific values—and just plain terrific. There are a few choices each of veal, chicken and seafood entrees, nearly all under $10. Veal marsala ($8.95) and chicken balsamic ($6.95) are just two of the better examples; and each entree includes a side order of pasta. Only with the fish can you go over Mr. C's limit, with daily specials priced at market value; even so, there are several dinners at $9.95, including brook trout, broiled swordfish and shrimp scampi. No wonder it's often difficult to get a table here.

One reason for the low prices is the fact that Cucina Stagionale has no liquor license; patrons are welcome to bring their own, of course, and Mr. C's friend invariably stops into the corner grocery directly across from the restaurant for something from their small but serviceable collection.

Dallas Jones Bar-B-Q—622 Broadway (West Houston St.); 212/228-6400, and 315 Sixth Ave. (3rd St.); 212/741-7390. Dallas Jones is considered by many to be one of New York's best take-out rib joints. (Although these small restaurants do have some seating, take-out is definitely the best option.) Start yourself off right with a bowl of chili con carne topped with scallions, cheese, and sour cream ($3.95). Baby-back-rib platters start at just $5.75 for the junior size; half-rack orders are $8.75, and the full rack, which will keep even hearty appetites busy for a good long time, is $14.95. A barbecued quarter-chicken is just $3.95; a half-chicken is $5.95. These platters include cornbread, coleslaw, and your choice of baked potato, steak fries, or white rice. Dallas also makes fried-chicken platters starting from just $3.95. You can mix and match all of these elements in various combination plates.

All of the ingredients here are fresh; fried foods are prepared in 100 percent vegetable oil to keep the cholesterol down (not that this is exactly health food), and the coleslaw has a distinct home-style taste. For lighter appetites, there are plenty of burgers and sandwiches—and even some Tex-Mex foods like tacos and burritos. But Mr. C advises you to stick to the ribs. They will surely stick to yours.

ESP—135 Christopher St.; 212/255-1240. No, it's not a magic act—unless you consider it a feat of legerdemain to find a truly elegant restaurant offering food at such reasonable prices. ESP is a Thai restaurant in the West Village that offers exotic dinners seven nights a week in a luxurious setting of dark wood paneling, a handsome bar area, and luminous white tablecloths on candlelit tables. If you make your way to the back, you will find that the rear section of the restaurant has floor-to-ceiling glass windows that look out onto an attractive brick courtyard area with a stone waterfall. (That part's open to diners during the summer.)

The menu boasts dozens of dishes in the $7.95 to $8.95 range. All of the beef dishes, for instance, are $8.95; all of the pork and chicken dishes are $7.95. The vegetarian dishes are even less. Start off with an appetizer of chicken or beef satay ($4.95) or stuffed Thai dumplings ($3.95). The traditional pad Thai noodle dish is $7.95 and quite good at ESP; this is a hefty plate. If you're bold, try the *gang neau*—red-hot curried beef in a coconut milk sauce—for $8.95. It's delectable, but not for the faint of heart (read: pass the fire extinguisher).

Among the many pork dishes, you might try *moo gratiem prik thai*, sauteed pork with garlic and pepper sauce. As for the chicken dishes, Mr. C recommends *preow warn gai*, a sweet-and-sour chicken served with diced pineapple, cucumber, onion, and scallions. A nice vegetarian selection would be the mixed vegetables in oyster sauce ($6.50). ESP boasts a vast menu that also features a wealth of seafood dishes, but these are priced a little too high for Mr. C's budgetary tastes.

For dessert, try the banana flambee, a banana wrapped in a spring roll skin, deep fried, topped with honey, and set ablaze just before it's brought to your table. Quite dramatic, and delicious. Another good dessert option is the cold, sweet, and refreshing Thai iced coffee. ESP also features a happy hour special—from 5:00 to 7:00 p.m. daily, you can get two dinners for the price of one at the bar. This will not feel a bit like slumming; the bar is elegantly appointed and tastefully lit.

Eva's Natural Foods—11 West 8th St.; 212/677-3496. Flash! Successful health food store in Village opens up kitchen for all-natural alternative to fast-food chains. Eva's has a bright, friendly atmosphere and a big menu that goes well beyond alfalfa sprouts. There's plenty here for just about anyone, not just vegetarians. Among the sandwiches, choose from burgers, tuna , seafood salad, falafel and lemon chicken. There are also, of course, burgers made from turkey and from spiced kufta. Most of these range from $3.00 to $6.00.

Much of the food here leans toward Middle Eastern cuisine. The sandwiches are served in pita bread, with a salad stuffed in; for a dollar more you can add fries. Salad plates are of a good size, whether they feature guacamole, tofu, pasta, or fruit. In fact, for $5.10 you can get a "Meatless Combination" sampler that will stuff you—with falafel, tofu, dollops of eggplant and chick pea salads, and brown rice, all on a bed of lettuce and vegetables. Or try broccoli and cheddar quiche, made with farm-fresh ingredients, or the carrot-broccoli tortilla pie (each $5.00).

For serious health fans there are special diet protein meals, fresh-squeezed juices, and lots of healthy yogurt and fruit shakes. At the rear of the restaurant you'll find the original Eva's store, with all kinds of natural foods and vitamins on sale at good prices. As they like to say, you can dine and shop under one roof until 11:30 every night.

Koo Koo Roo—2161 Broadway (72nd St.); 212/787-4600. It may have a funny name, but this California-style restaurant is one of the brightest, cleanest, and healthiest fast-food restaurants you're likely to find in New York. What's more, the food is delicious.

You'll find a cafeteria-style setup where chicken is the main dish . . . and where there's lots to choose from: skinless flame-broiled, rotisseried (in country herbs), and barbecue-style. The discriminating poultry fan can choose quarter, half, or whole birds; those readers who always fight with dining companions over the rights to the white meat should consider the double-breast combo. (No, it's not a suit, and it tastes a whole lot better.) The half-chicken (four pieces), whether skinless or barbecued, is only $5.59. For a dollar more, you can add two of the many wonderful Koo Koo Roo side dishes. Mr. C. was especially fond of the tangy tomato salad and honest-to-goodness mashed potatoes with gravy; California health food afficionados may wish to opt for the cracked-wheat rice.

The chicken comes wrapped in thin, soft-baked lavash bread—another distinctly West Coast touch. Koo Koo Roo makes up large quantities for picnic baskets and such; this can make for a nice treat on a warm day in nearby Riverside Park.

The Lost Diner—357 West St.; 212/691-4332. Well, *somebody* found this traditional old stainless-steel diner all the way over on West Street by the Hudson River—and turned it into a sensational dining spot. The Lost Diner combines classic American diner-style food with a touch of nouvelle cuisine at very affordable prices.

Start your meal off with a bowl of firehouse chili ($3.95); the quesadilla of the day ($4.95) is another good pick. Or try something as unusual as Cajun egg rolls (no kidding) for $4.50. There are plenty of salads and sandwiches here, including the Lost Burger, the chicken-salad sandwich (both $3.95), and the grilled three-cheese sandwich ($3.95).

The section of the menu simply entitled "Breakfast Stuff" includes any style of eggs for $2.50, steak and eggs for $7.50, and omelettes starting at $4.50. Meanwhile, on the "Entree" side, there are several commendable main dishes priced under $10.00. Try the traditional meat loaf ($7.95), the chicken and shrimp jambalaya with andouille sausage ($8.95), the southern fried chicken ($8.95), or the pleasantly assertive Louisiana fried catfish.

If you have room, you may want to hang out for the desserts, nearly all of which have a distinctly homemade look. There are a number of daily specials; Mr. C can vouch for the fruit cobbler ($3.95). Also worth exploring: the fudge pecan pie. Find the Lost Diner; you'll be glad you did.

MacDougal's Cafe—89 MacDougal St.; 212/477-4021. The NYU area of Greenwich Village is lined with one cafe/bar after another. One of the more popular, wrapped around the corner of MacDougal and Bleecker, is the MacDougal Cafe. Here you can sit inside at one of zillions of tables, or outside on their sidewalk patio, if the elements will allow, and while away an hour over lunch, brunch, dinner, or just a cappuccino and pastry.

The burger deluxe is very reasonable, at $5.25, with lettuce, tomato, and steak fries. Same price for a multitude of omelettes. Packed triple-decker sandwiches are mostly $7.95 in many combinations, again with fries. Lots of dinner entrees are in the $6.00 to $8.00 range; dinner specials may include such items as broiled flounder over rice for just $7.50. MacDougal's is open nice and late, like so many others in the area, making it a good place to stop into on your way to or from an off-Broadway theater, a movie, or the rock clubs further along Bleecker Street.

Mamoun's Falafel—119 MacDougal St.; 212/674-8685. "If you go to the Village, you have to eat at Mamoun's," insisted a friend of Mr. C's. He was right. It's just one of what seem to be a zillion or so Middle Eastern take-outs along this stretch of MacDougal, but Mamoun's is easily one of the best. Why they're all here together is as mysterious as the recipes for the delicacies found therein. No less a mystery is the fact that Mamoun's will give you a huge falafel sandwich, rolled up in pita bread with lettuce and tahini sauce, for a mere $1.75. There's plenty in there. Or get a falafel dinner plate, with more salad veggies on the side, for $5.00.

Same deal for shawarma, the spicy ground lamb and beef that's sliced from a rotisserie; the sandwich is $4.00, the platter is $8.00. Add a cup of hearty homemade lentil soup for $2.00; or finish off with a wedge of baklava pastry for a buck. It doesn't get much cheaper for such filling, tasty food. And like everything else in Greenwich Village, Mamoun's is open nice and late. Would you believe 10:00 a.m. until 4:00 a.m. on weekdays—and until 5:00 a.m. on weekends? *That's* New York.

Marnie's Noodle Shop—466 Hudson St.; 212/741-3214. Noodles continue to be all the rage in New York these days, and Marnie's, a cozy and comfortable West Village spot, offers the best of all worlds. They have Chinese noodles, Japanese noodles, Thai noodles, and a host of intriguing combinations and innovations, some of which may come as pleasant surprises to the noodle afficionado. Have you heard, for example, of Asian pesto? They've got it. It's a cold noodle dish combining basil, mint, and a tangy coriander sauce served over fresh noodles; a large plate is only $5.95.

On the hot side, you might want to try the Southeast Asian Sautee: wheat noodles in a spicy sauce of spinach, ginger, and coconut milk, served with your choice of vegtables, sliced chicken breast, or shrimp. A large plate is $7.95; a small one, $6.95. Marnie's has pad Thai for $7.95, and a vegetarian version for $6.95. If for some strange reason you wandered in here looking for something other than noodles, try the Chinese barbecued pork sandwich ($5.50), or a Thai beef salad, with sliced beef marinated in coriander sauce and served cold, for $6.95. The shop is great for take-out, although there are a few tables if you wish to stick around. Marnie's is closed on Sundays.

Miami Subs—305 Sixth Ave. (3rd St.); 212/807-0005, and 114 Liberty St.; 212/227-3003. "Great food, served fast," boasts this Florida-based chain that has recently begun flying north. Mr. C finds both of these claims to fall a bit flat, but Miami Subs is still a step up on the fast food chain from, say, the McDonald's just across Sixth Avenue. With this place, at least, you have more interesting choices, and they start from more recognizable—if prepackaged—ingredients.

In addition to hot and cold subs (maybe a novelty in Palm Beach, but certainly not here), Miami serves up chicken wings, in platters of ten ($4.99, with good, crispy fries) and buckets of twenty ($7.99) or forty ($14.99). Flame-broiled burgers start at $2.45, up to $3.95 for a double. These are larger and fresher than the flat things that pass for burgers at McD's. Another good bet is the chicken breast sandwich, also flame-broiled, which you can top with cheese, mushrooms, or bacon ($3.75 to $4.45), on a real bulkie roll. Gyros, fried clams, and the like round out the menu. They also serve breakfast from 7:00 a.m. to 11:00 a.m. on weekdays; the "Miami Slam" gives you two each of eggs, bacon and sausage for $2.75.

Bright tropical colors are the decor, of course; there is ample seating on two levels. Also good to know is the fact that Miami Subs is open until 3:00 a.m. every night.

One Potato—518 Hudson St.; 212/691-6260. Mr. C has always said that bar food is one of the best options for good cheap eats, and One Potato in Greenwich Village is a good example of this. The roadhouse-style bar has several tables set up across the room where you can eat lunch, dinner, and also brunch at ridiculously low prices. Nothing on the dinner menu is priced above $7.95, and while this menu is limited, there are several different kinds of entrees to choose from.

London broil and barbecued pork chops are the top items on the menu ($7.95 each); these are served with potato (natch) and the vegetable of the day. Burgers start at $4.95 for a complete platter, and you can have sauteed boneless breast of chicken with potato and vegetables for $6.95. For starters, a cup of chili is $2.50; a plate of guacamole and chips is $3.95.

For $2.00 extra, you can make a complete dinner out of any entree after 5:30 p.m.—adding a salad and dessert. The lunch menu is similar, with steak and chicken sandwiches, burgers, and so on, all in the $5.00-to-$7.00 range. These, interestingly, include your choice of a cocktail, glass of wine, or bottle of beer. The same deal applies to the weekend brunches, most of which are priced between $6.00 and $8.00. One Potato is fairly small, and the atmosphere can get pretty rowdy for the West Village, but it's a convivial and fun place. And cheap.

Pita Cuisine—535 LaGuardia Place; 212/254-1417, and 65 Spring St.; 212/966-2529. Perhaps as nice a health food cafeteria as you'll ever see, Pita Cuisine serves up all-natural food stuffed into, you guessed it, pita pockets. This doesn't mean exclusively vegetarian, though there are lots of meatless choices; it's good common ground. And the place is lovely—track lighting, lots of ferns and greenery, natural wood decor. Order your food from the pickup counter and find a table.

The cuisine is primarily Middle Eastern. Most items divide into two options: Stuffers, sandwiches filled with your choice of item plus greens and tahini dressing, and platters, which add tabouleh, chick peas, red cabbage salad and pita bread on the side. Thus, a baba ghanoush stuffer is $3.25, while a platter is $6.25. Mr. C recommends a Middle East Combo, offering of hummus, falafel, and baba. Die-hard vegetarians may want to try the Veggie Cutlet, Veggie Burger, or the Veggie Nuggets. All of these are in the same price range as above.

Meat items include a turkey burger, sliced hot turkey, and even good ol' beef burgers; again, same prices. Or, dodge the whole issue with a pasta (and vegetable) salad for $6.00, or a spinach and cheese lasagna for $6.50. They also make lots of homemade soups, $2.25 per bowl, including lentil, split pea, and chicken noodle. Plus sugar/salt free muffins, herbal teas, cappuccino for $1.50, and beers on tap for $1.75. In short, this is a place everybody can love.

Quantum Leap—88 West 3rd St.; 212/677-8050. Of the Village's many vegetarian restaurants, this is a real favorite of Mr. C's vegetarian expert. QL takes a novel approach to the subject, offering something for everyone. The atmosphere inside is nicely laid-back. Start off with a cup of house tea (Kukicha) for 75¢, and the waitress will refill it for you—just the way coffee drinkers get at diners.

It may take you a while to decide what to eat—the menu is suprisingly diverse. It includes seafood, making this convenient for vegetarians to take their non-veggie friends. As an example, let's imagine just such a couple: One could start off with a fresh salad of carrots, sprouts and cucumbers on a bed of Romaine ($2.50), while the other goes for "Sea and Land" ($2.95), combining red and green cabbage with carrots and hijiki—that's seaweed, folks. Quite tasty, and high in protein. Anyway...

The veg eater goes on to spicy Szechuan bean curd, sauteed with onions, peas, carrots, brocolli and cashews in a zesty peanut sauce. Or, perhaps the seitan (wheat gluten), again mixed with vegetables and sauteed in a garlic and ginger sauce. Both are priced at $8.95, and give you enough to make finishing difficult.

The non-veg has plenty of options too: Spinach ravioli filled with ricotta cheese, served over vegetables ($8.50), fish and vegetable tempura ($9.50), and pan-fried vegetarian dumplings ($8.95). Hey, they serve that at *regular* Chinese restaurants. And there are several fish entrees daily, priced around $9.50; choose teriyaki, garlic sauce, lemon herb sauce, and more. All come with brown rice and steamed vegetables; but our fictitious carnivore can just scoop these off and hand them to his partner.

Certain items are up for grabs, as far as which side of the fence they should be on; Tempura a la Parmigiana ($8.95) may sound like it won't work, but it's a tasty and filling platter of deep-fried vegetables with cheese baked on and tomato sauce over the top. And "Spaghetti and Wheatballs" ($8.95) seems self-explanatory—though you probably wouldn't expect artichoke pasta.

For dessert, both our diners may grab a slice of banana cream crumb pie ($3.50)—no argument there. Other pies and cakes change daily, and all are made with no eggs or refined sugar.

Quantum Leap offers weekday lunch specials, from $3.95 to $4.95, various combinations of soups, salads, breads and pastas. They also serve brunch on Saturdays and Sundays from 11:00 a.m. to 4:00 p.m., with enough varieties of omelettes, pancakes and waffles to make *anyone* forget this is a vegetarian restaurant in the first place.

Ray's Pizza—465 Sixth Ave. (11th St.); 212/243-2253. It's been Mr. C's rule not to explore the vast world of New York's pizzerias; mainly because A) we *know* they're cheap, and B) there are more pizza shops in the city than stray dogs—or even lawyers. Still, rules were made to be broken. Here goes.

Ray's is perhaps the one pizzeria everyone in New York has heard of. These days, if you walk just one block in any direction, you're bound to see something called "Ray's Famous Pizza." Or "Famous Ray's Pizza." Or "The Original Famous Ray's Pizza"....you get the idea. These may be okay, but they're all just trying to copy the *true* original. Experts know that this humble establishment in Greenwich Village is the genuine article, the one that started them all off—well before anyone even thought of cloning it.

Ray's is an authentic pizza joint; the ovens go non-stop, service is fast, and there are no tables or booths—just those inconvenient but space-saving tall standup tables. Never mind. No one comes here for the ambiance. But the food is great, and can be as hearty a meal as you've ever gotten on a wedge of bread. The basic slice is $1.75, but for $2.50, you can get toppings of eggplant and cheese or broccoli and cheese (yes, even the original has changed with the times). Of course, *all* pizzas have cheese, but no one puts as much on as Ray's. And these are not skinny little triangles, mind you; a slice here is a serious slice.

For the truly monstrous appetite, go for "The Works" ($3.75 a slice), which combines all of the above elements, and then some. One or two of these, and it's your stomach that'll be doing all the work for quite a while. Ray's Pizza is good stuff indeed, using the best ingredients. Oh, and you can get whole pies here too, of course.

Now, pizza becomes a very personal matter for some folks; and Ray's has its detractors. It certainly won't please the coal oven/sun-dried tomato and pesto crowd. But, if you want to see what the fuss is about, this is the location to try.

Rumbul's—20 Christopher St.; 212/924-8900. 559 Hudson St.; 212/929-8783, 128 East 7th St.; 212/472-8696. These Village cafes are widely renowned for their fabulous homemade desserts, cakes, pies, and related exotic creations. However, they also serve inexpensive meals that are quick and hearty.

Stuffed shells and shepherd's pie, all made on the premises, are priced between $5.00 and $6.00. Sandwiches, such as tuna or chicken salad served on a croissant, run only $4.75. Add a cappucino and you have a very simple, elegant and inexpensive repast—after which, of course, you'll still have a couple of bucks left over for one of those famous desserts. Seating is limited; take-out is a good option here.

Spain Restaurant—113 West 13th St.; 212/929-9580. Here's a tucked-away gem at the top of the Village. As you can guess from the name, this restaurant serves up truly authentic Spanish cuisine, in hearty portions that have been winning raves for years.

The place divides into a bar-and-table area up front, joined by a narrow hallway to a larger dining room at the back. Both rooms are quite plain, not to mention a bit worn; but that's how you can tell that this is a genuine neighborhood place, not spiffed up for tourists. And the prices will further confirm this.

Start your meal off with a bowl of *gazpacho* for $2.75. This is the famous Spanish "cold" soup. Moving on to the main courses, you may choose from such entrees as trout amandine (a low $7.25), or one of the many rice dishes. Chicken or shrimp over rice are just $8.50 each. Getting fancier,

Mr. C recommends barbecued filet of pork with fruit sauce ($7.75), which comes with Spanish saffron rice and a salad.

But the real native dish of Spain (both the restaurant and the country) is *paella*, and if you like seafood, you must try it here. This heaping platter combines clams, mussels, shrimp, chicken and sausage into a stew that's big enough to share, all for $9.50. When in Spain, to paraphrase a well-known cliche....

Finish off your meal with another famous Spanish delicacy, flan ($3.00)—a wedge of egg custard topped with sweet caramel sauce. Scrumptious. If you can't afford a trip to Barcelona at the moment, you can enjoy Spain without leaving the city. This is about as close as you can get to the restaurants you'd find over there anyway.

Temple in the Village—74 West 3rd St.; 212/475-5670. Temple in the Village is a modest-sized eatery near NYU, a simple, quick, eat-in-or-take-out spot specializing in macrobiotic and vegetarian food. The specialty of the house is the large and extensive buffet of vegetables, rice dishes, and a wealth of other vegetarian items, all available at $4.49 per pound. Take as much as you like. If you prefer, try something like the Bibim Rice Special ($5.95); this offers you your choice of five different vegetables, brown rice with a hot sauce, and a steaming bowl of miso soup.

The decor is spare (after the Japanese, with rice paper decorations and such). Classical music plays over the sound system; the tables are small and plain. In other words, nothing fancy. But if you're in the area and looking for a quick, simple, and healthy meal, this is a great spot. Temple in the Village is open daily from 11:00 a.m. until 9:30 p.m.

Tutta Pasta—26 Carmine St.; 212/463-9653, and 504 LaGuardia Place; 212/420-0652. This Greenwich Village pair is a longtime hit with students, professionals, and visitors alike. Tutta Pasta offers, of course, lots and lots of pasta dishes, most of which are a healthy $6.95; among these are linguine carbonara, tricolored penne with broccoli, fettucine Alfredo, manicotti filled with spinach and cheese, and many others.

The menu, though, isn't just tutta pasta. There is a good variety of veal, chicken, and seafood entrees; all of which are a bit steep at around $11.00 and up, though that does include a side order of linguine. An inexpensive alternative, besides pasta, is the individual pizzas, baked to order in a traditional brick oven. Their basic is $6.95; the same price, though, gets you the Panzarotti (isn't he that opera singer?), topped with prosciutto, salami, ricotta, mozzarella, and tomato. These range all the way up to the seafood pizza ($10.95), with mussels, shrimp, crabmeat, calamari, and scungilli. These are big enough to be a single meal, or to be split as an appetizer.

There are lots of apps, by the way—from a hot antipasto for two ($6.95) to stuffed mushrooms ($4.75). Not to mention a full complement of wines and beers. Of course, the old saying goes: When in Rome, have the spaghetti—or something like that. If that's the name of the place, it must be the right thing to order.

Village Natural Restaurant—46 Greenwich Ave.; 212/727-0968. See "Good Health Cafe" listing under "Upper East Side."

West 4th Street Saloon—174 West 4th St.; 212/255-0518. Another of the Village's many, many pub-style restaurants, W4S is one of the larger and more comfortable choices—just a block in from Avenue of the Americas. This sprawling establishment has tables outside in good weather, a long bar area inside the door, and two separate rooms in the back—with cozy high-backed wooden booths, candles, and a fireplace.

The menu is nearly as large. Go for a Saloon Burger ($5.95), topped with bacon, cheddar cheese, fried onions and Russian dressing; add a plate of jalapeno fries for $3.00. Homemade chicken pot pie is $6.95; same price for rigatoni and sausage, or a sliced steak sandwich. There are lots of dinner entrees well under $10.00, such as tricolored linguine with seafood ($7.95) and grilled peppered chicken breast, further seasoned with rosemary and garlic ($8.95). Plenty of good beers accompany all this, of course, and the service is very quick and attentive. It's an attractive and relaxed spot to mellow out from the bustling Village scene.

LOWER MANHATTAN

(Including Chinatown, Financial District, Little Italy, SoHo, TriBeCa)

Ballato's—55 East Houston St.; 212/226-9683. Since coming under new management in 1992, Ballato's has become one of the city's hottest Italian restaurants, and it's not uncommon for people who are waiting for a table to be asked to come back to this intimate yet elegant storefront another evening. Reservations, therefore, are recommended.

If you do manage to get a table, you will be in a position to enjoy some delicious and very reasonably priced pasta dishes (most are $8.50) or some of the other entrees, such as veal scallopini or trout cooked in garlic and rosemary. Most of the meat and seafood dishes are priced at $9.50, and are thus a little steep by Mr. C's standards, but you may decide to splurge. Better yet, Ballato's offers a *prix-fixe* dinner (fixed-price to you and me) Mondays through Saturdays from 4:00 to 6:30 p.m.: Appetizer, entree, dessert, and coffee, tea, espresso, or cappucino for $12.50 per person. Sure, it breaks the in-and-out-for-under-ten-bucks rule, but this meal could easily cost twice as much at some of New York's swankier Italian restaurants . . . and it would still be worth it at those prices.

Bell Caffe—310 Spring St.; 212/334-2355 (BELL). SoHo is known for its cafes, bohemian sanctums where people can sit over a pot of herbal tea and discuss the fate of man's existence—or the latest French film. Such places in SoHo are also known to be very expensive. But here on Spring Street near the river, there are two cafes a block apart, each with its own unique style, and both quite affordable.

The bigger and more renowned of these is the Bell Caffe. It's a wild-looking mish-mash of a place, with old wooden tables and chairs, no two of which match. Toward the rear, the food prep counter looks like a bar Mondrian might have designed—and it lights up. The walls display the work of local artists, a different show each month, with an opening-night artists' reception the first Monday of each month. You're all invited.

The food at Bell Caffe is loosely vegetarian; call it creative. The ever-changing menu does include some seafood and poultry dishes, like linguine with shrimp sauce ($9.50) or cornish game hen ($9.00), glistening with an apricot-mustard-ginger glaze. Stir-fry veggies over rice or noodles, in sesame oil, $7.00, is always a good bet. And "The Works" house salad, just $5.50, is a piece of art itself. This towering bowl is filled with lettuce, spinach, feta cheese, fresh vegetables, black olives, orange slices, apple wedges, grapes, stuffed grape leaves, and banana slices, with a tangy vinaigrette on the side. It also comes with slices of homemade carrot-

Mr. Cheap's Picks
Chinatown

✔ **Chef Ho's Dumpling House**—Fabulous dumplings and other Chinese snack foods, soups, etc. A real Chinatown find.

✔ **Meung Thai**—Chinese food ain't the only game in Chinatown anymore: Here's a Thai place that's high in quality and low in prices.

raisin bread, moist and sweet.

Bell offers live music in the evenings, with no cover charge. They serve many unusual brews, from Celtic Ale and Dragon Stout to a gourmet-blended house coffee spiked with cinnamon. There are plenty of appetizers, sandwiches, and desserts like chocolate Kahlua cake. If this is your kind of scene, they'll take good care of you.

Meanwhile, just down the street is another great hangout, the **Ear Inn**, at 326 Spring Street (212/226-9060). Formerly a good ol' New York saloon, established in 1817, the Ear now features great food and live music on weeknights—mostly blues and jazz. The neon sign over the door, which should light up as "BAR," has been blacked out slightly to read "EAR" instead. The food here includes more exotic salads, but also eight-ounce sirloin burgers for $6.25, pasta and seafood dinners around $10.00, and omelettes from $4.25 at lunch. Call ahead to find out their music schedule for the week.

Bo Ky—80 Bayard St.; 212/406-2292. There are only about fifty-kazillion restaurants lining the streets of Chinatown, and they're not just Chinese anymore; plenty of Thai and Vietnamese places have cropped up in recent years as well. They can be simple or lavish, touristy or authentic. It's difficult to pick the good ones out from the bunch, and even a reliable recommendation can pose problems. Take Bo Ky, for example.

If you want to impress people with your knowledge of the neighborhood, guiding them through the crowded streets to a genuine Vietnamese kitchen where the natives eat simply and well, this is such a place. But, once you sit down and look at the menu, you'll find it largely incomprehensible—some thirty dishes with generic names like "Special Beef Flat Noodle Soup" or "Country Style Duck." If you ask the waiter what any of these is like, his English may not allow him to shed much light on the subject. It's frustrating.

The best approach is to be open-minded. Check out what folks at the other tables are having, and point. The joint is always busy, so you know it's good. And with nearly everything priced between $2.50 and $4.00—whether it's a giant bowl of soup crammed with chicken, noodles, and bean sprouts, or a platter of shrimp rolls served over white rice—you can afford to be adventurous.

Broome Street Bar—363 West Broadway (Broome St.); 212/925-2086. From its vantage point at the corner of Broome and West Broadway, this cozy SoHo joint serves up tremendous burgers and sandwiches. Considering the price levels at the other restaurants in the area, the Broome Street Bar's offerings are very cheap indeed.

Burgers are priced from $6.00 and, in an interesting twist, come served in pita bread. Potato chips and pickles are served on the side. There are a number of appealing burger varieties to choose from. Sandwiches are in the $5.00-to-$6.00 range, and the categories here—ham, turkey, tuna—are relatively familiar; sandwiches are served with lettuce, tomato and chips. You may opt instead for a crispy grilled cheese sandwich, which is in the same price range, or an omelette and salad. This last selection, just $5.00, is a particularly good weekend brunch choice. Don't miss out on the chili; it's mild but tasty and will run you $2.50 for a cup and $4.25 for a bowl.

As you would expect, there are plenty of great beers available here at Broome Street, including Foster's Lager and Brooklyn Brown Lager. This place has been serving up burgers and beers in high style for over twenty years, and in this case that's a definite plus. There's a very funky jukebox in the back with plenty of vintage rock and soul tunes; the hanging plants also lend a commendable coziness to the proceedings. Interestingly enough, although it can be very difficult to secure a table during the dinner hour, the crowd seems to peter out about 9:00 p.m. This makes the Broome Street Bar an easy top-notch choice for a late-night snack. Check it out.

Cafe Limor—303 West Broadway; 212/334-6816. Here's a delightful little hole-in-the-wall that's perfect for a quick bite whether you're browsing the art galleries of SoHo or the electronics shops of Canal Street—for it's right on the border of both. Limor offers a variety of Mediterranean food, which doesn't fit either neighborhood; but that makes it all the more fun to have it there.

For a quick snack, there are all manner of filled sandwiches, from spinach pies ($2.50) to a mozzarella and prosciutto roll ($2.75) and a vegetable croissant ($3.50). If you want something more filling, look no further than the potato pancake sandwich, stuffed into a homemade pita pocket along with Greek salad and a spicy sauce, all for $3.00. It's big and delicious. And for a fun meal, try the combination box ($4.00): Baba ghanoush, tabouleh, one of those big potato pancakes, and salad.

Add some fresh-squeezed orange or apple juice, or a cappuccino; for dessert there are plenty of homemade pastries, baklava, and more. What there aren't plenty of are tables—just four, so lingering over your espresso can be tough. No matter;

Mr. Cheap's Picks
Financial District

✔ **Recession Cafe**—Name-wise, perhaps the most philosophically satisfying of all Mr. C's Picks. A wide range of Italian and American foods—in a trendy Eurosomething setting below Broadway.

✔ **White Horse Tavern**—Not the famous one, but a terrific little Irish pub near South Ferry, doling out piping hot meals to go with your Guinness.

if the weather's nice, you've got your choice of interesting strolls close by.

Chef Ho Dumpling House—9 Pell St.; 212/349-0503. Two blocks below Canal Street, in the true heart of Chinatown, Chef Ho's is frequently singled out as one of the area's very finest dumpling houses. It is a simple, spare, no-frills establishment, but the food is indeed first-rate—and you can't argue with a menu that barely makes its way past $6.00 on any item.

Most of the specialties here are, as you'd expect, dumpling dishes of one kind or another. Whether you order the Three Delights Plate (dumplings filled with leeks, pork, and shrimp) or the Homemade Meat Buns (ground pork in a doughier-than-average shell), you'll be getting very good food for not much money at all. The meat buns struck Mr. C as a particularly good deal; you can get a decent-sized plate of them, steamed or fried, for just $3.75. Standard-variety dumplings come boiled, steamed, or fried at $3.65 for a plate of eight. The wonton soup, an excellent way to begin your meal, is also $3.65, and a nice big scallion pancake is only $1.50. Various noodle plates are priced from $3.00 to $6.00. All of the items are very fresh and have a delightful homemade taste. The surroundings are clean and bright. Chef Ho's is a quick, dependable stop among the myriad offerings in Chinatown.

El Sombrero—108 & 117 Stanton St.; 212/254-4188 or 212/674-2998. This restaurant, known to some of the more oblivious gringos as "The Hat," is in fact a very authentic Mexican restaurant that somehow found its way onto the extreme eastern end of the Lower East Side. Very little English is even spoken, so this is a good place to go if you're either, A) already somewhat familiar with the cuisine and don't need to ask too many questions that require translation, or B) a former Spanish major looking to show off.

Once you order what you want, you'll get a very large platter of it, most likely for between $5.00 and $8.00. The selections include such traditional specialties as *carne asada* (fried steak), tacos *al carbon*, or a seafood quesadilla. The *pescado frito* (fried fish) is another good example; it's just $6.50. Like all of these plates, it includes rice and beans. There is a bar, but you won't have to wait there too long, as the food comes out fast and piping hot. The all-Spanish jukebox, like the all-Spanish chatter, keeps the atmosphere lively and, for non-majors, pleasantly incomprehensible.

Hamburger Harry's—157 Chambers St.; 212/267-4446, and 145 West 45th St.; 212/840-2756. See listing under Midtown West.

Hudson Grill—350 Hudson St.; 212/691-9060. In the midst of fashionable TriBeCa, a fashionable restaurant without the high-chic prices. Hudson Grill is an attractive, casual restaurant and bar offering a large menu of carefully prepared items best described as nouvelle bar food. Reasonable prices, too.

The large restaurant is divided into several connected rooms, all off of a central bar area à la *"Cheers."* The resemblance ends quickly, however: Each wall of the place is done in a different rich, deep hue, like a sweeping blue or a terra cotta red. One room features a pool table; another has booths by the windows; another boasts a cocktail area. The opulent feel of the place even extends to the restrooms, which feature handsome wooden countertops.

Oh, yes, the food. It's terrific. The menu features lots of salads and sandwiches, all priced between $5.00 and $7.00. Some of the options include a warm chicken tarragon salad or a Sloppy-Joe-style barbecued pork sandwich. Burgers start at

Mr. Cheap's Pick
Little Italy

✔ **Il Fornaio**—A cheap alternative to the glitzy tourist spots; just a modern, open-kitchen pizza and pasta house.

$6.25; burgers and sandwiches come with dark and spicy hand-cut French fries. There are lots of pasta dishes to choose from; they start at $7.25. Burritos are $6.50.

Moving on to the dinner plates, you'll find such selections as barbecued baby back ribs, or shrimp on skewers ($8.95 each). The bar offers beers from around the world, including Bass, Dos Equis, and Haake Beck's.

Check out the scene on Friday evenings, when Hudson Grill offers live music from an eclectic array of local rock bands. It's also important to note that this establishment, located as it is in a primarily commercial area, is not open on weekends.

Il Fornaio—132A Mulberry St.; 212/226-8306. Making your way through the maze of eateries in Little Italy can be daunting, not to mention expensive (okay, let's not mention it). One place dares to be different: Il Fornaio offers super-cheap, good food in a clean, bright little cafe. Their white-tiled open kitchen cranks out brick-oven-baked pizzas and calzones, along with pasta dinners; in the more cozy room beside it, you can chow down in a casual setting.

Individual (meaning small, yes) pizzas are just $3.00, with various toppings extra; and a pepperoni calzone is $4.00. Moving up the scale, they have lasagna for $4.95 and veal parmigiana with spaghetti for $7.50. There is also a chalkboard of daily specials, including soups and salads, all of which are à la carte, for a truly inexpensive and quick alternative to the bigger showplace restaurants.

By the way, this place is not related to a newer Il Fornaio at 1505 Lexington Avenue (at 97th Street; 212/876-0683). They happen to share a similar menu and prices, along with the name. The Upper East Side one is good too; but of course that won't help you if you're doing the Little Italy tour.

Joey's Paesano—136 Mulberry St.; 212/966-3337. A couple of doors along from Il Fornaio, Joey's Paesano is a more traditional restaurant, which proves that you can find a good deal in Little Italy and still get an authentic "experience." Joey's Paesano has been doing this successfully for years, and it's easy to see why they're always busy. The fairly small tavern-style room packs happy diners into long tables; they don't seem to mind. The music of Italian pop crooners adds to the festive feel. And the menu, specializing in Neapolitan fare, seems bigger than the restaurant itself.

There are nine different veal dinners, all $9.95, from scallopine to parmigiana; seven more chicken choices, all priced at $8.95; and over a dozen different pasta dishes, each $6.95. Pasta is not included as a side on the meat entrees; but at these rates you can go ahead and add it—or leave a bit of room for dessert. In any case, you won't go away hungry from Joey's.

Katie O'Toole's—134 Reade St.; 212/226-8928. A friendly neighborhood restaurant and bar that boasts a casual, almost collegiate party atmosphere. The sprawling layout allows you to wander from room to room; there is a small band area where, on weekends, live music can be heard well into the evening. The music leans toward rhythm and blues; there is no cover charge. (Note: Katie's is a popular partying spot, so quiet, contemplative weekend meals are probably not in the cards.)

The menu consists mainly of burgers and sandwiches, along with full entrees, most of which are priced at $7.95. (The glazed Hawaiian-style ham, in particular, is well worth investigating.) Daily dinner specials reflect the pub-style atmosphere: fish and chips for $7.95, or bangers and mash (sausage and mashed potatoes) for $6.95. The dinner specials are available as a full meal for $9.95; you get salad and coffee as sides.

There are dozens of burgers to choose from, ranging from the All-American Burger ($4.95) to the Apple Knocker Burger ($6.25), which features cheese and fresh Granny Smith apple slices atop the patty. Don't knock it till you've tried it. O'Toole's also boasts a full complement of desserts, coffee drinks, and, of course, many varieties of beer on tap. (Hey—it's a college crowd.)

L'Ecole—462 Broadway (Grand St.); 212/219-3300. New York City has many hidden treasures, and this is one that even the thriftiest among us can enjoy. L'Ecole, in SoHo, is the restaurant portion of the French Culinary Institute, which trains future French chefs in the fine art of classical cuisine. Here you can sample their work at a fraction of the cost of some uptown *brasserie*. Where else but at such a place will you find a full three-course meal of the very classiest sort for only $15.00 per person? That's the price of a *prix-fixe* lunch, served Monday through Friday; it includes your choice of appetizer, main course, and dessert, plus coffee or tea. (Tax and tip, of course, are extra.) Menus change with each season and there is a different selection available each day of the week. Your appetizers may include Roquefort soufflé, diced vegetable soup with gruyere toast, or *paté de campagne*.

Moving on to the entrees, you'll have a choice of two, and these may include roast leg of lamb with spinach flàn and potatoes amandine; seared tuna with white beans, arugula, and lemon confit; or boneless breast of duck with lime. Desserts are as wonderful as you would expect. Your choice may include a flaky strawberry tart, *soufflé au chocolat*, white/dark chocolate mousse, or pears with butterscotch sauce.

You can also expand your meal to five courses, trying all of the choices on the menu, for $20.00 at lunchtime. Dinners are available at three courses for $26.00, or five courses for $32.00. There are also à la carte

Mr. Cheap's Pick
Lower East Side

✔ **Ludlow Street Cafe**—After the Lower East Side bargain shops close up, this coffeehouse-style restaurant and bar wakes up with good food and great live music.

menus, but these are not such a good bargain. The restaurant offers one seating for each meal: at lunch that means noon, Monday through Friday; while dinners are served Mondays, Wednesdays, and Fridays at 8:00 p.m. The meals last one to two hours, and you'll be seated at a single community table, which affords you the chance to meet other fans of French cuisine. You'll also get the chance to take home many of the recipes, so you can try putting together some of these delectable dishes at home if you're so inclined.

While the prices are unbelievably low for this kind of food, you will not be skimping at all on atmosphere. L'Ecole has a grand dining room with high ceilings, large windows, and a handsome bar. The entire room is decorated in an up-to-the-minute contemporary European style. If you arrive early, you may wish to take a tour of the French Culinary Institute's classroom facilities.

Some important tips. Lunches at L'Ecole, in addition to being better priced, are also easier to get into, since they are offered every day. Remember this: you must reserve in advance for dinners, and you might keep in mind, too, that some people end up booking as much as a full month ahead of time. Finally, even though the prices here "break" Mr. C's semi-sacrosanct $10.00-per-head rule—and by a fair bit when taxes and tips are added—it is nevertheless highly recommended if you can pony up the few extra bucks. L'Ecole is one of the Big Apple's unique dining experiences, and a truly breathtaking value as well.

Le Petit Cafe—156 Spring St.; 212/219-9723. It's difficult to find anything that's reasonably priced in SoHo, but if you're spending the day wandering among the galleries and boutiques and want to stop in for a quick and inexpensive bite, this crazy eat-in/take-out shop is just the thing.

They have a variety of sandwiches and salads, most of which are priced between $4.50 and $6.00, served up in a casual atmosphere where you order from a counter and then find yourself a seat. A fresh mozzarella sandwich with grilled eggplant and marinated peppers is just $4.50; add a garden salad on the side for $1.25. The sandwich comes on French bread. Quiche of the Day is $6.50 and comes with a side salad and small order of pasta. Pasta of the Day, likewise, comes with a side salad for $5.75. The salads range from your basic chef's salad to Middle Eastern varieties, such as an engaging hummus and tahini number served with pita bread ($5.75).

There are daily specials offering such bargains as soup and salad for $4.95. Le Petit Cafe also offers lots of fresh-baked muffins and croissants made on the premises, as well as fresh-squeezed juices and a vast array of hot and cold coffee and tea drinks. The restaurant is great for take-out, and they deliver to the surrounding area.

Ludlow Street Cafe—165 Ludlow St.; 212/353-0536. You'd hardly expect to find a 1960s-style coffeehouse this far down on the Lower East Side—mixed in with the super-cheap clothing shops that leave this area a ghost-town after business hours—but in fact there are some really hip finds on these blocks. Ludlow Street Cafe opens nightly for dinner from 6:00 to midnight; walk down a couple of steps into this humble and cozy restaurant/bar which is also known for great local music. On just about any night the place is jammed by late evening—and jamming with folks enjoying the sounds and the food.

Entrees here are full and delicious platters, from the Cafe Special Burrito (beef, chicken, or vegetarian, filled with beans, rice, cheeses and guacamole, for $7.50) to chicken dijon ($8.50) and linguine primavera ($8.75). Plus warm and cold salads, burgers, appetizer snacks, and homemade soups and desserts. Wash it down with cappucino, espresso, or herbal tea; beers include Brooklyn Lager in bottles, and Yuengling on tap. Drafts are just $1.50, and the service is very friendly.

Also friendly is the nightly entertainment, which gets underway by ten. The styles include all kinds of popular music, different on any given night, and there's no cover charge. They just pass the hat.

Another great idea: Ludlow's $7.95 brunch, served not only on Saturday and Sunday from 11:00 a.m. to 4:00 p.m., but also on Friday and Saturday nights from 3:00 a.m. to 8:00 a.m. for true night owls. After all, what's the point of getting your Sunday Times on Saturday night, if you can't hang out somewhere cool with it until the next morning?

Lupe's East L.A. Kitchen—110 Sixth Ave. (Watts St.); 212/966-1326. East L.A. has come to the west side of SoHo in the form of this affordable and decidedly unfancy Mexican restaurant. Burritos and enchiladas are the order of the day at Lupe's, where big platters of each are available for both lunch and dinner for between $5.00 and $8.00 per. Among the exuberantly spicy options are a Beef Burrito Colorado, which has beef, beans, cheese, and red chili sauce rolled up inside; and the Super Burrito, which offers you beef or chicken along with beans, cheese, guacamole, rice, tomatoes, sour cream, and red or green chili sauce. (There's a vegetarian version of the Super Burrito, as well as a nondairy vegetarian entry. Take your pick.)

All of these are served with rice and salad on the side, making up a very large and filling meal. Some of the other platters include enchiladas (again, with your choice of chili sauce), quesadillas, and huevos rancheros—the Mexican equivalent of eggs and hash, but served with rice and beans. That last item is tasty but mighty, mighty big, and if you're like Mr. C you will have a hard time finishing it. Lupe's serves the real stuff.

Mangez avec Moi—71-73 West Broadway; 212/385-0008. No, not French—Indochinese. Mangez avec Moi is a simple TriBeCa storefront serving up great foods from all over Southeast Asia: A lot of Thai and Vietnamese, along with Laotian, Japanese, and Chinese too. Thus, you have one restaurant that can offer pad Thai, Laotian ginger shrimp, eggplant tempura with teriyaki sauce, and Vietnamese spring rolls. In fact, you may even choose between several chicken curries: Thai red curry, Saigon curry, Taj Mahal curry, and more, each subtly different. All of the entrees are plentiful and delicious.

If you're a fan of pad Thai, that most basic of Siamese dishes, you'll love it here—a moist, heaping plate topped with your choice of chicken, beef, pork or vegetables, all for $5.95. Indeed, many of the dishes allow you to match the cooking style with any main ingredient. One of the more interesting preparations is prig Lao, a spicy sauce made with roasted chili peppers. Mr. C tried it with slices of beef, tender and tasty (the kitchen will be happy to turn down the "heat" if you wish, so that even a delicate palate can enjoy it).

Being near the financial district, this place draws a big lunch crowd—during which service is done cafeteria-style from a steam table buffet. This makes things quick, easy, and even cheaper, with daily specials (most around $5.00, and no tips necessary). At night the restaurant is more subdued, with table service and a family atmosphere. Most of the dinners

Mr. Cheap's Picks
SoHo

✔ **Ballato's**—Their recently reworked menu has made this a tough place to get into without reservations. Great Italian food, and very reasonably priced.

✔ **Bell Caffe**—The veggie haven of the lower West Side. A real 1960s throwback.

✔ **Broome Street Bar**—This SoHo joint has been around long enough to watch the chic life grow up around it. Meanwhile, you can still get a great burger and a beer at "real" prices.

✔ **Hudson Grill**—Artsy, hip, and relaxed. A restaurant bar featuring a casual menu of sandwiches and entrees.

✔ **L'Ecole**—Prepare for one of the best dining bargains in New York or anywhere else on the planet. The French Culinary Institute is training the chefs of the future. Somebody has to eat all that "practice" food—and it's great! (Call ahead.)

range up to about $8.50, with some seafood dishes going up over $10.00. Decor is minimal, but clean; and you may opt to bring your own liquor. The friendly staff will even put it on ice for you.

Meung Thai—23 Pell St.; 212/406-4259. Chinatown hardly seems an appropriate name for the area these days, what with the recent proliferation of Thai and Vietnamese restaurants in the neighborhood. For Thai food, Meung Thai is one of the standouts in this part of town. A fairly small (or, if you prefer, "intimate") restaurant, this place boasts a decor that is pleasant, modern, and not terribly overdone.

Much the same can be said for the food on the large and extensive menu. It lists appetizers like chicken or beef satay grilled in peanut sauce ($4.95), as well as some wonderful thick soups, including chicken bean curd and hot and sour soup with shrimps (all soups are around $3.00). Main courses include a number of curries, all $7.00 to $8.00; unlike Indian versions, these are made from coconut milk.

There are half-a-dozen meat preparations, all $6.95: choose chicken, beef, or pork as the base, then add Chinese broccoli, oyster sauce, pad Thai with chilis and garlic, or one of the other accompaniments offered. Meung Thai has a good many seafood choices, too, most of which have to do with shrimp or squid and go for $8.95. For something simple and inexpensive, try the shrimp pineapple fried rice ($6.95). This features rice that's similar to Chinese fried rice but not quite as heavy. An entire section of the menu is devoted to recasting all of the restaurant's standard offerings as vegetarian entrees. These are all in the $5.95-to-$7.95 range.

Weekly lunch specials are served from 12:00 noon to 3:00 p.m.; most are $3.95 and a terrific value. You can choose among, for instance, shrimp and rice soup, pad Thai, and rice noodles with Chinese noodles and chicken. At Meung Thai, all foods (including the curries) are lightly spiced so as not to incinerate you, a thoughtful touch considering the unwarranted incandescence of much Thai food. However, if you like your food very spicy, you can order it extra hot.

Just around the corner from Meung Thai is another popular Chinatown spot for Thai food, the **Thailand Restaurant** (106 Bayard St. at the corner of Baxter; 212/349-3132). This is more the sort of place to visit for a big night out; it's a large and ornate restaurant some people may find a bit on the hokey side. The food is quite good, though, and very inexpensive. Almost no entrees on the à la carte menu top $8.95, and there are plenty of options in the $4.00-to-$6.00 range, especially noodle and vegetarian dishes.

Miami Subs—114 Liberty St.; 212/227-3003, and 305 Sixth Ave. (3rd St.); 212/807-0005. See listing under "Greenwich Village."

Ottomanelli's Cafe—62 Reade St.; 212/349-3430. See listing under "Midtown Manhattan East."

Piccola—594 Broadway (Houston St.); 212/274-1818. Right on the border of SoHo and NoHo, this new eatery is an oustanding example of fast-food that isn't junk food. Piccola bakes up tasty individual pizzas in its brick oven, which takes up one wall of this large but narrow space, giving it a homey feeling. As you walk your tray along the cafeteria-style counter, you can also survey freshly-made sandwiches, salads, and full entrees, all very good and very cheap.

The pizzas come in a dozen varieties, from good ol' pepperoni to spinach to a "white pizza" topped with only mozzarella and ricotta cheeses. All of these are $4.99, except for the basic cheese, which is a dollar less. An eggplant parmigiana sandwich, on more of that brick oven bread, is just $4.49; and the dinners, all large-sized platters, start at $3.99 for spaghetti and meatballs to baked ziti for $4.99 and daily specials for $5.99. Mr. C loved the grilled chicken over pasta, smothered in a thick tomato/vegetable sauce. These come with bread and butter, and you can get various sodas, mineral waters, and coffees along with it all. Not a late-night place; Piccola closes up around 8:00.

Pita Cuisine—65 Spring St.; 212/966-2529, and 535 LaGuardia Place; 212/254-1417. See listing under "Greenwich Village."

The Recession Cafe—182 Broadway (Cortlandt St.); 212/791-4040. Deep in the heart of the financial district, the wryly named Recession Cafe is a good place to escape from the pressures of economic downturn. If your stocks aren't doing so well, you can still eat here in high style. The gleaming lounge-style eating area is just past a refreshing miniature waterfall at the entrance; mirrors and a subtle European lighting scheme add to the ambience. There is also a bar, which comes in handy on those losers-outnumbered-gainers days.

As for the menu, it inclines toward the Italian and offers a wide variety of items, most of them on the casual side. Check out the appetizers: Mr. C can vouch for the mozzarella and prosciutto with fresh tomato and basil ($4.95). Main courses include a barrage of pasta dishes (fifteen, to be exact), most priced between $6.50 and $8.50; try the angel hair pomodoro with mushrooms and green peas ($6.50) or the carrot fettucine with green peas in a white wine sauce (also $6.50). There are also individual-sized (ten-inch) pizzas, all either $5.50 or $6.50, that carry toppings like fresh-cooked vegetables and cheese, or tomato, meatball, and sweet sausage.

Burgers start at $4.50; Mr. C suggests the pizza burger

($5.50) or, for the adventurous, Hopping John's Hot Atomic Burger ($5.95). That last one is something. The Recession Cafe offers catering and free delivery, and claims that the consumer confidence index has risen 30% since they've opened. Clearly a cause-and-effect relationship.

Royal Canadian Pancake House—145 Hudson St.; 212/219-3038, and 1004 Second Ave. (53rd St.); 212/980-4131. $8.75 for pancakes? Is this really a cheap place to eat? Well, this ain't just any ol' pancake house. Wait until you see what you get. Everything about RCPH is surprising—from the size of these flapjacks to the dozens of varieties from which to choose. Ever tried cappuccino pancakes, or oat bran and peanut butter, or broccoli and cheddar? Ever even thought of them? That's what this place is all about. "Pancakes Make People Happy" says the sign overhead; judging by the crowds, it must be true. They're also overwhelmed by Royal Canadian's mega-portions—gigantic cakes the size of a record album, done on the griddle or roasted in the oven. Complimentary cornbread, warm and made with chocolate chips, may also have something to do with the smiles on people's faces.

Don't worry if your taste is less exotic; they do have old-fashioned buckwheat, buttermilk, and blueberry. Also waffles, omelettes, soups and salads, coffees, teas and fresh-squeezed juices. Seating can be at their long luncheonette counter, or at tables. It's a highly popular brunch spot, of course, especially with families, so expect to wait for a table at peak times.

All their pancakes are light, fresh, and tasty, and all varieties go for the same $8.75. Needless to say, you should plan to share. In that respect, the place is definitely in keeping with this book.

Spaghetti Western—59 Reade St.; 212/513-1333. As you might gather, pasta is the specialty of this bar-with-restaurant just around the corner from City Hall. Though it looks like an old-time saloon, this place shoots from the hip—complete with posters of Clint Eastwood movies over the bar. The posters, of course, are in Italian.

All of the pasta dishes, such as homemade spinach lasagna, gnocchi, or cheese ravioli, are $8.95. If you haven't been told to get out of town by sundown, drop in for an early bird prix-fixe special (Monday through Friday, 5:00 to 7:30), when the same dinners—at the same price—include salad, coffee, and dessert. The menu also takes in the Wild West, with various burrito dinners from $6.95 to $8.95. Go for the chile colorado (beef with red chile sauce) if you dare. And there are burgers, pizzas, salads, and Tex-Mex appetizers, all reasonably priced.

Wash 'em down with one of several good beers, including Dos Equis and Tecate. If there is a noticeable bias toward Mexican brands, well, heck—all those Italians make is wine!

White Horse Tavern & Restaurant—25 Bridge St.; 212/668-9046. For starters, this pub bears no relation to the better-known White Horse Tavern in Greenwich Village—the one Dylan Thomas was said to have frequented. Still, way down near the Staten Island Ferry terminal, this hideaway offers lots of old Gotham character.

It's basically a bar with terrific hot meals, which you get on a tray, cafeteria-style. Just point to what you want, and the friendly woman will happily heap mounds of it onto your plate, just as she's probably been doing for years. Or, ask her to toss a burger on the flame grill for you. The meals are hearty and delicious. Those burgers—get ready, now—are a mere $2.00 . . . eat that, McD's! Add cheese and bacon for a dollar, and thick-cut fries for another dollar. Total, $4.00—greasy and good. Other luncheon plates are mostly $4.75,

Mr. Cheap's Picks
TriBeCa

✔ **Mangez avec Moi**—A cozy, family-style restaurant in which the varied cuisines of the Orient are well represented.

with half-a-dozen choices daily, such as pot roast or chicken scampi. Add a brew, or just a soda; find a well-worn table and enjoy the bustling atmosphere.

Wong Kee—113 Mott St.; 212/966-1160. This is another place to go if you want to impress someone with your knowledge of "where the good spots are" in Chinatown. Wong Kee is a small, family-style restaurant; the no-frills decor may be a bit offputting, but the accompanying menu prices and excellent fare more than make up for it. That part about the family-style atmosphere also means (during the dinner hour, at least) kids, kids, kids. Mr. C recommends that you prepare yourself for a boisterous dining experience. The food, however, will calm you right down. Order a heaping platter of Wong Kee's Special Chicken ($7.60) or pineapple roast duck ($8.00). There is also a good selection of soups in the $2.00-to-$3.00 range. Appetizers generally run from $4.00 to $5.00. Service is prompt, the restaurant is quite clean, and the clientele is diverse—a good sign—although some of its number are given to runny noses and the occasional tantrum.

Yip's Restaurant—10 Liberty Place (off Maiden Lane); 212/732-8264. Down an alley, off a narrow side street, in what appears to be the middle of nothing, lies Yip's—a divey Chinese hole-in-the-wall. Even if you were to notice it as you walked past, you might well dismiss it as one of zillions like it. Why, then, does Mr. C mention it? Simply because everyone who works around the Wall Street-World Trade Center area seems to go there.

The place may look grungy, but the food is good. And although take-out is a big business here, you can carry your food upstairs to a seating area that is actually quite clean and pleasant. Besides—and here's the clincher—the prices just can't be beat. Mr. C was delighted to reward the friend who had brought him there by picking up the tab—especially since it came to an extravagant $6.75 for the both of them.

There are a dozen basic platters, each of which can be ordered over white rice, pork fried rice, vegetable lo mein, or shrimp fried rice. Pepper steak, sesame chicken, shrimp with broccoli, and others are among the options for such a platter. Nothing, repeat nothing, on this menu costs more than $3.90. Period. There are also four or five daily specials, such as General Tso's chicken or Szechuan beef, served on the same beds. Chicken with garlic sauce over lo mein noodles was particularly good, though not spicy as the menu indicated; barbecued chicken with veggies was also good.

Yip's is only open Monday through Friday, from 10:00 a.m. to 4:00 p.m.; at the height of the lunch hour, lines can be out the door. Be sure you know what you want before you step up to the counter, or they'll bark at you! Mr. C's insider source also noted that the quality, like the customers, tends to drop off by around 2:00.

MIDTOWN MANHATTAN EAST

(14th Street to 59th Street, East of Fifth Avenue)

Baby Bo's Burritos—627 Second Ave. (34th St.); 212/779-2656. This Murray Hill Mexican spot seems to have taken its lead from the tremendously popular Benny's Burritos (see separate listing in East Village section), offering a simple menu of a dozen or so Mexican specialties, most of which are priced between $6.50 and $8.95. Burritos, of course, are the house specialty, a prime selection being the Venice Burrito ($7.50), a fourteen-inch tortilla filled with beef, chicken, or spinach, plus beans, rice, cheese, sour cream, and guacamole. The Super Vegetarian (also $7.50) can be ordered mild or spicy, and is well worth checking out.

Other dinner entrees include chimichangas, enchiladas, a taco salad, and arroz con pollo. This last item, which runs $8.50, is, of course, a chicken and rice dish; they prepare it here with tomatoes, green peppers, onions, garlic, and olives. There's also a good beef casserole ($8.95) that offers marinated strips of beef baked in a casserole dish and covered with melted cheese.

Feeling adventurous? Try Marietta's "Boom-Boom" chili ($6.50); it comes in both meat and vegetarian varieties. Baby Bo's takes a tip from a variety of Chinese restaurants in the area by offering a number of lunch specials; these are $4.95 and a heck of a bargain. Mr. C proposes the spinach or tuna quesadilla. Lunch specials come with nacho chips and fresh homemade salsa and are served weekdays from 11:30 am to 3:00 pm. Finish your meal off with an order of flan ($2.25) or one of the battidos (also $2.25), the house's own all-natural fruit shakes. Baby Bo's offers free delivery and is open nightly until "around eleven." Hey, it's a casual place.

Christine's—462 Second Ave. (26th St.); 212/779-2220, and 208 First Ave. (12th St.); 212/505-0376. See "Little Poland" listing under "East Village."

Cucina & Co.—200 Park Ave. (Pan Am Building lobby, 45th St. entrance); 212/682-2700. Here's an interesting twist—a restaurant that is less expensive for dinner than for lunch. Cucina & Co. is great at any time, but since it thrives on the teeming thousands of businesspeople who pass by during the day, it offers some very enticing two-for-one specials at night—a mere escalator ride above Grand Central.

This bright and lively cafe, with its spotless Mediterranean decor, serves a variety of salads, sandwiches, pastas and meats. Baked pastas ($8.95) are made with different fillings each day, such as cannelloni with spinach and ricotta cheese or penne with vegetables and mozzarella. Sandwiches, alas, are a bit overpriced, though wonderful; go for the "Baguette"

($5.95), with grilled chicken breast and roast peppers. They're all served on fresh, crusty bread, with great shoestring fries on the side.

There is also a roast of the day, like rotisseried leg of lamb ($9.50), served with flageolet beans and roast potatoes. But it's at dinner time that these dishes become a real bargain, when $18.95 gets you boneless veal shank with red potato salad—for two. Or, $16.95 for a pair of cannelloni platters, served with stuffed zucchini and mixed greens. There are four or five such deals to choose from, available from 5:00 to 9:00 p.m., Monday through Friday; the restaurant's only weekend hours are Saturdays from 8:00 a.m to 4:00 p.m., with the regular menu.

The front of the restaurant, by the way, is a take-out heaven for anyone on the move—a mouth-watering array of fresh pastries, hot teas and coffees, sandwiches and soups, with fast check-out lanes.

Dosanko—329 Fifth Ave. (32nd St.); 212/686-9259, 135 East 45th St.; 212/697-2967, 423 Madison Ave. (48th St.); 212/688-8575, 10 East 52nd St.; 212/759-6361, and 217 East 59th St.; 212/752-3936. As you can see, midtown is well-stocked with this chain of Japanese noodle houses, though Dosanko was around long before the current "noodle craze" struck big. It's a quick and easy place to get a nice hot meal for under $10.00—and it's healthy to boot. As with most such restaurants, you have lots of noodles, broths and other toss-ins to choose from. Larmen, one of the basic options, gives you a miso (clear) or shoyu (soy sauce) broth, with noodles, carrots, celery, scallions, and slices of beef or pork—a large, tasty bowl, all for $5.10. It's tough to finish, and can be a meal in itself. Don't underestimate this just because it's soup!

Many other noodle dinners are priced between $5.00 to $7.00. For non-soup entrees, try the katayaki ($5.50)—a bed of crisp fried noodles with beef, vegetables, and sauce over the top. And a platter of fish and shrimp over rice, with vegetables and a salad, is just $6.60. Beer, wine, and sake are among the offerings from the full bar. Dosanko is a dependable network of restaurants for a simple meal; the service is fast, and the food will fill you up without weighing you down.

Giovi—8 East 18th St.; 212/620-4182. If you're roaming around the Flatiron District, snapping up one of the area's many fine bargains in furniture, perfumes, or men's suits, stop in to Giovi for a quick getaway to an Italian piazza. This recently opened cafe looks like a courtyard somewhere in Venice, with pink pastel walls and lots of tables for two. The walls are decorated with three-dimensional art made from wooden shutters and windows, while high ceilings and silk trees add to the outdoor feeling.

The specialty here, of course, is cappuccino and pastries—the latter displayed in a glass case full of wonderful cakes, pies, and tarts. These are, alas, rather expensive; $3.95 for a slice of cake, for example. Meals, however, are more reasonable, not to mention creative, and also very good. There are several pasta dishes, all priced at $7.45, such as ravioli "in an amusingly sweet and spicy tomato sauce"; as well as penne pesto, which consists of pasta marinated in pesto and tossed with roasted red peppers.

Another selection of dinners, each $7.95, includes a scrumptious eggplant rolatini, which Mr. C thoroughly enjoyed—delicately fried eggplant slices over three warm, soft cheeses, with a bean salad on the side. Among the other choices are Vietnamese peanut noodles, veggie burritos, and curried tuna salad. The portions are not huge, but enough.

Giovi is also a neat-freak's delight, with perfectly matched cups and saucers and creamers for your caffe. Each Euro-modern dish is carefully placed upon the clean white tabletop. It's a nice place to stop in for a calm breather amid the bustle of Fifth Avenue.

The Great American Health Bar—2 Park Ave. (33rd St.); 212/685-7117, 10 East 44th St.; 212/573-6350, and other locations. This is a coffee-shop-style chain of inexpensive restaurants serving food prepared with all-natural ingredients: salads, sandwiches, and dinner entrees. Sit at the gleaming, spiffy counter or find yourself a table.

Sandwiches (served with a side salad) come on your choice of seven-grain pita or whole-wheat bread. For those in the mood, there's a Swiss cheese, cucumber, tomato, and alfalfa sprout sandwich for just $5.60. Falafel enthusiasts can secure a pita bread sandwich with generous portions of falafel and tahine for $4.75. Your basic tuna melt, made with cheddar cheese and tomato, runs $5.90. Salads are served with seven-grain bread; the cold pasta primavera ($5.95) is worth checking out, as is the Great American Salad (also $5.95), replete with shredded cheese, walnuts, hard-boiled egg, tomato, sprouts, cucumber, carrots, and fresh greens.

Dinner entrees range from fresh steamed vegetables on brown rice covered with cheese sauce ($5.95) to a tasty vegetarian burrito ($6.95). Ask about the daily pasta specials, which, in their richness, seemed to Mr. C to push the health-food envelope to the outer edge. In the best way, of course.

Jackson Hole Wyoming—521 Third Ave. (35th St.); 212/679-3264. Burgers, burgers, burgers! That's the specialty at Jackson Hole, and they're huge. There are also over thirty different varieties to choose from: The basic beefburger starts at just $4.00 ($6.00 if you want a side of lettuce, tomatoes, and French fries); the Texan burger ($4.60 or $6.60) comes complete with fried egg; a bacon pizza burger ($6.05 or $8.05) arrives with three strips of bacon on top; the Copsegmore ($6.75 and $8.75) features fried onions, tomato, ham, mushroom, and Swiss cheese. (Who knows what Copsegmore means? It's a full meal in itself.)

Tired of burgers? It *is* possible to get something different at Jackson Hole, including a number of good Mexican dishes. Southern fried chicken ($7.50) is another good bet here, and Jackson Hole offers a wide variety of omelettes that start at just $3.35 (such a deal!), as well as a full selection of sandwiches and salads. The atmosphere is lively and bright; the decor is best described as an exotic stainless-steel diner transported to a deserted stretch of two-lane somewhere in, well, Wyoming. The crowd, however, is definitely urban, and the lively, eclectic feel of the place is one of the best reasons to jump into Jackson Hole.

K-Dee's—551 Second Ave. (31st St.); 212/684-6919. K-Dees is kind of like an old-time pub with a modern style. The handsome, dark-wood bar area just inside the door gives way to a brighter, more contemporary dining room further back. Since these are both tucked into a somewhat narrow building, each area feels separate from the other and offers its own atmosphere.

At the bar, that means Monday Night Football (with an open buffet) and Guinness on draft. In the tables section, the extensive menu has lots of sandwiches from $4.00 to $6.50, soups and salads, pastas for $8.00 a plate, and meat and seafood entrees. These include sliced steak ($7.95), broiled pork chops or chicken piccata (each $8.95) and shrimp scampi ($9.95). The food is tasty and filling.

Not much more to say—K-Dee's is a fine place to relax over good eats and drinks, a neighborhood spot that's warm n' friendly. New York can never have too many of these.

Le Cafe—725 Third Ave. (46th St.); 212/972-1200. If you like to eat lighter food that's trendy and healthy, but often find yourself short of time, cash, or both, Le Cafe may be the spot for you. It takes the fast-food approach to today's chic food styles, and the East Side of midtown is an area that offers few such dining options.

Choose among a variety of thick sandwiches priced at from $4.00 to $5.00 each, including chicken salad, turkey, and cheddar, a warm chicken filet, and even a chicken "fajita in a pita." This sandwich consists of grilled chicken mixed together with melted cheddar, greens, and tomatoes—all for $4.75. Salads are also in the $5.00 price range, whether you go with a chef salad, chicken pasta salad, or fresh fruit salad. Hot entrees include quiche and salad for $4.95, a turkey-melt open-faced sandwich with a salad for $5.50, and vegetable lasagna, also with a salad, for $5.95. A bakery on the premises offers up plenty of inexpensive treats, from zucchini bread and low-fat muffins to good old traditional high-fat muffins and brownies.

Le Cafe is clean and bright, with fast-food-style tables done in natural wood finish. There are a counter and some tables at street level, and another seating area upstairs with room for a hundred more patrons.

Moonstruck East—449 Third Ave. (31st St.); 212/213-1100 and 400 West 23rd St.; 212/924-3709. So many diners, so little time! In fact, the menu at either of these Chelsea and Murray Hill spots is a massive book in itself. Page after page listing breakfasts, salads, sandwiches, burgers, dinners, desserts, the works. There are nearly three dozen varieties of omelettes alone. And you get an amount of food that may be just as hard to finish.

Choosing from over twenty hamburger options, Mr. C's companion selected a mushroom burger ($4.55) a plump seven-ouncer (as they all are), they came piled high with equally plump grilled mushroom halves. Good French fries, too. Mr. C had a "Victoria House" sandwich ($6.95): grilled chicken breast on a bulkie roll topped with melted mozzarella and fried onions and served with fries, cole slaw, and pickle. You can get breakfast all day, full dinners, and, of course, Greek specialties.

Moonstruck has a liquor license and also offers a Saturday or Sunday brunch for $7.95 that includes a Bloody Mary or Mimosa, one of many three-egg omelettes, toast, home fries, and coffee or tea. There is also a special children's menu available.

Mumbles—603 Second Ave. (33rd St.); 212/889-0750, and 1622 Third Ave. (91st St.); 212/427-4355. See listing under "Upper East Side."

Old Town Bar—45 East 18th St.; 212/473-8874. Lower midtown is well-known for its many nineteenth-century saloons: All dark wood, brass, and hearty food. Most of these, alas, can also be fairly expensive—especially if you figure in a hefty liquor tab. For this reason, many such bars can also be mistaken for a Brooks Brothers showroom.

One alternative that just about anyone can afford is the Old Town Bar. It's a long, high-ceilinged place with two floors of that same turn-of-the-century New York charm—and a great place to hang out over beers and a simple menu of inexpensive fare. These are mostly sandwiches, whether cold deli varieties such as smoked turkey,

Mr. Cheap's Picks

✔ **Giovi**—You'll feel like you've been tranported to a piazza in Florence. Inexpensive light meals and pastries.

✔ **Moonstruck Diner**—One of those mega-diners: You don't get a menu, you get a tome. Good food cheap, and don't forget its Chelsea counterpart.

✔ **Shaheen**—Buffet-style Indian food means low prices in a pleasant atmosphere.

✔ **Tibetan Kitchen**—The food is a cross between Chinese and Indian; it's incredibly cheap, and the ambience is quiet enough to meditate in.

bacon, and muenster cheese ($6.00) or a hot fish sandwich made with fried flounder ($5.75). You can also get a bowl of chili for $4.75, and a fresh, plump burger for $5.50 (with French fries or new potato salad).

The beer, of course, is not so cheap, but that's where they make their money. If you're really watching your wallet, nurse a Ballantine Ale ($2.75) and enjoy the food—and the bustling atmosphere. It is, to say the least, a popular (read: crowded) watering hole, especially after 5:00 p.m. The place also has the distinction of being immortalized in the minds of late-night television viewers everywhere; it's the bar you used to see every night during the opening of David Letterman's show. The intro has since changed, but let's hope this Gotham landmark never does.

Oh, and if you must wear a fancy pinstripe suit here, for goodness sake, get it at Rothman's (see listing under "Clothing"). It's just around the corner.

Ottomanelli's Cafe—119 East 18th St.; 212/979-1200, 337 Third Avenue (25th St.); 212/532-2929, 538 Third Ave. (36th St.); 212/686-6660, 237 Park Ave. (45th St.); 212/986-6886, and 951 First Ave. (52nd St.); 212/758-3725. Branches of this popular chain are springing up faster than the dough in their pizza. Ottomanelli began as a meat market in New York at the turn of the century, but more recently has made the transition to a successful series of restaurants serving pastas, pizza, burgers, and other main courses. The prices for this popular fare are not, perhaps, the cheapest in New York, but they are quite reasonable, considering the hefty portions. At Ottomanelli's you get a lot of their dough for your dough.

Most pasta dishes are priced at $8.75, which includes wonderful toasted garlic bread; and tasty, if not exactly trailblazing spaghetti and meat balls, fettucine Alfredo, and so on. Pizza at Ottomanelli's comes in a basic ten-inch individual size starting at a very reasonable $5.95, with additional toppings only a dollar each. Then there are special combination pizzas, like the primavera, which comes topped with fresh vegetables ($7.95).

Fresh-ground steakburgers (between $5.00 and $7.00) also offer a number of variations, such as the super cheese steakburger, which is topped with three different cheeses ($6.95).

All of these burgers come with an order of ultra-crispy "cross-hatch" fries. Other quality entrees at Ottomanelli's can be obtained for less than $10.00 apiece, but these consist mainly of sandwiches and salads, and so Mr. C. finds them a tad overpriced. Stick with the more generous items, such as the barbecued half-chicken with those fries; it runs only $7.75, a very good deal. For a dependable (if casual) Italian or American meal, the lively Ottomanelli Cafes are a good bet. And you sure can't go very far around town without bumping into one.

Papa Bear—210 East 23rd St.; 212/685-0727. The East Village may have cornered the market in super-filling, super-inexpensive Polish coffee shops, but that's not the only place to find them. Papa Bear is a Gramercy Park version of the same kind of restaurant. Don't go expecting much in the way of decor, but rest assured that you won't spend very much money and you won't go away hungry.

Start off with a bowl of hearty soup, such as red borscht with meat dumplings or white borscht with kielbasa. These come with a nice hunk of bread and slab of butter; most soups are $1.50 by the cup and $2.50 by the bowl. Moving on to the dinner items, there are a couple of dozen to choose from, all priced under $8.00: chicken Kiev, wiener schnitzel, stuffed peppers, Polish kielbasa with onions, beef stroganoff—the list goes on. It's all hearty, and the main meal includes your choice of two side orders such as kasha, French fries, sauerkraut, coleslaw, potato salad, spinach, cucumber salad, etcetera. Quite a dinner.

You can combine all of this into a daily special at lunchtime: a cup of soup, the main entree, two side orders, and a beverage, all for just $5.95. That's available Monday through Friday between 11:30 and 3:00. Of course, there are plenty of hot and cold sandwiches, as well as the obligatory blintzes and boiled or fried pierogies. Papa Bear is also a great place for breakfast: two eggs any style with toast and homefries for just $1.95, or challah French toast for $3.25. You can always add ham, bacon, sausage, or good old Polish kielbasa to breakfast plates for a nominal charge. Whatever you get and whatever time of day you get it, the good food here will definitely stick to your ribs.

Royal Canadian Pancake House—1004 Second Ave. (53rd St.); 212/980-4131, and 145 Hudson St.; 212/219-3038.

See listing under "Lower Manhattan."

Rupali—715 Second Ave. (37th St.); 212/599-8979. From the folks who brought you Sonali, one of the standout restaurants on the East Village's "Curry Row," comes this Murray Hill spinoff, which has drawn just as much attention for the quality of its food. All of the standards are here, including tandoori and biryani, both of which run a bit on the expensive side. However, you can still do very well for yourself with Rupali's vegetarian specialties, all of which run under $8.00, and the lamb, beef, and chicken entrees, which are served over rice and vegetables and which are all in the $8.00-to-$9.00 range.

As is usually the case at these kinds of restaurants, lunch offers the best deals, the most flamboyant of these is probably the Sizzling Tandoori Lunch ($7.95), which includes tandoori chicken, shish kebab, rice, and vegetables. There are half-a-dozen curry lunch specials (offered from 11:30 to 3:00 every weekday); these are full platters featuring curried versions of everything from shrimp and crab to lamb and beef, all in the $6.50-to-$7.50 range. Rupali also has a weekend brunch, served from noon to 3:30 p.m.:

It's an all-you-can-eat buffet for $7.95. You may not often find yourself in this mostly residential neighborhood, but if you do, stop in.

Sam's Noodle Shop—411 Third Ave. (29th St.); 212/213-2288. One of the latest rages on the city dining scene, noodle shops are just what Mr. C loves—casual, clean places in which you can get a table full of different foods for very little money. Sam's is such a place. Start off with a dish of cold sesame noodles for just $3.50, or a bowl of hot and sour soup for a mere $1.25. Egg rolls filled with chicken, shrimp, or vegetables are $1.35; and speaking of fillings, there are similar variations in the steamed dumpling department—a platter of eight for about $4.00.

Entrees range from hearty bowls of Cantonese wonton soups stocked with sliced meats, each a meal in itself, to fried rice and lo mein dishes; all of these cost around $4.00 to $6.00. Or move on to the many beef, chicken, pork, and seafood offerings, such as diced peanut chicken with hot peppers ($6.75), good ol' beef and broccoli ($7.25), shredded pork in garlic sauce ($6.50), and a casserole of mussels, black beans, and more peppers ($7.95). Plenty of vegetarian options too, of course.

Sam's also features a "grill bar," serving up individual veggies or cubes of meat and fish on skewers, not unlike a sushi bar. All are $1.00 to $3.00 each, allowing you to get just as much as you want—though this does not strike Mr. C as a cost-effective way to go. Far better, by the way, are the weekday lunch specials—twenty choices, each $3.95, from 11:30 a.m. to 4:00 p.m.

Shaheen—99 Lexington Ave. (27th St.); 212/683-2139. The area just above Gramercy Park on the East Side is often referred to as "Little India," filled as it is with Indian restaurants and food markets. Not all of these eateries are as inexpensive as one might hope, but Mr. C has located a couple for you. Shaheen takes a fast-food approach to Indian food, with everything on its menu displayed buffet-style, allowing you to choose what looks good and take it back to your table. In fact, just about everything here does look very good, and what's more, it doesn't cost much.

The appetizers, whether meat or vegetarian, are all between $1.50 and $3.00. Deep-fried turnovers filled with green peas and potatoes, for instance, are $1.50 per plate; a meat version filled with ground beef is $2.50. You can even get tandoori chicken, often an expensive entree, as an inexpensive ($2.50) appetizer.

At these prices you can sample your way through the rest of the menu as well. The meat and poultry entrees include alloo gosht, a ground lamb dish cooked with potatoes ($3.25); murgh masala, a mildly spicy chicken and tomato concoction (also $3.25), and shahi murgh badami, an unusual chicken dish cooked up in a white almond sauce ($4.95). The vegetable entrees are even better deals: a mixed vegetable plate is just $2.50, and palek taneer, a heaping portion of cooked spinach mixed with a soft, sweet cheese, is $3.00. Yogurt karhee, a northern Indian specialty, is fried vegetables in a spicy yogurt curry sauce. That's only $2.75. There are also more expensive items on the menu. The house specialties range from $7.00 to $8.00 for a full plate; these include baby lamb chops and tambouri chicken kebabs. You may also want to try a combination platter, such as the meat or vegetable thalee ($6.00 each). These feature a meat or vegetable curry dish served up with rice, roti bread, a vegetable, and a side salad.

Although Indian restaurants are not especially noted for their desserts, Shaheen has a very colorful array from which to choose. Try the russ malaee, homemade cheese balls baked and soaked in a sweetened milk and nut mixture ($2.00), for an unusual finish to your meal. By the way, Shaheen also offers a buffet lunch, which is served Monday through Friday from 11:00 a.m. to 3:00 p.m.—$5.95 gets you all you can eat. This is also a place you can invite a friend to. While it may take the fast-food angle, it does not look like a fast-food joint: the tables are covered with tablecloths, the interior is quite comfortable, and the service is as gracious as at any fine Indian restaurant.

Just around the corner, two blocks up from Lexington Avenue, is another fast-food-style Indian restaurant, **Curry in a Hurry** (130 East 29th St.; 212/889-1159). This one even manages to look like a McDonald's, and follows the same format: you walk up to the counter, look up at the menu board, and place your order. But don't be fooled! While the decor is minimal, the food is often recommended just as highly as that of other area restaurants. If you're in a hurry yourself, it will probably serve you quite well.

Tibetan Kitchen—444 Third Avenue (33rd St.); 212/679-6286. As Mr. C has noted elsewhere in this book, New York has at least one restaurant for every country in the world. Tibet is ably represented by this humble, quiet restaurant in Murray Hill. Just stepping in the door takes you into a serene world of soft lighting, Eastern music, and polite, attentive service. A pot of black Tibetan tea is instantly brought to your table and poured for you. The small room is simply decorated in dark wood, with a spiral staircase down to a second dining room with a bar.

The menu divides almost evenly into vegetarian and meat dishes, most of which are priced between $6.00 to $8.00. Start with a tasty bowl of thang soup ($2.00), a variation on egg-drop with spinach and a clear, light broth base. Move on to a plate of steamed dumplings filled with vegetables or beef ($6.50 and $7.25), which the menu notes as Tibet's most popular dish (good to know in case you ever get on "Jeopardy"). Or, try a huge plate of tentsel ($6.95), sauteed peas with bits of fried egg and shredded beef. Tibetan chicken curry is $8.25; for anyone looking for a quick description of this cuisine, Indian food is probably the nearest relative. Another interesting curry dish, Himalayan Khatsa ($5.90), consists of curried chunks of cauliflower, peas and tofu—served cold and spicy on a bed of lettuce.

By the time you leave, you're sure to feel warm and relaxed—as though you'd been much further away from it all. Tibetan Kitchen does not open for lunch on Saturdays, and is closed all day Sundays.

MIDTOWN MANHATTAN WEST

(14th Street to 59th Street, West of Fifth Avenue)

Afghan Kebab House—764 Ninth Ave. (51st St.); 212/307-1612, and 1345 Second Ave. (70th St.); 212/517-2776. You can travel the world by walking along Ninth Avenue in midtown. Eastern, Middle Eastern, Mexican, Cuban, South American...you name it. Of all the ethnic restaurants one can sample here, the Afghan Kebab House is frequently singled out for good food and value. If you've never tried Afghan cuisine, it's sort of a cross between Greek and Indian—lots of grilled meats, cooked with spices and served with rice.

Most of the main dishes here are in the $8.00 range and offer good portions of lamb, beef, chicken, or even fish—cooked up in shish kebab form, but served without the skewers. Half-spiced chicken (that's half a chicken, all of which is spiced) offers up plenty of food, as does the spicy fish kebab plate; for vegetarians there's palau baudinjan—grilled eggplant with onions, tomato and herbs. Meat dishes are grilled over wood charcoal, for a delicious and mildly spicy taste. All plates come with brown basmati rice, a side salad with a mint-yogurt sauce, and a slice of warm Afghan bread, similar to pita bread, over the top.

For appetizers, try the mishawa soup (lentils and vegetables) or the aushak—boiled dumplings with scallions and herbs in a mint-yogurt sauce. Each is $2.50, and evidence that all cultures basically serve their own versions of the same foods! The restaurant itself is tiny, narrow, with a floor that slants a bit at the rear. The decor is minimal and a bit rundown, but offers some authentic touches from the Far East. Customers are encouraged to bring their own wine or beer, if they so desire.

Baby Fox Cafe—12 West 55th St.; 212/397-2020. In the midtown and Fifth Avenue shopping area, it can be quite a challenge to find a quick place to stop in for a bite to eat without shattering your budget. Baby Fox Cafe is a bright, clean deli/cafeteria with a decor that reminds one of nothing so much as an ice cream parlor complete with ceiling fans. Here you will find home-style soups, sandwiches, and pastries at very reasonable prices. Try the chicken pasta primavera salad ($5.95), made with chunks of chicken breast, tricolor pasta, and fresh vegetables. Another winning selection: a slice of quiche florentine filled with spinach, mushrooms, and Swiss cheese. It's only $4.95; for a dollar more you can add a side salad.

Soups are made from scratch on the premises (no MSG); each day you can choose from a dozen or so varieties. The list changes daily, but typical entries include split pea, lentil, eggplant parmesan, asparagus, black bean, and tarragon tomato. Baby Fox offers a number of gourmet salads—for instance, a chicken salad with water chestnuts and cashews—priced at $5.95. The menu is large and sensibly health-conscious; even the pastries are sugar-free. Mr. C was especially enamored of the muffins (pineapple-orange, banana-raisin bran) and scones (apricot-almond-cranberry). This is a good breakfast or lunch spot that is open seven days a week, from 7:00 a.m. to approximately 5:30 p.m.

Bali Burma—651 Ninth Ave. (45th St.); 212/265-9868. Elsewhere along the international stroll that is Ninth Avenue, Bali Burma serves up Burmese and Indonesian food in an elegant setting that looks as if it should cost you more than it does. Linen tablecloths, a couple of fresh flowers on each table (in the obligatory mineral-water-bottle vase) and exposed-brick walls make this a nice, relaxed place to dine. The food, meanwhile, resembles the other cuisines from this part of the world—particularly Thai—but with its own distinctive twists.

A prime example is the "Burmese Royal Chicken" ($8.95), which is made with coconut milk curry. But anyone timid about spicy food need not worry about the word "curry"; this dish isn't hot at all. It's more like a very tasty stew, filled with tender chunks of meat and potatoes. The sauce is good for sopping up with the rice on the side.

There are, of course, spicier entrees, such as duck with lemon grass and "Flaming Beef," in a red chili pepper and coconut sauce. All of the chicken, duck, beef, and pork dinner entrees are priced at $8.95; rice dishes, noodles (good ol' Pad Thai), and vegetarian entrees range from $5.95 to $7.95.

Lunch specials are a particularly good deal at Bali Burma; over twenty options, each $4.95, give you plenty of meat or vegetables, along with soup or salad (go for the soup), red Indonesian rice (mildly spicy) and a small, crispy spring roll. The specials are offered from 11:30 a.m. to 4:00 p.m. on weekdays.

Bella Napoli—150 West 49th St.; 212/719-2819. Nothing fancy here—just good, old-fashioned, southern Italian food. Order it at the counter and get it to go, or bring it to one of the small tables. The moment you walk in, though, you won't mind the lack of decor; the air just smells too good.

There are twenty different pastas, all $5.95 each: Capellini primavera, baked lasagna, fettucine Alfredo, spaghetti in shrimp sauce, and more. Or go for a nine-inch pizza ($3.50, toppings $1.00 each) or the newest rage, a "stuffed pie" slice ($3.00). They have full-size pizzas too, with regular or whole-wheat crusts.

Chicken dishes are all $7.95, whether you choose Francese, Parmagiana, Paillard, or one of half-a-dozen more. Veal dishes are $8.95, and all of these include spaghetti or a salad on the side. There's so much more—fried calamari ($8.50), seafood appetizers, calzones, you name it. If you're wandering around Times Square and you're tired of the Italian food cranked out factory-style at Sbarros and other chains, then stop into Bella Napoli for the real thing.

Cabana Carioca—133 West 45th St.; 212/730-8375. Take a look at the menu for this popular, long-time Brazilian restaurant and you may wonder what it's doing in this book. It's just outside of Times Square, where everything is expensive. The dinners—steaks and fish, mostly—are around $15.00 and up. Ah, but wait! Next to the entrance is another sign, with handwritten daily specials, and they are all less than half the price of the regular menu. Why? Because you can only get them at the bar.

And that's the secret of cheap dining at this fine restaurant, a favorite of native Brazilians and Portuguese, and of native New Yorkers as well. The bar is small, perhaps a dozen seats or so; but you can usually find a seat except at peak times (they get a huge pre-theater crowd). Is it worth squeezing in? Absolutely.

First of all, wherever you sit, you're entitled to the salad bar, which is small but well stocked with greens, chick peas, vegetables, tuna, and fresh bread. This itself could fill you up, but wait—don't forget that you've also ordered the *feijoada*, which the waiters simply call the "Brazilian National Dish" to save time and embarrassing pronounciation questions. And here comes your plate, a thick dark stew piled atop a mound of white rice, garnished with orange wedges and more salad on the side. The stew consists of large chunks of grilled pork, slices of mild sausage, and black beans. If you'd sat at a table, it would have cost you $14.95. Now get ready. At the bar, the whole thing—salad, dinner, and all—costs a mere $4.95. Unbelievable.

There are half a dozen other choices on any given day, such as a pot of cooked mussels for $5.75; shell steak or grilled shrimp, each $8.00; and for some reason, pot roast for $4.75. The shrimp appetizer alone costs $7.95 at the tables.

So is there a catch? Sure—the drinks. Unless you get a soda, which will still be overpriced, one drink can cost you almost as much as the rest of the meal. Hey, they have to stay in business somehow. Meanwhile, when you get so much great food for five bucks, what the heck?

Cafe Edison—228 West 47th St.; 212/840-5000. Theatergoers have known about this Times Square institution for years. Located within the Hotel Edison on 47th St., the Cafe Edison offers deli-style food in good portions and with relatively quick service, making it a great spot for a thrifty pre-theater meal or an inexpensive lunch. There aren't many such non-touristy options in this area. The burgers here are cheap, certainly, but nothing to rave about; Mr. C advises going instead with the triple-decker club sandwich—sliced turkey with chopped liver, lettuce, and tomato. Another good bet: the fresh chicken salad with bacon, lettuce, tomato, coleslaw, and Russian dressing. All of these sandwiches are priced between $5.25 and $6.95.

There are plenty of salad platters to choose from, too; they're all priced between $5.75 and $8.00, and in addition to the tuna, shrimp, or salmon, you get potato salad, coleslaw, lettuce, tomato, hard-boiled egg, and your choice of bread. For a hot meal, try a plate of good old New York cheese blintzes with sour cream ($5.25); browned corned-beef hash with a poached egg over the top ($4.95); or broiled chopped sirloin steak ($7.95). Dinner entrees come with a side salad, french fries, roll, and butter. Desserts are warm, but not baked on the premises; you are best advised to try something like the Skyscraper Ice Cream Soda ($2.45), one of a number of creditable ice cream drinks and dishes on the menu.

Cupcake Cafe—522 Ninth Ave. (39th St.); 212/465-1530. Want to impress people with a real "insider's" discovery? Just a block down from the Port Authority, amidst the terrific seafood shops and butchers (profiled in the "Food Stores" section of this book), is a hidden treat. Even from across the street the Cupcake Cafe looks like a dingy old bakery—but inside it has a handful of small tables, where you can sip herbal teas or rich coffees while nibbling on yummy sweets and other delights. The cupcakes, of course, are wonderful. They come in small and large sizes ($1.00 and $2.00), and in such flavors as chocolate with mocha frosting and maple walnut with maple frosting.

The cafe also offers an array of other goodies: Chocolate chip cookies (three for $1.00), lemon poppyseed muffins ($1.25), and homemade quiche and individual pizzas with fresh toppings (each $3.00). The surroundings are strictly no-frills; that's part of the bohemian charm. The bakery is at the back of the store, and you can watch the latest batches being carted out to the counter.

Cynthiya and Robert—Sixth Ave. at 50th St. (southwest corner); no phone. If there are fifteen thousand restaurants in New York City, there must be twice as many pushcart vendors, hawking every kind of food from knishes to kebabs. There are far too many, and they are far too transient, for Mr. C to deal with in this book; one wagon, however, has hitched itself to the same midtown corner for the last twenty years or more. This husband-and-wife team have sold enough sandwiches to put their children through college—and the kids' names on the cart.

Located right across the street from Radio City Music Hall, these folks crank out hot and tasty subs faster than the Rockettes can kick. The basic chicken sandwich is just $3.00; chicken parmigiana is $4.00. Steak subs are $3.25, and steak parmigiana is $4.25; sausage and peppers is $3.00, sausage parm is $3.75 . . . and so on. You can request extras, like onions and a tangy, spicy sauce slathered on top. Then take your

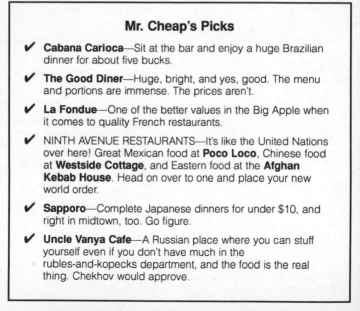

Mr. Cheap's Picks

- ✔ **Cabana Carioca**—Sit at the bar and enjoy a huge Brazilian dinner for about five bucks.
- ✔ **The Good Diner**—Huge, bright, and yes, good. The menu and portions are immense. The prices aren't.
- ✔ **La Fondue**—One of the better values in the Big Apple when it comes to quality French restaurants.
- ✔ NINTH AVENUE RESTAURANTS—It's like the United Nations over here! Great Mexican food at **Poco Loco**, Chinese food at **Westside Cottage**, and Eastern food at the **Afghan Kebab House**. Head on over to one and place your new world order.
- ✔ **Sapporo**—Complete Japanese dinners for under $10, and right in midtown, too. Go figure.
- ✔ **Uncle Vanya Cafe**—A Russian place where you can stuff yourself even if you don't have much in the rubles-and-kopecks department, and the food is the real thing. Chekhov would approve.

lunch over to one of Sixth Avenue's many large, outdoor fountains and engage in the two best activities in New York: Eating and people-watching.

Check 'em out. Mr. C's expert in the neighborhood, a man who has dined al fresco there on a regular basis for much of his adult life, calls them "absolutely the class of the area." They've even been written up in the New York Times, no less. These folks are here for good—and they are good.

Dosanko—1500 Broadway (43rd St.); 212/354-2550, 123 West 49th St.; 212/245-4090, and 24 West 56th St.; 212/757-4339. See listing under "Manhattan East."

Film Center Cafe—635 Ninth Ave. (44th St.); 212/262-2525. Here's a very cool place to hang out. The prices are a bit above Mr. C's $10.00 limit, but not too far; and, if you're a showbiz fan, Film Center Cafe will make you feel like you're in "Chinatown" (the Jack Nicholson movie, that is). Walk in through the dark, laid-back bar, past a genuine wooden telephone booth, into the dining room at the back. The walls are painted with the trademarks of the major film studios—Paramount's peak, MGM's lion. These are illuminated by special lights that create the look of venetian blinds, as if you're in sunny L.A. with the shades drawn. Bring your own shades if you wish, to add to the effect.

Hollywood illusion may be the backdrop, but the food is perfectly real and deserves top billing. Mr. C's dining co-star tried the broccoli ravioli ($10.95)—large dumplings carefully choreographed on the plate. They were tender and moist, filled with bits of broc and ricotta cheese, and topped with a tomato basil sauce. [Mr. C cast himself as the man with the chicken salad] ($7.95), a big plate with warm strips of white meat on top of mixed greens and vegetables.

Dinner entrees, like chicken Kiev and shell steak, go up into the $12.00-to-$14.00 range. Stick with something like the burgers ($6.95, including fries) or the vegetarian plate ($7.95) of steamed veggies over rice with a Thai peanut sauce; better yet, try the cafe at lunch, when the same menu is offered at several dollars less per entree. The atmosphere is fun, and makes this a unique experience.

The Good Diner—554 Eleventh Ave. (at 42nd St.); 212/967-2661. With the exception of its slightly out-of-the-way location (a healthy walk from the midtown theater district you were probably visiting), The Good Diner really is everything a good diner ought to be. It's big, bright, and colorful—and it serves up food from a menu to match. There are plenty of genuine, six-ounce, fresh-ground burgers to choose from, starting at $2.85. You'll also find a cornucopia of hot, cold, triple-decker, and open-faced sandwiches, and custom-made pizza available in three sizes and with a bewildering array of toppings, including broccoli and andouille sausage. The Good Diner also offers plenty of desserts and, of course, breakfast, which is served all day and includes such treats as challah bread French toast ($2.90), a stack of buttermilk pancakes ($2.90), and three-egg omelets served with homefries and toast (from $2.85). There are two dozen dinner entrees, most in the $7.00-to-$10.00 range; all include your choice of soup or salad, potato, and a vegetable or pasta side dish. Good old spaghetti and meatballs ($6.95) at the Diner is a frugal classic. Mr. C's dining companion ordered one of the daily specials: a roasted half-chicken served with spicy Yankee bean soup, plenty of stuffing, home-style mashed potatoes, steamed vegetables, and a rice pudding dessert—all for $7.45. There was enough here to feed, if not an army, at least the

Japanese bobsled team. The Good Diner, which is open twenty-four hours a day, also offers a children's menu—appropriate, considering the near-universal appeal of the place.

The Great American Health Bar—123 West 39th St.; 212/354-1100. See listing under "Midtown Manhattan East."

Hamburger Harry's—145 West 45th St.; 212/840-2756, and 157 Chambers St.; 212/267-4446. This pair of eateries offers up a good, dependable burger and fries—along with other dishes at reasonable prices. The burgers are made from seven ounces of fresh ground beef, cooked to order over a coal-and-wood grill. There are over a dozen varieties. These start at $3.95 for your basic; add American, cheddar, Monterey Jack, Jarlsberg etc. for a dollar more; and another buck for fancier models, such as the Hollywood, with avocado slices and alfalfa sprouts. Any one you choose can be made into a "platter" for two dollars extra; this gets you a mildly spicy red cole slaw and your choice of new potato salad or curly French fries.

Harry's also offers other kinds of food, such as Cajun fried chicken ($5.95), beef or chicken burritos ($7.95), and various daily specials. The food is good, if not outstanding, and the service is prompt and polite. There is a curving counter for the lunch crowd, and bottled beers include Samuel Adams and Corona. The atmosphere is not much like a bar, though; more like the kind of restaurant you'd see at a suburban mall, making a good blend for families who want to stay a step or two above the fast-food chains. Even Mr. C, who prefers to save money on good food, keeps away from those.

Kosher Delight—1359 Broadway (36th St.); 212/563-3366, and 1156 Sixth Ave. (45th St.) ; 212/869-6699. Kosher, it may be; as for the delight part, well....This looks like a great idea—a fast-food restaurant in midtown where you can really depend on the quality. They're clean, have a large and varied menu, and deliver to offices in the area at no charge. But alas, be careful what you choose. "Glatt kosher" may mean healthy, but it doesn't guarantee good quality here. Mr. C tried a hamburger and found it to be no more appealing than the bland, thin, soggy patties at Burger King.

You'll be better off with a sandwich, like turkey or hot corned beef; but at $6.25 they're a bit overpriced. The hot, open-faced versions, with KD's good French fries, are a better bet. So are the Middle Eastern choices, such as a falafel sandwich ($3.35), to which you can add your own fixings at the salad bar. The salad bar itself is filled with lots of good things—greens, veggies, chick peas, pastas.

They even have a Chinese menu, with beef and broccoli, lemon chicken, and more—but again, pricy at $7.95 and up. These, at least, are freshly made and, of course, use no M.S.G. Grab an egg roll and some chicken soup ($1.85 and $2.95, respectively) and have a snack here instead of a full meal. Kosher Delight is included in this book more because of high hopes; a healthy, no-tip alternative to expensive midtown restaurants and junk food. Give 'em a try; just choose carefully.

La Fondue—43 West 55th St.; 212/581-0820. A New York landmark for many years, La Fondue sits in the middle of a mini-"Restaurant Row" of continental bistros near Fifth Avenue. The difference is that La Fondue is much less expensive and a heck of a lot more fun. The atmosphere is festive, with everyone seated at long tables as in a tavern somewhere in the French countryside. This does allow the place to pack in a lot of folks, in the front room, the back room, and the upstairs rooms.

The food, meanwhile, is

first-rate. This is also of the simple and rustic variety, in hearty portions. Croque Monsieur ($9.75) is the classic made with Danish ham and Swiss Gruyere cheese, a sort of deep-dish Monte Cristo sandwich covered in a creamy sauce and baked until the whole platter is brown and bubbling on top. Croque Madame is a similar treatment of a boneless chicken breast. All entrees, by the way, come with a green salad and fresh sourdough bread.

The restaurant also boasts huge salads, like the Crab Klondike salad ($8.95), heaped with chunks of Alaskan crab meat, fruits, vegetables, greens and bread. Soups may be ordered as an appetizer or an entree with bread and salad. Quiches and pastas are also available.

But the real treat here, of course, is the house specialty: Fondue! Priced from $14.00 to $17.00, with enough for two to share, there are several varieties to enjoy as a meal, or for dessert. Cheese fondue blends Swiss Gruyere and Emmenthal cheeses with wine and seasonings in a pot; dip in some crusty bread, or apple wedges. Filet mignon or crab claws fondue allow you to dip pieces of meat into hot oil and flash-cook them to your own taste. And everyone knows what to do with chocolate fondue. La F's Swiss chocolate is blended with honey, almonds, sweet cream, and brandy. Très romantique, non?

La Fondue's prices are even better at lunchtime, and they also serve up a number of lunch specials. The "Soup-er Stockpot" ($7.95) offers you a choice of international soups, from French onion to gazpacho, along with salad, sourdough bread, a pot of tea or glass of wine, and a slice of homemade "Chocolate Whipped Cream Icebox Cake" for dessert. But then, you'd miss the fondue.

Little Saigon Cafe—374 West 46th St.; 212/956-0639. How this tiny spot nestled its way onto pricey Restaurant Row seems a marvel of diplomacy. The little Vietnamese woman who runs it can barely speak English; but she keeps smiling while she cooks up a storm. The shop is basically a kitchen storefront geared to take-out, with just a few neatly-decorated tables. Her menu consists of two dozen items, and none is priced higher than $6.00; she cooks everything to order, and the food is delicious.

The choices cover both Viet and Chinese cuisines, ranging from stir-fried shrimp with vegetables ($5.00) to lemon grass beef with rice ($4.00). Kimting shrimp rolls are the house specialty, combining shrimp and crab meat with vegetables, wrapped in delicate rice paper, and deep-fried. You get six of these piping-hot babies for $6.00. For something a little different, try pork sauteed with green peppers in tomato sauce ($5.00) or the mildly spicy vegetable soup—just a buck. Little Saigon, a few steps in from Ninth Avenue, is a pleasant and cheap alternative to the ritzy French and Italian bistros up and down the block. The cafe is closed on Sundays; and alas, the 9:00 a.m. to 7:00 p.m. hours make it better for lunch than pre-theater.

Manhattan Plaza Cafe—482 West 43rd St., Third Floor; 212/695-5808. Want to find a great theater district secret that actors have known about for years? Manhattan Plaza is a complex of red-brick buildings that offer subsidized housing for artists; this corner, at 10th Avenue, includes a rather elegant health club and restaurant that are out of the way and relatively inexpensive.

The cafe is upstairs, through the health club, taking you into a lush, bright atrium with a bar and small tables. One more flight (don't worry, they're short), and you're in the restaurant area. This affords a lovely view of the bar/atrium and of the swimming pool, surrounded by palms and ferns. The pool is in the next building, accessible by an outdoor walkway; in winter it's a funny sight to watch people wrapped in heavy coats passing between these two tropical oases. As a matter of fact, if you can't get to Florida during the cold months, passing an hour or two in this cafe feels like a quick (cheap!) getaway.

The food is casual, leaning toward the trendy nouvelle styles; it's not super cheap, but it's close. Salads, sandwiches, and pastas all stay around the $5.00-to-$9.00 range, with entrees going up to $12.50. But that's for a ribeye steak in a porcini mushroom sauce, complete with baked potato and three other vegetables. Similar deals are found with grilled tuna ($11.00), chicken pie ($8.50) and other daily specials.

Stick with the simpler fare and you'll do even better. "Uncle Andy's Hamburger" ($5.25) comes with French fries, lettuce, tomato, and onion; the grilled chicken breast sandwich ($5.50) includes shoestring fries, and your choice of cilantro yogurt or honey-mustard spread. Pasta Puttanesca ($6.00) is a good-sized platter of fusilli noodles in a tomato sauce flavored with garlic, pepper, and black olives. Among the many interesting salads, try the ratatouille ($6.00) or the hot chicken salad ($7.50), served over mixed greens and grilled vegetables.

Manhattan Plaza Cafe also serves a dandy $8.95/$9.95 brunch on weekends, with such choices as eggs Florentine, whole-wheat pancakes with blueberries, and a smoked salmon plate. Adding to the fun is the possibility of rubbing elbows with someone you've seen on the stage or on television. Who says the actor's life has to be tough?

Metro Delicatessen—790 Eighth Ave. (48th St.); 212/581-9100. A block over from the Theater District at the corner of 48th Street, the Metro Deli is a part of the Midtown Ramada Hotel—and offers a hefty taste of New York for either the tourist or the theatergoer. It's big and spacious, with plenty of tables and an open deli counter. Service is fast and courteous. After dining here, you may cover as much ground as the menu; soups, salads, sandwiches, eggs, burgers, full meat and fish dinners, desserts, and more.

There are lots of "Old World" specialties, such as potato pancakes, pirogies, and cheese blintzes, each $6.95 per plate (for a dollar more, you can get a combination platter). Other main dishes include Hungarian beef goulash ($9.95), in a tasty brown gravy with vegetables, served over wide noodles. A roasted half-chicken with potato and vegetable is $8.95, as is a hearty corned beef and cabbage dinner.

Burgers start at $3.95 plain, ranging up to about $8 for a bacon cheddar deluxe with all the fixings. Also at $8.95, a hot open-face turkey sandwich comes piled high with real roast turkey meat, and French fries on the side. Among the huge cold sandwiches, try the triple-decker corned beef, turkey, and pastrami at $8.25. And, if you have room for dessert, go for the homemade cheesecake ($2.95).

The Metro Delicatessen may not seem all that "cheap," but you get a lot of food, and prices here check in well under the recently opened Roxy Delicatessen, just a block over in Times Square. The Metro even adds a piano bar, with no cover charge, on Wednesday through Saturday evenings.

Mom's Bagels of New York—15 West 45th St.; 212/764-1566. This is what a midtown quick-food joint should be like. Whether or not there is a Mom making the bagels, bialys and onion breads, they are made fresh on the premises under religious supervision. That means kosher dairy; there is no meat on the menu, though they do serve fish. Can't have bagels without lox, after all, or smoked whitefish either.

A basic bagel and cream cheese is $1.45; fancier cheeses include walnut and raisin, blueberry, and others. The bagels themselves don't go far beyond the familiar, but they're good. Sandwiches on a bagel or bialy (sort of a filled-in, flatter bagel) include tuna salad ($4.20), sable ($4.75), gouda cheese ($3.25), and many others. All of these are also available as platters, with your bread on the side, for a few dollars more; nothing tops $7.45.

Mom's also makes other old-world treats, like cheese blintzes and potato pancakes (each $4.50), apple-noodle pudding ($2.50) and homemade soups. And, until 11:00 a.m., you can get a breakfast special of scrambled eggs, home fries, coffee, and a bagel or bialy for $1.85. Being a breakfast and lunch kind of place, catering largely to the business crowd, Mom's closes by 6:00 p.m. Being kosher, they close at 2:30 p.m. on Fridays, and their only weekend hours are Sundays from 10:00 a.m. to 3:30 p.m.

Moonstruck West—400 West 23rd St.; 212/924-3709 and 449 Third Ave. (31st St.); 212/213-1100. See listing under "Midtown Manhattan East."

Ngone—823 Sixth Ave. (29th St.); 212/967-7899. There are probably not too many Senegalese restaurants in the city—much less any which could almost be mistaken for a fast-food restaurant. But that's what Ngone is, right in the heart of the Garment District (and just across the street from a terrific vintage clothing store, The Family Jewels; check them out elsewhere in this book). It's quite a find.

You can place your order at the counter, looking at the display of wonderful stews behind the glass, and then take your tray to a table. So what is the cuisine of Senegal like? Well, the music on the sound system is hot, but the food, surprisingly, is not. There are some spicy dishes, like Thiou curry ($7.95), lamb with boiled potatoes and carrots. But most of the preparations, such as chicken Mafe($7.95), which is served in a peanut sauce, are tasty without being sharp to the tongue. This chicken is served on the bone, again with cooked vegetables, and couscous on the side—great for finishing off the sauce.

There are various other meat and vegetarian entrees, as well as appetizers like legume soup ($3.25), or fataya—a kind of dough filled with chopped meat or fish and a mildly zingy sauce (also $3.25). Lunchtime, from 11:00 a.m. to 4:00 p.m., offers one of the best bargains in town: Any entree is just $5.00—and they even throw in the coffee. Very friendly folks, too.

Oakwood Cafe—291 Seventh Ave. (27th St.); 212/627-2157. Across from the Fashion Institute of Technology (and a block up from the equally legendary S & W Clothing store) this trendy cafe has recently sprung up, with a fabulous assortment of baked goods, sandwiches, and quiches. Yes, it's yuppie, and not super-cheap; however, for a pleasant and dependable bite to eat in this hard-working neighborhood, stop in.

The first thing you see are brownies, cookies, and other pastries—a display case packed with 'em. You can order take-out here, and there's even a selection of newspapers and magazines being sold as well. If you prefer, move past all this and have a seat at one of the dozens of small cafe tables further back in the store. Sandwiches range from $3.95 for a BLT to $6.25 for shrimp salad;

there are some interesting choices, too, such as lemon chicken salad ($5.75)—large chunks of chicken in a tangy sauce, with strips of red and green peppers. All sandwiches come on your choice of thick-sliced white, wheat, rye or pumpernickel. A "Muenster Melt" (hmm, sounds like a Halloween song), $4.25, comes on an open-face bagel with cream cheese, tomato, and alfalfa sprouts.

Plus various quiches ($5.50), smoked fish platters, soups and salads, and a large selection of coffees, teas, cappuccinos, fruit juices, and sodas. The dining area is clean and bright, with high ceilings, and makes a good place to meet for conversation over a quick lunch.

Ollie's Noodle Shop—190 West 44th St.; 212/921-5988, 2315 Broadway (84th St.); 212/362-3111, and 2957 Broadway (116th St.); 212/362-3712. See listing under "Upper West Side."

Poco Loco—598 Ninth Ave. (43rd St.); 212/765-7626. Who would expect such a hip hangout only a block away from the Port Authority Bus Terminal? Poco Loco is a funky, lively Mexican restaurant with an attitude that makes it seem more like you're in the Village. Of course, the location is also close to Off-Broadway's Theater Row and cabaret scene, so that explains it. Music is loud and soulful—definitely not the Tijuana Brass. There is a small, friendly bar up front; half-a-dozen fine Mexican beers are proffered. The walls are painted in hot colors, adorned with wacky "Day of the Dead" artwork. The waiters' work area was decorated with a "Lite-Brite" toy—remember those? On certain nights, you may even have your palm read.

The food also distinguishes Poco Loco from the rest; they use all-natural ingredients, and will even substitute marinated tofu for meat and fish in most of their dishes. And they like to experiment. So, while a quesadilla is always on the menu ($5.50, made with roasted garlic and topped with guacamole), you may also find a version filled with smoked chicken as the daily special ($1.00 more). The "Seizure Salad," a peppered-up Caesar's, and the Poco Loco Burrito (each $5.50), will keep you busy for a while too.

Moving on to larger meals, try the "Ponderosa Pie" ($7.25), flour tortillas layered with chicken, salsa, cheese and vegetables. Mr. C's companion chose to try the most gringo dish on the menu, "Chicken Strips al Mojo de Ajo" ($7.50), tender chunks of meat in a creamy white wine and garlic sauce, served with cilantro rice. It was fabulous, and not at all your typical Mexican—but you see, that's the point. This place is not content to serve the same food as all the other south-of-the-border joints in town. They're obviously a little crazy—and very successful.

Sam's—263 West 45th St.; 212/719-5416. If you're in the heart of the Manhattan theater district not long before curtain time, you shouldn't expect to find too many cheap dining options. Sam's is a happy exception, however, and one that will serve you well. It's right across the street from the Royale Theater. This cozy, brick-walled restaurant/bar serves a $14.95 pre-theater dinner. While this is above Mr. C's normal budgetary guidelines, we should note that the dinner includes soup or salad, one of many entrees, *and dessert and coffee.* More to the point, they'll get you in and out in time for the show.

The large menu of entrees includes steaks, all sorts of chicken dinners (most of which lean toward the Italian), and seafood. If you are looking for something lighter, take a look at the burger selection ($5.95 each) or the array of good, thick sandwiches, like corned beef from $5.95 to $7.95. Sandwiches and burgers are served with thick-cut French fries. The homemade lasagna is $7.95; stir-fried chicken served over egg noodles is just $8.95.

Sam's also stays open late for a bite right after the show. If you're still eating around midnight, you'll find your repast at Sam's extended by one of the city's most unusual floor shows as the waiters celebrate the end of their shift. Hard to describe, but worth staying up for.

Sapporo—152 West 49th St.; 212/956-4678. Sapporo is another of midtown's many inexpensive Japanese restaurants. Here you can get a large meal for well under $10.00 and come away feeling healthy as well as full. The emphasis is on noodle dishes; try the ramen noodles in a curry soup ($5.30). Also of interest is the Sapporo Special Ramen, an assortment of meats and vegetables combined with the noodle soup ($5.65). There are, in addition, a number of substantial meat-or-seafood-on-rice entrees, priced around $5.75; the menu also features items like sauteed pork in a ginger and soy sauce ($6.45). There are lots of great selections here, and the food at Sapporo comes with high recommendations from both Mr. C and his network of Manhattan Japanese restaurant junkies. Definitely worth a visit.

Tenth Avenue Jukebox Cafe—637 Tenth Ave. (45th St.); 212/315-4690. The name says it all, folks. This is a comfortable and cozy neighborhood cafe and bar—and a very nice place to end up if you find yourself wandering aimlessly around the Hell's Kitchen area, which can sometimes happen to the best of us.

This place is definitely a step above the rest of the neighborhood. You'll find good beers (Guinness, Foster's Lager) on tap, and plenty of snack foods and substantial meals, all at very good prices. Appetizers include French onion soup ($3.25) or a half-dozen baked littleneck clams ($5.95). Also available: salads and ten-inch pizzas ($5.95 for the basic model, with additional toppings $1.00 each). Pasta dishes are all priced from $7.95 to $8.95, including tricolor cheese tortellini Alfredo and chicken primavera over spaghetti in a light tomato sauce (each $8.95).

The Cafe has plenty of good old burgers and sandwiches, too. A bacon cheese steakburger is $6.75 and comes with French fries, as does the grilled turkey, bacon, and cheddar sandwich on rye bread, priced at $6.95. Want a full dinner? There are a number to choose from, and they all come with pasta. Chicken parmigiana and stuffed eggplant are $8.95 each. The atmosphere is informal, relaxed, and even a little artsy—but never pretentious.

Uncle Vanya Cafe—315 West 54th St.; 212/262-0542. Tucked away on a side street just off of Eighth Avenue in midtown, Uncle Vanya is another great New York find that will give you a real experience of the Old Country—namely Russia. Since the restaurant is actually secondary to the catering and take-out business that operates here, the food is sometimes offered in ways you may consider unusual. If you want chicken cutlets, for example, you will need to order them individually at $3.75 apiece. (The chicken cutlet sandwich is $5.50. Bread included.) A similar approach holds for items like stuffed cabbages ($2.50 apiece) and salmon pojharski, which is a cutlet of ground fresh salmon in a dill and lemon sauce ($3.50 apiece). A hearty serving of beef stroganoff is $7.00, and a small portion of Russian meatballs in a sour cream sauce is $2.50. (You'll probably want to order a double serving of that one, as it's quite modest in size.) This unusual serving style gives you the opportunity to mix and match a larger dinner that fits both your appetite and your budget—and lets you sample a good many Old-World delicacies in a single visit. You might want to experiment with some of Uncle Vanya's intriguing salads, for example. The herring forshmak salad is a chopped herring salad with bits of apple and lemon; that goes for $1.75 per quarter pound. The Salad Olivier, which is the same price, may not have anything to do with the late Sir Laurence, but it is a tasty and refreshing chicken salad featuring potatoes, onions, cucumbers, and apples. There are also sandwiches, smoked fish by the piece, and lots of dinner pastries like piroshki, a delicious meat, cheese, or cabbage dumpling. As for dessert pastries, try a poppyseed pierogi for $1.95. Many of these, as you can probably tell, are fairly unusual Russian specialties.

All in all, Mr. C finds Uncle Vanya's well worth a try. The service is very friendly and the accents are just about as heavy as the food—usually a pretty good sign when it comes to chasing down authentic ethnic cooking.

Urban Grill—330 West 58th St.; 212/586-3300, and 1613 Second Ave. (84th St.); 212/744-2122. Lots of burgers here, and they're good, too. Nothing fancy, just your basic half-pounders of real beef grilled over an open flame. The (very) basic burger is just $3.50; add lettuce, tomatoes, and fries for the deluxe platter at $5.50. Then there are the variations: cheeseburger ($3.95/$5.95), baconburger ($4.95/$6.95), and the high-end model, the Urban Burger, which boasts bacon, cheese, mushrooms, and fried onions ($5.95/$7.95).

The Urban Grill also offers sandwiches, like a chicken salad melt on pita bread ($6.50), and salads, like the grilled-vegetable salad ($6.95). Also worth checking out: the marinated, skinless, and boneless chicken breast sandwiches, cooked over charcoal like the burgers and offered with much the same options (and prices). A pretty good selection of beers (including Sam Adams) is available in bottles and on tap.

While the decor is nothing to speak of—pretty much a cross between a coffee shop and a neighborhood bar, complete with the television up in the corner broadcasting sports—you're not going there for atmosphere. You're going for good food that doesn't cost too much, and in that respect the Urban Grill comes through.

Vegetarian Heaven—304 West 58th St.; 212/956-4678. Located at the very southern tip of Columbus Circle, Vegetarian Heaven is an odd mixture of styles: A vegetarian Chinese restaurant with an emphasis on light, healthy cuisine that's also—no kidding—kosher. As if that weren't enough, the spot it occupies was former home to an English-style pub restaurant, which means you'll be enjoying your kosher Chinese food while looking up at walls laden with golf clubs, rowing oars, and, most intriguing of all, stuffed and mounted game. Yes, the target market for this restaurant is *vegetarians*. You figure it out. At any rate, the food is generally quite good, the prices are reasonable, and the service is refreshingly quick and attentive.

The menu boasts over a hundred items, some of which are converted meat and poultry dishes that purport to have found a convincing substitute for their prime ingredients in various tofu preparations. Just to keep things interesting, these pseudo-beef and pseudo-chicken items are listed on the menu as though there were no substitution at all: sliced beef sauteed with peanuts and hot peppers ($8.50), sweet and sour ribs ($8.50), and so on. Some of these efforts are more successful than others; Mr. C and his dining companions were of the opinion that the "beef" dishes were the more successful copies, with "chicken" falling afoul of anything recognizably fowl. You may reach different conclusions about this, but Mr. C doubts it. Meat imitations aside, any number of good, standard vegetarian Chinese dishes can be had here. You'll find a wealth of fried rice dishes (all $5.50) and noodle entrees (around $6.00 each), as well as seafood items that use *real* fish, like the spicy Crispy Whole Fish ($9.50). Ample lunch specials ($4.95) are available Monday through Saturday between 11:00 a.m. and 3:30 p.m.; these may represent the best way for aficionados to sample the more creative concoctions available at Vegetarian Heaven.

Westside Cottage—689 Ninth Ave. (47th St.); 212/245-0800, and 788 Ninth Ave. (52nd St). There must be several billion Chinese restaurants in New York City. Singling any of them out is a tricky exercise; but Westside Cottage, with its two midtown locations, definitely rises above the pack. The decor is trendy and modern continental, with marble-top tables and track lighting; but the menu is far less expensive than the surroundings would suggest, and the portions are substantial indeed. Case in point: Mr. C started with a bowl of Cantonese noodle soup; the waiter brought out a spoon and a small empty bowl. Things looked bleak for a moment, considering the $4.50 price listed on the menu, but presently, the waiter returned with a large metal tureen that seemed, at first glance, only slightly smaller than a Ford Festiva. It was packed with soup, noodles, vegetables, and chicken-filled wontons; as the waiter doled a portion into the smaller bowl, Mr. C quickly repented, realizing that this menu item could easily have served as an entire meal. Indeed, every time the waiter passed by, he took a moment to ladle more from the large bowl to the smaller.

The vast menu at Westside extends to some two-hundred dishes, including a wealth of chicken, pork, seafood, and vegetable entrees priced between $5.00 and $8.00. The chicken items in particular are first-rate; whether you order sesame-flavored, ginger, lemon, or barbecued pineapple chicken, you won't be disappointed. All of these chicken entrees are priced between $6.75 and $7.95. Vegetarian entrees—such as sauteed snow peas, zucchini, and tomatoes—are all priced at $5.95. Rice and noodle dishes begin at just $4.50 for a gargantuan serving that will definitely provide leftovers to take home.

Westside Cottage uses no MSG, ever, makes a point of using only fresh ingredients in all its menu items, and offers a special "Health and Diet Menu" of a half-dozen entrees prepared with no oil, cornstarch, or salt. As if that weren't enough, Westside offers a choice of nearly fifty lunch specials with an entree, rice, and your choice of soup or egg roll, priced between $4.50 and $5.50—featuring pepper steak, shrimp with lobster sauce, and scallops with broccoli. Available weekdays between 11:30 a.m. and 4:30 p.m., this is a lunch deal you will be hard pressed to beat. It's easy to see why Westside Cottage is regularly named by local newspaper and magazine writers as one of the best Chinese restaurants in the city. What's refreshing is that its prices are (easily) low enough to be included in this book as well.

UPPER EAST SIDE

Afghan Kebab House—1345 Second Ave. (70th St.); 212/517-2776, and 764 Ninth Ave. (51st St.); 212/307-1612. See listing under "Midtown Manhattan West."

Atomic Wings—At Name This Joint, 1644 Third Ave. (92nd St.); 212/410-3800, Spanky's, 1446 First Ave. (75th St.); 212/772-8400, Down the Hatch, 179 West 4th St.; 212/627-9500, Blondie's, 2180 Broadway (77th St.); 212/877-1010, and Cannon's, Broadway and 108th St.; 212/316-2300. See listing under "Greenwich Village."

Burritoville—1489 First Ave. (at 77th St.); 212/472-8800, and 1606 Third Ave. (at 91st St); 212/410-2255. See listing under "Greenwich Village."

The Carriage House—219 East 59th St.; 212/838-9464. Admittedly there aren't too many dining options on the Upper East Side for those engaged in the relentless search for lots of good, fresh food that costs very little. The Carriage House, however, which is just around the corner from Bloomingdale's, offers chicken and burgers at super-low prices. This is basically a bar, but they do have a cozy dining area up front that is well separated from the rest of the place; with its natural wood tables and casual decor, it's an easy place to stop in for a quick lunch or dinner.

Wings are the main attraction here, whether you get them Buffalo-style, barbecued, or slathered with one of a variety of imaginative sauces. A dozen wings costs just $4.95; a double order, with up to twenty-eight pieces, (enough for two people) is only $9.25. Buffalo wings come in various grades of spiciness, from "Mild" to "Super Wow." Barbecue flavors include sweet, Chinese, and Smoky Mountain; also (in a category the proprietors simply label "Unique") apricot chutney, honey mustard, and cajun spice. Add an order of seasoned fries, dipped in a light, crispy, and very tasty batter, for $1.95. If wings aren't your fancy, the Carriage House also offers a good chicken breast sandwich ($4.95) and fresh hamburgers ($4.25). Their chicken breast salad ($4.95), includes boneless and skinless chicken breast grilled with any of the above-mentioned sauces, atop a salad of fresh vegetables and lettuce. The Carriage House offers free delivery and is open seven days a week from lunchtime to the wee hours of the morning.

Dino's Kitchen—400 East 74th St.; 212/879-4749. Mr. C was merely walking past the window of this newly opened establishment when he heard someone exclaim, "Hey, my friend, come in. Don't cost to look!" No one has to say that twice to this correspondent. Dino's Kitchen really is little more than an open kitchen, adorned with a few checkered-tablecloth tables. It's a good place to stop in for a quick bite or for take-out. All of the Italian specialties here are made on the premises (you'll be able to verify as much yourself from any seat in the place), and the prices are

Mr. Cheap's Picks

✔ **EJ's Luncheonette**—Perhaps the top of the heap when it comes to trendy, fun, nostalgic diners. That makes it popular, and that means it's often hard to get in—but once you do you'll find good food at moderate prices.

✔ **El Pollo**—A no-frills eat-in or take-out joint serving hearty South American-style chicken.

✔ **Pastappunto**—One of the East Side's many alternatives to that overpriced boutique food for which Mr. C has no patience. Plenty of good pasta dishes here, all around five bucks.

✔ **Rathbone's**—A comfy neighborhood bar and restaurant with inexpensive meals, good beer, and free (!) jazz in the evenings.

✔ **Sotto Cinque**—Another good cheap pasta joint. The name, which translates as "under five," says it all.

great. The baked ziti plate is just $4.50; lasagna is $5.25.

Among the larger dinners, chicken parmigiana is $7.50, veal marsala is $5.25, and linguine with clams in red or white sauce is just $6.50. All of these dinners are served with side orders of spaghetti and garlic bread. Dino's also makes up sandwiches, salads, and appetizers: mozzarella sticks, for instance, are $3.00, and baked clams are $4.50. On the other end of your meal, you can linger over fresh-made espresso or cappucino and home-style pastries. Dino's offers catering services as well, although once you discover this place you may just make it your little neighborhood stop-in. Lunch is served daily from 11:00 to 3:00 except for Sundays. Dinner is available seven nights a week from 5:00 to 10:00.

EJ's Luncheonette—1271 Third Ave. (73rd St.); 212/472-0600, and 433 Amsterdam Ave. (80th St.); 212/873-3444. See listing under "Upper West Side."

El Pollo—1746 First Ave. (90th St.); 212/996-7810. South American cuisine, a basic, unadorned style of cooking that often yields exquisite results, has been gaining a foothold in the city for a couple of years now. El Pollo is a Peruvian restaurant with a simple but elegant atmosphere that specializes in a barbecue-style chicken grilled with a mild blend of spices and seasonings. The prices here are phenomenally low for the Upper East Side, and the portion sizes are more than adequate. A whole chicken is $8.75; a half-chicken only $5.00. You can get a hefty breast and wing for a mere $2.75.

These are all à la carte, so you'll need to add side dishes—and there are some wonderful ones at El Pollo. Mr. C encourages you to try the thin curly French fries ($2.50), fried sweet plantains (also $2.50), or a nice house salad ($3.00). For dessert, try the flan ($3.00) or a helping of quinua pudding, a sort of South American rice pudding flavored with raisins, cloves, and cinnamon. Lunch specials are served weekdays from 11:30 a.m. to 3:00 p.m.; they offer all of the above choices at slightly lower prices. El Pollo is open seven days a week until 11:00 p.m.

Good Health Cafe—324 East 86th St.; 212/439-9680. A veggie palace outside of the Village? On the Upper East Side, yet? It's true. For ardent vegetarians, this is about the only option in the area. Fortunately, it's good enough to eat here often. The atmosphere is pleasant and laid-back, as you'd expect; the staff is very friendly and helpful, with a good knowledge of healthy eating.

At lunchtime there are several specials, from $3.95 to $5.95. Mr. C's health food expert stops in often for the millet croquette platter, lightly-fried cakes served with steamed vegetables and soba noodles. Like many dishes, it's accompanied by a wonderful carrot-ginger sauce. Soups, salads, and sandwiches start around $2.50.

Dinners come in a wide variety. There are Oriental dishes such as yasai soba, stir-fried buckwheat noodles with shiitake mushrooms and shredded vegetables; continental dishes, like vegetable and fettucine parmigiana; and several seafood dinners, such as flounder tempura. All are priced between $8.50 and $9.50. Yes, even the non-Birkenstock crowd can eat comfortably here—and everything is prepared with all-natural ingredients.

Good Health Cafe also has locations in the East and West Villages: **Village East**, 2 St. Mark's Place (212/533-9898) and **Village Natural**, 46 Greenwich Avenue (212/727-0968); it also offers an in-house store with good prices on vitamins and packaged foods.

Googie's Luncheonette—1491 Second Ave. (78th St.); 212/717-1122. Some restaurants exist for their customers; at other restaurants, the opposite is true. Popular from the day it opened in late '92, Googie's is more about itself as a "scene" than about good dining, but the masses who flock to this glorified diner don't seem to mind. The decor is flashy, the platters are oversized, and people at the tables keep craning their necks to see what just whizzed by.

It's all part of the diner revolution—along with EJ's Luncheonette, Ed Debevic's, and others—fashionably retro joints that are fun, lively, and suitable for breakfast, lunch, or dinner. For the most part, Googie's is a fine addition to this roster, though with certain drawbacks. One is that, with the place so popular, there can be as much as a half-hour wait for a table on a busy weekend night or brunch. There's really nowhere to stand without being in the way, and of course they do not take reservations.

Once you get a seat, service is very efficient. They have a large staff of waiters, runners, and station chefs, so that food is served promptly. It's quite good, fairly health-oriented (lots of pastas and salads) and moderately priced—again, with some caveats. Dinner entrees offer good portions at decent prices; pastas are all under $10.00, salads between $5.00 and $7.00. The salads, in particular, are wonderful, made with fresh vegetables, greens, arugula, radicchio, and other such ingredients.

Burgers and sandwiches, however, start a bit high at $6.50 and up; though the burgers, at least, are ten ounces and juicy. The sandwiches are not such a bargain—good, but not huge. All of these come with mounds of the skinniest Idaho shoestring fries you've ever seen (very salty on Mr. C's visit, though), which look great and do add to the "fun" of it all.

Desserts are fine, though again a bit pricey; but for $2.50, you can enjoy a double-sized cup of cappuccino with an Italian biscuit on the side. There are also tall glasses of cold chocolate drinks with lots of froth on top. Go for the fun atmosphere and good food at moderate prices, but not—strictly speaking—for the value.

Jackson Hole Wyoming—232 East 64th St.; 212/371-7187, 1611 Second Ave. (83rd St); 212/737-8788, and 1270 Madison Ave. (91st St.); 212/427-2820. See listing under "Midtown Manhattan East."

Lee and Elle—999 Third Ave. (59th St.); 212/758-2018. If you've spent the day shopping at Bloomie's (or anywhere else in this area), chances are you've already blown a substantial portion of your budget and you'd like to rest up over a nice inexpensive meal. As Mr. C has noted, there aren't too many options in the neighborhood, but Lee and Elle is one of a few happy exceptions. It's a gourmet deli and cafeteria featuring a hot and cold buffet with over three dozen salads—and a similarly bewildering array of vegetable, pasta, and Chinese dishes, hot soups, and fresh-baked pastries.

There's a simple little system here: Fill up a plastic container with as much of anything as you want for $3.99 a pound. Mr. C is a big, big proponent of this kind of unadorned operating style, even though it means that the restaurant makes out on some dishes. The key, of course, is selection—but whether you choose the cold pesto salad, the sesame noodles with sauteed beef, or something in between, chances are you will eat very heartily for not much cash. Of course, such buffets have sprung up in seemingly every corner deli in the city; what makes Lee and Elle different is the second-floor seating area, with its neat, small, cafeteria-style tables. The dining area is bright and spotless, the seats up front offer a birds-eye view of all those people still bustling up and down Third Avenue, and you won't even have to leave a tip.

Leo's Diner—128 East 86th St.; 212/876-9100. Mr. C hasn't covered too many of the Big Apple's approximately ten trillion diners, mainly because the food tends to be pretty much identical from one to the next. Leo's is something of a special case in that it's an inexpensive dining option on the expensive Upper East Side. Granted, the quality is your standard-issue diner level, but the location certainly sets the place apart in a corner of the city that could use a few more affordable dining options.

There are lots of early-bird dinner specials at Leo's; they are available between 4:00 and 6:00 p.m. and are priced between $6.95 and $7.95. These may include such selections as a roasted half-chicken, veal and peppers, or chicken tarragon, and they all come with a vegetable on the side as well as a drink of your choice and dessert. There are also a good many affordable pasta dinners to choose from; these are priced at just $5.50. Other daily specials include various diet plates (priced from $6.00 to $7.00) and the inevitable Blue Plate Special ($9.00 to $10.00). Also worth noting is that all baking at Leo's is done on the premises, so save a little room for dessert.

The decor is a notch or two above that of your average New York coffee shop, with walls and tables done up in natural wood finish. The counter area is faintly reminiscent of a cocktail bar; the booths and tables are clean and attractive. Nothing spectacular, but certainly affordable enough and worth stopping at if you're in the area.

Luke's Bar and Grill—1394 Third Ave. (80th St.); 212/249-7070. With a not-too-overpriced menu of simple food in a casual setting, Luke's is a welcome recent addition to the Upper East Side.

It's like a *really* nice Ground Round—green walls and brass decor, with a handsome wooden bar up front. The bar, by the way, features Foster's Lager, Samuel Adams, and Beck's beers on tap. The food is just what you'd expect to go with these: Lots of appetizers, sandwiches, and dinners too.

The dinners, unfortunately, can get a bit pricey; though you can find such choices as a half roast-chicken dinner for $7.95 or fried calamari for $8.95. Better off with the "fun foods"—juicy hamburgers start at $4.95—though you'll have to add the great fries for $2.50. There's a grilled chicken and guacamole sandwich for $6.95, and daily specials as well. For dessert, the "Utterly Deadly Pecan Pie" says it all. Luke's also serves a fine weekend brunch, with big omelette plates for $5.25 and most other items priced from $4.00 to $7.00.

Oh, sure, you can get huge burgers elsewhere in town for less, with the fries—but not too many in this area and with this kind of style and attentive service.

Mangia Mangia—1293 Lexington Ave. (87th St.); 212/289-1361. Yes, yes! Eat here and you'll get a big meal for just a little money. This is one of the many "family-style" pasta shops that have popped up in the Upper East Side as a great alternative to the fancier restaurants there. Mangia Mangia looks a bit like a large coffee shop: it has a dining counter as well as tables with the requisite red-checked tablecloths.

It focuses mainly on pastas, such as fettucine Alfredo ($6.95); capellini primavera, an angel-hair pasta mixed with vegetables in a light cream sauce (also $6.95); and chicken parmigiana with linguine ($8.95). If you're hungry, you can start off with antipasti, like fried calamari for $4.95 or a Caesar salad for $3.95. Mangia Mangia also offers pizza: the basic model is $6.95 for a small pie that is still big enough for two people to share. If you like early bird specials, stop in between 4:30 and 6:30 pm for soup, salad, and a pasta dish of your choice—all just $6.95. (By the way, all pasta dishes include a serving of Mangia Mangia's delicious garlic bread.) This may not exactly be an intimate place, but it is a lively spot where you're sure to get a lot of pasta for your dough.

Mumbles—1622 Third Ave. (91st St.); 212/427-4355, and 603 Second Avenue (33rd St.); 212/889-0750. These popular neighborhood joints have been around for almost twenty years, and it's easy to see the reason for their staying power. The atmosphere is casual, and lively without being noisy. The large interior is dark and pub-like, with natural wood and brass decor. And the menu covers all the bases, from soups and salads to sandwiches to dinners.

Burgers are a staple here, of course; at $5.95, they are half-pounders and include lettuce, tomato, and fries. For a dollar more you can choose two other toppings. Sandwiches and salads are in the same price range, with lots of choices in each category. Plenty of appetizers too.

Entrees—fish, chicken and steak— are $10.00 and up, but come with rice or potato and another vegetable; you can also get fish and chips for $7.50, honey-dipped chicken for $6.50, and several pastas, each $8.95. Mix and match your favorite pasta and sauce. Half-orders are also available for just $4.95.

Mumbles also offers a children's menu (nothing over $3.25) and regular specials throughout the week—including happy hour drinks at reduced prices and early bird dinner specials every day.

Ottomanelli's Cafe—1370 York Ave. (73rd St.); 212/794-9696,

1518 First Ave. (79th St.); 212/734-5544, 439 East 82nd St.; 212/737-1888, 1626 York Ave. (85th St.); 212/772-7722, and 1404 Madison Ave. (97th St.); 212/996-7000. See listing under "Midtown Manhattan East."

Pastappunto—1427 Second Ave. (75th St.); 212/362-0203. Pastappunto is another one of the Upper East Side's pasta houses offering a welcome respite from expensive, "fancy" meals when all you want is something quick, good, and cheap. They have a wide variety of pasta dishes—more than a dozen to choose from, in fact—all single-priced at $4.95. Among these are cappellini primavera, angel-hair pasta with fresh sauteed vegetables; good old fettucine Alfredo, and meat or vegetarian lasagna.

Start off with one of the many inexpensive antipasti dishes, such as bruschetta, that wonderful grilled bread with tomatoes on top ($2.95), a Caesar salad ($3.95), or grilled Italian sausage with a side salad ($4.25). There are also plenty of sandwiches, all priced around $5.00: consider the pollo Romano, a lightly breaded chicken breast sandwich topped with melted mozzarella and spices.

This is a terrific place to linger over a cappucino and one of the many desserts. A tasty example of the latter would be the Italian ricotta cheesecake ($3.75 a slice). The restaurant itself is artsy and modern, but very comfortable; the walls are painted in rich dark colors, ceiling fans whir high overhead, and there are plenty of lush hanging plants in the windows. If you're going to be in this pricey neighborhood, this is the kind of place to visit when it's time to eat.

Rathbone's—1702 Second Ave. (88th St.); 212/369-7361. For over twenty years Rathbone's has been a simple neighborhood restaurant that's a relaxing alternative to East Side chic. It's a dark, wooden, saloon-style restaurant bar, with lots of good beers on tap and in bottles; and the sawdust on the floor makes it feel even more like a throwback to older times.

And if that's not enough, the prices are definitely nostalgic. Can you believe getting a burger on an English muffin, with French fries, for just $4.50—in this neighborhood? Actually, there are a few others, but they don't have this atmosphere. They also don't have live jazz with no cover charge or minimum, as Rathbone's does four nights a week.

Getting back to the food, the large menu ranges from fettucine Alfredo ($5.95) to a broiled half-chicken ($7.95) and wiener schnitzel ($9.95). All entrees come with salad or fresh vegetables, and baked potato, fries, or rice. Plus, there are sandwiches, appetizers, and desserts (Peach Marnier or Blackout cake for $2.95!). This is a place where you can really hang out and become a regular—even on a budget.

Ruppert's—1662 Third Ave. (93rd St.); 212/831-1900, and 269 Columbus Ave. (72nd St.); 212/873-9400. Not far from Mumbles on the Upper reaches of Third Avenue, Ruppert's offers another option for cheap neighborhood dining on the East Side. Again, it's a large, comfortable establishment, with a bar up front and several dining areas on two levels. The menu ranges all over the culinary landscape, from veggies to burgers to seafood. The prices are fantastic.

At the time of this writing, in fact, Ruppert's has settled into its "1980s Prices" promotion, offering several entrees from just $3.95 daily. These include a burger and fries, linguini, eggplant parmesan, and quiche of the day with salad. Many other dinners are only a dollar or two more, like blackened chicken breast ($5.95), grilled fresh tuna steak ($6.75) and chilled seafood and pasta salad with shrimp, scallops, mussels, and calamari. Even a 1 1/4-pound lobster dinner is only $10.95—one of the cheapest around!

For appetizers or just plain nibbling, chicken fingers are just $2.95, nachos "supreme" are $3.25, and a Caesar salad is $2.95. Desserts include home-made apple-strawberry pie, Mississippi Mud Cake, and Sedutto's ice cream. There's a Ruppert's on either side of the park. How can you go wrong?

Sotto Cinque—1644 Second Ave. (85th St.); 212/472-5563. How can you beat this? For those of you who don't speak fluent Italian, "Sotto Cinque" means "under five"—and they're not talking about kiddies. This basic pasta house offers over a dozen different entrees, all at the unbeatable price of $4.95. Choose from linguine with pesto, fettucine Alfredo, vegetarian lasagna, and more.

Penne ortolane gives you short tubes of pasta with broccoli and zucchini, in a garlicky cream sauce; Cappellini primavera offers several mixed vegetables sauteed and served with a light tomato sauce. There are also lots of appetizers and antipasti, such as minestrone, stuffed mushrooms, and baked clams; again, nothing over $4.95. Same with sandwiches and desserts. The portions are good, and while you can undoubtedly get better pasta around town, you probably can't get a better deal.

Sotto Cinque is especially good for quick and easy take-out, and the restaurant also offers free delivery.

Tony's Di Napoli—1606 Second Ave. (83rd St.); 212/861-8686. Although Tony's has been around since 1959, it moved just last year into this spacious, handsome location—bringing "family-style dining" to the Upper East Side. As popularized by the wildly successful (and more expensive) Carmine's, this means that you pay more for an entree than anything else Mr. C ever recommends; but each one is a huge central plate that has enough food to serve two people, or even three with smaller appetites. Or one person who wants to take it all home and not have to cook for a month.

There are a dozen pasta dishes to choose from, ranging from $10.00 for basic spaghetti to $13.00 for rigatoni with vodka and mushrooms. Try eating anything after that! Several chicken and veal dishes are $15.00 to $22.00, including chicken scarpiello and broiled veal chops. Seafood dinners (mostly shrimp) cost about the same, topping out at $24.00 for a mixed plate of lobster tail, shrimp, clams, and mussels. Don't forget, you'll be getting enough to start your own ocean.

The restaurant covers a couple of storefronts, with a bright, spacious interior, natural wood, and the ever-popular red and white checkered tablecloths. Tony's also accepts food orders by phone, which you can then pick up for an instant and inexpensive party buffet.

Trattoria Bella Donna—307 East 77th St.; 212/585-2866. This is a very cozy, very popular Upper East Side restaurant that focuses on moderately priced pasta dishes. Although it's not by any means the cheapest place in town, you do get a huge amount for your dollar. There are literally dozens of good options to choose from here. Start off with an antipasto; the basic green salad ($4.00), is a fresh and creative mix of arugula, watercress, endive, and sliced fresh tomatoes. The bella vista salad ($5.00) combines two kinds of mozzarella cheese, fresh and smoked, with roasted peppers, tomatoes, lettuce, and radicchio.

Now in most traditional Italian restaurants, the pasta course is supposed to lead up to something else; here it is the main course, and, as noted above, there are a lot of main courses to choose from. Like Mr. C, you'll just have to dive in and make a choice. The penne alla erbe combines pasta with spinach, broccoli, leeks, and garlic ($7.50); farfalle osteria is bow-tie pasta with sauteed zucchini in a tomato arugula sauce (also $7.50). Moving up the price scale a bit, the capellini mediterranea ($9.25) is angel-hair pasta with shrimp, white wine, and shallots in a spiced olive oil sauce. The menu tops out at $10.95, which will get you a platter of black tagliarini, black-colored noodles mixed together with crabmeat in a scampi sauce.

Mr. C counted up about thirty different pasta dishes here, most priced under $10.00. As you may be able to tell from the dishes cited here, the kitchen is a creative one, and the people here are justly proud of that. More to the point, the place is famous—meaning it is quite possible you will have some difficulty securing a table. If you get shut out, come back and give it another try sometime soon.

Triangolo—345 East 83rd St.; 212/472-4488. Of the East Side's many affordable Italian restaurants, Triangolo is one of the most appealing for its simplicity and great food. There's nothing wrong with the ultra-modern looks of Ecco-La, but sometimes Mr. C just likes a simple, quiet restaurant for a special meal without the hype. This is it.

Triangolo is small, spare, and elegant inside; the walls are painted in rich Mediterranean colors but remain undecorated. The staff is extremely attentive and friendly, watching over you without creating any pressure. The menu features over a dozen pasta dishes priced under $10.00, apart from daily specials, and the antipasti are around $6.00 to $8.00.

The pastas are beautifully cooked, whether you go basic or fancy. Conchiglio sarde ($8.50) are shells and sausage; the sauce is packed with ground sausage that's just a bit spicy. One of Mr. C's companions made the real find on the menu, though: Rotolo di pasta Montanaro ($9.50) features dark porcini mushrooms sauteed in virgin olive oil and rolled up in a large pasta tube; this is then sliced into four sections, which are cooked flat and smothered in sauce. The mushrooms are so rich and tasty, you'll think it's a meat dish. Intense.

Portions are very big, so there can be some to take home. It tastes just as good the next day. The restaurant also has a fine selection of wines. Good place for a romantic, quiet date. Because the place is small, reservations are a good idea on the weekends.

Urban Grill—1613 Second Ave. (84th St.), Manhattan; 212/744-2122, and 330 West 58th St.; 212/586-3300. See listing under "Midtown Manhattan West."

UPPER WEST SIDE

Atomic Wings—Blondie's, 2180 Broadway (77th St.); 212/877-1010, Cannon's, Broadway and 108th St.; 212/316-2300, Name This Joint, 1644 Third Ave. (92nd St.); 212/410-3800, Spanky's, 1446 First Ave. (75th St.); 212/772-8400, and Down the Hatch, 179 West 4th St.; 212/627-9500.

See listing under "Greenwich Village."

Blue Coyote—2381 Broadway (87th St.); 212/874-7532. A neighborhood bar with good, simple food at reasonable prices, the Blue Coyote is a fun place to call your hangout. For atmosphere, a huge inflatable cactus stands by the well-stocked jukebox. A cozy cluster of tables offers a more secluded conversation area away from the bar and in from the bustling street scene outside.

The waiters and bartenders definitely contribute to the fun feeling of the place; some of the bartenders even like to experiment behind the counter, offering shots of their latest cocktail concoctions to nearby patrons. They could even teach "Cheers" a thing or two about gregariousness. Hey, it's research—someone's got to try it.

Food consists mainly of appetizers, burgers, sandwiches and salads. A big, fresh burger with French fries, lettuce, tomato, onion, and pickles is just $5.50; 25¢ more gets you a California chicken sandwich, grilled chicken breast topped with sliced avocado and Swiss cheese. And the "Omelette du Jour" seems to translate as, "whatever you want in your omelette". It comes with fries and toast for a fine $4.50. The appetizers include Buffalo wings ($4.50), fried calamari or peel 'n' eat shrimp (each $5.50), and nachos "with the works" ($4.95). Blue Coyote also serves up a $6.95 Sunday brunch, including a selection of mixed drinks and of entrees—one of the best-priced brunches in the area.

Border Cafe—2637 Broadway (100th St.); 212/864-3037. No, not *that* Border Cafe—that East Side one with the East Side prices. Upper West Siders know about this humbler Tex-Mex; same name, no relation, and much better prices. Where else can you get a barbecued half-chicken dinner, with fried, mashed, or baked potato, and cornbread, for $4.95? Or a chicken and ribs combo, same fixin's, for $6.95? Not many places—and it's good stuff.

Fresh half-pound burgers start at just $3.95, with French fries, lettuce, and tomato. Mexican platters are big, too. Go for any combination of chicken chimichangas, cheese enchiladas, and bean burritos, served with rice and beans: one item for $3.95, two for $4.95, three for $5.95. Wash them down with a ten-ounce margarita for just $4.50, or a bottle of Corona for $2.50. Pitchers and other bottled imports make this a good hangout for students, yuppies, and just about anyone. The bar area up front is separated from the dining tables, so everybody gets along fine together.

Cafe Bel Canto—1991 Broadway (68th St.); 212/362-4642. Here in the pricy environs of Lincoln Center, Cafe Bel Canto offers an inexpensive dining option that is every bit as delightful as those offered by its upscale competitors. And it's very, very New York. The cafe is open to the street during the summer months for al fresco dining and glassed in at night and during colder times of year. It's open daily from 8:00 a.m. to midnight; as a public plaza, technically, you can even bring your own food and simply order wine from the bar. But then you'd miss out on the pastas, salads, and light sandwiches the cafe offers. Salads are priced from $6.00 to $7.50; the fresh Caesar salad ($6.75) is very large and quite good. You can get an individual pizza for $6.50 and a variety of pastas—such as an exemplary linguine with mussels in white wine sauce—for $8.50.

Most sandwiches are in the $7.00 to $8.00 range, a little steep for Mr. C's tastes, but quite good. The panino di Bel Canto puts grilled chicken, zucchini, tomato, onions, and smoked mozzarella between two delicious slabs of crusty bread. The more reasonably priced bruschetta ($4.95) comes on a similar crusty roll and is topped with avocado, goat cheese, basil, and olive oil. Give it a try. A pastry cart features baked goods and a variety of other desserts. For a light snack or a full meal before sneaking in to catch the second act of the opera you can't afford tickets to, Cafe Bel Canto may be just the thing.

Cafe Bloom—321 Amsterdam Ave. (75th St.); 212/874-3032. The sight of the freshly prepared foods in the window of Cafe Bloom should be enough to draw you inside immediately. Heaping bowls of curried chicken, pasta salads, and rice salads form a palette of delicious-looking colors. There are some two dozen dishes to choose from, and the pricing is simple: Combine any three for just $4.95. Chicken is the only meat on the bill—but there's lemon chicken, sesame, ginger, avocado, and more. Pastas include cheese tortellini in pesto sauce. Among the many salads are baba ghanoush or lentils with lemon and garlic, and the other vegetarian entrees feature roasted potatoes with garlic, coriander, and lemon; okra in tomato sauce; and vegetable lasagna.

They do a lot of take-out business here, since it's the perfect sort of place to stop into on your way home from work. You can do so frequently and never get tired of the choices. There are tables at the back, though, and the interior is quite handsome in dark wood paneling. Cafe Bloom stays open until 10:00 p.m.

Cafe 112—2885 Broadway (112th St.); 212/662-8470. Up in the Columbia area, Cafe 112 is one of the most popular student hangouts. This restaurant and bakery has a coffeehouse atmosphere and serves up plenty of casual food at very casual prices. Start off with such appetizers as lentil soup ($2.50) or a basket of fried zucchini sticks ($3.75). Follow it with a seven-ounce burger plus French fries and salad (just $3.99) or get fancy with the Special Burger, which is cooked in white wine and topped with parsley, onions, and tomato—a real treat at $5.25.

A plate of fettucine Alfredo is just $5.50; a huge serving of ratatouille over rice is just $4.99. Or go Middle Eastern with a plate of foujedara for $5.99—it's a vegetarian dish of rice and lentils cooked with baked onions and served with a minced cucumber and yogurt salad. The Chicken New Orleans ($6.95) is a delicious grilled chicken breast topped with pesto and grilled mozzarella on rye toast with salad. What this has to do with Louisianna is beyond Mr. C, but it certainly makes for a very filling and affordable meal.

Lots of vegetarian choices here, as well as a full selection of coffees, pastries, and other goodies. The weekend brunches, which start at $2.95, are a particularly good bet at Cafe 112, not least because of the classical guitarist who will serenade you as you dine.

Cafe Pertutti—2862 Broadway (111th St.); 212/289-1361. Here's another cozy and intimate neighborhood place in the Columbia area. Cafe Pertutti offers traditional Italian fare, focusing primarily on pasta, and just about all its pasta plates are priced at $7.00. You can choose from rigatoni, tortellini, ravioli, and tortelone, which are green and white dumplings filled with chopped vegetables. (This last item is $8.00.) Having chosen your pasta, you may then choose your sauce—boscaiola, a thin tomato sauce mixed with pieces of sauteed vegetables; puttanesca, which mixes spicy stuff like anchovies, capers, and garlic; or carciofo, a creamy tomato sauce with artichoke. Meat dishes are more limited, with only a few to choose from: chicken parmigiana, chicken cacciatore, and chicken in white wine sauce. All are $7.95 and come with a side order of pasta. Other daily specials may add to the list.

Cafe Pertutti also offers a selection of inexpensive sandwiches and salads, as well as wine by the glass and several very good beers (such as New Amsterdam). Eat light and save some room for the cafe's wonderful desserts! There's always a lot to choose from every day, going well beyond the traditional Italian spumoni. You may instead opt for a pecan tart served with fresh cream, or an amaretto mousse pie. Order one of these with a double espresso or a mocha cappucino and you'll be in dessert heaven.

Caffe Popolo—351 Columbus Ave. (76th St.); 212/362-1777. Making its debut in the summer of '92, this intimate little cafe is a hit with local residents. "I'm going to hang here all the time," said Mr. C's area pal, who was making

Mr. Cheap's Picks

✔ **Cafe Bloom**—Heaping bowls of salad, curries, and other prepared foods to eat there or take home. Choose any three for $4.95!

✔ **Caffe Pertutti**—Near Columbia. A fun, friendly, Italian joint. Check out the magnificent desserts.

✔ **Las Marcias**—One of the Upper West Side's many Hispanic restaurants, Las Marcias offers staggering values on dinner orders: full plates for around $5.00. Tough to beat.

✔ **Ollie's Noodle Shop**—The new Chinese kid on the block has taken New York by storm. Consistently good food, family atmosphere, reasonable prices.

✔ **Patzo**—A big, artsy place on Broadway. A visit here is a little like journeying to a Venetian palace. Very affordable food, and quite good.

his second visit that week. The small marble-top tables, the exposed-brick walls, and the laid-back jazz music on the stereo all make it a New York natural.

Oh, and don't forget the food. There are few such cafes in this neighborhood serving such elegantly casual meals, and at such good prices. Ten-inch pizzas on very thin crusts are the house specialty, in ten varieties; also sandwiches made on long rolls that crackle with crispiness. All of the breads are baked in Popolo's own brick oven, you see. These are then filled or topped with the freshest of ingredients: mixed greens, arugula, wild mushrooms, proscuitto, sun-dried tomatoes, whatever.

Yes, it's yuppified, but it's great, so what the heck. Try a "Melanzane" pizza ($7.00), with baby eggplant, tomato, oregano, roasted garlic, and goat cheese. Or a sandwich made with fresh mozzarella, pesto, and Italian sausage ($5.25). There are also a dozen different pasta dishes, each $8.00, which give you enough to take some home. Several chicken entrees ($9.00 each), salads, and antipasti round out the menu. Of course, you should try and leave room for one of the gorgeous-looking desserts in the glass case at the back (a bit expensive, but all homemade on the premises) and a cappuccino. Mr. C sipped a delightful variation, the caramel latte ($2.75)—a triple-layered coffee drink spiked with caramel sauce. Sweet!

Eden Rock—2325 Broadway (84th St.); 212/873-1361. Middle Eastern food comes to the Upper West Side at Eden Rock, which offers moderately priced entrees and a wide range of inexpensive appetizers and snacks. This is good if you're dining with a large group; there are well over a dozen appetizers, all of which seem to be priced at the same $3.00. Whether you choose some of the time-honored favorites, like stuffed grape leaves, baba ghanoush, or spinach pie, or decide to get adventurous with bamai (a kind of deep-fried okra) or modardara (baked lentils mixed with bits of fried onion and served with rice), you'll probably like what comes out of the kitchen. An even better deal is the combination special: any three appetizer items for just $5.95.

Eden Rock has plenty of sandwiches, and they're the kind you'd expect: falafel ($2.75), chicken shawarma ($3.75), and chicken kebab (also $3.75). Moving on to full dinners, the lamb shish kebab dinner is $8.50; the more unusual shrimp kebab is $9.50. All dinners come with rice and salad, and you can substitute hummus or baba ghanoush. The top-priced item for a single diner would be the broiled lamb chops, served with potatoes ($15.00). The Mazza Plate, designed for two, offers you nine different dishes on one large platter for $23.00.

The food at Eden Rock is fine, though Mr. C's Upper West Side sources point out, and rightly, that you may emerge from the place smelling of the oil that is used in so many of the dishes and that permeates the surroundings. Take-out may be a better option.

88 Noodle House—565 Columbus Ave. (88th St.); 212/362-0203. You may not have noticed the 88 Noodle House in Columbus Avenue's restaurant section, being in a non-descript building on a non-descript block well above the main stretch. But one of Mr. C's foremost restaurant experts says he dines here almost once a week, and with over two hundred different items to choose from, it's easy to see why. This is a full Chinese menu with all of the standard options, from sweet and sour chicken to mu shu pork and orange beef. However, Mr. C always recommends that you go with the specialties of the house, which means starting with something like an order of cold sesame noodles ($4.25) or spinach or whole-wheat noodles ($4.75). Among the many other noodle dishes are lo mein and chow fun, of course; mei fun, the wonderful thin rice noodle dish, is worth looking into as well. You can order them here with chicken, beef, pork, or shrimp for just $5.25. Try sampling noodles from many parts of the Far East, such as tom men—a Hong Kong-style noodle soup containing roast pork or fish ($5.25)—and lar men—a Japanese version of a similar soup ($4.25 for a nice large bowl).

There are plenty of vegetarian options here, as well as the obligatory Chinese restaurant lunch deals, which are served daily from 12:00 noon to 2:30 p.m. There are two dozen different lunch options, all of which include egg roll, fried rice, and a choice of soup. Worth looking into are garlic shrimp ($4.25), pepper steak (also $4.25), and chow fun noodles with beef or chicken ($4.95). 88 Noodle House is a terrific example of your basic no-frills, good-food, not-a-lot-of-bucks noodle joint, and heaven knows we need more of them these days.

EJ's Luncheonette—433 Amsterdam Ave. (80th St.); 212/873-3444, and 1271 Third Ave. (73rd St.); 212/472-0600. What a wild scene this is. EJ's has grabbed hold of New York's passion for nostalgic diners, and has created a campy, funky joint that's like a time-warp to the 1950s. These establishments are covered with clocks, old-fashioned advertisements, ceiling fans, and the other accouterments for anyone interested in going back to the future—and in eating well along the way.

The menu ranges all over the diner repertoire, but always with a modern twist. Breakfasts include oat bran Belgian waffles ($5.00) and "Health Kick" omelettes ($5.75), made with egg whites only, mushrooms, tomatoes, and herbs. Challah bread, fruit, and home fries come on the side. Lunch, meanwhile, brings on huge burgers ($5.75 to $6.95) served on a toasted bulkie roll with thin, crispy fries, lettuce, tomato, onion and pickles. Add gruyere cheese, Canadian bacon, chili, and other trendy toppings. The grilled chicken breast sandwich ($6.50) is done up Cajun-style, with barbecue sauce, pepper, and onion. Or go for giant grilled cheese sandwiches of all varieties, on thick slabs of challah bread. Big salads, too, with fresh greens and vegetables. There are half a dozen "Blue Plate" specials every day, actually served on blue plates; beer and wine are also available. Try to save room for dessert—a traditional chocolate egg cream, or perhaps a banana split.

The result of all this is that EJ's is a monster hit; until the rage dies down, at least, you may have to wait for a table even in the middle of the afternoon. It'll be worth your while. EJ's is open daily until 11:00 p.m., weekends until midnight.

Finfinae Ethiopian Cuisine—710 Amsterdam Ave. (95th St.); 212/866-4868. At first hearing, "Ethiopian cuisine" may sound like some cruel joke. In fact, Finfinae is quite an elegant restaurant, with a clean, white interior, linen tablecloths, and the smell of incense hanging in the air. The food, is hearty, spicy, and inexpensive. All of the dishes are served with *injera* bread, a sort of flat, open crepe. What you do is tear off a piece, drape it over your fingers, and scoop up your food with it. There are no other utensils—unless you request some.

The cuisine itself reminds Mr. C of Indian food; lots of stews involving ground, marinated meat in spicy sauces. Beef and lamb are the most common, and these entrees are all around $9.00 to $11.00. Yabeg Alicha, lamb in a green pepper sauce, is also seasoned with rosemary and ginger; it's one of the milder dishes. Doro Wat is one of the few chicken dishes, marinated in lemon sauce and cooked in red pepper sauce for a complex taste. There are also many vegetarian entrees—the real bargains at $6.25 to $7.95. Yeshimbra Assa Wat, for example, is made of ground chick peas, rolled up and cooked in a spicy red sauce—kind of an African falafel.

Finfinae's *injera*, unlike that of some other such restaurants, is a whole-grain bread; it's made from a grain called teff, which is said to be very rich in nutrients. Surprisingly, perhaps, *you'll* feel quite rich—without having to be—when you eat here.

Firehouse—522 Columbus Ave. (85th St.); 212/787-3473. A relatively recent addition to this hopping block of late-night bar/restaurants, Firehouse is really just a bar with good food—and a rowdy one, at that. Red siren lights flash and bounce off the walls, and a raised area of tables at the rear offers monitors and a giant-screen TV showing sports—but don't expect to hear any of the play-by-play. This place packs 'em in, though during the warm months you can also grab a patio-style table out front.

What's good here? All sorts of bar foods, including a variety of wings (Buffalo, BBQ, Jamaican Jerk, boneless, etc.) in portions starting at $4.95, $9.50, and up. Homemade ten-inch pizzas, with crispy, thin crusts, $5.95 to $7.95, with such toppings as pineapple chicken, Oriental shrimp, or grilled veggie. Salads, burgers, and sandwiches in the $6.00-to-$8.00 range. And appetizers like "Jalapeno Poppers" ($3.95), fried peppers filled with cheese, for the adventurous.

Firehouse also offers a variety of special deals, like the weekday happy hour from 4:30 to 7:00, when drafts start at $1.00 and margaritas at $3.00. Mondays are "All U Can Eat" nights, with as many wings as you can flap for $8.50. And, of course, "Fireman Appreciation" on Tuesdays, when drinks are half-price with a fireman's identification (what does that mean—they have to wear their hats?)

Brunch is a little more laid-back, Saturdays and Sundays from 11:00 a.m. to 4:00 p.m. Firehouse has also begun putting out blazes on the East Side, serving its menu at a bar called Etc. (1470 First Avenue, 212/382-0122).

Harriet's Kitchen—502 Amsterdam Ave. (84th St.); 212/721-0045. Harriet's Kitchen is just that—a take-out place that strives to be just like your own kitchen at home (or better!). All the food is fresh and homemade, with an eye toward healthy preparations, like skinless chicken fried in cholesterol-free vegetable oil. Chicken, in fact, is the main item here, in such entrees as a barbecued half-bird ($4.55), boneless lemon chicken with linguine ($6.50), and "Harriet's Famous" chicken pot pie ($6.50), as well as in main-course salads, like mixed greens with sliced chicken, apples, and walnuts ($4.95).

If you're not after things with wings, don't despair. There are six-ounce hamburgers for $3.95 and homemeade meatloaf with real mashed potatoes for $6.50. Plus appetizers from gazpacho ($2.95) to zucchini sticks with horseradish sauce ($3.25), vegetable side dishes, and desserts too. Extra bargains are the children's special—two pieces of chicken with fries and cornbread for $4.50 (available from 4:30 to 6:30 p.m. only)—and the family dinner, with enough chicken, potatoes, cole slaw, and cornbread to feed four to six people for just $23.95. Harriet's also does catering, as well as delivery on the

Upper West Side (free with orders of $8.00 or more).

Hi-Life Bar and Grill—477 Amsterdam Ave. (83rd St.); 212/787-7199. Definitely one of the hipper spots on this restaurant-packed stretch of Amsterdam, Hi-Life feels like a scene out of some 1950s movie. From the martini-glass sign outside to the black leather upholstered walls inside (try to get the cozy booth just inside the front door), this is a good old-fashioned lounge. There should be a beaded curtain, through which you would hear some torch singer crooning away. And yet there is a slightly modern skew to the decor; check out the bizarre lamps, for instance.

Hi-Life is kind of small, adding to the intimate atmosphere, although they compensate by squeezing in as many tables as they can. Once you're seated though, the food makes it all worthwhile. The menu is modern and eclectic, with burgers, pastas, steaks, salads, and desserts. The prices are at the top of Mr. C's budget range, particularly the daily specials; but you get a lot of delicious eats, and after all, it's an experience. Appetizers are reasonable, such as nachos for $3.75, black bean soup for $3.00, and cheese fondue for $5.00. During happy hour, these are half-price.

Among the lower-priced dinners: Southern fried chicken—the genuine, greasy down-home recipe—is a large portion for $8.95, with good mashed potatoes and a vegetable of the day. Big, juicy burgers start at $5.50, but you'll have to add the shoestring fries. Pastas are also a good bet, in the ubiquitous large white bowls for $8.00 to $9.00.

Brunch runs all day on the weekends; otherwise lunch is not served at Hi-Life. Just dinner, from 5:00 p.m. to midnight. No respectable lounge lizard would be up and out any earlier.

The Hungarian Pastry Shop—1030 Amsterdam Ave. (111th St); 212/866-4230. In the Columbia University area, folks know about this extremely laid-back establishment, famous for its coffee and pastries. It is also known as a spot where you can literally sit all day over refills while dawdling over Dostoevsky. If anyone bothers you at all, it's likely to the be the cafe's cat. In short, the Hungarian Pastry Shop offers a mellow and pleasantly homey scene. Service is mellow, too, which some of the more uptight patrons may be tempted to read as "minimal," but then again, sometimes you just want to be left alone. A variety of simple pastries—cookies, tarts, etc.—are all priced around $2.00 and under. Fresh-brewed coffee is $1.30, but remember, this is a bottomless cup that can see you through an entire day.

Indian Cafe—201 West 95th St.; 212/222-1600 and 2791 Broadway (107th St.); 212/749-9200. Of New York's many, many Indian restaurants, the Indian Cafe has often been singled out by reviewers as a pleasant and dependable eatery for good food on a budget. Mr. C confirmed this on his own visit to the 95th Street branch. The interior is small but comfortable, the atmosphere subdued, and the service very attentive and quick. The menu offers a wide variety of chicken, beef, seafood, and vegetarian dishes, with nothing priced higher than $8.95; the food is delicious, so it's pretty hard to go wrong.

Good ol' chicken curry ($6.95) was tasty, though not too spicy; the standard practice here is to walk on the mild side unless you request otherwise. If you like your food hot, be sure to ask for it. Meanwhile, the portion was nice and large. The same price fetched a yummy order of Mutter Paneer, peas with chunks of mild cheese cooked in a thick brown sauce. For an inexpensive entree, curried rice pilaf and mixed vegetables with shredded coconut and almonds

($5.25) is hard to beat. The restaurant has a liquor license, with authentic Indian beers available.

Especially worth noting is the lunch special menu, which offers no less than ten different entrees from vegetables to beef, lamb and even goat curry—along with an appetizer, salad, rice and chutney—for only $4.95. And, unlike many such luncheon deals, it's available from 11:30 a.m. right up to 4:00 p.m.

Indian Delhi—392 Columbus Ave. (79th St.); 212/362-8760. Is this meant to be a pun? If so, it works. Indian Delhi is a small take-out place with just enough tables to qualify as a dining spot too. But as at a deli, you gather your order at the counter and take your tray to a table by the window. Simplicity is key, with all-disposable plates and utensils. Still, if you want a quick, easy nosh of Indian food that will spice your palate and spare your wallet, this is the place.

The food is authentic and homemade, using all-natural ingredients cooked in low-fat oil. A cup of vegetarian curry soup is $1.50; a small yogurt and cucumber Raitha salad topped with raisins is $2.50. Hot and cold sandwiches include an "Indian Veggie Burger" for $4.95, tucked into pita bread. Hot plates are the best deals, though, like the vegetable combo for $5.50—choose any three items from the daily selection, served over jasmine rice. Chicken curry gives you plenty of meat, on the bone, with rice and a vegetable for $5.95. And the Methi Masala bread plate is that wonderful, hot, grainy bread cooked with spinach, broccoli, carrots, onions, tomatoes, and spices—all for $3.95.

Kamel's Cafe—370 Columbus Ave. (78th St.); 212/496-6532. Kamel's is an unheralded find tucked into this popular stretch of Columbus. Its narrow interior is much like a European patisserie, cozy and bustling. During the warm months, though, when the avenue becomes one long boulevard of browsing and eating, you can sit at one of the tables out front and eat much less expensively than at most of Kamel's neighbors. And you get the same view—looking across the street to the park behind the Museum of Natural History, plus lots of people-watching.

The menu is an eclectic mix of Continental and Middle Eastern. A delicious quiche and fresh salad platter is filling at $5.75; so is the Salad Nicoise, with vegetables, tuna, egg, and anchovies ($7.25). The assortment of baguette sandwiches seems a bit overpriced for what you get, but the hummus or baba ghanoush sandwiches are each $3.50.

Meanwhile, this is a great place to sit over a cappuccino (chocolate, mocha, sambuca and more) and pastry. Pain au chocolat is just $1.50; or choose a pecan danish, apple turnover, tiramisu, eclair, baklava. . . .or a piece of delices cake—almond meringue layered with dark chocolate cream, mocha butter cream, and whipped cream. At $3.00 a slice, you can afford the cake—if not the calories.

La Caridad—2199 Broadway (78th St.); 212/874-2780. The paper menu at this restaurant features a decorative map of Cuba filled with legend and lore about the island and has the quote, "Cuba is known as the pearl of the Antilles because of its beauty and natural wealth." New York is known as one of the few places in the world where you will find a wealth of Cuban-Chinese restaurants, and La Caridad is one of the city's best. You'll be able to keep a good portion of your own natural wealth by eating very cheaply here, and the food is certainly beautiful. Most dinners, whether Hispanic or Oriental, are priced from $5.00 to $7.00 and come in staggering quantities on heaping plates. The *arroz con pollo*, for instance, is indeed beautiful to look at: a large mound of saffron-colored rice in bright orange, laced with large chunks of chicken and topped with green peas and pieces of red pepper. Tastes great too, and there's plenty of it; this is one selection that will not leave you hungry.

On the Oriental side, fried rice plates start at $4.00, as do chop suey and lo mein; a plate of mixed Chinese vegetables is just $5.35. Bouncing back to the Caribbean side, consider the *calimares enchiladas* for $5.95. Sit at the counter, find a table, or just grab food to take out. The atmosphere is bustling at La Caridad; it has a reputation as a good place for a quick, tasty, and inexpensive meal, and it deserves it.

Las Marcias Restaurant—588 Amsterdam Ave. (89th St.); 212/595-8121. Las Marcias, a neighborhood-type shop, is one of the many Hispanic restaurants along this stretch of Amsterdam. Each can be counted upon to serve up huge, tasty meals at low prices. The cuisine here is Dominican, with quite a large menu of choices. A small luncheon counter and glass-topped tables make the small place neat and bright.

As at most such restaurants, the good deals start right up with a *bilingual* breakfast. From 7:00 to 11:00 a.m., just $2.95 will get you two eggs (any style) with bacon, ham or salami; home fries or cassava; toast; and coffee, tea or hot chocolate. For lunch, try an avocado salad ($2.00), with fresh slices over lettuce, or a chicken salad plate ($5.95). Chicken, of course, figures in a major way here. How about a whole roasted chicken—with rice, beans, and fried plantain—for just $7.50? The half-chicken, same sides, is a mere $5.50. And there are seven or eight different specials each day of the week, such as whole red snapper with salsa ($7.95), baked pork ribs ($5.95) and spicy "Caribbean meatballs" ($5.95). For more exotic tastes, you may enjoy the stewed goat ($6.50) and cow feet soup ($2.95). Whatever you fancy, these specials all come with white or yellow rice, plantains, and beans or cassava. The portions are huge, so you can take some home.

You'll find similar deals at several other wonderful Latin American restaurants along this mile. Among them are **La Sarten**, 564 Amsterdam Avenue (88th St.); 212/787-6448, a Caribbean house offering many entrees from $7.00 to $10.00 and a $5.95 lunch special that's hard to beat—choose from ten dishes including pepper steak, pork cutlets in garlic, and codfish stew. **Angelo's Express** next door (also 564 Amsterdam; 212/580-1700) somehow combines Mexican and Italian foods—like chile relleno ($6.25), peppers stuffed with chicken, beef or cheese, alongside penne with chicken ($7.50), made with sun-dried tomatoes, mushrooms, and red peppers.

Further up the street, try **Casilda Restaurant**, 764 Amsterdam Avenue (97th St.), 212/864-5648; a hopping Dominican joint with many daily dinner specials priced from $6.00 to $8.00 for full meals. They also have lots of imported Latin beers and wines.

Mingala West—325 Amsterdam Ave. (76th St.); 212/873-0787. Mingala bills itself as the only Burmese restaurant on the Upper West Side (though Mr. C has written about Bali Burma in the "Midtown" section). Burmese cuisine is similar to Indian in flavor, with both meat and vegetarian dishes treated in a spicy manner. More importantly, the prices are great! Nothing on the menu tops $8.95, except in the seafood category. But there are lots of beef, chicken, and pork dishes, along with rice, noodle, and salad dinners as well. The names are as creative as the food: "Rangoon Night Market

Noodles," for example ($6.95), combine egg noodles with roast duck in a garlic and scallion sauce. "Mountain Ruby Chicken" ($8.95) is a spicy stir-fry with chili peppers, zucchini, and peanuts mixed in. And "Pineapple Pork Balls" ($8.50) explain themselves. No giggling, now.

Soups and salads are wonderful and cheap. Try the "Twelve Ingredient Hot Pot for Two" ($5.75) filled with shrimp, chicken, pork, mushrooms, tofu, snow peas, and other vegetables. Or a string beans and peanut salad ($4.50), with steamed veggies, roast peanuts, sesame seeds, and a zingy lemon sauce.

But wait, it gets better. Mingala offers two dozen lunch specials for just $4.50 each, Monday through Friday from noon to 4:00 p.m.; these are drawn from all sections of the menu and come with vegetable fried rice and a salad or soup. Then, from 4:30 to 6:30 p.m., you can order from ten different early bird specials, each just $5.95. These bargains make good food even better.

Ollie's Noodle Shop—2315 Broadway (84th St.); 212/362-3111, 2957 Broadway (116th St.); 212/362-3712, and 190 West 44th St.; 212/921-5988. Success breeds more success. In just a few years this upscale Chinese restaurant has become the favorite of so many Westsiders that it has spawned two copies—including one right in the heart of Times Square (a much-needed addition of dependable, affordable dining there!). Ollie's gives you a ton of food at great prices in a lively atmosphere. In fact, they're so busy that waiting for a table is not uncommon during the dinner hour.

The vast menu offers lots of different kinds of appetizers, which can become the whole meal in themselves. Be sure to get some kind of dumplings (you can watch them being made in Ollie's open kitchen while waiting for that table); a platter of eight goes for around $4.00—whether meat, veggie, seafood, or shrimp—steamed in a green wrapper dough. Sesame wontons, scallion pancakes, and roast pork buns are some of the other fine specialties.

Follow this with a heaping bowl of Cantonese wonton or Mandarin noodle soup, and you're all set. Most are between $4.00 to $6.00, packed with vegetables, strips of meat, noodles and all kinds of goodies. These vast bowls are hard to finish!

Of course, if you want to go on to a main dish, there is another huge selection to ponder. A dozen or more choices each of chicken, seafood, beef, pork, and vegetarian dishes all check in from about $6.50 to $8.75. But really—don't you think the all-appetizer meal is more fun?

Ottomanelli's Cafe—50 West 72nd St.; 212/787-9493. See listing under "Midtown Manhattan East."

Patzo—2330 Broadway (85th St.); 212/496-9240. One of the more elaborate restaurants on the Upper West Side, Patzo looks like it should be much more expensive than it really is. Lots of dinner options around $10.00 or less, plus a $4.95 brunch until 4:30 on weekends make this large, lavish restaurant an affordable one.

"Palazzo" might be just as good a name for the vast Mediterranean interior, with three open floors of dining rooms leading up to a high, vaulted ceiling. Just inside the main door is an elegant bar area, which offers its own inexpensive menu until 2:00 a.m., Fridays through Sundays (1:00 a.m. on weeknights). The place is decorated everywhere with food: Crusty loaves of bread, wine bottles, jars of dried pasta in various colors, and huge copper pots. Italian painted tiles are set into the walls, which are also adorned with theater posters and artsy European lighting.

The food they actually *serve* looks just as good. Start off with the antipasto ($4.95), mixed from a changing daily selection of greens and vegetables. There are a dozen pastas, most around $8.95, including tricolored cheese tortelloni Alfredo. There are also several good-sized individual pizzas, on fresh thin crusts, which will fill you up for about $8.00.

Other dinner entrees include eggplant rollatini ($7.95), sauteed breast of chicken in a lemon and pepper sauce ($8.95) served with rice and vegetable, and veal parmesan with linguine ($11.50). Baskets brimming with a variety of fresh-baked breads are brought immediately to the table, each of which is also equipped with a bottle of extra-virgin olive oil and balsamic vinegar. At the other end of the meal, desserts—like Tirami Su and Mississippi Mud Pie—are baked on the premises.

Along with a regular à la carte menu, Saturday and Sunday brunch offer a selection of $4.95 entrees, from a heaping bowl of pasta and vegetable salad to ricotta and vegetable quiche and a charcoal-grilled turkey burger with thin, hand-cut French fries. Whether you go for lunch, brunch, dinner, or late-night snacking, Patzo will be a grand experience at reasonable prices.

Puccini Cafe—475 Columbus Ave. (83rd St.); 212/875-9533. Dining at Puccini is like a quick trip to Europe—all of it. The decor could be that of any bright, clean cafe in Paris or Rome; Spanish guitar music plays on the sound system; and the menu ranges from pasta to quiche to blintzes to cappuccino and pastries. The food is all fresh and attractive, and the atmosphere is lively and bustling.

It's the light nature of the foods offered that keeps this trendy-looking place affordable; salads and sandwiches are the main fare, though there are some larger entrees too. Half-a-dozen pasta dinners are all in the $7.50 to $9.50 range, including lasagna and spinach fettucine with mushrooms and olives. The large variety of salads are similarly priced: Nicoise, Waldorf, avocado citrus, Angelas (fusili pasta, tuna, tomato, black olives, cucumber and pearl onions, $7.50), and more.

Omelettes, served through breakfast and lunch, are sizeable and come with home fries or delicately-cooked French fries, and toast made from homemade bread. Mr. C enjoyed the Puccini, made with bits of salmon, asparagus, and mozzarella cheese ($7.75). Blintzes ($5.00 to $6.00) are a turn on the traditional; they are filled with vegetables, mushrooms, scallions, and such. The closest variety to the sweet kind found in Jewish delis has a filling of sweet cheese and raisins, with fruit over the top.

Puccini has lots of hot and cold beverages, from fresh-squeezed fruit juices and iced cappuccino to hot coffees and teas. And just try to keep from looking at the long pastry case, with such delights as flan, profiteroles, and cappuccino mousse cake. These are pricier, but worth the splurge!

Ruppert's—269 Columbus Ave. (72nd St.); 212/873-9400, and 1662 Second Ave. (93rd St.); 212/831-1900. See listing under "Upper East Side."

West Side Storey—700 Columbus Ave. (95th St.); 212/749-1900. Way up on Columbus, past the well-known restaurant mile, is one more gem. West Side Storey is a cozy, bright, and bustling update on diner-style food that is upscale without being overpriced. Brunches here are hard to beat, with huge omelettes filled with things like Spanish sausage, garden vegetables, smoked salmon, and even caviar (*there's* a word you won't find too often in Mr. Cheap's books). All are priced between $5.95 and $7.95, with home fries and bread baked in-house.

Of course, you can get

these omelettes any day of the week, along with salads, giant sandwiches (Genoa salami, fresh mozzarella and roasted peppers on focaccia bread, $6.95), pastas, burgers, and homemade deep-dish pizzas (split one, as low as $10.95, for a real bargain). There is also a small globetrotter of an entree list: Thai chicken, Moroccan chili, burritos, and good ol' American meatloaf dinners, all under $10.00. Portions are ample indeed.

This neighborhood place is always packed on the weekends, with families, couples, and visitors from the suburbs. Even the Sharks and the Jets, presumably, would break some fresh bread here and chow down.

Zabar's Cafe—2245 Broadway (80th St.); 212/787-2000. If you're one of the many who love shopping at Zabar's for their fresh-baked breads and pastries, cream cheeses, smoked fish, and so forth—but you can't wait to get home to tear into this great food—stop into Zabar's Cafe. It's next door to the main market and provides both stand-up counter eating and take-out service. Here you'll find all the bagels and cream cheeses you've come to love, as well as muffins, pastries, and the like. The cafe also has a number of breakfast specials. On Mr. C's visit, one of these was a fresh-made omelette croissant (choose from ham and egg, or egg and cheese) plus coffee and orange juice, for just *two bucks.* Quick, hard to beat price-wise, and a great way to start the day. There are a number of similar specials at Zabar's, including their terrific home-style soups. Be forewarned: There's almost always a line to get to the counter, but it moves quickly. Like any good New Yorker, you should, too, when you finally reach the front. With any luck, you'll then be able to find an open stool at one of the side counters; otherwise, you can be even *more* like a New Yorker—eating and walking down the street at the same time.

OUTER BOROUGHS

Cousin John's Cafe and Bakery—70 Seventh Ave., Park Slope, Brooklyn; 718/622-7333, and 343 Seventh Ave., Park Slope, Brooklyn; 718/768-2020. With two locations in Brooklyn's up-and-coming Park Slope district, Cousin John's offers simple fare for a snack or light meal. Order three eggs, any style, with a croissant (fresh-baked on the premises) and a salad—it will run you just $4.25. Or try the soup of the day (Mr. C was impressed by the hearty vegetable variety offered on the day of his visit)—that comes with a salad as well, and is just $4.75.

The ingredients are fresh, the food is quite tasty, and the prices are tough to beat. If you're not in the mood for a meal, check out the pastry counter. There's plenty to choose from, and coupled with an herbal tea or a capuccino, one of these can make for a nice midmorning or midafternoon snack. All in all, a good spot for a quick, cheap bite between window-shopping visits to those entertaining shops on Seventh Avenue.

Egidio Cafe—622 East 187th St., Belmont, Bronx; 718/295-6077. The Arthur Avenue section of the Bronx is known to many as an outer-borough Little Italy. The intersection of Arthur and 187th Street is lined with expensive Italian restaurants that are probably worth the prices they charge; however, if you're looking for a simpler dining option, consider the Egidio, which Mr. C thinks is every bit as good as its fancier neighbors. This is really two stops in one: a bakery on the corner and a sit-down cafe that serves lunch and dinner next door. (The cafe also features a gelati take-out counter.)

The food is truly wonderful. Start off with a bowl of chicken soup crammed with pasta and vegetables for $3.50. Follow that with a large plate of stuffed shells for just $4.50, or fettucine with meat sauce for $6.95. The daily specials are all listed up front, and may include such items as veal parmigiana for just $6.95. Orders come out quickly and are accompanied by fresh, warm bread that's crusty on the outside and soft and delicious on the inside.

You won't believe how full you can get at these prices; still, you should probably save room for some gelati after your meal—and perhaps a cup of the espresso, which is particularly good here. If you've got an espresso maker at home and are eager to use it to generate some top-notch brew, you can buy some of the fine Egidio house grind for just $2.75 a pound, another fantastic bargain. The cafe is open until 8:00 pm.

El Gran Castillo de Jagua—345 Flatbush Ave., Park Slope, Brooklyn; 718/622-8700. In Park Slope's melting pot, this Dominican/Spanish diner is plain and very authentic—with fabulous food that's among the cheapest and best *anywhere*. In fact, Mr. C and his Brooklyn expert had a tasty, filling meal here for $13.00.... *together*. There are two rooms: A lunch counter area first, and then a larger dining room. It's not elegant (it shouldn't be), but it's clean and colorful. A jukebox blares out Spanish CDs, with everyone from Julio Iglesias to Ruben Sierra—yes, the baseball star. Who knew?

The menu is vast, starting with breakfast (two eggs any style with toast and home fries, $1.75) and moving on to lunch and dinner. Warm, fresh bread and butter are brought to the table first, always a good sign. Then there are soups, like chicken ($2.50), which included a whole leg sitting in a tomatoey broth with potatoes, carrots and noodles. Almost a meal in itself. Then, you can try the Caribbean specialty, mofongo ($3.50) a mountain of mashed green plantains with ground roast pork mixed in. Too much to finish.

There are about twenty meat selections, almost all of which are $5.25 to $7.50. These include Spanish pepper steak, barbecued chicken, and two breaded pork chops, each served with rice and beans or fried plantains and salad. Then there's seafood, like sauteed fish filets ($6.95); rice dishes, like chorizo sausage and rice ($4.95); sandwiches and salads. Beer and wine are also available.

If you can manage, save room for the homemade flan ($1.50) often dressed in unusual flavors. And you won't find it any cheaper. El Gran Castillo is a friendly neighborhood place or an exotic trip to faraway lands—whichever you prefer.

Fountain Cafe—183 Atlantic Ave., Brooklyn; 718/624-6764. In the midst of downtown Brooklyn's Middle Eastern shopping district, along Atlantic Avenue, the Fountain Cafe is a clean, bright, and very inexpensive restaurant specializing in sandwiches, kebabs, and vegetarian entrees.

It's good whether you're looking for a quick bite or a full meal; if you're stopping in for a snack, try one of the Syrian meat or spinach pies (just $1.50) or perhaps a bowl of lentil soup ($2.00). A large variety of meat and vegetarian sandwiches are priced between $3.00 and $4.00; these include such choices as barbecued lamb kebab for $3.75 or a falafel sandwich for $2.85. Whichever you choose, it's going to come wrapped up in pita bread and stuffed with salad and tahini sauce. Quite a handful, and very filling.

Full-size platters, which come with salad, rice, and vegetables on the side, start as low as $3.25 for stuffed grape leaves; other vegetarian options include a falafel, hoummos, and baba ghanouj platter for just

Mr. Cheap's Picks
Brooklyn

✔ **El Gran Castillo de Jagua**—In Park Slope, a great neighborhood Hispanic restaurant. Incredible amounts of food, super-cheap. Mr. C's kind of place.

✔ **Monika**—A Polish find near the Sunset Park area. Tiny, quiet, and wonderful.

✔ **Patsy's Pizza**—Many consider this the best pizza in the city. Right at the Brooklyn Bridge, it's lively and reasonably priced.

Mr. Cheap's Pick
The Bronx

✔ **Egidio Cafe**—In the Arthur Avenue area, which boasts so many Italian restaurants, this cozy little bakery and cafe is a cheaper alternative to the big "mangia" scenes.

$6.00. Meat entrees are mostly priced around $8.00, whether you get shawarma, a spiced ground lamb dish, chicken kebabs, or even a combination plate of two different kinds of meats. Follow this with one of the Fountain's intriguing coffee or tea selections— and for dessert you must try the baklava. It's just $1.25 a slice.

Down the block from the Fountain is a newer entry in the field called **Maroosh** (107 Atlantic Avenue; 718/330-0423). Mr. C enjoyed it quite a bit. This place specializes in sandwiches, salads, and lighter fare, and also offers a bewildering array of French pastries, tarts, and other delights brought in from the nearby Marquet Patisserie. You can eat in or take out. Both restaurants are open seven days a week.

Healthy Henrietta's Burritos—60 Henry St., Brooklyn Heights; 718/858-8478. A macrobiotic Mexican restaurant? Yup. Henrietta's offers familiar dishes done in "Northern California" vegetarian style, using all-natural ingredients, free of chemicals. Some items are also free of taste; but there are plenty of things here that are just fine—even for old-fashioned, additive-loving diners.

Certainly, a vegetarian burrito is a vegetarian burrito. For $6.25, this is made with a tortilla the size of a record album (speaking of old-fashioned), into which is rolled: Beans, rice, guacamole, and your choice of Monterey jack, sour cream or, yes, tofu sour cream. Quesadillas start at $4.25 for the basic. And the menu tops out at $8.00, with the "Super Enchilada"—beans, rice, and cheese (or tofu!) baked in one of three varieties of picante sauce and topped with guac, lettuce, and tomatoes.

Then, there are the special platters, complete meals for $9.00. There are three variations of sauteed veggies, with rice, corn bread, spinach, and hijiki—that's seaweed, son. Actually, it's not bad. The same cannot be said for the corn bread, alas—the macro version comes out dry and grainy. Oh well. Still, the name doesn't lie; Henrietta's is healthy.

Jackson Hole Wyoming—69-35 Astoria Blvd., Queens; 718/204-7070. See listing under "Midtown Manhattan East."

Junior's Restaurant—386 Flatbush Ave. Extension at DeKalb Ave., Brooklyn; 718/852-5257. "Junior's Most Fabulous Restaurant" may perhaps symbolize the transition that takes place in so many of New York's neighborhoods. This huge, sprawling establishment, opened in 1929, is a wacky mix of old-time Jewish coffee shop and modern urban barbecue house. The clientele is similarly made up of blacks, Hispanics, and Jews, all chowing down on blintzes, chopped liver, Buffalo wings, and ribs. The atmosphere is bright and boisterous, with lots of groups out for big dinners during Mr. C's visit.

"May I recommend this table, sir?" said the extremely polite maitre d', with all the attention he might have given to a fine bottle of wine. The waitstaff was equally attentive and efficient, setting out onion rolls, pickles and cole slaw upon arrival—the tradition of a good Jewish deli. Indeed, for those looking for the best bargains, the "overstuffed" sandwiches are the winners—over forty options, ranging from egg salad and bacon ($5.25) to lake sturgeon, Nova Scotia salmon, sliced tomato and Bermuda onion ($8.95).

Mr. C, however, seeing that the Old World side was in good hands, ordered a platter of barbecued baby back ribs ($11.95). What promptly came out was about a rack and a half of meaty, juicy ribs smothered with a tangy sauce, along with a baked potato and more cole slaw. It was too much to finish. Saving room for dessert, though, is important. Of the two dozen treats offered, many baked in-house, the cheesecake ($3.25 a slice) is a big winner. Huge is more the word for this creamy slab with a cookie crumb crust. Have it topped with strawberries. If you didn't leave room, you can always pick some up to take home from Junior's retail bakery. In fact, the cheesecake is the restaurant's calling card; you can have one shipped anywhere in the country.

Junior's has a separate cafe lounge with a full bar and more tables for dining. It's all open seven days a week.

Monika—643 Fifth Ave., Sunset Park, Brooklyn; 718/788-6930. Walking into this tiny storefront restaurant is like walking straight from the street into someone's dining room. Monika is a Polish restaurant that fills your stomach with hearty home cooking and leaves your wallet full at the end as well. Nothing on this menu is priced any higher than $4.60—the tab for a large platter of potato dumplings with meat. These small potato dumplings are called *kopytka*, and they can be had as a separate order for $3.60 or added to any other entree for $1.00. Among the other entrees are half a dozen varieties of pierogies, which come filled with meat, sauerkraut, cheese, or even blueberries. Whatever filling you select, your plate will cost just $3.20. Yes, you read right: $3.20.

The menu is made up of nothing *but* bargains. A baked half-chicken is just $3.70; roast pork chops are $4.00; the Polish kielbasa (which should not be missed), either boiled or fried, runs just $4.30. As for appetizers, there are a number of soups to choose from, most of which are priced betwen $1.00 and $2.00 a cup. Whether you get the sauerkraut soup ($1.00), the pea soup ($1.00), or the borscht with mushrooms ($1.90), you won't go away disappointed.

Cheese blintzes, already an inexpensive delicacy at so many Polish restaurants in Manhattan, are priced even lower here: just $3.00. They make an intriguing dessert, not unlike an Italian cannoli, but you may end up considering them a meal in themselves. Another dessert option: Compote made from sliced peaches, just 70¢ a serving. When was the last time you got *any* dessert for that price? They'll take good care of you here; the servings are ample, the ingredients are the genuine article, and the prices are *bardzo tano*—loosely translated, that means "surrealistically low." Monika is open daily from 10:00 a.m. until 8:00 p.m.

Moustache—405 Atlantic Ave., Brooklyn; 718/852-5555. This simple spot on the "antiques mile" of Atlantic Avenue is, like many of its neighboring eateries, Middle Eastern. And there the resemblance ends. The specialty here is something owner Salam al-Rawi calls a "pitza"—individual ten-inch pies made on pita bread. It works. The bread is homemade, freshly baked, thin and crispy; the basic, tomato and cheese, is just $5.00. Familiar toppings, like mushrooms or peppers, are $1.00 each.

But why be ordinary here? For $2.00, you can top your pitza with shrimp or scallops in garlic and parsley. And then it really gets exotic. The *laham-bazin* features ground lamb, beef, and onions, still $5.00; sort of a cross between pizza and gyros. Chicken pitza ($7.00) tops it with lemon-marinated chicken plus garlic, red peppers and scallions. And the *merguez* ($6.00) has a spicy lamb sausage on top.

There are sandwiches and salads too, most $5.00 or less. For dessert, try a variation of baklava filled with walnuts and raisins, $1.25. The surroundings are clean and humble, and quite friendly.

Ottomanelli's Cafe—92-65 Fourth Ave., Brooklyn (94th St.); 718/680-2100, and 96-24 Queens Blvd., Rego Park; 718/459-7427. See listing under "Midtown Manhattan East."

Pastrami King—124-24 Queens Blvd., Kew Gardens, Queens; 718/263-1717. An old-style Jewish deli serving up—what else?—tasty pastrami sandwiches. Also corned beef sandwiches, brisket sandwiches, turkey sandwiches, and combinations thereof. Not to mention hot open-face versions of same, as well as soups, Hungarian-style dinners, and other filling fare. Pastrami King cures its own corned beef, garlicky pastrami, and other meats on the premises, and they are good!

The dinners are a bit overpriced; so stick with the sandwiches (they'll certainly stick with you), about $6.00 for the two-fisted basic varieties. These are nicely-sized, but you can probably polish them off if you have a healthy appetite. Or step up to the combos, such as roast turkey with chopped liver and chicken fat (that'll harden your arteries) or corned beef and pastrami with cole slaw and Russian dressing. These run up to $8.25.

If you think you'll have room, order up some appetizers or side dishes too, like kasha varnishkas with gravy or thick, crispy French fries—each $2.25.

Don't look for spiffy decor or sparkling service here—the restaurant has been around awhile and so, it seems, has the staff. But they're friendly, if you can get their attention. If you're in the neighborhood, this is a neighborhood kind of place.

Patsy's Pizza—19 Old Fulton St., Brooklyn Heights; 718/858-4300. In the shadow of the Brooklyn Bridge, on the Brooklyn side, there are several fine restaurants offering great food with dramatic views of Manhattan. Unfortunately, if you're reading this book, you may not be able to afford the dramatic prices they charge. But because you *are* reading this book, you're in luck.

Mr. Cheap's Picks
Queens

✔ **Pastrami King**—So this old-time Jewish deli has seen better days—it's still got great food. A little heavy, but great. You were expecting maybe tofu and those fancy-shmancy rabbit-food sandwiches?

✔ **Uncle George's**—The best deal to be found among the Greek restaurants in Astoria. Filling, friendly, and cheap.

There are less expensive, just as delicious, alternatives. Tops on this list has to be Patsy's.

A very close personal acquaintance of Mr. C's recently pronounced this "the best pizza I've ever had." And he's eaten quite a few in his day. Indeed, Patsy's pizza is thin-crusted, coal-oven-baked, and topped with the freshest ingredients. This means a pie that is crisp, not oily or greasy, on which sauces and cheese are placed, not smeared on. The mozzarella is homemade, the tomatoes are freshly crushed. It's good stuff.

Patsy's is a restaurant, not a sub shop; the decor is bright and clean. A 1940s-style jukebox plays plenty of Sinatra, and his picture adorns the pastel-colored walls. Beer and wine are served, and the place is open six nights a week until 11:00 or 12:00 p.m. (closed Tuesdays). You cannot order slices here; whole pies only. At $10.50 for a small pie, and $12.00 for a large—with extra toppings $2.00 each—this is not the cheapest pizza in town. But two people can share the small, three can share the large, and don't forget the superior quality—or the location. You can still eat here for around $10.00 or less; and if you can't enjoy the view while you eat, just walk the food off on a short stroll to the river.

San Burrito Bay Taqueria—140 Montague St., Brooklyn Heights; 718/875-8846. Oh wow, California comes to, like, Brooklyn Heights. Check out the natural wood tables and the bay window overlooking chic Montague Street. This second-floor Tex-Mex restaurant is fresh and new, with prices that are hard to match. Burrito plates range from $4.25 to $6.95, including rice and beans; the simplest, "L.A.," gives you a choice of meat filling, just your basic. At the other end of the scale, the "Outrageous" offers a choice of two meats (or a double helping of one) with guacamole, cheese, pico de gallo, and sour cream.

Tacos *al carbon* may be ordered individually, most just $2.50 each. Fillings include grilled marinated beef or pork, with a bit of spice to them. Or go for the Chile Colorado, cubes of pork in a zingy chili sauce. Nacho plates and quesadillas are $5.50 each, or $4.50 for meatless versions. There are, of course, plenty of vegetarian items on the menu, and lots of combination options.

San Burrito is open seven days a week until 10:00 p.m., and until 11:00 p.m. on weekends.

Teresa's Restaurant—80 Montague St., Brooklyn Heights; 718/797-3996, and 103 First Ave. (6th St.), Manhattan; 212/228-0604. All the way at the end of Montague, just before the Promenade, Teresa's hides a hearty, home-style diner behind a sleek white facade. Inside, the restaurant—with its booths, tables and lunch counter—is a handsome, slightly upscale variation on the Russian/Polish diners of the East Village. And though the interior is nicer than Kiev or Veselka (or even Teresa's own Manhattan branch), the prices are pretty much the same.

Belly up to the counter and order a piece of steak sitting in a pot of mushroom gravy ($6.95), or a breaded veal cutlet ($7.25). A pair of stuffed cabbages are $6.50, and a roast half-chicken is $6.95. All of these, and many other dinners, include bread and two side orders of the day's vegetables. You'll be stuffed yourself. This is also true at lunch, when the same entrees are a dollar cheaper.

Each day there is a different soup, from Ukranian borscht to potato soup to pickle soup (!), all $2.00 for a large bowl. Homemade blintzes, $5.95, are fabulous—long, crisply-fried on the outside, sweet on the inside, and dusted on top with confectioners' sugar. And don't forget the pierogies, filled with cheese, meat, potato, or sauerkraut and mushrooms. Get 'em boiled or fried, just $4.75 for seven heavy dumplings. *Ess, mein kind!*

Tony's Pier—1 City Island Ave., City Island, Bronx; 718/885-1424. Bet you didn't know you could find a little touch of New England in the Bronx. It's called City Island. Located near the Westchester border, it may require a bit of a drive, but once you get there you'll find one long stretch of wonderful seafood restaurants that will make you feel as if you're on Cape Cod. Tony's Pier is the very last one, all the way out by the water, with a large open patio in back that offers a tremendous view across Long Island Sound. (If you can make out any land on the other side, that's Great Neck.)

This is your basic no-frills clam bar. Walk up to the counter and order yourself a generous plate of fried shrimp ($10.00), calamari ($9.00), oysters or clam strips (each $8.00). All of these dinners come with French fries, cole slaw, pickles, and tartar sauce. A little heavy, perhaps, but perfectly appropriate for the surroundings. Unlike many of the other restaurants hereabouts, Tony's is open year-round; during the cold winter months you can camp yourself in front of a big roaring fire as you eat. The restaurant is open seven days a week.

Tripoli—156 Atlantic Ave., Brooklyn; 718/596-5800. A long-time landmark in Brooklyn's Middle Eastern district, Tripoli is a large and lavish restaurant and bar that looks a lot more expensive than it actually is. The decore features a nautical theme, with wood-paneled walls and ornate seafaring decorations. Even the very high ceilings have been painted with blue skies and puffy white clouds. These sailors must have gotten a bit confused on the voyage to Brooklyn, though Tripoli offers foods originating not in Libya, as the dutiful map-consulter might expect, but in Lebanon.

The extensive menu offers many traditional Lebanese foods and dozens of entrees. Most of these main dishes are priced between $7.00 and $9.00. Kibbee mishwiye ($8.75) is lean and finely ground leg of lamb mixed with cracked wheat and further stuffed with chopped nuts and onion, then charcoal broiled. Or try minuzli ($7.75), which is sauteed eggplant stuffed with ground lamb and pine nuts, cooked in a spicy tomato sauce and served over rice. In addition to the lamb dishes you will find chicken, steak, and seafood entrees such as suumuk b'tahini ($9.50)—sauteed fish filets cooked in a spicy tahini sauce, topped with almonds and walnuts and served over rice. The vegetarian entrees are even better bargains: most run between $5.25 and $7.00. The kibet b'ziat ($7.00) is a platter of cooked potatoes and onions stuffed with walnuts and raisins; the whole mixture is then baked in olive oil. A most exotic offering!

After your meal you can choose from dozens of desserts, all priced at $2.00 or less, including baklava, almond cakes, and other treats. Tripoli has a full bar, including a fairly extensive and reasonably priced wine list. The downstairs function room offers traditional Middle Eastern entertainment on Friday nights. Yes, that means belly dancing. Although there is a $20.00-per-person food and drink minimum for those wishing to enjoy this entertainment, there is (no pun intended here) no cover.

Uncle George's—33-19 Broadway, Astoria, Queens; 718/626-0593. Of all the Greek *tavernas* along these few blocks of Broadway, Uncle George's has got to be Mr. C's favorite—as it clearly is for many other people. Racks of lamb and spits of whole chickens are turning above open fires as you walk in. A large diner with long, family-style tables, George's is open twenty-four hours a day and is regularly packed. The natives know a good deal when they see one.

The menu is large, too, with most entrees well under $10.00. Choices range from traditional favorites like roast leg of lamb ($7.00, with orzo or vegetable) and a barbecued half-chicken with potatoes ($5.00) to such seafood delicacies as a platter of baby smelts ($7.00). Then there is the Pandora's Box of daily specials, each available on certain days of the week. On Mondays you'll find stuffed squid for $6.00; on Wednesdays and Sundays, roast pork with spinach rice for $5.00; and Saturdays include rabbit stew with onions, $7.00. Whether your tastes are basic or exotic, you're sure to find something yummy.

Portions here are enormous. When Mr. C asked the waiter how many lamb chops came in the regular entree (one of the more expensive items at $10.00), the reply was, "Well, it depends on the size of the chops. If they're big, you get three. If they're small, you get four." What you definitely get here is full. Indeed, the authenticity of Uncle George's was confirmed by one of Mr. C's dining companions, a person of Greek descent herself, who pronounced the restaurant a winner—very much like family restaurants in the old country.

Afterward, if you have room, walk across the street and to the right a bit for dessert at the **Omonia Cafe** (32-20 Broadway; 718/274-6650). A fine restaurant in its own right, recently expanded and renovated, Omonia's bakery/cafe offers dozens of wonderful pastries and hot beverages. A giant wedge of baklava here costs just $1.50; most other places around town give you a piece that's half the size and more expensive. The cafe also has a gorgeous white grand piano at the back, with free music nightly. What a deal! You can enjoy an entire evening out, including dinner, dessert and entertainment—affordably—without even leaving the block.

LODGING

For starters, let's establish one important point: Mr. Cheap has not attempted to identify the best ways to secure inexpensive *long-term* digs in and around the Big Apple. That's a book in itself. What follows is a brief survey of some of the more attractive bargains for those who are visiting Manhattan and environs on a short-term basis. In general, this section is designed for those who are eager to find a good cheap spot to spend a long weekend, vacation, or somewhat longer stay. A recent travel survey found that, London and Hong Kong, New York City is the *most expensive place in the world* when it comes to lodging and meals. But there are certainly deals to be found, and Mr. C has done the legwork for you.

Two categories here: "Off the Beaten Track" and "Hotels." The first passes along some ideas for rock-bottom prices in non-hotel settings. (Of course, that's a comparative "rock-bottom"; the assumption here is that you're not interested in, say, free emergency shelter.) In the second section you'll find leads on some of the most affordable hotel settings in the midtown area.

Of course, the hotels cost more than the off-the-beaten-track places. Only you can determine how much of a criterion a luxury accoutrement like an ice bucket should be. For the author's tastes, a friend's couch, with the occasional visit from a friendly pooch, has both options beaten cold. Maybe you could just buy an ice bucket and keep it by the couch at your pal's place. No? Okay, then. Here's the lowdown.

OFF THE BEATEN TRACK

Abode Bed and Breakfast—P.O. Box 20022, New York, NY 10028; 212/472-2000. Okay, okay, it's not really a place you can stay. (It was probably the P.O. box that tipped you off, right?) This is a service that, by phone or mail, will connect you with short-term vacancies in apartments in residential buildings around the city, which Mr. C considers to be a capital piece of creative thinking on someone's part. Although prices vary widely, it's safe to say that there's something here for just about every price range. Some rooms are available with a host on the premises; it's less expensive, but presumably also less like having the place to yourself. An interesting idea that's worth looking into when a hotel room seems unlikely for logistical or financial reasons. Similar services are offered by **City Lights Bed and Breakfast** (212/737-7049), **Bed and Breakfast Network of New York** (212/645-8134), and **Brooklyn's own Brownstone Bed and Breakfast** (718/857-0196).

The Leo House—332 West 23rd St., Manhattan, New York NY 10011; 212/929-1010. The Leo House was originally established in the Battery Park area in 1899 by the St. Raphael Society, a group dedicated to aiding German Catholic immigrants. Today, at its West 23rd St. location, it

Mr. Cheap's Pick

✔ **Short-Term Housing**—Quite a find for those spending some time in the city: An owner or lessee is out of town for a spell, so you agree to keep an eye on his or her place. If the match is good, this can be a win/win situation for everyone.

serves as a Catholic hospice for out-of-state visitors. It is safe, clean, and ideally suited to visitors on a tight budget ... or at least, to those visitors on a tight budget who can plan their stay approximately three months in advance. (That's the estimated wait.) It perhaps bears repeating that the premises are meant for *out-of-staters only*—although people of all faiths and from all countries are welcome. Breakfast is served in the Leo's tidy little cafeteria every morning except Sunday; laundry facilities are available on the premises, as is a chapel, which holds daily Mass. Single rooms run between $52.00 and $58.00 per night; double rooms are priced from $60.00 to $67.00. Quite affordable indeed. The maximum stay is three weeks, although openings for short-term residencies do come up from time to time. *Note well*: You have to play by the rules at the Leo. Only registered guests are allowed in rooms, and smoking is restricted to a few common areas and the garden. This is certainly not your typical lodging establishment, but then you get the feeling that's just how the Sisters of St. Agnes, who have been running the place for the last century, like it.

92nd St. "Y" Residence—1395 Lexington Ave., Manhattan; 212/415-5650. If you're young (that means men and women ages eighteen to twenty-six), you can stay here for extended periods of time at very low rates indeed. All they ask is that you don't make any jokes about the Village People. Seriously, though, the Y is a good inexpensive option to explore if you're going to be in town for a spell, although, to borrow a phrase from the world of advertising, certain restrictions apply. There is a minimum requirement to your stay that can vary from a few weeks to three months, depending on the time of year. Both single and double rooms are available, but you should apply well in advance by calling or writing in for a form. Security guards monitor all visitors.

Short-Term Housing—849 Lexington Ave., Manhattan; 212/570-2288. Looking to make an extended—but not permanent—stay in the city? Short-Term Housing can match you up with private apartments that are temporarily vacant. No, this doesn't mean "abandoned"—typically, the space arises because the owner or lessee is out of town. Many of these arrangements are made as sublets. Call for more details. If your visit to New York will be too lengthy to make hotel rates practical—maybe you're looking to try the Apple out for a few months—this could well be the solution.

HOTELS

Important Note: The hotels listed below will all take good care of you for under $100 per night—in midtown, no less. However, honesty compels Mr. C to acknowledge here that these are the most recent announced pre-tax prices as of press time. Actual hotel rates seem to change with the wind—well, certainly with the seasons. A book like this cannot stay truly accurate for long, so if you don't find these exact prices, please don't demand to see the manager (or Mr. C, for that matter). Instead, think of these listings as general guidelines for comparison as you search around. They do prove, at least, that there are some alternatives to $400 a night at the St. Regis.

Best Western President Hotel—234 West 48th St., Manhattan; 212/246-8800, or 1-800/528-1234. The Best Western President boasts four hundred rooms, including two deluxe penthouses and twelve executive suites. These last items are probably not the rooms you can secure for $85.00 a night for a single and $95.00 for a double, but they're no doubt close enough for some of the razzmatazz to rub off. This is quite a nice place—complete with coffee shop, atrium-style bar, and in-house Italian restaurant—that manages to stay under Mr. C's magic $100.00 nightly mark for its basic rooms. It's also got a heck of an advantage over even some of the pricier places when it comes to location: the President is close to Times Square, the Museum of Modern Art, Rockefeller Center, and the Jacob K. Javits Convention Center.

Edison Hotel—228 West 47th St., Manhattan; 212/840-5000, 1-800/221-4083. Smack in the middle of the theater district, the estimable Edison offers some very competitive rates for an overnight stay. Singles start at just $93.00 per night, doubles at $99.00. The food at the Cafe Edison (located within the hotel) is a great bargain, too; see the separate listing in the Restaurant section, under "Midtown Manhattan West."

Herald Square Hotel—19 West 31st St, Manhattan; 212/279-4017, 1-800/727-1888. Remember James Cagney as George M. Cohan in *Yankee Doodle Dandy*? Remember how, when he sang "Give My Regards to Broadway", he referred to having someone remember him to Herald Square? Wouldn't you like to be able to stay in the very hotel in which Cohan wrote that famous line? Well, so would Mr. C, but unfortunately this ain't the place. What the Herald Square Hotel *is* is a clean, dependable place to spend the night in New York for not very much money. The hotel boasts 120 rooms; singles start at just $65 per night, doubles at $70.00.

Jolly Madison Towers—22 East 38th St., Manhattan; 212/685-3700, 1-800/225-4340. This elderly but still quite appealing

Mr. Cheap's Picks

✔ **The Jolly Madison**—In midtown, but not of it, this Murray Hill spot offers some very competitive weekend specials. Perfect for that long-overdue getaway.

✔ **The Portland Square Hotel**—Nothing fancy, but where else can you find a base of operations for a Broadway weekend for well under $90 and live to tell the tale? Shared everything, including bathrooms. Still, you'd rather spend the money on theater tickets, right?

establishment can be found in the Murray Hill area, which out-of-towners remember primarily as a telephone prefix from 1950s films and TV shows. The district actually takes its name from one Robert Murray, an eighteenth-century bigwig whose place once stood at the intersection we know now as 37th Street and Park Avenue. Murray Hill is an oasis of relatively calm domesticity in the frenetic mix that is Business Manhattan; although the area around the Jolly Madison can get quite boisterous during weekday rush hour periods—thanks to the traffic coursing through the Queens-Midtown Tunnel—a weekend stay hereabouts will yield the opportunity for a welcome escape from the chaos of midtown without actually leaving it. Mr. C was attracted not so much by the supply of famous landmarks near the Jolly Madison (the United Nations, Grand Central Station, and those swanky Fifth Avenue boutiques are all within walking distance) as by the prices for nightly lodging here, which start at a competitive $99.00 for some single *and* some double rooms. Weekend specials start at just $85.00, a true New York bargain.

Pickwick Arms—230 East 51st St., Manhattan; 212/355-0300, 1-800/755-5029. Location, along with price, is the main selling point of the Pickwick. It's situated almost directly between Rockefeller Center, to the west, and the United Nations, to the east. It's a pleasant enough place that offers some very impressive rates: just $65.00 per night for a single and $80.00 for a double. Approximately four hundred rooms.

The Portland Square Hotel—132 West 47th St., Manhattan; 212/382-0600, 1-800/388-8988. "ROOMS FROM $40 - $95 PER NIGHT!" That's the screaming headline on the brochures for the Portland Square Hotel, and it's true enough. The fine print on the rate card, however, will clue you in to the fact that the $40.00 rate—which is, granted, very nearly impossible to beat, given the hotel's Times Square location—entails "shared bathroom facilities" for "one person only." Certainly it's still an impressive deal, but the provisos are worth keeping in mind if you had visions of, say, taking a nice, long hot bath at your leisure. The standard one-person room, with shower, tub, and one bed, runs $60.00 a night; a double room (one bed) is $75.00. These are still pretty amazing rates for well-kept rooms in this locale. All rooms include color TV and air conditioning. And that's about it. The Portland Square takes pride in its status as a "classic limited-service budget hotel since 1904." If you're up for that, and if you're looking for a good base of operations for a Broadway weekend, you should probably give the Portland Square a look.

Roger Williams Hotel—28 East 31st St, Manhattan; 212/684-7500, 1-800/637-9773. Located near Herald Square, this comparatively small (seventy-five rooms) establishment has been in business for over forty years. Part of the reason for its current popularity may be the extremely aggressive pricing structure: singles start at $55.00 per night, doubles at $60.00. Worth checking out.

The location also puts it close to the Empire State Building, just three blocks away. More importantly for readers of this book: About ten blocks down Fifth Avenue lies the Flatiron District, which is laced with bargain shops. Men's suits, furniture, books and perfumes are in abundance at discount, and many of these shops are profiled in preceding chapters.

INDEX

ALPHABETICAL INDEX

- A -

- B -

- C -

- D -

- E -

- F -

- G -

- H -

- I -

- J -

- K -

- L -

- M -

- N -

- O -

- P -

- Q -

- R -

- S -

- T -

- U -

- V -

- W -

- Y -

- Z -

SUBJECT INDEX

What? Mr. C left you out?
Missed your favorite cheap spot?

Mr. Cheap® tries to be everywhere, but hey—it's a big city. If you've got a bargain-priced shop, restaurant, hotel, or entertainment activity (or if there's one you just enjoy), send it in for the next edition of *Mr. Cheap's® New York*!

CHAPTER HEADING: ________________________________

NAME OF BUSINESS/ORGANIZATION:

____

ADDRESS: ________________________________

____

PHONE: ________________________________

WHAT'S GREAT ABOUT IT: ________________________________

____

____

____

____

YOUR NAME: ________________________________

ADDRESS: ________________________________

____

Clip this page out and send it to:

Mr. Cheap®
c/o Adams Media Corporation
260 Center Street
Holbrook, MA 02343

Thanks, fellow cheapsters!

Mr. C

DISC. RMS. N.Y.C. -
SHOREHAM HOTEL
GOTHAM "

HOTEL ROOMS DISCOUNT 40% AVG.

1-800-781-9887 - ENG. FRANCE

" - 576-0003 - CALIFORNIA